Framing the Polish Home

Ohio University Press Polish and Polish-American Studies Series

General Editor: John J. Bukowczyk, Wayne State University

Framing the Polish Home: Postwar Cultural Constructions of Hearth, Nation, and Self, edited by Bożena Shallcross

Framing the Polish Home

Postwar Cultural Constructions of Hearth, Nation, and Self

Edited by
Bożena Shallcross

OHIO UNIVERSITY PRESS
ATHENS

Ohio University Press, Athens, Ohio 45701

Printed in the United States of America

Ohio University Press books are printed on acid-free paper ♾

10 09 08 07 06 05 04 03 02 5 4 3 2 1

The chapters by Ryszard Nycz, Madeline G. Levine, and Jerzy Jarzębski have been published in the Polish periodical *Teksty Drugie*. The chapter by Marek Zaleski has been published in *Respublica Nowa* and a portion of the chapter by Anna Nasiłowska has been published in *Jarosłav Ivaškievič i Ukraina. Zbirnik naukovich prac* (Jarosław Iwaszkiewicz and Ukraine: A collected volume of articles).

Library of Congress Cataloging-in-Publication Data

Framing the Polish home: postwar cultural constructions of hearth, nation, and self / edited by Bożena Shallcross.

p. cm. — (Ohio University Press Polish and Polish-American studies series)

Includes bibliographical references and index.

ISBN 0-8214-1436-4 (cloth : alk. paper) — ISBN 0-8214-1437-2 (pbk. : alk. paper)

1. Poland—Intellectual life—20th century. 2. Polish literature—20th century—History and criticism. 3. Home—Poland. 4. Home in literature. 5. Ethnicity—Poland. 6. Identity (Psychology) in literature. I. Mądra-Shallcross, Bożena. II. Series.

DK4382 .F73 2002
943.805—dc21

2002066282

Publication of books in the Polish and Polish-American Studies Series has been made possible in part by the generous support of the following organizations:

Polish American Historical Association,
Orchard Lake, Michigan

Stanislaus A. Blejwas Endowed Chair in Polish and Polish American Studies,
Central Connecticut State University, New Britain, Connecticut

St. Mary's College of Ave Maria University,
Orchard Lake, Michigan

The Polish Institute of Arts and Sciences of America, Inc.,
New York, New York

Additional support for this book has been provided by the following institutions:

The University of Chicago

Polish Studies Center,
Indiana University, Bloomington, Indiana

Contents

Series Editor's Preface

The idea of home spans human societies, but its specific articulation, meaning, and significance invariably have been framed by time, place, and culture: the concreteness of geography and history. For many Americans, perhaps home has been understood as a comfortable, uncomplicated commonplace—as in home plate, homesick, homespun—but not so for the Poles, for whom it has been a concept of paradox and contradiction through the past two centuries of nationalist striving, war, homelessness and exile, foreign occupation, and nation-building.

In assembling the work of a group of distinguished American and Polish scholars, *Framing the Polish Home: Postwar Cultural Constructions of Hearth, Nation, and Self,* edited by University of Chicago Slavicist Bożena Shallcross, for the first time explores the concept of home in the literary and cultural world of a European country whose culture and history bear the marks of its position as a borderland and crossroads between East and West. The essays examine the theme of home in the works of modern Polish writers whose names read like a who's who in modern Polish letters. They locate the Polish concept of home at the nexus of nationalist longing and postcolonial de/re-construction, involving subjectivity, otherness, loss, self-discovery, and personal and national identity.

Ironically, many of the authors treated in this volume are little known to the Western reading public, despite the fact that their work resonates with Western European literary themes at the same time possessing a pathbreaking, iconoclastic quality and cultural edginess. The cultural products they created undermined the Soviet-era canon but now serve to challenge contemporary Polish cultural conventions. In developing the theme that forms a central focus of this volume, perhaps they also may shed new light on a human universal which offers rich opportunities for interdisciplinary approaches.

We are pleased to offer *Framing the Polish Home* as the first volume in the new Ohio University Press Polish and Polish-American Studies Series. The series revisits the historical and contemporary experience of one of

America's largest European ethnic groups and the history of a European homeland which has played a disproportionately important role in twentieth-century world affairs. The series will publish innovative monographs and more general works that investigate under- or unexplored topics or themes or offer new, critical, revisionist, or comparative perspectives in the area of Polish and Polish-American Studies. Interdisciplinary or multidisciplinary in profile, the series seeks manuscripts on Polish immigration and ethnic communities, the country of origin, and its various peoples in history, anthropology, cultural studies, political economy, current politics, and related fields.

Supported by a series advisory board of accomplished Polonists and Polish-Americanists, the Polish and Polish-American Studies Series has been made possible through generous financial assistance from the Polish American Historical Association, the Polish Institute of Arts and Sciences of America, the Stanislaus A. Blejwas Endowed Chair in Polish and Polish American Studies at Central Connecticut State University, and St. Mary's College of Ave Maria University and through institutional support from Wayne State University. Publication of this particular series volume also has been aided by grants from the University of Chicago and Indiana University. As an ambitious new undertaking, the series meanwhile has benefitted from the warm encouragement of a number of persons, including Gillian Berchowitz, Stanislaus Blejwas, Thomas Gladsky, Thaddeus Gromada, James S. Pula, David Sanders, and Thaddeus Radzilowski. The moral and material support from all of these institutions and individuals is gratefully acknowledged. As is that from Ohio University Press. I would like to extend a personal word of thanks and deep appreciation to Ohio University Press—for believing in the series, providing the advice and good counsel that helped bring it forth, and investing the time and resources to make it a reality.

The appearance of the first volume of this series marks a milestone in the maturation of the Polish Studies field and stands as a fitting tribute to the scholars and organizations whose efforts have brought it to fruition. Sadly, though, it has become a special memorial to one of its most enthusiastic supporters. Perhaps more than any scholar, Stanislaus A. Blejwas, University Professor and holder of the Polish Chair at Central Connecticut State University, dedicated himself to advancing Polish Studies through his own work, his support of talented colleagues and worthy projects, and his conscientious advocacy of scholarly objectivity and academic honesty. Professor Blejwas, a member of the series advisory board, passed away suddenly as this volume was being prepared for production. While this volume demonstrates the intellectual vibrancy of Polish Studies, may it also memorialize Professor Blejwas's own contributions to this burgeoning and important field.

John J. Bukowczyk

Acknowledgments

THIS VOLUME'S ORIGINS date back to Home/Less: The Polish Experience, a conference organized in December 1998 at Indiana University in Bloomington. The conference was supported by a grant from the American Council of Learned Societies, given to me and Sven Spieker as the conference organizers. I thank Sven Spieker for his impact on the conference.

Despite its origin in the conference, *Framing the Polish Home* is not a volume of proceedings. Not only has its conceptual framework been substantially revised and the list of contributors changed, but also the entire collection was anonymously refereed. Therefore, I thank the outside readers for their suggestions.

I appreciate the generosity of the American Council of Learned Societies and the Division of Humanities at the University of Chicago for subsidizing the preparation of the volume for publication, as well as the Polish Studies Center and the International Programs at Indiana University for their financial and administrative support.

I had the good fortune to prepare this volume for publication with a few excellent friends, whose competence helped me shape the book and whose patience made the whole process seemingly effortless.

My most cordial thanks go to Russell Coon, whose careful proofreading of the volume turned out to be an insightful critique. Also, I thank George Fowler for rescuing me from the numerous pitfalls of computer technology.

I owe special thanks to Dave Shallcross—my most faithful reader.

Bożena Shallcross

Guide to Pronunciation

THE FOLLOWING KEY provides a guide to the pronunciation of Polish words and names.

a is pronounced as in *father*
c as ts in *cats*
ch like a guttural h
cz as hard ch in *church*
g always hard, as in *get*
i as ee
j as y in *yellow*
rz like French j in *jardin*
sz as sh in *ship*
szcz as shch, enunciating both sounds, as in *fresh cheese*
u as oo in *boot*
w as v
ć as soft ch
ś as sh
ż, ź both as zh, the former higher in pitch than the latter
ó as oo in boot
ą as French *on*
ę as French *en*
ł as w
ṅ changes the combinations -in to -ine, -en to -ene, and -on to -oyne

The accent in Polish words always falls on the penultimate syllable.

Framing the Polish Home

Baltic Sea
Gdańsk
Wilno
U.S.S.R.
GERMANY
Poznań
Warsaw
Łódź
Lublin
Wrocław
Kraków
Lwów
POLAND
Territorial Changes
1939 – 1952
Poland 1939
Postwar Poland
0
100
MILES

INTRODUCTION

Home Truths

Toward a Definition of the Polish Home

Bożena Shallcross

Wherever we can point to human beings, there we point to somebody's *home*—with all the kindly meaning of that word.

—Yi-Fu Tuan

Horses, razors, alphabet blocks,
warm green lamps, women, manners, burning
conversations, and the yellow ashes of the books. . . .
Over an étagère, a swarthy Tatar Madonna,
immobile, like a hummingbird.
A huge family reunion. The children are sent
to the garden. Vodka bitter as wormwood
and the Old Testament of jokes. A shrill
eternity of laughter. Apples and cherries.
Bread. Take it all away from them.

—Adam Zagajewski

Few concepts seem to have such universal appeal as the notion of the home, an appeal that transcends cultures, languages, and cultural settings. With its seemingly infinite power to symbolize the whole range of nostalgic desires and values, the notion of the home has been extraordinarily prone to rhetorical and political exploitation—the most recent of which is the much-quoted phrase: the "house of Europe." Surprisingly, very little critical attention has been dedicated to this area, particularly in the field of Polish studies.[1]

Occasionally labeled home studies,[2] the discourse on the home is a truly cross-, inter-, and multidisciplinary entity that has evolved simultaneously from anthropology, sociology, philosophy, psychology, architecture, and cultural studies. The relatively new discourse on the home as a legitimate area of study has been substantially stimulated, if not pioneered, by a number of philosophical contributions: Martin Heidegger's existential notion of the home, Mircea Eliade's symbolic content of the home, and its oneiric image as envisioned by Gaston Bachelard. Each of these thinkers considers as fundamental different aspects of a human abode, and thus each expands the discourse's range and reach. In literary theory, the representation of the home is a rich—if not inconvenient—meeting ground for all these disciplines: it may encompass the poetics of space (Bachelard), the question of identity (often closely fused to a specific national architectural tradition), and an array of positive and negative topophilic emotions and existential statuses that inform the rooted and stable form of life as well as the condition called homelessness.

Home interpreted through its architectural framework is a house—the semantic distinction that is absent in the Polish language, where the single word *dom* signifies both a home and a house: a place where one belongs as well as its material embodiment, a mortar-and-brick building. A house translated into a narrative is a home, and, if we follow this, home in the Polish sense of the word is both a place one identifies with and a place one built and furnished to inhabit. And, to push this correlation even further, the process of framing one's own home also functions in two dimensions, for the home's frame can be both real and textual, physical and interpretive. The notion that the home is a cultural text—explored as early as in Romanticism by Théophile Gautier, who described Victor Hugo's home at rue de la Tour d'Auvergne as "a domestic poem" (Mądra-Shallcross 1992, 91)—has its counterpart in the concept of the text as home. And every home, narrated or built, needs an underlying construction system, a skeleton that gives shape to its structure and constitutes its frame. Such a frame is not a simple sum of our separate inquiries as collected in this volume; it is rather a conceptual frame—the result of these inquiries' most insightful and poignant discoveries that buttress and delineate the essence of what is the Polish home.

So, what is the Polish home? Its living entity encompasses home as *locus amoenus,* with its memory and customs that hark back to Renaissance poet Jan Kochanowski's hospitable invitation to his abode; a nostalgic—but vividly visualized manor house—projection of the conservative and elitist past; a steady dwelling, yet all too frequently open to invasion; therefore a domicile whose stability and safety is a sheer fantasy; a space of Otherness conquered from the neighbors and subsequently domesticated (polonized) as well as a place of cultural resistance or estrangement (or both) from an imposed ideology; a restored space of displacement amid all that is Other in exilic writing. Is the Polish home then—as represented in literature—a system of at once mutually exclusive and compatible dynamics and definitions? Or is it a victim of ever-changing ideologies, especially if one considers its post-totalitarian/postmodernist chapter?[3] Certainly, the Polish home is a strangely malleable and changeable idea that entails both kindly—as Yi-Fu Tuan wants it—and unkindly meanings of the phenomenon. Despite their dual nature, topophilic feelings or our homing instincts ("uczucie domowe," as the Romantic poet Zygmunt Krasiński calls it) deny, resist, and hide homelessness and a mobile type of dwelling. Only the global perspective changes the traditional perception/illusion of the Polish home as a stable domicile. Indeed, compared to the nomadic nation, such as the Roma, or to the diasporic history of Jewry, Poles are not wanderers. Most of the time they stay put. However, their homeland's boundaries have frequently moved under their feet.[4] Subversively, the mobile homeland of the relatively immobile people shaped its inhabitants' identity and difference, while, in turn, they determined their home(land)'s cultural and national profile.

The present volume opens with the notion fundamental to any discussion of home: an inquiry into the fusion of home and the self's attachment to a (chosen, given, inherited, invented, appropriated) place. For, as Rosemary Marangoly George writes, "The conflation of the home and the self is one of the threads that runs through the examination of 'home'" (1996, 20) and derives from the union (Romantic in its origin and even stronger) between the self/body and home.[5] More specifically, in part 1, home is viewed in terms of identity and identification sought by Polish writers in their particularly isolating experiences such as alienation, exile, emigration, and homoeroticism. In his study, Ryszard Nycz explores those questions that constitute the conceptual core of the entire volume, for he examines the changing attitudes toward the self, home, and outsideness throughout the twentieth century. He proposes to view the question of identity in terms of two opposing strategies: one founded on the Romantic sense of Polishness and Polish "soul" that clings parochially to one's home(land), risking a complete alienation from world culture, and the second based on permanent homelessness and its variants—nomadism, exile, expatriation, dispossession, and alienation. These negative experiences of uprootedness, paradoxically, heighten and complicate the sense of the self, of what is "truly alien" and "truly actual," to use Nycz's terms, in regard to one's identity.

Kim Jastremski proposes a reading of Czesław Miłosz's strategy toward home from two compatible perspectives: home is the point of departure to the world and the destination point he reaches in his journey through the world. Home thus is a hermeneutic idea through which Miłosz embraces the Other and a compulsion to settle down amid Otherness. Grażyna Borkowska's chapter examines the dialectics of the alienating homoerotic experience combined with the desire to belong, as articulated by Julian Stryjkowski's prose writing. The relationship between the self and the community—or, in Tamara Trojanowska's words, "individuality and social relations"—is tested by her within the domestic space evoked in Tadeusz Różewicz's and Witold Gombrowicz's plays and posited against modernist and postmodernist discourse on identity.

The volume explores the subject of the home from a rigorous critical perspective. Its geographic and historical territory is Poland between World War II and the end of the communist regime—a time and place where wars and mass genocide, forced displacement and emigration, totalitarianism and poverty were prevalent. Those who survived were often deprived of the sense of place and identity that comes with a rooted existence. Therefore, the volume pays special attention to the impact that various ideologies, fascism and communism in particular, had on the cultural and literary representation of the home and humans' identity with their private space. For the same reason, one of the volume's premises is based on the antinomy between dwelling and the condition called homelessness. This opposition is characteristic of the Polish experience, and ultimately of the representation of the home in the literature of that period.

The problem of the home in Polish literature cannot be fully understood without an examination of its place in the history and culture of Polish Jewry. The question of the Jewish home, its promise and its denial, became one of the most complex and painful chapters in the history of the home in Poland. Indeed, it is this chapter and its stark opposition to the idyllic and Romantic roots of the home in Poland that makes this phenomenon so distinctive. Madeline G. Levine discusses several texts that offer testimony of the destruction of the sheltering home during World War II, the phenomenon of the "domicide," as she aptly calls it. Among them are Miron Białoszewski's *A Memoir of the Warsaw Uprising,* Bogdan Wojdowski's *Bread for the Departed,* and Ida Fink's *A Scrap of Time.* Levine's scrutiny of the literary reflections of domicide is twofold: the most memorable perversion of the notion of the home, the ghetto, is juxtaposed to the home experience on the Aryan side of Nazi-occupied Poland. As such, it demonstrates the basic difference between the two sides of the ghetto wall; although home is only a provisional shelter for the Polish writers, for Polish Jewish writers and poets it lost its distinction from the streets: it is open and equal to violation. In ghettos, people were deprived of their livelihood and their homes, their sense of place, and their privacy. Deprived of what Heidegger described as one of its basic conditions, its usefulness *(Dienlichkeit),* a home was frequently reduced to nothing more than a hovel or dugout, providing only minimum shelter from the elements.

The impact of the war and the new postwar political order is also examined from the perspective of ownership: in Poland, not only were borders redrawn, but houses changed hands as well, when the lost territories in the eastern borderlands were "replaced" by the "regained" territories in the west. In my chapter, I trace how the discourse on the home is related to the process of mythologizing history and private home(land) in Stefan Chwin's acclaimed novel *Hanemann,* and to what extent the appropriation of the home that belonged to the Other is conditioned by apologetic strategies. Katarzyna Zechenter argues that the postwar loss of Tadeusz Konwicki's Lithuanian home(land), and the experience he shared with his generation, became a pivotal event in his fiction. Through this loss he expressed the notion of a domicile as persistently shaped and invaded by history and ideology.

In part 3, the disintegration of the urban home that occurred between the late 1940s and the 1960s, along with the desperate attempt to rebuild the privacy that was lost in communal living, is discussed by Henryk Dasko. The official communist battle against the home took the form of an all-out attack on every aspect of privacy and individuality—for Witold Rybczynski (1986) the defining factors for the idea of the home—both of which were crucial prerequisites for the survival of the home. Dasko discusses the vision of the Polish home in socialist-realist fiction (Aleksander Ścibor-Rylski) and contrasts it with an analogous image in post-Stalinist literature (Marek Hłasko and Janusz Głowacki).

Jerzy Jarzębski investigates how the destructive impact of the Stalinist housing policy on the individual home and large urban centers of Kraków and Warsaw was represented in the prose produced during that period. In Stalinist Poland the notion of the home assumed gigantically ideological proportions as the country became the "homeland for workers." The infamous "communal apartments" replaced the individual home as the symbol of the regime's battle with the "bourgeois" ideal of the home as an expression of individual subjectivity, stabilization, and material culture. Contextualized within the city discourse, the processes of invalidating and even destroying the traditional housing policy and disintegrating urban center demonstrate a shift to the periphery as the place of universal dwelling in Polish literature of the communist period best manifested in prose by Marek Nowakowski, Tadeusz Konwicki, and Janusz Anderman.

The Palace of Culture and Science in Warsaw is a negative locus of Magdalena J. Zaborowska's examination of the posttotalitarian crisis of representation, homelessness, and life in transit induced by various ideologies. Using a feminist reading of Maria Kuncewicz's prose and the visual arts of Zofia Kulik and Beata Wehr, the author explores the fact that the dwelling is both a location as well as a never complete process and passage.

In part 4, the investigation of the home harks back to the nineteenth-century origins of the archetypal Polish abode as represented by the manor house. Given by the Polish nation to its leading writers, such as Henryk Sienkiewicz, the manors symbolized the partitioned homeland. Even today, they epitomize the most exclusive aspects of what defines the Polish "homing instinct." Beth Holmgren traces how Sienkiewicz's manor was institutionalized and transformed into a museum and appropriated to serve the propagandistic needs of the communist authorities. A few notable exceptions, such as Jarosław Iwaszkiewicz's house in Stawisko (which remained in his hands throughout the period of nationalization of private property), illustrate the concept of the writer's home as home(land), a peculiar intimate space that implies Polishness. Here, Anna Nasiłowska answers the question of how the regime gave certain privileges to Iwaszkiewicz, a writer and poet who was willing—to a certain extent—to collaborate. The elusive utopia of the home, of Iwaszkiewicz's beloved abode in Stawisko, proved resistant to all attempts at diminishing or eradicating it. In Marek Zaleski's article the notion of the home is examined from the point of view of the ideological corruption of this idea as epitomized in the home for creative work ("dom pracy twórczej"), even though at the origin of this idea was a utopian experimentation and an aesthetic (European avant-garde) belief in art as mechanism for remodeling society and "improving" mankind.

The possibility of creating one's home in exile as attempted by Polish émigré writers as the aesthetic, political, and existential reinvention of the lost home and homeland is examined in part 5. In this regard, the home created in an exilic dwelling and writing is not a place to be conquered or colonized but a place in the mind. Here, Halina Filipowicz's feminist perspective on the home in exile—based on three émigré plays—opens the last section of the volume. In her gendered reading of domesticity—still a rare enterprise in Polish studies—Filipowicz does not dwell on exilic politics and the home(land) as its center but revises the traditional view of exilic existence and writing. While Alina Witkowska (1997, 31) argues that Romantic émigré life was a typically masculine form of Polish culture—the "culture of lonely men," as she puts it—Filipowicz renegotiates the relationship between the contemporary émigré perspective and the identity-bearing home(land) along gender lines in order to bring the status of woman, gender, and sexuality into the discourse.

David Goldfarb chooses one of the props that Witold Gombrowicz kept on his desk to demonstrate how the writer mediated the outside/inside trope of his status as émigré. The binoculars that Gombrowicz purchased in West Berlin allowed him to see from a distance how people lived on the other side of the wall, and, ultimately, in communist Poland. Thus, the relationship between Witold Gombrowicz and his home country can be defined as pornographic: its detached representation is something that can be fantasized about, but never touched.

The volume concludes with Włodzimierz Bolecki's interpretation of Gustaw Herling's mythology of the home. In Bolecki's view the nostalgia for the lost homeland reveals the deeper paradigmatic meaning in the working of the writer's memory: the striking (especially in the context of the numerous precise descriptions of Italian landscapes) absence of descriptions evoking the landscapes of his childhood combines in Herling's writing with various processes of recollection that stop short of description. Bolecki posits that this characteristic gap is a part of the broader phenomenon in Herling's writing: the rhetoric of the indescribable. The writer's text of the home belongs to this ineffable sphere.

Remarkably, the prose of the nineties displays a shift from the text of the home to the textual home. Seconded by another transformation, the textual (narrated) home does not exist anymore within the "homeland narrative" but the "narrative homeland." As Przemysław Czapliński says,

> a place can be a homeland only on the condition that it can tell us a story; and it can speak only as text, plot, narration. The inhabitant of that place, who wants also to have a homeland—and who knows that this must always entail work (today: narrative work)—must above all posit himself as reader. In today's world, to be an inhabitant of a particular place means to become conscious that we exist on the pages of a palimpsest. We are walking on the traces left by others, who lived here before us. . . . With these stories as his roots, the reader-inhabitant grows down into the soil of his homeland, drawing from literary memory his models for reading, and from historical memory, the material for his plot. (2000, 364–65)

These small individualized home(land)s replaced exilic writing and its nostalgic evocation of the home. The political changes initiated in 1998 transformed (once again) the status and functioning of both the literature produced in Poland and its émigré counterpart. And critics have already bid farewell to this division.[6]

The broad ramifications of the concept of the home allowed the contributors to bring together in one volume an array of disciplines that manifest their interconnectedness. Polish literature, architecture, interior design, cultural tradition, ideologies, aesthetics, and various strategies of identification, all combine to play a part in this critical effort at "framing" the Polish abode in its diversity. Through these themes and points of view the present collection not only delineates the recent historical development of the home in Polish literature, but also captures its universal meaning.

Notes

1. With very few exceptions (e.g., Mądra-Shallcross 1992, Benedyktowicz and Benedyktowicz 1992, Legeżyńska 1996), no research has been carried out on this sub-

ject. The Benedyktowiczes' work is a contribution to a very specific type of ethnographic inquiry, while Legeżyńska focuses on select readings of postwar Polish poetry. Moreover, these monographs—written in Polish and published in Poland—had little or no impact on the discourse on the home in the United States.

2. In its awkwardness this term equals "body studies"; see Leitch 2000, 128.

3. For a discussion of the posttotalitarian revival of manor architecture in Poland, see Bożena Shallcross 1999.

4. For this distinction I thank Judith Kornblatt, who commented on the concept of the Polish home during the conference Polonophilia and Polonophobia of the Russians at Indiana University, Bloomington, in 2000.

5. In spectacularly synecdochal fashion, Zygmunt Krasiński equated the villa he purchased and decorated for his mistress with his own body (Mądra-Shallcross 1992, 7).

6. For an in-depth analysis of this process, see Jarzębski 1998.

Works Cited

Benedyktowicz, Zbigniew, and Danuta Benedyktowicz. 1992. *Dom w tradycji ludowej* (Home in the folk tradition). Kraków: "Wiedza o Kulturze."

Czapliński, Przemysław. 2000. "The 'Mythic Homeland' in Contemporary Polish Prose." Trans. Karen Underhill, with Tomasz Tabako. *Chicago Review* (special issue: *New Polish Writing,* ed. W. Martin) 46, 3–4: 357–65.

George, Rosemary Marangoly. 1996. *The Politics of Home: Postcolonial Relocations and Twentieth-Century Fiction.* Cambridge: Cambridge University Press.

Jarzębski, Jerzy. 1998. *Pożegnanie z emigracją: O powojennej prozie polskiej* (Farewell to emigration: On postwar Polish prose). Kraków: Wydawnictwo Literackie.

Legeżyńska, Anna. 1996. *Dom i poetycka bezdomność w liryce polskiej* (Home and poetic homelessness in Polish lyrics). Warsaw: Wydawnictwo Naukowe PWN.

Leitch, Vincent B. 2000. "Postmodern Interdisciplinarity." *Profession*: 124–31.

Mądra-Shallcross, Bożena. 1992. *Dom romantycznego artysty* (Home of the Romantic artists). Kraków: Wydawnictwo Literackie.

Rybczynski, Witold. 1986. *Home: A Short History of an Idea.* New York: Penguin.

Shallcross, Bożena. 1999. "Re/Constructing the Manor." *Polish Review* 4: 439–44.

Witkowska, Alina. 1997. *Cześć i skandale* (Honor and scandals). Gdańsk: Słowo/Obraz Terytoria.

PART I

Home and the Question of Identity

1 ||| "Every One of Us Is a Stranger"

Patterns of Identity in Twentieth-Century Polish Literature

Ryszard Nycz

POLISH LITERATURE ENTERED the twentieth century under the star of a disturbing experience of modernity through which the traditional patterns of identity were thoroughly reassessed. The global process of modernization, gradually affecting all spheres of life, branded modernist European literature of that period much more extensively than Polish literature. Irrespective of the differing rates of change in technology and civilization, however, similar perceptions of the new situation, as well as their reflection in the literatures of various countries, rose roughly at the same time—around 1910.

That was the year in which, according to Virginia Woolf, "human character changed" (1968, 1:320); the year during which, as Gottfried Benn purported, "everything started to shatter" (1951, 7). It was in precisely that period that the crises of representation, expression, language, and communication were scrutinized by the Vienna circle of writers and philosophers of language (Janik and Toulmin 1973). It was then that Rilke completed *The Notebook of Malte Laurids Brigge,* an insightful confirmation of the alienation and disintegration of the modern person. To sum up the change with the memorable phrase from his first *Duino Elegy,* "we are not comfortably at home in our translated world" (Rilke 1977, 5).[1] It was also at that critical moment of the early crystallization of modern identity that Stanisław Brzozowski wrote, "*Every one of us is a stranger from one abyss* headed toward another; silence sustains and surrounds us" (1990, 483; emphasis mine). Several months later he supplemented this universal reflection with an observation that was specifically local and Polish: "Today, every thinking Pole must feel the same: our thoughts decay overnight. They do not survive any contact with air and land—the same air and the same land that our forebears have bequeathed us—our only land. . . . At this moment I have no connection whatsoever with life" (Brzozowski 2000, 93; entry for January 10, 1911).

The quotes above—and many similar—reflect the presence of motifs that characterize the human condition using essentially identical categories: estrangement from the world, alienation from one's roots, a sense of not belonging to any place that might serve as a point of reference for establishing one's identity. They also indicate a profound change in anthropological self-knowledge. The authentic human condition is fundamentally determined by the conviction that "the *mode* of existence of 'I' towards the 'alien' world, consists in *being there,* in *identifying oneself* through existing there, feeling *at home.* But in the world that is different at first glance, it is 'I' that is native to it, that subdues and removes the dissimilarity. In such a world, the 'I' finds in the world a site (*lieu*) and a home (*maison*)" (Levinas 1979, 37). The home is never an ordinary place of residence, a physical object, a singular tool for living in or an aim of human activity. Home is, first of all, the primary condition for this human activity. People always go out into the world from a sort of at-homeness, and may always come back and find shelter there. Settling in is a basic relationship that reflects biological origin and symbolic belonging to one particular place—within geographical space, within a national community, within society, within culture—from which people obtain a sense of permanent identity.

Such a *genius loci,* founding the sense of national and cultural identity, was established in Polish literature by Romantic thought and imagination. It reacted to the historical experience of the partitions by forming the notion of the Polish soul—one that is born out of a mysterious union between the community spirit and the spirit of place as well as the notion of "our (Polish) land," which preserves its mystic and cultural identity regardless of all political changes and shifting boundaries (cf. Chwin 1997, 27–28). At the turn of the century, Brzozowski contemplated the farcical efforts to preserve "the national substance," the ostentatious locking of oneself in the "Polish home," the firm holding on to the familiar, which sentenced the Pole to imprisonment in "Polishness" and, as a result, to a dangerous alienation from the world, a fatal exclusion from civilization and spiritual changes in the modern world.

In the modern world, however, "each one of us is a stranger," that is, every one of us is both someone foreign (from the vantage point of indigenous peoples) and someone who is not at home (in our own perception). Essentially, strangers are not where they should be, having been deprived of their "place on earth" (and looking toward it with melancholy and nostalgia), or else, they promise themselves that they will recover such a place—and approach it in terms of future conquests, "winning" or "occupying" a position. At any rate, the newcomer-stranger is someone permanently displaced, who has lost his stature of a "native in being" (to use Levinas's term) and must set off to seek his own identity. His initial condition is determined by severe homelessness (dispossession, exile, alienation).

I conclude that the pervading sense of displacement, which constitutes a key experience of modernist consciousness, also determines the position of man at the starting point of modern Polish literature, while the concept of a newcomer-stranger, as introduced by Brzozowski, allows us to discover the hero's condition and basic characteristics. The character's subsequent fate can be perceived in terms of a double-track attempt at outlining the fundamental patterns of life and the finding of ways for self-identification. It also reflects the testing of two basic routes to gaining one's identity, which demonstrate their consistency and influence as peculiar reactions to the diverse consequences that ensue from the quality of not settling in that characterizes the starting position of an individual who enters the stage of the modern epoch.

| I |

IF I WERE to seek the simplest, and yet at the same time, the most generalized differentiation of such an identity, I would see its discernible evidence first of all in formulations by two classics of twentieth-century Polish literature made at roughly the same time (mid-century) and in the same émigré conditions. The first, by Czesław Miłosz, resounds with mild persuasion: "Wherever you are, you could never be an alien." The second, by Witold Gombrowicz, sounds like a command: "Be foreign forever!" It takes little effort to note that those views are neither incompatible nor mutually exclusive. Both appear to assume the sense of not settling in as an intrinsic feature of the condition of modern man. The solutions proposed by them do not so much have an antinomic character as a complementary one. They assume the guise of a dialogue, of a dispute without hopes for an early settlement. ("Be foreign forever," says one; "you could never be an alien," explains the other.)

Miłosz's formula is to be found in his important poem *Po ziemi naszej* (Walking our land), whose title alone invokes the intertext crucial for an understanding of this work for nostalgic and polemical reasons: the Romantic myth of the geographic and mystical symbiosis of man with his place of origin, the Polish soul eternally rooted in Polish soil, the myth spread by the then enormously popular works of the "lesser bards" of Polish poetry. Among them were Wincenty Pol with his *Pieśń o ziemi naszej* (A song about our land) and Teofil Lenartowicz, so many of whose poems have become a virtual treasure trove of quotations, such as "mnie wszystko tak cieszy, co polskie, co nasze." In Miłosz's *The History of Polish Literature*, Pol's poem is described as "a kind of patriotic 'treatise' in verse (a work full of charm, incidentally) on the geography and customs of various Polish provinces" (Miłosz 1983, 266).

A certain degree of familiarity with the nineteenth-century context, which is uncommon among Polish interpreters of Miłosz's work, appears to be indispensable for the comprehension of the work. It unfolds as an inner polemic, in which the Romantic tradition of self-identification, achieved by settling into "Polishness," is from the very beginning contrasted with the liberating force of Whitman's model of universal humanity, in which the rustic tradition is contrasted with the experience of a big city, and ethnocentrism contrasted with anthropocentrism.

> Wherever you are, colors of the sky envelop you
> Just as here . . .
> . . . .
> . . . birds are named
> in the language of that place: a *towhee* came to the kitchen,
> scatter some bread on the lawn, *juncos* have arrived.
> Wherever you are, you touch the bark of trees
> Testing its roughness different yet familiar.
> Grateful for a rising and a setting sun
> Wherever you are, you could never be an alien.
>
> (Miłosz 1981, 86)[2]

"Niemnie, domowa rzeko moja!" (Neman, you river of my home!), wrote Adam Mickiewicz, contributing to the myth of the unique aura of belonging to one's place of origin. "Rough bark of trees, different yet familiar," says Miłosz, not so much denying as multiplying and relativizing the unique values of what is specific to home. Such a perspective imbues *our land* with a new, perhaps double, meaning. It acquires a universal sense that consists of—or preserves within itself—an ethnic concretization of the significance of every kind of "our land," a local community, regardless of whether it refers to the small homeland of a Native American tribe or the author's homeland. For Miłosz, the first and foremost repository of such historicality is language, since language can best preserve the traces of human presence in its discursive properties, in proper names, and in local designations. This is always the "language of the place," in which the specific is grafted onto the universal, and consequently permits the preservation of opportunities to settle in, whether it be a nostalgic dream about returning to "places lost," or hope for overcoming the remoteness of the other experience.

Despite frequently reluctant comments about modernity and avant-garde, the process of gaining personal self-knowledge by Miłosz's "alien" is a model realization of the twentieth-century subject: the modernist traveler, who sets off to seek the Remote in order to discover its familiar aspects, his alter ego. He seeks the Remote in order to persuade it to cooperate, though only on his own terms, since, having accepted them himself, he regards them as universally valid. In Miłosz's stranger, one recognizes some characteristic qualities of an anthropological model of the participant-observer, who, endowed with both personal experience and the ability for intellectual generalization, is capable of discovering the universal in the local (e.g., is capable of finding an example of Culture in an alien, exotic culture), as well as the common and the personal in the peculiar and the dissimilar (e.g., finding a man with the same human qualities in a native). Both as an individual and a universal property, dissimilarity/otherness is a guise for unrecognized familiarity, the source of fear of the state of unintegrated foreignness, an epiphanic experience of contact with the "unattainable" or a nostalgic experience of antithesis and loss.

The importunate closeness to the "other" eventually results in one's resignation from "imperial" aspirations to transcend oneself, to dominate and seize whatever is different, leading to the acceptance of one's own boundaries, and thereby the external presence of the Other. "We have remained what we were when we left the home village or city of our youth," says Miłosz, "and *we are a traveling monad* that absorbs images and sounds, but that at the same time remains indifferent to outside influences" (1997, 81; emphasis mine). To be oneself means to accept that whatever circumscribes one also isolates one from others, that one's limitations at the same time constitute the boundaries of one's identity. This, in turn, leads to a reversal of perspective of the anthropological model of behavior and to a looking at oneself in terms of otherness, if only as an incidental case, a local peculiarity among other cases. "After all, Nature was not the object of my contemplation. It was human society in the great cities of the modern era. . . . I was unable to fathom that element, I was unable to embrace and comprehend it, and to think meant to *move in it, observing at the same time and from a distance myself and others*" (Miłosz 1986, 137; emphasis mine).

| I |

A SIMILAR EVOLUTION, though based on different premises, can also be perceived in the other influential alternative available for seeking one's identity. "Be foreign forever!" urges Gombrowicz in his *Diary* (1988, 1:123). But what is this really supposed to mean? To be a stranger in Gombrowicz's world certainly entails a steadfast refusal to acknowledge identification with social roles, with images of an individual's "self" imposed by others. After all, it should always be "removed from what one is doing" (2:219). We are strangers if we change our place of residence, as are those who enter the sphere of our world and do not fall into the traditionally dichotomous classification of friends and enemies, into "us" and "them." Thanks to the peculiarity of the situation (at the expense of "double" alienation), the stranger acquires the privilege of universal and objective perception and the power to extricate himself from the overpowering ties imposed by the community. Like the "third man" invoked by *Ferdydurke*'s main character: "Come, *third person,* come to the two of us, appear, so that I may cling to you, rescue me! May he appear instantly, this third person, a stranger, as fresh and cool and pure as a wave of the sea, may he shatter with his strangeness this vaporizing intimacy" (1961, 271).

The stranger is also someone whose presence is not acknowledged by the "natives," someone who is constantly threatened with social nonexistence, someone kept at a distance of anonymity. Any association with such a stranger might lead to the removal of the barrier of strangeness, closing the gap, opening up the possibility of transforming the stranger into a "fellow citizen," who, having changed so much, would contribute to the life of the community and thereby find an opportunity to avoid bitter alienation and loneliness, on condition that he give up his uniqueness. But, inasmuch as a house that one may not leave becomes a prison, such excessive attachment to familiarity may develop into a form of xenophobic discrediting of the alien or of one's own incapacitation. Thus Gombrowicz's stranger is someone who does not belong to the community by choice, who is denied the rights enjoyed by individuals within that community, but rather someone who does not feel obliged to perform any duties within the community. As someone actually *free,* he cultivates his freedom even at the expense of being excluded from every native community. This explains Gombrowicz's comments in an interview with Piero Sanavio: "I think that every writer, without exception, is always in exile for the simple reason that by his very nature he does not fit in with existing patterns. Artists have always been exiles. . . . I am sure that if I were living in Poland, I would be the same kind of exile as here and as I was in Argentina" (Gombrowicz 1991, 42–43).

What is, then, the ultimate significance of his urging each of us to remain a stranger? One hypothesis has been proposed by Adorno: "If the alien were no longer ostracized, there hardly would be any more alienation" (1973, 172). A similar motivation appears to underlie Gombrowicz's acceptance of alienation. "Alienation? Let us leave the beaten track and assume that it is not so dreadful, that we actually know such alienation inside out, in our reasonable and technical inside" (Gombrowicz 1996, 79). Gombrowicz perceives the world in negative terms, associated with the existential anthropology of the first half of the twentieth century. It is not settling in that is universally experienced, but uprooting, which opens up space for the creation of an artificial interpersonal world. In this context an individual is forced to make an effort at *self-creation.* Assuming that no community and no "ethnic spirit of place" can provide a natural set of reference points to construct one's own personality, Gombrowicz's stroller, who wanders about the peripheries of reality, is obliged to establish such a reference point within himself or else to conceive of a situation that will determine his identity through relationships with others.

To persist in alienation under such conditions means not only to resist the integrative bonds of cultural orders, the mythology of the familiar, the temptation to fraternize with others, but also to acknowledge the right of every "other" to exist, to affirm the very presence of the Other, the separateness of what is radically different. Man seen from such a vantage point, an envoy of the inhuman in a supposedly human world of everyday experience, is thus a "compatriot" in the process of becoming a stranger. He is a potential stranger, who discovers his alienation within himself and respects its rights outside himself. Ultimately, this approach also demonstrates a singular reversal of perspective of the anthropological pattern: from the defense of one's independence thanks to the effort of being different from everything else to the recognition thereof in the otherness found in oneself.

| | |

The relationship between man and his place of origin and residence, as well as the lifestyles and identity models related to it, has already been highlighted in quite a few insightful analyses and original systematizations in Polish writing on the subject. This subject involves different branches of scientific pursuit: from Zygmunt Bauman's philosophical sociology of modernity and postmodernity, through the studies of Ewa Rewers devoted to the cultural philosophy of space and Wojciech Burszta's analysis of anthropology of the present time, up to the current discussion about identity patterns in recent literature by authors like Przemysław Czapliński and Krzysztof Uniłowski.[3]

The reason for my attempt to outline the two types of the stranger figure, which in Polish literature determine man's condition on the threshold of the twentieth century, is that I am convinced of their broader appeal. They may be treated as distinct manifestations of the two most important routes followed by Polish contemporary literature in the search for identity patterns.

The Miłosz variant—let us call it the *settling-in strategy*—reflects an important regional-ethnocentric approach, whose past reveals at least three central issues. The first one occurred in the 1930s in the works of the Authentysts, the Lublin Czechowicz circle, the Vilnius-Żagarysts, among others, and posits a regional and rustic character as a distinctive reaction against the vicissitudes of modern life and the defense of provincial rights against centralization. The second wave appeared both in Poland and in exile in the sixties. Examples include the works of Andrzej Chciuk, Tadeusz Konwicki, Andrzej Kuśniewicz, Józef Mackiewicz, Włodzimierz Odojewski, and Julian Stryjkowski. The main feature of this variant is the mixed nostalgic and ironic approach to the "lost places" (Polish eastern provinces), treated as a counterbalance to the uprooting space and the homelessness of where the writers currently live. The third wave appeared in the early nineties, mainly in the works of the younger generation—Kazimierz Brakoniecki, Stefan Chwin, Paweł Huelle, Aleksander Jurewicz, Feliks Netz, Jerzy Pilch, Janusz Rudnicki, Andrzej Stasiuk, Olga Tokarczuk, and many others. Such literature of "small homelands" is focused, generally speaking, on discovering peculiarities (otherness, singularities) where the writers currently live. This eventually leads to a reassessment of both customary bonds between people and place and of traditional identity patterns.

The Gombrowicz variant—let us call it the *alienation strategy*—may serve as a summary for the search of individual routes for self-creation present in the writings of the Polish avant-garde in the interwar period. It documented the consequences of alienation and uprooting that resulted from experiencing modernity and then found its idiomatic fulfillment in the works of such diverse writers as Andrzej Bobkowski, Tadeusz Różewicz, and Adam Zagajewski. Eventually it conformed autonomous attempts at self-identification of the youngest generation of the above-mentioned group: Chwin, Pilch, and Rudnicki. Obviously, this should not be taken to mean that the twofold model of discovering or creating identity through people's relationship to where they live has been an exclusively Polish invention. On the contrary, it constitutes a feature common to modern literature in its entirety.[4] Its Polish character comes from local (historical and cultural) motivations and tangible forms of seeking identity: either through spiritual contact with physical places to ensure self-identification, or through establishing an identifying factor within oneself, that is, through a constant projection and reinterpretation of one's own existence.

From today's perspective we can clearly see that the initially distinct and diverse strategies have become more and more similar, largely owing to literary pursuits within an area of prevailing convictions that are gradually becoming more and more alike. The first such feature is the acknowledgment of dislocation as a natural and permanent feature of individual modes of existence. "We travel and live on the road here and there," writes Różewicz (1991, 37). "I see myself as a walking tree," says Miron Białoszewski, in an ingenious transposition of the classical metaphor of the symbiotic link between man and his place of residence. He adds, "It is we who give birth to those homes"

(1980, 64). Likewise, the state of being uprooted loses its exceptional and discriminating stamp of contemporary human condition. Instead, it becomes more and more often affirmed as a characteristic of universal and positive experience. Chwin confesses, "I treat uprooting not only as a natural state, but also a state in which values are or can be born" (in Wojciechowski 1996, 71). Lastly, the sense of alienation and its circumstances cease to determine only nonauthentic and negative modes of individual existence in its relationships with the external world. Instead, they become a positive manifestation of one's own actuality. Adam Zagajewski writes, "*I was foreign to them too, but I also became a little foreign to myself, and thus a little more real,* as if made of slightly sturdier stuff. . . . I found foreignness in my hometown. I found foreignness within me" (2000, 59; emphasis mine).

| | |

What we are is where we are from—a nineteenth-century person, either a Positivist or a Romantic might say about himself. I have no connection whatever with life, so I do not know who I am—said the desperate modernist on the threshold of the twentieth century. I feel I am a stranger, therefore I am—Zagajewski seems to be saying at the end of this century. Even such a cursory glance at the main stages of the journey undertaken by the modern wandering "stranger" permits us to see, in a metaphorical shortcut, the distance that has been covered, the magnitude of changes as well as the different contemporary forms of identity. That modernist "stranger who comes from an abyss" had the soul of a modern anthropologist—he set out to conquer the remote in order to discover himself in it. Conversely, today's surprised stranger eyes himself and his local community from the position of an anthropologist and ethnographer. Eventually, he returns home or has never left it in the first place, but cannot see in it anything exclusively his. Today's "strangers" not only perceive opportunities for themselves in settling in without taking root, in the compulsion to live somewhere only for a short period of time, they also discover that even the most familiar of all "our places" is marked with the presence of others (though they may be gone by now) and that even what is most mine, my "selfness," not only connects me with other people, but also with the extrahuman, truly alien, and truly actual.

Translated by Rafał Śmietana

Notes

Unless otherwise indicated, all translations from the Polish are by Rafał Śmietana.

1. In the original: "wir nicht sehr verlässlich zu Haus sind in der gedeuten Welt."

2. In the original:

> Gdziekolwiek jesteś, owijają ciebie kolory nieba,
> tak, jak tutaj, . . .
> ptaki są nazwane
> językiem tego miejsca: towhee przyszła do kuchni,
> posyp chleba na trawniku, przyleciały juncos.
>
> Gdziekolwiek jesteś, dotykasz kory drzew
> próbując jej chropowatości innej a domowej.
> Wdzięczny za wschody i zachody słońca
> gdziekolwiek jesteś, nie zdołasz być obcy.
>
> (Miłosz, 1984, 102)

3. I refer here to the following: Zygmunt Bauman, *Modernity and Ambiguity* (1995), Ewa Rewers, *Język i przestrzeń w poststrukturalistycznej filozofii kultury* (Language and space in the poststructuralist philosophy of culture) (1996); Wojciech J. Burszta, *Wymiary antropologicznego poznania kultury* (Dimensions of anthropological cultural cognition) (1992); Przemysław Czapliński, *Ślady przełomu: O prozie polskiej 1976–1996* (Vestiges of change: On Polish prose, 1976–1996) (1997); Krzysztof Uniłowski, *Skądinąd: Zapiski krytyczne* (Elsewhere: Critical notes) (1998).

4. To realize this more fully, it is sufficient to quote the memorable phrases from the expositions of two great novels of the twentieth century. Marcel Proust in *Remembrance of Things Past* says, "when I awoke at midnight, not knowing where I was, I could not be sure at first who I was; . . . but then the memory, not yet of the place in which I was, but of various other places where I had lived and might now very possibly be, would come like a rope let down from heaven to draw me up out of the abyss of non-being, from which I could never have escaped by myself" (1970, 5). And Robert Musil writes, "We overestimate the importance of knowing where we are because in nomadic times it was essential to recognize the tribal feeding grounds" (1995, 3–4).

Works Cited

Adorno, Theodor W. 1973. *Negative Dialectics.* Trans. E. B. Ashton. New York: Seabury Press.

Benn, Gottfried. 1951. *Probleme der Lyrik.* Wiesbaden: Limes Verlag.

Białoszewski, Miron. 1980. *Rozkurz* (Maelstrom). Warsaw: PIW.

Brzozowski, Stanisław. 1990. "Bergson à Sorel." In *Idee: Wstęp do filozofii dojrzałości życiowej* (Ideas: Introduction to the philosophy of the maturity of life). Introduction by Andrzej Walicki. Kraków: Wydawnictwo Literackie.

———. 2000. *Pamiętnik.* Kraków: Czytelnik.

Chwin, Stefan. 1997. "Wyobraźnia i duch miejsca." *Tytuł* 3–4: 27–28.

Gombrowicz, Witold. 1961. *Ferdydurke.* Trans. Eric Mosbacher. New York: Grove Press.

———. 1988–89. *Diary.* Trans. Lillian Vallee. Gen. ed. Jan Kott. 3 vols. Evanston: Northwestern University Press.

———. 1991. "Gombrowicz: Forma i rytuał" (Gombrowicz: Form and ritual). Interview by Piero Sanavio. In *Gombrowicz filozof* (Gombrowicz the philosopher). Texts selected by Francesco Cataluccio and Jerzy Illg, 25–68. Kraków: Znak.

———. 1996. *Testament: Rozmowy z Dominique de Roux* (Last will: Conversations with Dominique de Roux). Kraków: Wydawnictwo Literackie.

Janik, Allan, and Toulmin, Stephen. 1973. *Wittgenstein's Vienna.* New York: Simon and Schuster.

Levinas, Emanuel. 1979. *Totality and Infinity: An Essay on Exteriority.* Trans. Alphonso Lingis. The Hague: Martinus Nijhoff.

Miłosz, Czesław. 1973. *Selected Poems.* Trans. by Peter Dale Scott et al. Introduction by K. Rexroth. New York: Seabury Press.

———. 1981. *Selected Poems: Revised.* New York: Ecco.

———. 1983. *The History of Polish Literature.* Berkeley: University of California Press.

———. 1984. *Wiersze.* Kraków: Wydawnictwo Literackie.

———. 1986. *Unattainable Earth.* Trans. Czesław Miłosz and Robert Hass. New York: Ecco Press.

———. 1997. "Być emigrantem" (To be an émigré). In *Życie na wyspach* (Life on islands). Kraków: Znak.

Musil, Robert. 1995. *The Man without Qualities.* Trans. Sophie Wilkins. New York: Knopf.

Proust, Marcel. 1970. *Swann's Way.* Trans. G. K. Scott Montcrieff. New York: Random House.

Rilke, Rainer Maria. 1977. *Duino Elegies and the Sonnets to Orpheus.* Trans. A. Poulin Jr. Boston: Houghton Mifflin.

Różewicz, Tadeusz. 1991. "Der Tod ist ein Meister aus Deutschland" (Death is a German master). In *Płaskorzeźba* (Bas-relief). Wrocław: Wydawnictwo Dolnośląskie.

Wojciechowski, Wojciech. 1996. "Uroki wykorzenienia: O narracji reistycznej, grach z losem i kilku innych pokusach: Rozmowa ze Stefanem Chwinem" (Pleasures of uprootedness: On the reistic narrative, playing with fate, and a few other temptations: Interview with Stefan Chwin). In *Rozmowy Tytułu,* ed. Krystyna Chwin, 32–41. Gdańsk: Biblioteka Tytułu.

Woolf, Virginia. 1968. *Collected Essays.* 2 vols. London: Hogarth Press.

Zagajewski, Adam. 2000. *Another Beauty.* Trans. Clare Cavanagh. New York: Farrar, Straus and Giroux.

2 Home as Other in the Work of Czesław Miłosz

Kim Jastremski

IN A 1979 essay, couched as a letter to the Lithuanian poet Tomas Venclova, Czesław Miłosz wrote:

> Recently one of my friends asked me why I return so insistently in my memories to Wilno and to Lithuania, as my poems and prose writings reveal. I replied that, in my opinion, this has nothing to do with an emigré's sentimentality, for I would not want to go back. What is at work here, no doubt, is a search for reality purified by the passage of time. . . . Wilno became a reference mark for me—of possibility. (1991, 23)

The possibility Miłosz finds in Wilno and Lithuania is that of a kind of poetic apokatastasis, in which there is a complete restoration of the land of his birth. For Miłosz, the "search for reality purified by the passage of time" takes the form of an ongoing literary creation of his homeland. His writing provides its map, showing both the way through and the contours of his imagined homeland—its flora and fauna, landscape and people, as well as its moral order, in all times and seasons. Before there can be a homecoming, however, or a reappropriation of the wholeness of home, the character of the original unity of his pre-exilic home must be established. For this reason, in his search for an end to the catastrophic ruptures of his adult reality—war, loss of home and family, exile—Miłosz frequently uses a child's naive point of view to access a time in which the world held for him a sacred and unutterable, but still tangible, meaning. The result is a collection of works, spanning the more than fifty years of Miłosz's publishing career, which describe the shape and feeling of Miłosz's personal Arcadia, the homeland that will bring salvation from the exile of adulthood and twentieth-century modernity.

Miłosz was born on June 30, 1911, in his family's former manorial village of Szetejnie, on the banks of the Niewiaża River, in what was then the Grand Duchy of Lithuania, within the Russian Empire.[1] His family was of the Polish-speaking gentry, a class that was politically and economically ruined by the time of Miłosz's birth, but whose grand heritage nonetheless persisted in collective memory. Miłosz counts himself among the last of the Polish-Lithuanians, recalling, "we were something else, Lithuanians, but not in the accepted twentieth-century sense, which says that to be a Lithuanian you have to speak Lithuanian" (1987a, 4). Miłosz's father, Aleksander Miłosz, was a highway engineer for the czar's army from 1914 to 1918; the family, including his mother, Weronika Miłosz (née Kunat), and his younger brother, Andrzej, traveled throughout Russia and Siberia when Miłosz was a child. They were in the Russian town of Rzhev, on the Volga River, at the outbreak of the 1917 October Revolution. After the revolution, the young Miłosz spent several formative years with his grandparents in the village of his birth and later moved to Wilno, the capital, for his higher education. The chaos of his early wanderings through war-torn Russia, countered by the peace he remembers in the pastoral setting of the Lithuanian river valley, would later become the frequent subject of his poetry and prose.

Although he did not actually leave Lithuania as a political exile until 1940, exile had been a state of mind for Miłosz at least since 1937, when he wrote from Warsaw, "W mojej ojczyźnie, do której nie wrócę" ("In my homeland, to which I shall not return") (1976, 41). Miłosz eventually emigrated from Poland to France in 1951, and to the United States in 1960. His constant return in his poetry to Szetejnie, to Wilno, and to Lithuania indicates the sense of rupture Miłosz incurred from his exile and his desire to recapture the sense of unity he once felt in his childhood home—a unity that might be compared to Lacan's concept of the imaginary, the time before the knowledge of division between self and other. The opposition between the chaos of exile and the half-remembered, half-imagined peace of home is a major leitmotif in Miłosz's poetry and provides the foundation for understanding the meaning of home in his oeuvre. In fact, the word *home* in Miłosz's writing marks two essential points: home as point of origin and home as destination, the future home that the exiled poet strives to reach through his writing. "In the sacral dimension," writes Aleksander Fiut, "the homeland is Paradise; in the historical dimension, it is Lithuania" (1990, 33).[2] These two homes, past and future, historical and spiritual, function in a triangular dynamic with the poet's state of exile. For Miłosz, home is constantly elsewhere and other, exile is constantly present and self, and the poet constantly strives but never succeeds in revising that relationship.[3]

Of the transformation of home that takes place in the imaginations of exiles, Miłosz writes, "their lands in the course of time are transformed in memory and take on outlines that are no longer verifiable" (1968, 106). Miłosz is a poet greatly concerned with outlines and boundary areas—imaginary borders where two opposing ideas meet: home/exile, self/other, matter/spirit, reality/illusion, being/action, despair/faith, male/female, humanity/animality. It is in these blurred border areas that such oppositions have the potential to disappear, with a restored unity reminiscent of the original one emerging in their place. In this way, the opposing ideas of home and exile merge in Miłosz's work to form a new home, Paradise. Often invoking the ideas of William Blake (but without adopting Blake's idealism), Miłosz's poetry strives to unite both the Innocence of his childhood home and his Experience of exile to form a new home, an Innocence regained that would be even more beautiful than the original because of its inclusiveness.[4] The poet's work is the pursuit of this new home and of a verifiable outline of its borders. This work takes place in the realm of the imagination, where syzygy of opposites is routine, as Miłosz relates:

> When Tomas brought the news that the house I was born in no longer exists,
> Neither the lane nor the park sloping to the river, nothing,
> I had a dream of return. Multicolored. Joyous. I was able to fly.
> (1984b, 71)

Loss and recovery exist simultaneously in the poet's dream, for the imagination facilitates the impossible: homecoming.

As Michael Seidel writes, "the task for the exile, especially the exiled artist, is to transform the figure of rupture back into a figure of connection" (1986, x). This transformation is facilitated by language. The poet Jane Hirshfield explains the particular ability poetry has to alter the state of division between self and other, such as is experienced by the exile:

> Human vision divides. Depending as it does on the clear perception of boundaries, it creates a feeling of the outer as opposed to the self, of distinct

> and separate being. We say, and feel, that we look "out": from the center of our being, vision travels away from us and into the world. But a sound is perceived as coming toward and entering us, bringing the outer within: sound lives in the movement of our own inner bones joining in the resonance of its outer source. (1997, 178)

In exile, division and boundaries form the "figure of rupture." Poetry, being born of the realm of sound, is the means by which the outer is brought within, by which the other breaks through the boundaries of the self, thereby creating a "figure of connection," which forms the space of the new home.

Poetry, then, provides Miłosz with the possibility for recreating the unity of his original home, as the following poem suggests:

> To find my home in one sentence, concise, as if hammered in metal. Not to enchant anybody. Not to earn a lasting name in posterity. An unnamed need for order, for rhythm, for form, which three words are opposed to chaos and nothingness. (1988, 441).

This short prose poem distills the myriad of meanings *home* acquires in Miłosz's poetry. The poem's designation of date and place ("Berkeley—Paris—Cambridge, Massachusetts, 1981–1983") indicates the transitory nature of Miłosz's geographical home, which we know to be Lithuania, or Poland, or France, or California. The strength of home—home as fortress or castle, a frequently encountered metaphor in Miłosz's poetry[5]—is evident in the force of the words that construct it: "as if hammered in metal." The potential for language to be that metal, hammered into the shape of home by the poet, indicates the importance of language in creating order (home) out of chaos (exile), connection from rupture. The form of words, the structure of sentences, the rhythm of stanzas and verse, all serve to combat the incomprehensible babble of the land of Ulro by overcoming the division between self and other. We find evidence of this in the fact that Miłosz writes all his poems in his native Polish,[6] despite having been banned from publishing in Poland for almost thirty years.

Fiut writes that Miłosz's "enchantment with physical beauty," demonstrated throughout his oeuvre, is "accompanied by a strong, erotically tinged desire for possession" (1990, 37). This desire for possession provides the impetus for Miłosz's poetic transports into the past, for it is only in the past, as a child, that he had the wholeness of vision necessary to know the names of things—the key to possessing them. The desire to recover the name of home is the impetus behind the poem "To find my home. . ." It is a poem of intimate desire; the repeated infinitives ("to find," "not to enchant," "not to earn") place the poem in the conditional mode, just one example of how Miłosz's poetic search for home often mirrors the language of erotic desire (see below). Home thus becomes the Lacanian Other, the woman to Miłosz's almost always masculine poetic voice, the thing that, paradoxically, must be distant to be named and brought closer, but that, once named, is even further divorced from the self. The language of the poem emphasizes the importance of finding the name of home; his home must be concisely rendered in order to be conjured into the present reality of the self.

"Esse" (1954), a prose poem, the bulk of which is one long paragraph describing the ecstasy of a vision of beauty in the Paris metro, depicts the recognition of the barrier between self and other, which is not only inherent in the romantic/erotic relationship, but in the exile's process of defining home. The poem's date indicates that it was written early in Miłosz's exile during an extremely lonely period in France. The male persona in "Esse" bemoans his inability to truly know the woman in the metro, the inability of a subject to absorb an object:

> I looked at that face, dumbfounded. The lights of the *métro* stations flew by; I didn't notice them. What can be done, if our sight lacks absolute power to devour objects ecstatically, in an instant, leaving nothing more than the void of an ideal form, a sign like a hieroglyph simplified from the drawing of an animal or a bird? (1988, 221)[7]

Miłosz's choice of form here, the prose poem over a more formal structure, reflects the hope that he will capture the rush of thoughts occurring in the mind of the persona all at once. There are no line or stanza breaks indicating pauses because there are no pauses in the persona's thoughts in the tumult of the moment depicted. The prose poem, then, is in this case the most appropriate medium to transmit the experience of being, of *esse.*

The persona recognizes that the object of his desire is unattainable, she—like his childhood home—moves quickly through time and space; it is out of his power to keep her from that motion forward. Instead, he is left with the empty shell of an ideal; a reference, perhaps, to Plato's notion of ideal forms, taken up by Jung in his idea of archetypes and discussed at length by Miłosz in *The Land of Ulro.* For the persona, as for Miłosz, the concept of the archetype, or ideal form of "the perfect woman" is not at all satisfying, when compared with the reality he knew for an instant on the metro. Listing her attributes, the persona is frustrated and again cries out, "but why isn't the power of sight absolute?" ("ale dlaczego wzrok nie ma siły absolutnej?").

The persona's unanswered question is followed by his attempt to describe how his understanding of the object would change, were he to have the power of absolute vision:

> A slightly snub nose, a high brow with sleekly brushed-back hair, the line of the chin—but why isn't the power of sight absolute?—and in a whiteness tinged with pink two sculpted holes, containing a dark, lustrous lava. To absorb that face but to have it simultaneously against the background of all spring boughs, walls, waves, in its weeping, its laughter, moving it back fifteen years, or ahead thirty. ("Esse," 1988, 221)[8]

Were the persona able to have the relationship with the object he desires, he would see her in all her complexity, in all times and in all places, in all moods and at all ages—removed from the human reality of fixed time and space. This is impossible, though, for the persona is capable of expressing his desire only in terms of possession and definition: "To have. It is not even a desire. Like a butterfly, a fish, the stem of a plant, only more mysterious" ("Mieć. To nawet nie pożądanie. Jak motyl, ryba, łodyga rośliny, tylko rzecz bardziej tajemnicza"). The subject's striving to merge with the object, although indicative of a desire to achieve the communion of dialogue with her, is characterized by the persona in possessive terms, denying the possibility of a true union of equals. The shift of verbal tense from past ("przyglądałemsię," "przebiegały," "nie zauważałem") to infinitive forms ("wchłonąć," "mieć") reinforces the distance between the persona and the object of his vision, as the fact-bearing, simple past tense dissolves into infinitives of desire such as were seen in "To find my home . . ."

The next section implies the persona's awareness not only that to name the object is impossible, but that any name he might find would be inadequate to express the joy he feels in the knowledge of their mutual existence:

> And so it befell me that after so many attempts at naming the world, I am able only to repeat, harping on one string, the highest, the unique avowal

> beyond which no power can attain: *I am, she is.* Shout, blow the trumpets, make thousands-strong marches, leap, rend your clothing, repeating only: *is!* (221)[9]

Even this joy is marred by the separation between the subject and object, expressed in the two pronoun-verb forms "I am—she is," and (in the Polish) marked graphically by the poet as a binary opposition by the use of the dash between the two. Thus, while there is a moment of joy in the poem (a significant one, where the change from "*I am, she is*" to "only: *is!*" signals a brief merging of subject and object, a moment of achievement of unity), it is concurrent with the knowledge that it is a false joy, that centuries of writers have already attempted and failed what the persona desires:

> And why have so many pages, tons, desksful of pages, been written, if I can only babble as though I were the first to emerge from the loam onto the shores of the ocean? What good were the civilizations of the Sun, the red dust of crumbling cities, armaments and engines in the dust of deserts, if they have added nothing to the sound *is?* (1987b, 2:47; my translation)[10]

This section recalls the references to Eliot's wasteland in the 1945 poem "Outskirts," signaling a return to the land of Ulro. The question mark after the last repetition of "jest?" (is?) marks the transition from the persona's joy to his painful realization that his momentary merging with the object is over. It is a foreboding question mark, anticipating the next section of the poem, in which the persona expresses his disillusionment and doubt in the possibility of reunion. In that question mark he relives the experience of the Fall from innocence experienced by the child, and the exile from home experienced by the adult.

The poem ends with a new, short paragraph, graphically signifying the interruption of the ecstasy, the rupture of the vision of beauty (a rupture made more clear in the English translation, which omits the above sentences on the efforts of civilization to express this joy, thereby emphasizing the sharp change in mood from the joy of the persona [powtarzając to jedno: jest!] to his despondency):

> She got out at Raspail. I was left behind with the immensity of existing things. A sponge, suffering because it cannot saturate itself; a river, suffering because reflections of clouds and trees are not clouds and trees. (221)[11]

The simplicity of the first short sentence of this paragraph, in which the woman leaves the metro, further dramatizes the abruptness of the shift in mood. Miłosz (1998a, 40) calls "Esse" "a short love poem" ("krótki wiersz miłosny"), revealing his assessment of erotic love, at least the kind that is preserved in this poem: the merging of self and other is real but temporary, fleeting; the brief experience of the new home is ecstatic but painful. Love, as experienced by the persona in the poem, is entirely reminiscent of Adam's experience of the Fall. The recognition of other and the attempt to cross the barrier between the self and other is momentarily successful, but ultimately a painful failure. The persona is violently returned to the land of Ulro, the land of suffering and insatiability, where the outside world approaches the surface of the self—in the way that trees and clouds imprint themselves on the surface of a river—but does not penetrate the self, and the self cannot contain it. Merging of self and other, of subject and object, is impossible, the end of "Esse" claims.[12]

As "Esse" illustrates, women in Miłosz's poetry often symbolize the unknown other, being one of the most obvious opposites of Miłosz's typically male lyrical personae. Like Mickiewicz's Zosia, women represent for Miłosz not only the typical feminine tropes of fertility and regeneration, but also a vision of the lost homeland, in that they carry the potential for a union of opposites and thus the connection necessary to transform the rupture of exile. While women are often found in the role of other in Miłosz's poetry, they are symbolic of a much larger desire—the desire of the self to merge with other.[13] Miłosz describes this desire, seen at work in "Esse," as "a spasm in the throat, staring at the face of every woman passing in the street. Wanting not her but all the earth" ("Do skurczu w gardle wpatrujący się w twarz każdej mijanej na ulicy kobiety. Pożądający nie jej, ale całej ziemi") (Miłosz 1984b, 47). For Miłosz, the other is very often female; but in addition to being objects of sexual desire, their sex is representative of a larger metaphysical desire to blend opposites, to destroy the boundaries separating the self from other and find the passage from exile.

Miłosz likens his role as a poet to that of a hunter of names, of the essence of things.[14] Miłosz traces his desire to name to his childhood, as seen in the anecdotes about keeping nature notebooks in *Rodzinna Europa* (1958; translated in 1968 as *Native Realm*). His 1955 novel *Dolina Issy* (translated in 1981 as *The Issa Valley*) is a semiautobiographical account of his boyhood in

Lithuania, which Miłosz says he wrote as a kind of "self-therapy" (Miłosz 1991, 24), a retreat to the time when he knew the names of things. The landscape of this novel, the manor house in which much of the action takes place, as well as the characters, are all drawn from Miłosz's memory of his own Lithuanian childhood. The character of Tomasz,[15] while admittedly semifictional, gives us important insight into Miłosz's summation of his own experiences during the difficult transition from childhood to adolescence, as Miłosz claims that *The Issa Valley* deals with "various problems and dilemmas of mine" (Gorczyńska and Fiut 1992, 103). Like Miłosz as a boy, Tomasz loves nature and spends much of his time studying the animals and plants of his region and drawing pictures of them in notebooks, labeling them in Latin. Tomasz too is a hunter of names:

> The notebook proved that Thomas had the gift of concentrating on things that excited him. To name a bird, to case it in letters, was tantamount to owning it forever. . . . In reality, everything about birds gave rise to unease. Was it enough, he wondered, to verify their existence? (Miłosz 1991, 151)

Tomasz's question marks the difference between the child, to whom such a question would never occur, and the adolescent, or the implied adult narrator. In adolescence, the child comes to recognize the boundary between self and other. The adolescent's growing awareness of this barrier awakens in him a desire to cross it. Eros awakens the knowledge of other in the self, a knowledge the child does not embody to the extent that the adult does.

Tomasz turns twelve in *The Issa Valley,* and he becomes a real hunter. The bird calls he had mastered to observe the birds of his forest now serve a different purpose. There is an essential barrier between Tomasz and the animals he hunts, a barrier that he hopes to destroy in the hunt, but that he finds indestructible. He cannot commune with the grouse the way he wants to, he can only come very close. In mastering a bird's call, Tomasz momentarily becomes the bird; he merges with it—only to kill it.

> Struck by a thunderbolt, [the grouse] had died instantly. But he, Thomas, still resided on this side of the thunderbolt. They had met in the only way possible, and he felt a twinge of remorse that it could never be otherwise. The truth was that Thomas hungered for a sort of impossible communion with living creatures. Why this barrier, and why become a hunter if one loved nature? (Miłosz 1981, 176)

Just as Tomasz's voice can mimic but never replicate the voices of the birds, so do the poet's words signal but not contain the thing he hopes to capture. Like Tomasz, the poet can only capture the thing when it is dead. He owns the thing, but learns that to possess something, to capture it, is to destroy exactly that which he was hunting—its essence, its reality. Why, then, become a poet?

Miłosz seems to recount Tomasz's lesson when, in discussing the architectural form of Eastern Orthodox Churches, he writes, "no doubt this fulfills a human need for an enclosed, delineated space, subject to its own laws and fenced off from that other, limitless space" (Miłosz 1991, 16). This enclosed space, safe from the chaos of the infinite world, is home. It is also a poem (as "Świat: Poema naiwne" [The world: A naive poem] attests; see below). In seeking the names of things, Miłosz strives to draw the boundaries of his home. Although defining an object, memory, or idea by placing it in the formal structure of a poem has the power to make it real by providing it with the physical form of language, it also destroys the very essence of its spiritual reality, of its eternal Truth, by denying it the fluidity of motion through time and space. Perhaps for this reason, Miłosz prefaces his essay about Wilno, "Zaczynając od moich ulic" (Beginning with my streets), with the poem "Miasto bez imienia" (City without a name). The poem illustrates that Wilno exists for Miłosz only in the realm of his imagination, only as an ideal, in the way that the animals, birds, and insects in young Miłosz's (and Tomasz's) nature notebooks "did not live in thickets but in an ideal space outside of time" (1982, 19). Indeed, Miłosz writes in the poem, "perhaps I am even glad not to find the desired word," for to find that word would be to expose his beloved Wilno—or Szetejnie, or Lithuania—to the flaw of poetry: constrictive definition. Naming a thing calls it into the present reality of the poet, but damages it, soils it, by denying it the metaphysical reality of fluid time and space.

The belief that it is possible to name a thing and not destroy it is perhaps naive; it constitutes childhood faith in existence. Miłosz writes, "the very act of naming things presupposes a faith in their existence and thus in a true world, whatever Nietzsche might say" (1983, 57). This childlike faith is Miłosz's response to Nietzsche's statement "God is dead." Childlikeness is something that the adult Miłosz must retain if he wants to survive his many exiles—from childhood, from innocence, from Lithuania, from Poland. His writing is an expression of his desire to believe in the existence of home, to believe that he can create a new home in his imagination and call it into being without "killing" it, without exiling himself all over again.

To invoke Lacan again, the only satisfaction of desire for the original home is a substitute home, the paradise of the imagination, which is invariably closer to myth or legend than to reality, but which comes to replace reality in the mind of the poet, so that the "quest for reality" Miłosz (1980, 6) describes in his Nobel speech is synonymous with the pursuit of home/ Paradise. Miłosz is understandably attracted to writers like Blake and Dante, who use the metaphor of worlds lost and worlds refound to represent our common human experience. He finds the comfort of an intellectual home in the work of other thinkers whose philosophies of the imagination have influenced his own. Much of Miłosz's own writing on the subject of the imagination centers around the phenomenon of imagining a new homeland for oneself. He explores the possibility of accessing the power of the imagination to create a refuge for himself, as an exile from Lithuania and Poland, and as Adam's descendant and exile from Eden.

> Homelessness, in the tribal as well as the geographical sense, became a *correspondence* of the spiritual exile of modern man, and his own quest for a homeland, for a place, acquired a double meaning. That the notion of homeland is born of the same realm as myth and fable we, above all, can appreciate—we as readers of *Pan Tadeusz* (. . . I finally understood it for what it was: a realized fairy tale). . . . Not all who are homeless wish to remain so . . . yet those in Carcassonne who publish novels in *langue d'oc* must be aware of the mythmaking, legendmaking aspect of their enterprise. I can sympathize with them; indeed . . . I understood that a homeland was both very much a need and a product of the imagination. (Miłosz 1984a, 76)

Miłosz is aware of the mythmaking aspect of his enterprise. His homeland as depicted in his poetry is both "a need and a product of [his] imagination," which implies on the one hand a strong desire for it to exist and a tacit acknowledgment that it does not exist—the desire and the knowledge are concurrent; thus, the literary creation of a homeland is for Miłosz a unifying experience, it acknowledges the conflict and rejoices in it.

In his writing on Mickiewicz's *Pan Tadeusz*, we see the literal description of a burgeoning opposition of soul to body at the same time as the text itself performs a blurring of oppositions on another level:

> In ancient, pre-Christian symbolism, the difference between a repentant spirit and a night bird, a moth, or an insect was blurred, the one being synonymous with the other, just as it is blurred in the early Mickiewicz, to the glory of his poetry. These same spirits take on a gelatinous solidity and commence to lead a life of their own. *So, too, one's native land.* At first it is a visible, palpable Lithuania: native landscapes, relatives, friends, *body and soul coalesced.* Later, the soul abandons the body, to become an Idea, a presence, until it is finally raised to the mythical. (Miłosz 1984a, 118; emphasis mine)

Historical past and present, self and other, subject and object, body and soul, home and exile, all converge in this passage, so that it is unclear whether Miłosz is speaking of Mickiewicz's Lithuania or his own. Both the Lithuania of *Pan Tadeusz* and of his own past are legends in Miłosz's imagination. Home, to the exile, becomes an ideal form whose pursuit is in and of itself a goal. The idea of home, the soul, becomes raised to the level of myth in the mind, a myth in which there is a reunion of soul and body, home and exile. In the realm of the imagination the opposition between home and exile contains within it the merging of the two.

Miłosz draws on other mystical traditions in his effort to strengthen the imagination in its pursuit of home. In *The Land of Ulro,* Miłosz explains his attraction to Blake and Swedenborg, as well as to older practices such as alchemy. The alchemists believed, Miłosz tells us, that by reasoned study of the nature of the elements of this world, humans could attain (or reattain) the knowledge of the spiritual world and thus a reunion of matter and spirit. The alchemical goal of the transmutation of matter is very much akin to the concept of poetic apokatastasis as the transformation of words to reunited spirit and flesh in "time redeemed." Miłosz writes that his kinsman, the French-Lithuanian metaphysical poet Oscar Milosz,

> envisioned the future of poetry as a transmutation both of the poet and of his art; hence the title [of his great metaphysical tract] *Ars Magna,* the Great Art—a synonym for alchemy in the Middle Ages. Now, alchemy, as we know, was premised . . . on the simultaneous regeneration of the adept and of the matter being transmuted. (Miłosz 1984a, 212)

This is the essence of Miłosz's poetic alchemy—it is based in the eschatological belief in a restoration of both his homeland and himself. While Miłosz (1985, 24) claims never to have had a "night of fire" like Oscar Milosz, Pascal, or Swedenborg, Miłosz is a hermetic poet in that he writes in the way the alchemist, the adept, conducted his experiments; his goal is to transmute matter, the object of his poem, into gold, into reality, so that it does not simply remain a sign on a page. Through this process, Miłosz, too, will be regenerated.

The poet's task, like the alchemist's, is a nearly impossible one, achieved only through great faith: to represent the eternal now with language, a human construct that by its very nature destroys the possibility of achieving unity of matter and spirit. In defining home with a word, language locks its essence into time and space, robbing it of its potential spiritual value. However impossible, though, it is the poet's quest to find a language for home that can break the bonds of time and space, just as the alchemist sought the formula to release the essence of matter from its shape. Miłosz writes of the relationship between alchemy and art:

> After the writings of C. G. Jung and Mircea Eliade it would be frivolous to dismiss as mere immaturity and pseudo-science the Sixteenth-Century thought strongly marked by hermetic writings and alchemy. . . . The greatness of many works of art created then is due to a mysterious web of meanings hidden beneath a representation of external reality. (1985, 30)

So, too, is Miłosz's poetry underpinned by a "mysterious web of meanings hidden beneath a representation of external reality." Indeed, Miłosz characterizes his own poetry as "a poetry of incantation . . . a sensitivity to the rhythmic structure of a line even if I'm writing prose" (Gorczyńska and Fiut, 1992, 316).

The alchemist is transported back to the moment of creation by means of the Philosopher's Stone:

> Ultimately, the real object of alchemical experimentation was that of creating the Philosopher's Stone, the physical vehicle for the "divine spark" necessary to the process of transmutation. . . . if a tiny piece of the Philosopher's Stone were placed on the surface of water, the complete process of creation would take place in miniature, so that the entire story of the unfolding of the universe could be perceived by the experimenter. (*Alchemy* 1994, 50)

The Philosopher's Stone represented for the alchemists the knowledge of the past. It represented the time before humans and knowledge were separated. The knowledge the alchemist sought was gnosis: spiritual knowledge, not rational, scientific knowledge, for which Miłosz derides Blake's Unholy Trinity:

> A scientist of the Baconian, Lockian, or Newtonian school suffers the illusion that knowledge is something impersonal, disembodied—that, in other words, only one faculty, the personal, suffices. The image of the world adduced by this science is a false one. To be free of its coercive power is to refute that false eternity (an endless succession of moments lapsing into nothingness) and false infinity (of illusory space, indefinite duration), and to know true eternity and infinity as the eternal now. (1984a, 175)

The knowledge of the alchemists and other mystics Miłosz consults refutes the idea of knowledge imposed by rational science and expands the ideas of time and space to include all time and all space in an eternal present of the imagination.

Miłosz's attempts to recover, in his words, "the broken unity of the internal and the external, spirit and matter, religion and science" (Miłosz 1985, 30) have led him to develop a philosophy of writing that finds its basis in an expansion of the concepts of time and space. For Miłosz, as for the alchemists, the modern idea of fixed time and space is a hindrance to reaching the "eternal now," which is the unity of matter and spirit. It can only be reached through the imagination, for only the imagination is capable of accommodating the necessary fluidity of time and space. Miłosz's vision of the eternal now—his personal Philosopher's Stone—has taken the shape of his imagined homeland, a homeland that does not exist anywhere except in his imagination, but that he strives to bring into existence through his constant literary invocation of it.

There are countless moments in Miłosz's poetry in which we are transported with his persona back into a moment in his Lithuanian childhood, to Miłosz's personal moment of creation.[16] An early example of this harking back to childhood is Miłosz's "The World: A Naive Poem," a cycle of poems from 1943 in which the persona describes the places and people of his childhood through the eyes of the child he once was. "The World" recreates the child's naive image of the world in Miłosz's adult world of Warsaw during the Occupation. In *Abecadło Miłosza* (Miłosz's ABC's), Miłosz describes the act of writing "The World" as a consciously defensive one:

> I wrote cheerful verses—*The World* and a couple of others—in the very midst of what was going on in *anus mundi,* and not in the least out of ignorance. . . . Cheerful verses written in the midst of horror declare themselves for life, they are the revolt of the body against its annihilation. They are *carmina* [songs], or incantations, cast so that in an instant atrocity would disappear and order would appear—the order of civilization, or of childhood peace, which, after all, amounts to the same thing. (1997, 40–41)

Miłosz's identification of "The World" with incantatory songs indicates the level of confidence Miłosz has in poetry, in the power of a particular rhythm and organization of words to preserve that which has been lost. The incantatory feel of "The World" is indeed interwoven in the rhythm of its language. Its cadences resemble those of a child's primer (Miłosz 1984b, 211) and it is evident that the poem is intended not simply to tell of "The World" from a child's point of view, but to teach that world, to encourage listeners and readers to memorize that world, so that they, too, will have access to its magical spell. Miłosz attempts to combat wartime doubt and despair with a child's faith in the essential meaning of the world. The invocation of the world of childhood resonates on many levels; it is of course an outcry against the moral decay that the evil of war demonstrates. At the same time, "The World" affirms Miłosz's belief in the essential goodness of the body, of the material world. In wartime, when the destruction of the material world, of bodies and buildings both, causes Miłosz to question the goodness of such weak, fleeting things, he reminds himself that the physical nature of humans is in partnership with their spiritual nature. Miłosz celebrates this unity through poetry that recalls a prior time of innocence, when knowledge of opposition did not assume a split between the two members of an oppositional pair, but rather a symbiotic, pre-exilic relationship.

Miłosz's acknowledgment, in the subtitle ("A Naive Poem"), of the poem's naiveté immediately addresses the conflict between the adult's education in the "true" mechanisms behind the phenomena we observe and the child's simple explanations for those phenomena, at the same time that it addresses the unbreakable union within this conflict between the child's naiveté and the adult's rationality. As Helen Vendler notes, the subtitle "is consciously set before us as though to disarm objection. The ignorantly naive does not call itself naive" (1999, 129). With this acknowledgment, Miłosz creates a space in which the poem can be written, safe from rational criticism, much as the child is safe from the knowledge of adult concepts. Before the poem even begins, then, we are aware of the freedom and safety the world of a child provides the adult poet.

The form the poet chooses to give his poem is a further signal to the reader of the poet's desire for a return to more innocent times. The whole poem primarily consists of smaller three- or four-stanza poems with eleven-syllable (5 + 6) lines ending in feminine rhyme.[17] Not only does Miłosz's choice of this stylized meter sound to the Polish reader like an elementary school primer, but, as Lucylla Pszczołowska (1997, 308) also notes, the meter recalls the poetry of Juliusz Słowacki and the Romantic period. As Miłosz has written, he is attracted to Romanticism for its concern with human subjectivity and the imagination, but is at the same time appalled by its disdain for rationality.[18] Fiut comments on the Romantic idealism and sublimation of "The World" that "in a *de profundis* of the greatest torment, shame, and despair, Miłosz's imagination turns toward the land of his childhood years, where home guaranteed safety, the imponderables were sacred, and nature, robed in all its gleaming colors, was a blessing to man" (1990, 46). In "The World," Miłosz borrows from the lessons of childhood as well as from highly formal Romantic poetics in his attempts to bring order to the chaos around him, as well as to remind himself and his reader that the objective truth of death and destruction need not be the only truth.

A close examination of "The World" reveals the nature of the recovery of the child's world and its importance to the poetic goal of recreating home. The poet uses the naive perspective of the child to access the child's world and the child's faith in the existence of that world. Jan Błoński reminds us that the apparent naiveté of the lyric voice in "The World" is deliberately chosen by the poet, "because there are some truths that can only be told by a child or a simpleton" (Błoński 1998, 24). Out of philosophical necessity, the educated, adult Miłosz adopts the simple voice of a child. Once the narrative point of view of the child is established in the opening poems of "The World," Miłosz inserts himself into the poem. This is most evident in the three poems—"Faith," "Hope," and "Love"—that form the moral and structural center of "The World," where the poet invites his adult self to enter the world of the poem and enjoy the perspective of the child. Only in this way can such a poem be written in such times: in "the asshole of the world" (*anus mundi*) (Miłosz 1997, 41) the cycle presents the simple hierarchy of existence, "from its humblest, most natural beings, to the highest, most spiritual," and "the pronouncement of a simpleton is actually the pronouncement of a sage" (Błoński 1998, 24).

The first poem of the cycle, "Droga" (The road),[19] confirms the idea that the child's world provides the poet with a space of freedom and safety. The world seems to have begun in this place, as seen in the rhyme linking "valley" and "begins" ("dolina," "zaczyna"), and it is thus immediately associated not only with Miłosz's birthplace in the Niewiaża River valley, but also with primordial Paradise. The spaciousness and fertility of the child's world is evident in the first verb, "expands" or "spreads out" ("ściele się"): "There, where you see a green valley" ("Tam, gdzie zielona ściele się dolina"), yet this expansiveness is not threatening; rather, it is manageable, as we see in the last line, "And from his flower bed [he] inspects the whole region" ("I z grządki całą widzi okolicę"). In keeping with the comfort and contentment the child feels at home, the child's travel on the road is *toward* home, and the world is something the child views *from* home. "The Road" presents the child's world as full of possibility, but that possibility is merely acknowledged and not exploited, as the child looks outward, choosing to remain within the confines of the gate articulated in the second poem, "Furtka" (The gate). In fact, in the child's view, the gate is more important for the static position it offers as a trellis for the wild hops that grow there, and as a chosen perch for the wild pigeon ("gołąb dziki").

The third poem, "Ganek" (The porch), introduces other thresholds, the doors of the porch and the windows, which offer the child a wide vision of the outside world ("from here, you can see north, south, east and west, / forests and rivers, fields and tree-lined lanes" ["widok szeroki stąd na wszystkie strony, na lasy, wody, pola i aleje"]), but that vision is not as interesting to the children as drawing a picture at the table. The possibility of leaving home, then, to explore the world, forms a backdrop to the child's life. In earliest memory, the outside world is available to the child in the form of thresholds on the world, but that possibility is not taken up, and the thresholds, in the child's mind, become less symbols of entry and exit than places for enjoying the view of the outside—like natural picture frames, framing the "widok" of the outside world.

The poem first moves inside the house with the fourth poem, "Jadalnia" (The dining room). Our attention is immediately called to the windows, but the light they provide from the outside is minimal, as they are shaded. Inside the house, things become artificial, unreal—the couch is covered with leather; the pastoral scene of the earlier poems, framed by the gate and the porch, is in "The Dining Room" a painting hanging on the dining room wall. This artificiality calls attention to the difference between the adult, material world and the child's natural world. The painting is of a winter scene, far removed from the real spring world of the first three outdoor poems. The world outside the child's region intrudes in the form of the clock from Gdańsk, a future site of the Nazi invasion of Poland. This unnatural foreignness indicates the presence of evil, supported by the image of the two laughing devils carved above the sofa and the ravens hovering over the ice-skating in the picture. Another clock stands in the corner, and we are further aware of the looming presence of evil—Mother brings the soup at the stroke of three o'clock (screeched by an artificial bird), and the regimentation of the adult world is opposed to the earlier, free world of the child in nature. The awareness of time is a feature of the adult world; the child is not concerned with the passage of time (and therefore not disturbed by his imminent death), but perceives that he should be if he wants to fit in with the grownups. The adult poet emphasizes that the adults in his childhood world are subjects of time; his attempt to sustain his child's vision of them is his attempt to save them from Chronos.

The poem "Zaklęcia ojca" (Father's incantations) begs a reading through the prism of alchemy and mysticism. It is Father's prayer, or, as the child sees it, his magic spell. Again, though, the role of father and child are blurred, and we might read the father's prayer as the adult poet speaking to God. It is set off in quotes (as is "Trwoga" [Fear] later in the cycle, also an address to God/Father). The prayer is a testament of faith ("I love you . . . even though I will never see your face" ["Kocham cię . . . choć nigdy twojej nie zobaczę twarzy"]), yet the fact that it is identified as an incantation causes us to question whether or not the utterer is speaking of faith he *has* or faith he *hopes to create* with his magic spell, through invocation. In this way the father mirrors the adult poet at work behind the poem, who hopes that his poem "The World" will call the world of the poem into reality and act as a ward against the horrors of the actual destruction of the world he sees taking place around him. "The World"'s picture of the world is not necessarily a statement of how things are, but an expression of desire for how things could be. It is an incantation, an alchemical formula being put to the test in the poet's laboratory.

The three poems "Wiara," "Nadzieja," and "Miłość" (Faith, Hope, Love) move from the outside world and the child's explanation of it to the inner world of humans, the soul, and the child's explanation of it. The three lessons of childhood are faith, hope, and love. In these poems, the child's perspective is drawn upon, but it is the adult poet who reaches the conclusions about what faith, hope, and love are, through analysis of what the child sees and feels. The adult learns from the child that faith is when one knows that things exist because they are necessary ("konieczne"). Faith is when one knows that, regardless of one's individual perception or particular vision of the world ("even if you close your eyes and dream up things" ["choćby się oczy zamknęło, marzyło"]), the world *is* what it was and what it will be ("The world will remain as it always has been" ["Na świecie będzie tylko to, co było"]). Despite our inability to capture it, to contain it and *see* its essence, the world *is.* The Heraclitic river, a source of endless frustration to the poet who attempts to capture reality in a word, is acknowledged and dismissed in the child's testament of faith: "And the leaf will be carried by the waters of the river" ("A liść uniosą dalej wody rzeczne").[20] The river is in constant motion, ever changing, but the child can still say with confidence that what it carries away is a leaf.

The poem "Hope" continues the theme of thresholds as being a place of possibility, but stresses that possibility exists because one has faith that the threshold can be crossed, not because one actually crosses it. This recalls the importance of the liminal areas in the earlier poems as simply a part of the space the child occupies, not as symbols of a departure from that space. Thus, thresholds in "The World" aren't symbols of boundaries, but of alchemical potential. They are connective spaces but not barriers, seams but not lines. Hope allows faith to continue; the two are linked in the child's mind: "Hope is with you when you believe" ("Nadzieja bywa, jeżeli ktoś wierzy"). This understanding of hope implies that faith undeniably has moments of doubt, which can be assuaged by hope. The child learns from his father's incantation that faith and doubt, although opposites, exist in a circular relationship, in harmony with one another. If we have faith, then in our moments of doubt we also have hope that our senses don't lie, that the earth exists because we can see it, touch it, smell it. The earth is not a dream, or shadows cast by Plato's ideal forms, but rather like the garden of the poet's childhood (as described in "Hope")—it exists because the poet can see it in his memory. Despite the fact that "you cannot enter" ("Wejść tam nie można"), hope lets us have faith that it *is,* for certain ("you're sure it's there" ["jest na pewno"]), just as the world outside the child's home certainly exists, not because he enters it but because he can see it and has faith that he *could* enter it if he chose. This line prosodically emphasizes the importance and certainty of both statements with an unprecedented eight stresses. While Miłosz has said, "I don't count the accents on my fingers when I write" (1987a, 316), his incantatory style, his innate feeling for the connection between the rhythm of the words and their meaning, is evident in this line. The caesura after "można" (which occurs after "enter" in the English translation) calls attention to the distance between the two statements and the difficulty in crossing the threshold from knowledge of fact ("You cannot enter" ["Wejść tam nie można"]) to faith ("But you're sure it's there" ["Ale jest na pewno"]).

This crossing is facilitated by hope, as the poem attests. Just as the world outside the child's exists, the past, too, is real. It exists because we can see it in our mind's eye. The power to see the past in reality, in the present, is denied us; however, "could we but look more clearly and wisely, we would see" ("Gdybyśmy lepiej i mądrzej patrzyli. . . byśmy zobaczyli"). Those who do not believe this are precisely those people who do not have hope, the Swedenborgian Propria and Blakean Spectres, who see not the continuity between faith and doubt but rather the barrier. Hope is a choice of double vision that allows faith to continue at the same time that it combats doubt.

The poem "Hope" has the first usage of the first person in the cycle: "A wszystkie rzeczy, które tutaj znałem, / Są niby ogród, kiedy stoisz w bramie." (The English translation loses the first person, and uses the verb "to see" in place of "znać," "to know": "all things you have ever seen here / are like a garden looked at from a gate.") The entrance of the persona with such language, in the moral center of the poem, emphasizes the importance the world of the poem, as well as the poem "The World," has for the poet. In this world the persona once had the knowledge ("znałem") of objects ("rzeczy"), of the essences of things. He was able to find names for everything he saw, both in the world around him and in his imagination. In the persona's world now, wherever and however it might be, this is not the case. He has lost the names of things. Clearly the persona in this poem is Miłosz, whose hope is for the return of the certain knowledge of the things of this world. His expression of faith in that hope is the poem "The World."

The third lesson of childhood involves the application of the first two lessons, of faith and hope. In the poem "Love," love is a way of seeing objects and oneself and understanding one's place in the grand scheme of the world.

> Love means to learn to look at yourself
> The way one looks at distant things.
> For you are only one thing among many.
> And whoever sees that way heals his heart,
> Without knowing it, from various ills—
> A bird and a tree say to him: Friend.[21]

The repetition of the forms of the verb "patrzeć" ("to look" or "to see") stresses the link between love and vision. This way of seeing is possible if one has faith and hope that the reality of the world includes oneself, as a little bit of nature, no more and no less. Seeing the world with love allows one to be accepted by the bird and the tree, to be accepted as a child of nature. The reward for such a vision of the world is light ("wypełnienia łunią"), which, as we have seen, is the life-giving energy of God. Fiut writes that "very likely [Saint Augustine's] *Confessions* are the source of the motif of a sudden entrance of light, of blinding brightness, a radiance [*blask*] that frees one from human limitations and allows one to comprehend the moment" (1990, 26). Such light is also reminiscent of other mystics Miłosz consults who claim to have had epiphanical experiences marked by visions of great light: Oscar Milosz, Swedenborg, Pascal (Miłosz 1985, 24; 1984a, 236).

The moments of illumination in "The World" signify the moments of vision of a world of love, so desired by the poet, whom we can presume to be suffering from the "various ills" ("zmartwień różnych") he hopes his poem will "heal" ("leczy"). Love is tantamount to empathy and facilitates the dissolution of barriers between self and other. Rather than think of oneself solely as a subject, the center of one's world's action and reaction, one should also think of oneself as an object like any other. In recognizing the other as a potential subject, one thereby recognizes oneself in other. Initially this self-recognition in other is driven by eros. Erotic love in turn has the potential to develop into the kind of love relationship between self and other that empowers the Spectre to move out of Ulro, as Miłosz writes:

> *Eros* is sexual love, but not only such, because it is an intermediary between gods and humans, an unlimited desire, a true motoric force of creativity in

> art and science. *Agape* is love of our fellow man, love-empathy, allowing us to see in another human being a creature as frail and as easily hurt as we are ourselves. (1996b, 177)

Miłosz defines *agape* as recognizing a being like yourself in another person. While erotic love gives humans a glimpse of the lost paradise of "the gods," agape comes closer to expressing the love of the poem "Love," in which the power of the ego is relinquished. As seen in the example of Tomasz in *The Issa Valley,* though, erotic love is an important stage in the process of achieving recognition of the self in other. The progression from eros to agape works to "heal the heart" of the wounds of exile.

Fear and doubt are addressed in the poem "Fear," and for the first time we think of the child as on the threshold of adulthood, on the verge of exile. This is the first instance in the poem in which we hear the child's voice directly, as he calls out to his father (although the child is not identified as the child). Set off in quotes, as was "Father's Incantations," it is possible to imagine the adult poet speaking to God in the frightened words of the abandoned child. The child is afraid of the dark in the forest in much the same way that the adult poet is afraid of the dark wilds of the boundless world: "The night has no borders. From now on darkness will last forever" ("Noc nie ma granicy, / Odtąd już zawsze ciemność będzie trwała"). The child also fears that he will go hungry and without shelter alone in the forest, just as the adult poet fears exile, the loss of home ("the travelers are homeless, they will die of hunger" ["Bezdomni, z głodu umrą podróżnicy"]). With the voice of a child, the poet questions God, asks him how he could abandon his children in the depth of the forest: "Where have you gone, Father? why do you not pity / Your children, lost in this murky wood?" ("Dokąd odszedłeś, ojcze, jak ci nie żal / Dzieci, w te głuche zabłąkanych knieje"). The poet uses his poem to voice his adult fears in a world where more than just those fears exist—in a world where hope and faith that fear will be relieved and Father will not abandon his children still exist. For, as Miłosz notes in "*Anus mundi,*" "The Lord God withdrew in 1941" ("Pan Bóg odszedł w 1941 roku") (Miłosz 1997, 41).

Father (although not identified as the Father) responds to the child's fears in the poem "Odnalezienie" (Recovery). The simple words "I am here" ("tu jestem") contain the promise that the child has not been abandoned and will not be abandoned. The child need simply give up his irrational fears and trust his Father. The adult poet again offers the words of the Father as an incantation, hoping that by providing the form of the words "tu jestem" for his God, who seems to have left the world behind in Warsaw in 1943, those words will be filled by a reality previously only imagined. This imagined reality is one in which "the path is straight" ("Ścieżka jest prosta"). Cocks greet the rising sun ("Roosters on fences greet the light" ["Koguty światło na płotach witają"]) and the earth is fertile and joyous ("bujna i szczęśliwa"). Miłosz opposes this scene to the darkness and fear of the previous poem, just as he opposes his vision of such a world to the wasteland of war in which he is writing. Even in war, the persona—and the poet—knows he must have faith that God will not abandon him, just as even in darkness, the child must trust the Father, and believe that day will come.

In a letter to the American Catholic monk Thomas Merton in 1961, Miłosz wrote that he had in mind a religious book that would honestly address the questions of faith both he and Merton struggled to answer, without relying on arrogant platitudes or absurd optimism that there are right answers, available to the right people:

> I see in the air the shape of such a book: somebody will write it. Perhaps you? It should be a book of great simplicity: what I believe and not why I believe but how I believe, namely, to draw a contour around what is hardly formulable, by images taken not from a religious experience. (A modern compendium, a sort of catechism.) (Merton and Miłosz 1997, 177)

Miłosz's formula for the proposed book provides a way of describing his poetics. His poetic output taken as a whole is this imagined book: it depicts what he believes and how he believes through images taken from his personal experience. Miłosz's poetry "draws a contour around what is hardly formulable," that is, it defines his vision of home recovered.

"The World" is at once an outline of Miłosz's faith and an expression of that faith. What "The World" says is the outline; the fact that it is being said, and under such circumstances, is the testament of faith. It is a combination of theoretical and practical faith. For Miłosz, faith first entails seeing the world—in the past, present, and future—through the eyes of love. Equipped with this vision, then, the poet must hope that the world he sees can be entered, and continue hoping even when he has reason to doubt the existence of that world. Similarly, the poet must have faith in the existence of that world in order to believe in the existence of the creator of that world, God. To think that he, the poet, is the only creator of that world, that it only exists on paper and in his mind, is to succumb to nihilism, so that no matter how beautiful and wondrous the poet's creation may seem, without God it is terrifying and amoral.

"Krzyś" ("Christopher Robin," written on the occasion of the death of A. A. Milne's son, the real Christopher Robin) illustrates the potential transcendence of exile using yet another juvenile form. In it we read of what happens to the characters from a child's storybook after the book is closed, when they are removed from human time and space and allowed to live entirely on the other side of the book's covers, entirely in the world of imagination:

> I must think suddenly of matters too difficult for a bear of little brain. I have never asked myself what lies beyond the place where we live, I and Rabbit, Piglet and Eeyore, with our friend Christopher Robin. That is, we continued to live here, and nothing changed and I just ate my little something. Only Christopher Robin left for a moment.
>
> Owl says that immediately beyond our garden Time begins, and that it is an awfully deep well. If you fall in it, you go down and down, very quickly, and no one knows what happens to you next. I was a bit worried about Christopher Robin falling in it, but he came back and then I asked him about the well. "Old bear"—he answered—"I was in it and I was falling and I was changing as I fell. My legs became long, I was a big person. I wore trousers down to the ground, I had a grey beard, then I grew old, hunched, and I walked with a cane, and then I died. It was probably just a dream, it was quite unreal. The only real thing was you, old bear, and our shared fun. Now I won't go anywhere, even if I'm called for an afternoon snack." (Miłosz 1998b, 144)

This entry from *Roadside Dog* recalls Vladimir Nabokov's statement that the Otherworld is the underside of Time, like the back side of the quilt. In describing the afterlife of the "real" Christopher Robin, "immortalized" ("uwieczniony") as a child in the pages of his father's books, Miłosz expresses his belief that the past exists somewhere, continuing on in its life and schedule as if the person you once were—a child—has just left for a little while, exiled into the land of adulthood, the land of Time. When he finds the right words, the alchemical formula known to the ancient adepts, Miłosz will have created his

Philosopher's Stone and found his way to that mythical, fairy-tale land of home. Once there, he will realize that it, the Otherworld, is the true reality, not the one he's in now: "The only real thing was you, old bear, and our shared fun." Miłosz's poetry is the expression of faith that his Hundred-Acre Woods, the Lithuania of his childhood, his Philosopher's Stone does exist, despite its elusive nature. A transformation of vision of the sort we see in "Christopher Robin," facilitated by the imaginative use of genre, makes such a transport to other worlds possible for both the writer and the reader. This entry into the other world of home through the imaginative use of language marks the achievement of Miłosz's desired poetic alchemy.

Notes

All translations, unless otherwise indicated, are my own.

1. Apart from Miłosz's own autobiographical admissions throughout his writing, biographical sources include Gorczyńska and Fiut 1992, Zawada 1996, Żak 1998.

2. See also the original Polish version, Fiut 1998.

3. This dynamic could be construed as Miłosz's response to the limitations of dialecticism. For a discussion of Miłosz's rejection of Marxist dialecticism, see Nathan and Quinn 1991, 31–64.

4. Blake's *Book of Thel* (1988, 7) outlines this progression from lower Innocence to Experience to a higher Innocence.

5. See, for example, "O byciu poetą" (On being a poet) 1997.

6. Miłosz (1988, 226) attests that the only exception to this is the 1969 poem "To Raja Rao," written in English.

7. Przyglądałem się tej twarzy w osłupieniu. Przebiegały światła stacji metra, nie zauważałem ich. Co można zrobić, jeżeli wzrok nie ma siły absolutnej, tak, żeby wciągał przedmioty z zachłyśnięciem się szybkości, zostawiając za sobą już tylko pustkę formy idealnej, znak, niby hieroglif, który uproszczono z rysunku zwierzęcia czy ptaka? Trans. Czesław Miłosz and Robert Pinsky.

8. Lekko zadarty nos, wysokie czoło z gładko zaczesanymi włosami, linia podbródka—ale dlaczego wzrok nie ma siły absolutnej?—i w różowawej bieli wycięte otwory, w których ciemna błyszcząca lawa. Wchłonąć tę twarz, ale równocześnie mieć ją na tle wszystkich gałęzi wiosennych, murów, fal, w płaczu, w śmiechu, w cofnięciu jej o piętnaście lat, w posunięciu naprzód o trzydzieści lat.

9. Na to mi przyszło, że po tylu próbach nazywania świata umiem już tylko powtarzać w kółko najwyższe, jedyne wyznanie, poza które żadna moc nie może

sięgnąć: ja jestem—ona jest. Krzyczcie, dmijcie w trąby, utwórzcie tysiączne pochody, skaczcie, rozdzierajcie sobie ubrania, powtarzając to jedno: jest!

10. The following two sentences are not included in the English version: I po co zapisano stronice, tony, katedry stronic, jeżeli bełkocę jakbym był pierwszym, który wyłonił się z iłu na brzegach oceanu? Na co zdały się cywilizacje Słońca, czerwony pył rozpadających się miast, zbroje i motory w pyle pustyń, jeżeli nie dodały nic do tego dźwięku: jest?

11. Wysiadła na Raspail. Zostałem z ogromem rzeczy istniejących. Gąbka, która cierpi bo nie może napełnić się wodą, rzeka, która cierpi bo odbicia obłoków i drzew nie są obłokami i drzewami. ("Esse," 1988, 221)

12. It is clear that Miłosz considers "*Esse*" to be a poem that reflects many of the essential themes of his oeuvre: in an interview with me in 1995, he stated that "Esse" is "a very important poem," and he claims: "I read this poem at all of my readings; both in Polish, and [when I'm in] America, in English" (1998a, 41). It is interesting to speculate as to why he omits the dark lines on the wasteland from his American readings—to protect the innocent? Out of a lack of faith that they will be understood by the naive? Both these entirely speculative reasons suggest Miłosz's attention to the distance between himself, an exile, and his American audiences.

13. See, for example, "Wtajemniczenie" (Initiation, 1986) or "Ogród ziemskich rozkoszy" (The Garden of Earthly Delights, 1986).

14. Thinking of himself as a hunter of the right word, Miłosz titled his published journal *Rok myśliwego* (1990) (English translation as *A Year of the Hunter*, 1994).

15. Tomasz's name relates him to the philosophy of Saint Thomas Aquinas, which was so important to Miłosz when he was writing "The World." See Błoński 1998, 24; Fiut 1990, 28–29; Zajas 1997, 124.

16. Bogdan Zeler (1995, 5) notes that in returning to childhood Miłosz continues a long tradition in Polish poetry, joining poets from Adam Mickiewicz (*Pan Tadeusz*, 1834) to Adam Zagajewski ("Dzikie czereśnie" [Wild cherries], 1985).

17. While in Miłosz's own English translation of "The World" he attempts to duplicate the original meter, all rhyme has been lost. Miłosz chose not to use Renata Gorczyńska, Robert Hass, and Robert Pinsky's translation, which preserves both the meter and the rhyme, in his *Collected Poems*. The Gorczyńska-Hass-Pinsky translation was published later in the dual-language *Poezje wybrane/Selected Poems* (1996).

18. See, for example, *The Witness of Poetry* or Miłosz's introduction to the collected works of O. V. de L. Milosz.

19. All excerpts from "Świat" are taken from *Utwory poetyckie*, 83–93. All English translations are by Czesław Miłosz (1988, 36–55).

20. The importance of river imagery in Miłosz's work is treated in depth by Aleksander Fiut (1998, 322–34).

21. Miłość to znaczy popatrzeć na siebie,
Tak jak się patrzy na obce nam rzeczy,
Bo jesteś tylko jedną z rzeczy wielu.
A kto tak patrzy, choć sam o tym nie wie,
Ze zmartwień różnych swoje serce leczy,
Ptak mu i drzewo mówią: przyjacielu.

Works Cited

Alchemy: The Art of Knowing. 1994. San Francisco: Chronicle Books.

Blake, William. 1988. *The Complete Poetry and Prose of William Blake.* New rev. ed. Ed. David V. Erdman. New York: Anchor Press.

Błoński, Jan. 1998. *Miłosz jak świat* (Miłosz like the world). Kraków: Znak.

Fiut, Aleksander. 1990. *The Eternal Moment: The Poetry of Czesław Miłosz.* Trans. Theodosia S. Robertson. Berkeley: University of California Press.

———. 1998. *Moment wieczny: Poezja Czesława Miłosza.* 2d ed. Kraków: Wydawnictwo Literackie.

Gorczyńska, Renata [Ewa Czarnecka], and Aleksander Fiut. 1992. *Podróżny świata: Rozmowy z Czesławem Miłoszem: Komentarze* (World Traveler: Conversations with Czesław Miłosz: Commentaries). Kraków: Wydawnictwo Literackie.

Hirshfield, Jane. 1997. *Nine Gates: Entering the Mind of Poetry.* New York: HarperCollins.

Merton, Thomas, and Czesław Miłosz. 1997. *Striving Towards Being: The Letters of Thomas Merton and Czesław Miłosz.* Ed. Robert Faggen. New York: Farrar, Straus and Giroux.

Miłosz, Czesław. 1955. *Dolina Issy.* Kraków: Wydawnictwo Literackie. 1981.

———. 1968. *Native Realm: A Search for Self-Definition.* Trans. Catherine S. Leach. Berkeley: University of California Press.

———. 1976. *Utwory poetyckie* (Poetic works). Ann Arbor: University of Michigan Press.

———. 1980. *Nobel Lecture.* New York: Farrar, Straus and Giroux.

———. 1981. *The Issa Valley.* Trans. Louis Iribarne. New York: Farrar, Straus and Giroux.

———. 1982. *Visions from San Francisco Bay.* New York: Farrar, Straus and Giroux.

———. 1983. *Witness of Poetry.* Cambridge, Mass.: Harvard University Press.

———. 1984a. *The Land of Ulro.* Trans. Louis Iribarne. New York: Farrar, Straus and Giroux.

———. 1984b. *The Separate Notebooks*. New York: Ecco Press.

———. 1985. Introduction to *The Noble Traveller: The Life and Writings of O. V. de L. Milosz*. Ed. Christopher Bamford. West Stockbridge, Mass.: Lindisfarne Press.

———. 1987a. *Conversations with Czesław Miłosz*. Interviews by Ewa Czarnecka and Aleksander Fiut. San Diego: Harcourt Brace Jovanovich.

———. 1987b. *Wiersze*. 2 vols. Kraków: Wydawnictwo Literackie.

———. 1988. *The Collected Poems, 1931–1987*. Hopewell, N.J.: Ecco Press.

———. 1991. *Beginning with My Streets*. Trans. Madeline G. Levine. New York: Farrar, Straus and Giroux.

———. 1996a. *Poezje wybrane/Selected Poems*. Kraków: Wydawnictwo Literackie.

———. 1997. *Abecadło Miłosza* (Miłosz's ABC's). Kraków: Wydawnictwo Literackie.

———. 1998a. *Antologia osobista* (A personal anthology). Kraków: Znak.

———. 1998b. *Roadside Dog*. Trans. Robert Hass. New York: Farrar, Straus and Giroux. (The poem "Christopher Robin" was first published in English as "Themes." Trans. Robert Hass. *New York Review of Books*, February 6, 1997, 10.)

———, ed. 1996b. *A Book of Luminous Things: An International Anthology of Poetry*. New York: Harcourt Brace.

Nathan, Leonard, and Arthur Quinn. 1991. *The Poet's Work: An Introduction to Czesław Miłosz*. Cambridge, Mass.: Harvard University Press.

Pszczołowska, Lucylla. 1997. *Wiersz polski: Zarys historyczny* (Polish verse: A historical survey). Monografie fundacji na rzecz nauki polskiej. Wrocław: Wydawnictwo Leopoldinum.

Seidel, Michael. 1986. *Exile and the Narrative Imagination*. New Haven: Yale University Press.

Vendler, Helen. 1999. "Understanding the World." *Partisan Review*, Spring.

Zajas, Krzysztof. 1997. *Miłosz i filozofia* (Miłosz and philosophy). Kraków: Wydawnictwo Baran i Suszczyński.

Zawada, Andrzej. 1996. *Miłosz*. Wrocław: Wydawnictwo Dolnośląskie.

Zeler, Bogdan. 1995. *Zrozumieć poezję współczesną* (To understand contemporary poetry). Katowice: Książnica.

Żak, Stanisław. 1998. *Polscy pisarze nobliści* (Polish Nobel prize-winning writers). Kielce, Ston 2.

3 The Homelessness of the Other

The Homoerotic Experience in the Prose of Julian Stryjkowski

Grażyna Borkowska

> He was still looking around as if he forgot that he could no longer hope. Until noontime that girl was the girl in a light-blue knit blouse and in the hotel Argentina, thanks to the actress Lonza, whom he saw a day before yesterday as Iphigenia and yesterday as Hamlet's mother, everything became confused. From the moment he heard her voice, the girl he looked for became the mother of the young actor. He played the role of Hamlet in yesterday's performance. The play took place in the Lovrjenac fortress erected on a cliff. Edward met Bombardelli a few days ago. He was introduced to him as a rising star. He was supposed to have shone in the role of Hamlet. His own mother worked the publicity from behind the scenes. She was absent from the banquet. The show was stunningly loud. Even the cannons were fired to make it real. Lovrjenac was real enough in its external robe—gloomy walls without roofing so that, during the performance, above one's head the real moon and stars shone. The ghost of Hamlet's father was more at home here than in the castle at Elsinore. (Stryjkowski 1961, 77–78)[1]

In this excerpt from Julian Stryjkowski's "Heinz," we see Edward, most likely a Jew, saved from the Lwów ghetto because of a daring escape and looking for a woman he loved once during the war. I suggest that Edward is most likely a Jew, because the question of origins is unsettled: he could be a Jew who decided to remain on the Aryan side but he could also be a Pole involved with a Jewish woman who, in a moment of crisis, decided to return to the ghetto. The heroes' conversation, recreated years later, settles nothing:

> "Lilka, don't go there," he begged her.
> "It can't be helped. At least over there I'll be among my own."
> "What about me?"

"You can conceal me only for so long. And then? I'd rather go on my own." (81)

The entire dialogue presents a pinnacle of towering double meaning as if the waves of the Adriatic were thrown against the walls of a Dubrovnik fortress. When Lilka says that she would like to be "among her own," Edward's reply: "And what about me?" can mean either "I'm a Jew as well" or, just as likely, "I am one of your own, even though I'm not Jewish." When Lilka says "I'd rather go by myself," it might mean that she does not want to have any intimate witnesses to her degradation and death and that she is glad that Edward is staying on the Aryan side. However, it might also mean that this Polish-Jewish love must be crushed so that others don't follow their example.

The multiplication of these ambiguities is Stryjkowski's narrative strategy. The story refuses to explain anything. On the contrary, it obscures a great deal. Conflicts remain unresolved and questions remain unanswered. Nothing comes to a point. The meaning will not reveal itself. The truth will not stand apart from semblance. In the story "Heinz," confusion and vagueness constitute the principle of the story. Figures and events appear as if in a fog. The girl in the light-blue knit blouse turns out to be Lilka. From up close one can see, of course, that she is not a young girl but a mature woman. She is the mother of the actor who plays the role of Hamlet. Who is Heinz's father? A German, the citizen of the country for which Lilka left after, or during, the war? Edward? Lilka is silent. She does not want to reveal the truth. She evades explanations, decisions, or declarations: "I want to have peace. I want to save Heinz from the ghetto, from you [i.e., Edward], from Govella, from Lonza. I want his father to be an unknown man with the odd name Bombardelli. I will defend him. I will watch over him. I will . . ." (Stryjkowski 1961, 117).

The drama of Edward and Lilka plays out against the backdrop of a different, Shakespearean, drama. Stryjkowski's heroes are actors. They played *Hamlet* together in Lwów. He, of course, played the leading role and she, of course, starred as Ophelia. Years later, they meet in Dubrovnik, where Lilka's son Heinz now plays the role once given to Edward. Why Shakespeare? Why Hamlet? Why the theater?

III

For Stryjkowski, the issue of identity and the sense of belonging to a community are pivotal. For other Jewish writers, the central concern is solidarity with those being killed or with those already put to death, the problem of responsibility, remembrance, the open wound, forgetting, testimony, the reality of extermination, life after death. Of course, Stryjkowski's mainly journalistic statements abound in opinions that point to the fact that such concerns are close to him and that he, in his own conscience, debated the much mythologized issue of guilt toward the dead and the necessity to commemorate their annihilation. Speaking about the beginnings of his literary output, Stryjkowski (1964) emphasizes that he started writing *Głosy w ciemności* (Voices in the darkness) in Moscow upon finding out that the ghetto had been annihilated and that this book functioned as a tombstone.

We have no basis on which to contest these startling admissions. However, we have plenty of reasons to say that erecting this tombstone did not mitigate the author's problems with self-definition. It did not settle them or make them less prominent. Of course, it was not just a matter of answering the question, Jew or Pole? Stryjkowski knew very well that there existed many variants of Jewishness and Polishness. He understood that, given all the difficulties, he could nonetheless make a choice. He did that. He learned to accept and to reject. He read the Old Testament in the original Hebrew as well as the twentieth-century poets writing in Hebrew. He hated the poverty and isolation of a small Jewish town closed up by the ritual of holidays and prayers. He was fascinated with Jewish spirituality imbued with the fire of mysticism, relentless and devoted to God. He was afraid of the Jewish dogmatism that disdained everything except the sphere of religion and spirit. He admired the Orthodox Jews, but he intuitively sensed that the twentieth century would not allow for the phenomenon of religious ecstasy and withdrawal and that it would demand consent, even of a priest or an artist, to wisely or coercively participate in history (see Stryjkowski 1991).

Stryjkowski allocated his sympathies on the Polish side in a similar way: selectively. Fascinated with the Polish language, in his childhood he was enchanted by the sounds of words unknown to him, learning the new language from his beautiful and elegant sister, Maria Stark. These new sounds seemed as beautiful and elegant as she herself was. The entire universe of his boyish imagination opened itself up under the impact of the Polish language: Karl May's Winnetou spoke to Stryjkowski in Polish, and thrilled by Sienkiewicz's books, he began to write.

All this mattered, but Stryjkowski also saw the negative effects of familiarizing oneself with Polishness. In school the little boy with side curls was the object of ridicule and jeering. Thus, he fenced himself off from the world with a wall of conceit. Agitated with his father, "God's policeman," he exhibited similar stubbornness, irreconcilability, and a sense of superiority toward the world. He was an unbearable child and an unbearable young man. The reason for this lay in his own personality rather than in the environment. He was unable to accept others as well as himself.

Stryjkowski's checkered biography lacks continuity. From a religiously Orthodox Jewish home, Stryjkowski goes to a Polish school. He abandons Hebrew in favor of Polish. He substitutes one form of exoticism for another. Soon afterward, he becomes a member of a Zionist organization, Szomer. He returns to the Hebrew language, the history of the Jews, and contemporary Hebrew literature. He confesses to Piotr Szewc: "Zionism easily replaced the faith that I lost earlier. It engaged me completely. Nothing was important, not even school or my parents. Only Szomer was important, as well as meetings, excursions, ideological discussions, scouting" (Stryjkowski 1991, 40).

He was a Zionist, but he did not want to go to Palestine, despite the fact that, after his father's death and his older brother's emigration there, his mother persistently urged him to leave. He promised to join her but ultimately he stayed: "There were many contradictions in me. I wanted to finish high school, pass the exit exam, and study Polish literature because I felt that God had given me a writer's talent. It sounds conceited but I can't help it" (Stryjkowski 1991, 43). He remained enchanted with Hebrew and Jewish culture—the poetry of Chaim Nachman Bialik and Shaul Czarnichowski as well as the prose of Shmuel Yosef Agnon. He did what he set out to do. He entered the Polish literature program at Jan Kazimierz University in Lwów. As he himself remarked, for him it seemed to be his road to Parnassus (60). He chose Professor Kleiner's seminar and wrote, under his direction, a dissertation entitled "Kobieta zbrodniarka w literaturze romantycznej" (The woman criminal in Romantic literature). He entered the Communist Party of western Ukraine. Back then, he understood his obligations and commitments toward Jewishness differently, for as he repeated numerous times, "A communist Jew ceases to be a Jew" (Stryjkowski 1991, 48).

Can one take this maxim literally, however? Can one regard some variants of one's biography as unchangeable if, in the thirties, Stryjkowski battled his creative impotence in two languages, if he participated in meetings with Jewish artists in Lwów, if he published in the Zionist daily *Chwila* (The moment), and finally if he perceived his career as a Polish writer in terms of chance rather than necessity?

It seems that he was trying to find a place for himself, a cultural and ideological system in which he could fully realize his interests and aspirations, unclear as they might be at the time. The latter made the poor, Orthodox family home seem too confining for him, as it was for many Jews at the time. Stepping outside the domestic space, Stryjkowski found himself faced with various choices. He could seek shelter in the Polish language or in Hebrew culture. He could choose to assimilate as a Pole while keeping the basic ties with the culture of his family home. He could go toward Zionism following in his brother's footsteps. Only one choice could not be considered: to remain in Stryj. If we take into account how much space Stryjkowski as a writer devoted to childhood, one can say that paradoxically even that variant played out.

| | |

He learned about the extermination of the Jews around 1943 in Moscow, which is when he began his mature literary output. It was as if he could write about the Jewish fate only in Polish and only in the shadows of the Red Kremlin. These facts are the most difficult to accept. The Jewish tragedy, the Polish language, and the Moscow umbrella—those were the peripheral considerations of Stryjkowski's creativity, as race, milieu, and the historical moment were in Hippolyte Taine's *History of English Literature.* In Taine, however, the crucial factors occur in a harmonious and affable symbiosis, aiding the birth of the creative works connected to them. In Stryjkowski's biography the decisive elements clearly did not harmonize. Why did he choose Polish in order to write about Jews in communist Russia? When did the communist in him lose out to his Jewish side? Why did his Jewishness seek out a language alien to itself?

Perhaps in this way it was easier for him to achieve a distance, which allowed him to write. We are talking here about the distance between the writer and his place of origin, about the language that possesses his self-expression, and the ideology that gives him a chance at survival. This distance must be understood as a need to balance oneself, as a kind of order imposed on external reality, as an attempt to hinder the destructive pressure of borderline elements, and as a refuge.

In Stryjkowski's case, maintaining such a distance means that we are dealing with a person's vicissitudes rather than with a tragedy of a man from a borderland who is entangled in a multitude of traditions, in a variety of ethnic, cultural, and ideological languages. In his stories, usually underpinned with autobiography, Stryjkowski manipulates the length of the distance vis-à-vis various segments of personal experience, expanding on some at the cost of others. Sometimes, he places a greater value on his Jewish origins, at others, he stresses his entanglements with communism.

The choice of different variants is not strictly a pragmatic tactic. It is a life strategy, a way of circumventing those problematic questions about one's identity, belonging, loyalties, and place of origin. It also constitutes, as can be clearly seen in subsequent stories, an attempt at establishing closer contacts in one's environment, an attempt at creating *a new home* in an alien world. As a rule, the efforts of Stryjkowski's heroes fail in this regard. Everywhere and always they feel alien. They don't form close bonds and their way of looking at the world remains cold and critical.

Stryjkowski's individual novels and his own biography lack an ideological basis of decision making. Why did he choose communism and why did he later abandon it? Why did he go in the direction of Hebrew culture and why did he then change that direction? Why was his stay in communist Russia so conducive to his well-being that he extended it by two years, unlike any other communist at the time, and why did he finally leave? One could pose the same questions to the heroes of his novels, in which case they would also remain unanswered. Neither the writer nor his heroes are strongly convinced about their own decisions. They search more than they find. They lack a strong sense of self-identification or any feeling of solidarity with an idea, a group, or a collective. They move around in a vicious circle. Stryjkowski's characters cannot find a place for themselves because they do not identify entirely with any given idea. They cannot bring themselves to such identification because they feel alien everywhere. Is there an explanation for this paradox?

Stryjkowski's narrative strategy consolidates the heroes in their nonspecificity. They barely recognize one another. Moreover, we are never entirely sure who they are versus whom they pretend to be. The "theatricality" of the story "Heinz" constantly blurs the identity of the characters, only because it allows them to act because, through the constant role changing, it creates only a possible conventionality of existence.

This convention of theater talk, absolved from the responsibility of testifying to a whole historical truth and contained within the logic of the role variant, also pertains to Stryjkowski himself, who describes himself as "an autobiographical writer par excellence."[2] In the story "Ajeleth," he explains his possible departure for Israel in a conversation with the daughter of his longtime friend:

> "If I were to go it would only be because of you. It depends on you."
> "So, you consider my country your own?"
> "No."
> "And I thought for a minute. Where then is your homeland?"
> "My language is my homeland."
> "Is your language the one you use speaking to me?"
> "My language is the one I write in. One can speak many languages."
> "Didn't they tell you yet to write only for Jews?"
> "Don't ask me such questions. For me all questions are extinguished." (Stryjkowski 1961, 61)

Questions dealing with identity became extinguished because the foundation for formulating answers has disappeared. It seems that in Stryjkowski's case the inability to arrive at self-definition is not connected with the tragedy of the Holocaust but precedes it. Speaking in many languages assumes giving many different answers, answers that are differently constructed and arranged. Therefore, Stryjkowski could answer: "I am a Polish writer," or "I am a Polish writer rescued in the East," or "I am a Polish writer saved in his Jewishness in the East."

A journey is the signal for Stryjkowski's attachment to the multitude of plot resolutions. In fact, it never signifies an interest in the new space. A journey facilitates a vague contouring of the abandoned biographical plot variant. For Lilka and Edward, it will be the variant of solidarity with the Jewish fate away from which they are now both running. For Ajeleth and her friend, it will be the choosing of the road proposed by the interwar Zionism. Stryjkowski does not make that choice in his own life. For the heroes of the American stories, it will be the grotesque attempt to recreate the Jewish Diaspora on foreign soil. A journey becomes synonymous with opening up, transgressing, and deconstructing only in the traditional cultural and psychosocial setup and only when the heroes feel that they are the depositories of commonly accepted values and when they go outside their domestic space. In the novels *Voices in the Darkness* (1956) and *Echo* (1988), going outside the closed system of the shtetl (see Stryjkowski 1994) causes the breakup of Tojwie's family. In *Austeria* (The inn, 1966), the act of solidarity with the followers of a different religion is an attempt to "save whatever one can."

The problem of sin and guilt surfaces only in those novels that rest on a strong foundation of traditional values. An observation made about the demonization of the concept of sin in Stryjkowski's prose misses the mark.[3] Sin in Stryjkowski is inseparably connected to love. The one who loves is the one who sins. Sin is equated with the loss of restraint, which is possibly forgivable and certainly very human.

The issue of guilt is delineated differently. It is always a matter of an individual's participation in another's salvation. There are no clearly marked boundaries here; everything is possible, necessary, and allowed. In the contemporary stories, which are overshadowed by the war, the issue of guilt and responsibility appears in phantomlike form, as do all the other affairs concerning the past. Jakub Stein accuses the main hero of failing to save his sister by not taking her to Russia. Lilka reproaches Edward for leaving her brother in prison, as if the threatened fugitive could choose his company and determine the conditions of his travel. These accusations are unfounded and nonsensical to anyone who, even to a minute degree, understands the reality of war. And yet, Stryjkowski makes them.

| | |

One cannot explain these peculiarities or other elements of Stryjkowski's narrative technique without referring to the crypto-homoeroticism of his prose. Homoeroticism is the key to understanding Stryjkowski's relation to the world, to history, to Jewishness. It is the measure of his presence in the world as well as the measure of his fear, distance, ineptitude, and homelessness. It is the true reason for his acceptance of various forms of avoidance and game playing, including those that encode erotic jealousy with the universal language of ethical obligations (Jakub Stein's grievances). It is the most logical explanation for his aversion toward all acts of self-identification that could create a permanent sense of identity.

It is only very cautiously and superficially that Stryjkowski refers to homoerotic experiences throughout the years. In his novel *Czarna róża* (Black rose, 1963), in the mini-narrative "Tommaso del Cavaliere," in *Na wierzbach . . . nasze skrzypce* (On willows . . . our violins), the narrator's inclinations are betrayed by the description of his partner's good looks, which, though fading, still retain the power of attraction: "For a long while we were looking at one another in silence. He stood unmoved. I gave him a hug first. Jakub Stein. I was still thinking that a woman would be a surprise. I recognized him by the splendid eyebrows joined together at the bridge of the nose—the sign of his strength, like Samson's hair. However, only this much remained from his good looks" (Stryjkowski 1974, 89).

Stryjkowski discusses the prototype for Jakub Stein more extensively in his overtly autobiographical story "Milczenie" (Silence), when he confesses his fascination with a school friend:

> In my class there was also another schoolmate, a close friend and a Jew, Jakub Wald, who, after passing his matriculation exam, left for Palestine. We were bonded in a strange kind of friendship. I would call it Manichaean, which is not entirely appropriate, if we take into account its clumsy religious sense. In order to fight the Arabs and to conquer Hitler, Jakub put on a brown shirt, not exactly of the Nazi shade, and illegally emigrated to Erech, as the biblical homeland was called. (1993, 6)

Most of all, they were rivals. What they had in common was envy, competitiveness, the need to dominate, excessive and unfulfilled ambitions. Jakub passed his matriculation exam with honors. He won the rivalry. It was then that the idea to study Polish literature was born. It was revenge and a painful blow delivered against an invincible friend. Stryjkowski informed him about his decision in an extensive letter written in Polish. The choice of the language must have come as a shock to Jakub, the member of Szomer. He answered in a letter full of hidden pain. Now, Julian felt like a conqueror. He did not cease to care for his friend. He asked his acquaintances about Jakub since he could no longer count on any gesture of interest or any sign of life from him. After many years, Stryjkowski visited Jakub in Israel. He met his faithful and unattractive wife. He wanted to believe that this marriage was a self-inflicted punishment for the separation. Nevertheless, he felt truly happy when he saw his letter and photographs kept for so many years. He thought: "My poor wretch! Who are you? You were the measure of all things for me. Your silence was a sham, like a deflated balloon or a torn spiderweb. I am liberated" (Stryjkowski 1993, 69). He seals this feeling of freedom by engaging in an intimate encounter with a man he meets randomly. Even if there were fictional elements in "Silence," intertwined with an autobiographical layer, the story would still shed a new light onto the key choices in Stryjkowski's biography and the biographies of his heroes.

The appearance of all sorts of biographical threads in the interviews and stories as well as their variance, complemented by new contexts and details, makes it hard to determine whether they belong to the sphere of truth or fabrication. However, repetitiveness is always a sign of importance. Therefore, it is worthwhile to look at the theater episode. That episode, which we could name after Balzac's *Lost Illusions* or Bolesław Prus's *Sins of Childhood,* appears in "Syriusz," from the collection *On Willows . . .* , and also in the conversation with Piotr Szewc. It pertains to the childhood performance of the hero (or the author, we can assume) on stage. A little boy is reciting his part when suddenly he notices that his friend, sitting in the first row, the friend for whom he cares the most, wiggles about in strange convulsions. It is uncertain whether he is crying or laughing or whether he is hiding his head out of shame or embarrassment. The juvenile actor cannot stand the tension. He puts down his copy of the play, leaves the stage, and faints. The unfortunate actor will remember this event for a long time and the injury will last a lifetime. Is it a coincidence that dabbling in theater will remain Stryjkowski's unfulfilled dream, that he will speak about the need to write a drama many times, and that publishing only one stage work, *Sodom,* will not bring this dream any closer to reality since all his other attempts will remain buried in his notebook?

Let us return to the question, Why theater? What role did Stryjkowski assign to such stage conventions as the metaphor of the play, the mask, or the costume? How did they relate to crypto-homoerotic narration? Was it the lack of a sense of identity, the impossibility of self-identification or a sense of homelessness? Why was the stage, adapted by so many as home, for him only an arena of estrangement and homelessness?

In the story "Heinz," the narrator says, "One can choose truthfulness for oneself since nothing is real. Everything is clothed, only nakedness is unreal. A naked body—that is a mask" (Stryjkowski 1961, 90).

According to Stryjkowski, only that which can be chosen is real; that is, only the variant of one's fate and the assumed role are real. What kinds of experiences dictate such an understanding of truth? In my opinion, two answers are possible. One is born of the conviction that despite historical and biographical determinants, a relatively free choice is possible. In Stryjkowski's prose the sphere of that choice is occupied by love, which, as in Shakespeare's *Hamlet,* is always entangled in hatred, sin, politics, threatened by death, and consistently tragic. A good example of this is the love between the newcomer from Narbona and the Christian Catalina, during the times of the Jewish persecution, or the love of Tag and Jewdocha during the Cossack raids, or the love of Maria and her married Polish lover.

The second answer originates in the experience of the escape. The need to conceal oneself is real, as is the fear that motivates that need. The rest is unreal, it does not count, it does not exist, since what we truly care about must be hidden deep down, disguised with a costume, and sealed with silence. "A silent theater is not a contradiction"—says Govella, one of the characters in the story "Heinz" (Stryjkowski 1961, 100). The essence of art lies in obliterating the barrier of the ineffable, in communicating without words, in exposing that which is unveiled. Stryjkowski tried to take on this challenge in "Heinz." He used theatrical and Shakespearean props for this reason. He signaled the touchiness of the homosexual theme by tying it to Hamlet's incestuous, yet culturally mitigated, perversion. In other crypto-homoerotic works—for example, in the story "Chiwu"—he no longer tried doing this. In this story, a woman encircled by another man is the partner for the unfulfilled and lost love.

In his last published work, Stryjkowski confesses: "I attacked this theme [of homosexuality] on many occasions. Never before did I do it frontally. I tore off the visor only in *Silence.* I thought, 'You are eighty years old.' Write it. Let it be your last book. Shut the door. Let there be no more words from you. Don't write anymore about anything" (Stryjkowski 1994, 143).

Let us first consider the phrase "to tear off the visor." It is a mix of two metaphors: "to lift up the visor" and "to tear off the mask." However, this imperfect fusion has its own deep meaning as a poetic metaphor that discloses the author's intentions, even those that are not conscious. Tearing off the mask exposes one to danger, just as wearing it is supposed to protect one against risks. Stryjkowski comprehends his life and writing as a struggle with that which is different, as a game played from a place that is hidden and protected, and as a camouflage. The lifting of the mask and showing one's face was an act of courage. At the same time, it naturally arrested the inner mechanism of Stryjkowski's prose oriented toward concealing its homoerotic essence or, in any case, toward concealing the entire truth, which was based on the experience of sexual otherness. It led to silence and a fundamental sense of not belonging.

| | |

STRYJKOWSKI WROTE QUITE a few good novels and collections of stories, starting with *Bieg do Fragalr* (A run to Fragalr, 1951) and ending with *Silence* (1993), but also one masterpiece, *Voices in the Darkness* (1956). It pained him later that he could not repeat the success of his début. Some of his other works, such as *The Inn* and the oneiric *Sen Azrila* (Azril's dream, 1975), come close. The biblical trilogy also strikes one with the beauty of stylized language. With the exception of this trilogy and his historical novel, *Przybysz z Narbony* (The newcomer from Narbona, 1978)—although I have my doubts about the latter—Stryjkowski made references to his own life, as did many other writers of the present era. What is surprising in Stryjkowski's literary output is the way he makes use of his biographical resources as well as the experiences, limitations, and opportunities dispensed by fate.

He was a Jew who grew up in a very traditional home. He was a follower of the Zionist ideology. He was a communist. He was a student of Polish literature. He was a party activist during the war, which he spent in the Soviet Union. He was a writer. He spent two years in the multicultural community of the Polish Kresy.[4] In Stryj and then in Lwów, he encountered not only Jews and Poles but also Ukrainians, Russians, and Germans. After the war, he acquainted himself with the world. He lived in Italy for a few years and spent some time in the United States.

Such multicultural encounters left only a minimal mark on his prose. They are almost absent from the linguistic configuration of his prose, which is consistently homogenous, with only traces of stylized conversation, as in *The Inn.* Stryjkowski's solution for life and for writing was always based on choosing some dominant or biographical thread while passing all the rest in silence. Henryk Jarosz from *The Black Rose* is none other than Stryjkowski with his Jewishness amputated. Artur Salz from *Wielki strach* (The great fear, 1979) is none other than Stryjkowski, who has no interest in the Polish culture and who constantly moves in the Zionist and communist circles of inspiration. For example, his hero intends to study medicine, not Polish literature. In the "Yugoslav" stories, such as *A Proper Name,* as well as in the "American" ones, such as *On Willows . . . Our Violins,* the hero does not call on any experiences pertaining to his party affiliation. His stay in Russia is described casually and does not entail any ideological debates; they are clearly superfluous. In addition, those different biographical variants, regardless of their plot and content, are told in the similar cold, well-balanced literary language of central Poland. Characteristic of this language is the absence of any dialectal, environmental, or territorial idiosyncrasies.

One is tempted somehow to name this unusual manner of narrating one's fate. However, it is not easy. In such cases it is useful to reach for a metaphor that, for example, has been drawn from other art forms. Two solutions come to mind, a music metaphor that compares Stryjkowski's narration to a structure of a variation and a theater metaphor that compares his primary narrational, or rather authorial, strategy to acting.

It seems that the latter proposition is closer to Stryjkowski. The theater, with its possibilities of choosing a particular role, corresponds to the biographical and psychological situation of the author. The theater serves as a stage for an indirect public self-introduction. It allows one to speak not entirely in one's own name. It dooms one to exposing the truth hidden under the scenic costume. It constitutes an endurance test that, at times, is impossible to pass.

In my opinion, Stryjkowski resigns himself to a theatrical convention not out of fear of exposing the sometimes undesirable elements of his biography and not even because of homosexuality itself; it is rather his inability to arrive at self-definition that creates a sense of alienation and homelessness that is tied to his homoerotic orientation. The difficulty with accepting one's "otherness" prevents Stryjkowski from accessing a collective experience that is unequivocally valorized. It pertains to Jewishness, Polishness, and his leftist tendencies in equal measure. Therefore, Artur Sandauer, who accused the author of *Voices in the Darkness* of an aversion toward the Jews, dictated by his attempts to gain popularity with a non-Semitic audience, is mistaken. Coolness and distance create the inner conditions of Stryjkowski's writing. They reenact a tormenting sense of alienation toward oneself and an overwhelming homelessness of the Other.

Translated by Katarzyna Owczarek

Notes

1. The volume was not scrupulously edited, as is evident from this passage. Errors in punctuation and syntax break the reader's concentration.

2. "Yes, I am an autobiographical writer par excellence. What does this autobiography depend on? On the fact that I never write about things I have not directly experienced" (Szymański 1964).

3. Jan Błoński (1982) even wrote that the Holocaust is a sort of punishment for sins that permeate the Jewish world.

4. Kresy (Borderlands): part of pre–World War II territories of easternmost Poland lost after the Yalta Conference in 1945. Culturally, ethnically, and linguistically they were quite a diverse territory (editor's note).

Works Cited

Błoński, Jan. 1982. "Autoportret żydowski" (A Jewish self-portrait). *Tygodnik Powszechny* 51.

Sandauer, Artur. 1982. *O sytuacji pisarza polskiego pochodzenia żydowskiego w dwudziestym wieku* (On the situation of a Polish writer of Jewish descent in the twentieth century). Warsaw: Czytelnik.

Stryjkowski, Julian. 1961. *Imię własne* (A proper name). Warsaw: Czytelnik.

———. 1964. "Rozmowa z Julianem Stryjkowskim" (A conversation with Julian Stryjkowski). Interview by Wiesław Paweł Szymański. *Tygodnik Powszechny* 21.

———. 1974. *Na wierzbach . . . nasze skrzypce* (On willows . . . our violins). Warsaw: Czytelnik.

———. 1991. *Ocalony na wschodzie: Z Julianem Stryjkowskim rozmawia Piotr Szewc* (Rescued in the East: A conversation between Julian Stryjkowski and Piotr Szewc). Cavaillon, Switzerland: Editions Noir sur Blanc.

———. 1993. *Milczenie* (Silence). Kraków: Wydawnictwo Literackie.

———. 1994. "Urodziłem się pisarzem, nie bohaterem. Rozmowa pomiędzy Julianem Stryjkowskim, Adamen Michnikiem i Romanem Kurkiewiczem" (I was born a writer, not a hero: A conversation between Julian Stryjkowski, Adam Michnik, and Roman Kurkiewicz). *Gazeta o książkach,* supplement to *Gazeta Wyborcza* 1. Reprinted in *Julian Stryjkowski* by Wiesław Kot. Poznań: Rebis, 1997, 143.

4 ||| Home/lessness and the Discourse of Subjectivity in Gombrowicz's *The Marriage* and Różewicz's *The Card Index*

Tamara Trojanowska

THE FOCUS OF this chapter is the relationship between the issue of home and homelessness and the discourse of subjectivity in two Polish plays: Witold Gombrowicz's *The Marriage* (*Ślub*) and Tadeusz Różewicz's *The Card Index* (*Kartoteka*).[1] The plays share more than the timing of their first productions in the theater, their success with audiences, readers, and critics, and the impact they have had over the years on Polish theater and drama.[2] Both propose a new vision of modern humans in the disenchanted world of disengaged freedom, or to put it in different terms, new ways of inquiring about and understanding the subject, its place, and the force of its agency in cultural history and meaning-making when the stability of traditional definitions disappeared. Both use a home setting, a primary site of initial tensions between individuality and social relations, as a locus of problematic subjectivity. This home is malleable, hybrid, and eccentric (in the double meaning of that word), lacking in intimacy and emotional dimension. It functions not as a location of family dramas, although the presence of a family is still important, but of the drama of subjectivity, of an individual's complex moral, cognitive, and creative relationship to oneself and to the world. This relationship is at the heart of the two plays and both playwrights use the techniques and strategies of subjective drama, closely related to the issues of identity, to explore it. I will pursue some aspects of this relationship by analyzing the figures of home and homelessness, understood in both texts as the inhabitation of and eviction from one's subjectivity in the context of spatial and familial relationships.

Considering that a sense of dispossession, of not being at home with oneself in the world is central to the modernist experience, the images of inhabitation and eviction are useful tools for addressing the most important questions about subjectivity, that is, how it understands and exercises itself and its relationship to the world, and how it acquires its force as agency.

At the Crossroads: Witold Gombrowicz's *The Marriage*

The Marriage is a dream of its protagonist. Henry, a Polish soldier in the last war in France, goes back home only to find it transformed into an inn, his father turned into an innkeeper, and his fiancée, Molly, into a disreputable maid. This oneiric homecoming and awkward family reunion is disrupted by his father's persecutors, the drunkards, whom Henry defeats by paying homage to his father and by changing him incidentally into a king. With his father's royalty comes a promise of a sacred marriage (and of a new home), but the ceremony never takes place. Henry, prompted by the chief drunkard and by his own doubts, dethrones his father and declares himself the king. He wants to marry without depending on a sacred sanction and therefore attempts to consecrate the celebration by the power of his own decision and by the sacrificial suicide of Johnny, Henry's friend, whom the Drunkard and Henry's parents implicate as Molly's lover. After Johnny's death, Henry imprisons himself.

This meandering, peculiar action begins in a murky, depressing, open space with the "disfigured" and "obscure" ruins of a church looming in the background—a relic of a distinctly theatrical setting and a sign of the modern challenge to metaphysics and transcendence in a postwar world.[3] This is the first degraded home in the play—the home of God, the first authority, source of order, and essentialist concept of identity that is undermined by being made homeless. In *The Marriage,* God has not died; he has been evicted. That eviction, a reversal of humanity's banishment from paradise, from an ideal, transcendent, and ultimate home, resonates throughout the play with multiple evictions of Henry's family, with degradations of other spaces, and with the destruction of the authority of God figures: a father and a king. On its opposite side are acts of inhabitation and sublimation of created spaces that are paired with restitutions of power and authority and are crowned with Henry's assertion of ultimate control over the life and death of others. These inhabitations and evictions also match the protagonist's sense of having and losing his individual autonomy.

The initial setting changes gradually and temporarily by Henry's creative effort, aided by the casual prompting of Johnny, into a family dining room in a gentry manor.[4] The wished for and at the same time feared appearance of Johnny helps to change the self of the solitary hero into a subject of interpersonal relations, while the deserted space of impossible transcendence transforms into a populated space of human, familial interaction. However, the shape of this room remains vague, its characteristics are ambiguous, caught between what is familiar, reminding Henry of his parental home and what is estranged, looking more like a tavern, a poor surrogate for a home, a public space of transitory and rudimentary existence.[5] Gombrowicz incorporates and immediately subverts the traditional setting of a family drama, which is usually associated with a private, secure space that directs attention to what is ordinary. In *The Marriage* nothing can remain ordinary.

Consequently the potentially intimate, emotionally charged, socially and culturally "sanctified" space of a home never materializes (see Ratajczakowa 1985). On the contrary, in a peculiar contest of spaces triggered by the appearance of other characters, a tavern defeats a home; a degraded surrogate mocks and displaces its prototype; a copy subverts the original. This degradation is remedied when in the second act the space takes its shape from more noble theatrical conventions, a tragedy or an opera, and the family inhabits a royal palace. Nothing indicates this change directly, except for only a few details (a column, an elevated platform, magnificent but burlesque costumes) and, most important, the changed roles of the characters: a father becomes a king, Henry's mother a queen, Henry is proclaimed a prince, and disgraced Molly is now a virginal fiancée to be married in a sacred, religious ceremony.

The final step in the process of inhabitation and eviction takes place in the third act. After dethroning his father, Henry seizes total power and imprisons his disruptive alter ego, the Drunkard, and his parents. That is, he banishes them, like God did the first parents, from his ideal home and for a moment enjoys the distilled essence of his theatrical universe. But in *The Marriage* such an essence evaporates quickly. It is not possible to inhabit completely even an immobilized and terrorized world, as it is impossible to inhabit oneself unequivocally. The space comes under siege when war is announced, and it deteriorates soon after.[6] The repressed forces reemerge, incite Henry's insecurities, suspicions, and jealousy that result in his demand of Johnny's suicide, and provoke the final eviction in the play. Henry, both the willing and involuntary murderer, imprisons himself and, as a self-proclaimed god in the "interhuman church," evicts himself from it. This self-banishment closes the play with a gesture that repeats and mocks the first eviction. The eviction of God has opened new possibilities of envisioning the self—no longer a free, autonomous, authentic, and rational modern individual whom we have inherited from the Enlightenment, but a more complicated self of interhuman subjects who imprison themselves in each other while trying to break free from such imposition, who form and shape each other, and are pained by such mutuality, and whose behavior is puzzling and unpredictable precisely because it is born in their "in-betweenness." Henry evicts himself from this "interhuman church" not because he rejects the idea of the interhuman. He recognizes it as both inevitable and dangerous, liberating and confining, exciting and overwhelming.[7] But in the end he has to recognize its unsurpassable limitations and its failure to constitute an alternative *modus vivendi.* His calling for another Man, directed against God and Reason ("May he be like me, troubled and immature / Confused and incomplete, dark and obscure / So I can dance with him! Play with him! Fight with / him! / Pretend to him! Ingratiate myself with him! / And rape him, love him and forge myself / Anew from him, so I can grow through him, and in / that way / Celebrate my marriage in the sacred human church!" [137]), is answered by death, and his "sacred human church" celebrates a funeral instead of a wedding.

In *The Marriage,* the process of appropriation and loss of family (and familiar) spaces, the shifts between peculiarity and familiarity, sanctity and profanity, the self and the other happen within the most intimate spaces of all: in the timeless realm that Freud ascribed to the unconscious mental processes. On the one hand, the oneiric convention of Gombrowicz's play points to the modernist concept of the vertical structure of human psyche resulting in the tensions between the surface behavior and the depth of their emotions and desires. Jan Błoński has followed this lead and analyzed Gombrowicz's play as a psychoanalytical tragedy. Dreams have also found a special place in the vocabulary of creativity and have even become a model for creation. In a famous passage in his *Diary,* Gombrowicz has compared his own creative method to a dream and to simultaneous following and controlling of its logic. Not surprisingly, the protagonist of *The Marriage* has often been interpreted not only as a dreaming subject but also as a creative artist.[8] However, the subjective structure of *The Marriage* offers Henry more than access to the subconscious or to the sources of creativity. It offers liberty from the constraints of rationality and responsibility in his experience of and experiments with his subjectivity, with moral and cultural codes, with taboos and hierarchies (so well embodied in family relationships). Such freedom gives the subject access to the fictional and the fantastic, but also implies impunity, which, according to Małgorzata Sugiera, belongs to the arsenal of Gombrowicz's "imaginary devil" (1995, 230–31). The temptation of impunity is essential to the understanding of Henry's phantasmagorias, but the notion of an imaginary devil in Gombrowicz's world has to be qualified. It does make sense so long as the concept of the divine, the idea of the sacred, is still valid, even if its validation comes from this, rather than the other, world. In other words, exiling transcendence exposes unceasing transcendental longings, whereas secularizing and controlling the world promises unattainable salvation.

Whether understood as a subconscious locus of the multiple (dis)placements of events, ordered by condensation and symbolization, or as a creative or dramatic strategy, the permanent liminality, unpredictability, and transformations of the oneiric world in *The Marriage* reflect the same qualities as the protagonist's three mental shifts. One such shift is between sublimation and desire (sanctification and degradation), which Błoński sees as two themes verbalized in two recurring lines: "Henry! Oh, Henry!" and "You pig" (1994, 128). The second is between spontaneity (participation) and self-reflection (withdrawal), and the third between the imperative to assess one's subjectivity and the pressure of the subjectivity of others. The first two shifts are of lesser importance to our considerations. The last one, heavily commented on by many critics, is still of interest. Henry both strives to inhabit himself (to be a coherent, rational, unique, autonomous, and authentic self) and is exiled into the world of human interaction, where he is no longer a substantively understood, unified, and essentialist subject. In this sense, Gombrowicz's character is both homeless and homebound, evicted from his subjectivity and thrown into the intersubjective, and obsessively returning to himself. By the same token, the play makes the distinction between the inside and the outside impossible to define. The inside (the subjective) is turned inside out, toward the intersubjective. The outside (the intersubjective) is turned inward, toward self-reflexivity. The provisionary self ends up not only with no fixed borders but also with little claim to knowledge about its relationship to the world. The relationship between subject and object is interdependent, and subjectivity can no longer be the legitimate source of the knowledge about it. The outside forms the inside as much as the inside gives meaning to the outside, and there is no way of verifying which takes precedence in this exchange.

It is significant that the other with and against whom Henry builds his phantasmagorias, and who in turn defines him, is his family. To put this situation in spatial terms again, the initial spaces of transcendence and of history collapse into a space of family relations, which are the most important locus, as Freud noted, of individual development (they share in our past) and which initiate us into a complex game of intersubjectivity. In this context, it is worth recalling Jerzy Jarzębski's observation that most of Gombrowicz's works "tell a story about a destruction of a family, about its purposeful dismantling, which becomes the primary goal of the protagonist" (1982, 374; 1992, 19–37). Such obsessive repetitiousness suggests that this dismantling can never be successful. Why isn't it successful in *The Marriage*? No matter how deformed and mistreated, the family maintains its central position in the play. Henry subverts its dismantling by his dependence on this initial frame of reference in his experience of the self and in his relations with others. He can no longer legitimize the subordination of his subjectivity to the traditional hierarchy of familial relations and asserts his self by denouncing the family. By exercising new rules of interaction and by creating a new social order, he hopes to become a source of their legitimacy. But his experiment goes too far and not far enough. It goes too far because the ultimate test of Henry's power is to make it constitutive of the sacred. In turn, the only way to consecrate his decision is through extreme violation—a murder, an act that cannot be legitimized. It does not go far enough because the new order, very much like the old one, still depends on the notion of the sacred. Granted, this sacred is interhuman rather than divine, but nonetheless by its sheer necessity it makes the denouncing of the family pointless. To put it differently, Henry's recreations of and violent reactions against his family cannot effectively exile what he desires to reject. There is no escape from home in *The Marriage*—an experience that Gombrowicz made his own in his permanent struggle with his home, both parental and national.[9]

The subjective poetics of the play and the intersubjective results of human interaction established in it constantly undermine the independence and finality of Henry's decisions. Many critics have noted that Henry rehearses his moves, that he tests the power of words, that his lethargy, hesitation, and doubts coexist with the mounting tension of the dynamic action assuming a life of its own. To put it simply, in a traditional sense Henry is an unreliable dramatic agent. But this changes considerably in Act Three, when the hero redefines his relationship to the world. His doubts do not disappear, but they often give way to decisive actions; his orders overcome hesitation. Henry still rehearses, but this time not only his own moves, but also the desired responses to his will (Johnny's suicide) and the ceremonies he is set to conduct (his wedding). He also presents his decisions as coming from his own deliberations during a sleepless night, and not resulting from his interactions with others, as was the case in the two previous acts.

Henry' contradictory understandings of subjectivity become particularly pronounced now. On the one hand, he tries to exercise his solitary self, modernist individualism independent of relations and based on instrumental rationality. He refers to himself as a modern man twice and each reference implies that he connects this notion with rationality. What must follow is the view that culture, social roles, and relationships are possessions of the self, that they do not constitute it. Such subjectivity constructs itself with multiple but removable costumes underneath which there is a private being ("Father is a title the same as King is. Can't you speak like an ordinary man?" [116]). On the other hand, he recognizes a subject that is constituted exclusively by human interaction. Henry's plans rely on the assumption that in each model of subjectivity an individual can maintain control either because such model is based on the principle of disengagement and instrumental rationality, and therefore justifies extreme individualism deprived of moral engagements (the modernist self), or because it is based on constant flux, which implies much room for satisfying human desire at the price of responsibility. His theory about "Holiness, majesty, power, law, morality, love, ridiculousness, stupidity, wisdom" coming "from people in the same way that wine comes from grapes," informs his decision to use this theory to his advantage ("I shall force these apes to produce everything my heart desires" [107]). He exercises this power during a rehearsal of Johnny's suicide. But in his lengthy and most important monologue, Henry realizes that the modernist self, and "a metaphysics of loneliness" (Luntley, 153) connected with it, has to succumb to the interhuman self and to metaphysics of positioning, both among human beings and in history. That is why the news of the war and the description of the killing is very much a part of the third act. The war introduces the historical dimension from which Henry's understanding of the self cannot break loose: "What does it matter (I ask) that I, I am in the very middle, the very center of everything, if I, I can never be / Myself? . . . I alone / I alone (Let's emphasize that once more) . . . while out / there/ Nothing but cries, screams and blood, alas, alas, and fear . . . No, I do not exist / I haven't any 'I,' alas, I forge myself / Outside myself, outside myself . . ." (135).

Although after discovering Johnny's corpse, Henry insists on his innocence, and therefore disregards a traditional moral code, he confesses to his participation in Johnny's death, and therefore restores the moral function of a decision. He concedes to his authorship of Johnny's suicide in an already familiar contradictory manner: "This corpse is my creation / But this creation is incomprehensible / Dark / Obscure . . . / More powerful than I, and / perhaps not even my own!" (156). His doubts result from the bewildering nature of this creation, from the intricate rules of interhuman relations and the resulting metaphysical crisis: "I have no control over my own deeds! / I know nothing, nothing, nothing, I understand / nothing, nothing, nothing! / Whoever says he understands is a liar! / [. . .] Being mutually united, we are forever arranging ourselves into new forms" (157). However, despite this confusion, Henry does not give up his creative, cognitive, and emancipatory potential. His claims to the authorship of Johnny's corpse make him a designer of its burial.[10] This authorship also voices different aspirations than did Henry's emancipatory gestures of seizing total control and asserting (unsuccessfully) his individual autonomy in the interhuman. Henry decides to place himself within the power of the intersubjective. The other is no longer a partner in the human church that Henry fantasized about in his famous monologue. The idea of such playful domination gives way to careful planning: "While I am standing here / and speaking . . . / Let your hands . . . / Touch . . . me . . . ," and to limited control of it: "Wait a minute. / I'm not through yet" (158).

The question remains why Henry gives up his impunity despite the declared innocence. Is it because he has encountered his conscience and has to recognize the value of human life and the subjectivity of the other? It probably is, since, as Johnny has once instructed Henry, pangs of conscience appear in solitude and evaporate in the company of others.[11] Henry may not feel responsible for Johnny's suicide, but he has no one with whom he can share his participation in it. Even the Drunkard, the only other possible partner in this crime, is surprised when he points his dirty finger at Johnny's corpse.

In that sense Henry reclaims his solitude, while giving himself up, and has to respond to conscience, even if conscience is understood only as pain of the violation. In the world of intersubjective existence, as is created in *The Marriage,* death becomes the ultimate limit of control and possession. Henry can no longer see his decision in the sphere of playful potentiality, but has to place it in the sphere of deeds, which cannot escape evaluation, no matter how sophisticated the system of evasion. Even when God is absent, killing remains a violation of life. No anthropological, historical, or philosophical experimentation can challenge the fundamental truth, formulated by Józef Tischner in his discussion of Emanuel Levinas's philosophy: "The commandment 'Thou shall not kill' has something absolute in it. It creates a relationship that can be destroyed by no other authority, because such authority does not exist. It does not mean that killing is physically impossible. It happens. But it violates what is absolute. Man can kill, but he cannot make killing cease to be a violation" (1990, 33).[12]

Gombrowicz does not situate Henry's decision in a Christian context—in which it is viewed as a "truly human moment that determines a unique, human, personal image that is shaped 'from the inside'" (Krąpiec 1974, 217)—but he nonetheless places the protagonist in the vicinity of its most important questions. Simply put, even though in Gombrowicz's play God has been evicted, he has left his belongings behind. By exiling himself from the human church, Henry acknowledges the validity of moral questions and undermines both the Nietzschean subjectivism of moral life and his own reductionism.

Nietzsche's dictum in the *Genealogy of Morals,* "there is no 'being' behind doing, effecting, becoming: 'the doer' is merely a fiction added to the deed—the deed is everything" (1989, 45), so appropriate for Henry's adventures, loses its appeal at the end. Henry marries the doer with the deed, even though he wishes them divorced: "If I am imprisoned here, then somewhere, somewhere far away, let *this deed of mine* be raised up on high" [my italics]. "The doer" has to materialize morally and while striving to "cut a path from Unreality to Reality," as his creator does, Henry meets the reality of a corpse.

The Marriage does not show "the drama of the self that discovers its own nonexistence" (Sugiera 1999, 46). It is this nonexistent self that obsessively searches for itself in Henry's experiments. Otherwise Henry wouldn't have reached for absolute power. True, the nonexistence of his self is one of Henry's own conclusions, but his assessments of his subjectivity change. He asserts his solitude unsuccessfully, acknowledges his substantiality while admitting its dependence on others, renounces his subjectivity, and finally becomes his own prisoner.[13] This last self-definition is particularly important as it confirms the fundamental impossibility of knowledge, an impasse in the relationship between subject and object, subject and others. What is nonexistent is a stable, authentic identity, not the "I-ness" itself. Henry's failure does not eliminate the self, it redefines it into a self that does not want to forsake the basic aspiration to inhabit itself while being constantly exiled from its subjectivity. This dramatic struggle makes Henry a moral subject, even if he does not follow Levinas's idea of responsibility and cannot identify the source of his moral imperatives.

Lyotard claims that what all metanarratives of modernity have in common is the notion of a universal finality, and he draws an important conclusion from this claim, namely that Christianity is modern in its very foundation. What is more, he believes that all "great stories" of modernity are secularized versions of the Christian paradigm. Gombrowicz's undertaking can thus be seen from a new perspective. Many critics have mentioned his seditious reliance on Christian rituals. *The Marriage* may be the best example of it. The liturgy of the mass, the play's imagery, the idea of the human church, and secular rituals all contribute to the play's blasphemous and subversive appeal. But this artistic and philosophical rebellion can be read as a disagreement with modernity's "great stories" and their false universal finality, whose source Gombrowicz pinpoints with great accuracy years before Lyotard's theory stirred waves in Western academia.

As a dreaming subject Henry realizes his struggles in language. He feels compelled to verbalize the "intensive laboring" of his spirit, as Gombrowicz puts it, to others and to himself (1969, 16). As both a process and a site of all contradictions, he constitutes himself as a multiple subject in and through language. He becomes a conscious subject that uses language and an unconscious subject that is spoken by it. He writes and interprets himself and others like a text, but he, as an author, is also determined by the text he creates; he is the creator and the created, the interpreter and the interpreted, the dreaming and the dreamt; he brings into being and undermines the existing; he shifts from inaccessible authenticity to excessive inauthenticity. In this process of double encoding he who speaks (writes) is not identical with he who is spoken (written), even though he speaks (writes) with himself, very much like "the sylleptic 'I,'" which Ryszard Nycz defines, among other things, as intersubjective and fragmentary (1995b, 386; 1997, 107–14). Nycz explains the concept of the "sylleptic I" as a double encoding of subjectivity: as true and invented, as empirical and textual, as authentic and fictional. It seems to fit best those texts in which the author enters his fictional works as one of the characters. Provided we read Henry's operations as textual and see him as both a character in and a creator of the text of his dream, the "sylleptic I" becomes a perfect match for his type of subjectivity. It also offers an explanation of Henry's last words, which have not, as yet, been adequately interpreted. "If I am imprisoned here, then somewhere, somewhere far away, let this deed of mine be raised up on high. And now let this funeral march of yours / Carry you away" (158). Henry's dictum parallels Gombrowicz's desire to "continue his life-in-writing" that reflects "the anxiety related to the future in which the name will remain as the only guarantee of the value of the written" (Longinovic 1998, 35).

Even though in *The Marriage* all creative operations are performed in the atemporal dimension of a dream, that dream is surprisingly well ordered and recovers the seemingly neglected temporality of Henry's life. It places Henry within history and brings forward his experiences as a soldier in war. It invokes his prewar family history and involves his marital plans for the future, which support individual yearning for social order and temporal continuity. Henry's dream is a new kind of autobiography, written not by a literary persona constructed by a writer but by an interhuman construct whose subjectivity realizes itself not only between Henry and others, but also between two levels of fictionality of his creation, between him and language, which links him with and separates him from the world.

In the final analysis, it becomes clear that *The Marriage* operates simultaneously along two axes that translate themselves into one another. One is vertical and explores the depth of the subconscious; another is horizontal and explores the expanse of the intersubjective. The vertical refers to modernist explorations of the structure of the self; the horizontal refers to the postmodern exploration of the conditioning of the self. In Brian McHale's terms, the play marries the celebrated subjectivity of high modernism (immersed in the problems of epistemology) with the ontological orientation of postmodernism (preoccupied with the modes of being) (McHale 1987). In a word, *The Marriage* engages a complex discourse of subjectivity that defines the subject both in terms of modernist individualism and in terms of a postmodern intersubjective, fragmentary, and contextualized entity. In the end, it becomes a battlefield of these two concepts of subjectivity and two definitions of identity.

The Reluctant Postmodernist: Tadeusz Różewicz's *The Card Index*

Tadeusz Różewicz approaches the problem of subjectivity from a different angle. While *The Marriage* examines the consequences (and the boundaries) of a new definition and experience of subjectivity and a new mode of being of the sylleptic I, *The Card Index* exposes the unsolvable perplexities of the modernist self and the internal conflicts of modernity that have made them possible. While Gombrowicz uses a home and a family as experimental sites for the contesting forces of this new experience and performance of the self, Różewicz contextualizes home and family historically, culturally, and ideologically. While there is no escape from home in Gombrowicz's play, there is no return to it in Różewicz's.

Różewicz makes homelessness a prevalent experience for the characters in many of his plays (*Wyszedł z domu* [He left home], *Stara kobieta wysiaduje* [Old woman broods], *Odejście głodomora* [The hunger artist departs]) and prose (*Moja córeczka* [My little daughter], *Śmierć w starych dekoracjach* [Death among the old stage sets]). Even for those physically bound within the four walls, the Hero in *The Card Index,* a home no longer serves as a center of orientation in the world. They are as homeless as the characters of Eliot's *Waste Land* and *Hollow Men,* Conrad's novels, or Beckett's plays.

While in *The Marriage* a dream is an impulsive autobiography that cowrites its subject, in *The Card Index* memory is a compulsive biography that refuses to be written. *The Marriage* presents an assault on the remembered, while *The Card Index* presents violence of the remembered.

The Card Index unfolds in a windowless bedroom through which people pass by as if it were a street. All doors to it are open and the Hero's bed ends up, as Jan Kott has it, on the main Warsaw intersection, "on the corner of Jerozolimskie Avenue and Marszałkowska Street" (1962, 299). Some may prefer to say that this most private of rooms is a figure of the Hero's self, opening up to the chaotic traffic of his individual past (which includes references to the playwright's biography and to the literary biography of the lyrical persona of his poetry),[14] and of his present. But most important, it opens to generational experiences of history (of those born, like Różewicz, in the 1920s),[15] and to the ideological options history has to offer. The interwar period (the Hero's childhood) is mediated in the play primarily through family relations and cultural codes. The war (his adolescence) is recounted, and its impact reassessed, in nightmarish images, mediated through the Hero's reactions, and in the witnesses' fragmentary stories, disjointed accounts, and accusations.[16] Stalinism (the Hero's maturity) finds its representation primarily in allusions. But its aftermath (the Hungarian revolution of 1956 and the succeeding thaw) is a subject of substantial confrontations.[17] That is to say, in *The Card Index*, the discourse of subjectivity meets Linda Hutcheon's description: it is situated and contextualized primarily within the framework of history and ideology (1988, 159).

As I have concluded elsewhere, the liminal character of such space neutralizes traditional distinctions between *le dedans* and *le dehors, ici* and *la,* which Bachelard associates with being and nonbeing; between the intimate and the public space; and most important, between others and I (Trojanowska 1996, 419). In Różewicz's play, both time and space resist such binary oppositions and clear demarcations. A bedroom, which is traditionally associated with a closed, private space, becomes public while remaining intimate. It repeats in a way the ambiguity of theater space used in an actual production. An interior extends into the outside, into the street and the space of history, but also becomes a figure of the inner space of memory. The present serves as a vehicle for the past, but also performs its dramatic function of immediacy in a self-conscious theatrical performance. Neither is the relationship between Others and I based on a clear-cut distinction, since it is the others who, as both independent dramatic agents and constructs of the remembering I, activate (rather than constitute) the Hero's subjectivity. In other words, time and space in *The Card Index* match Lyotard's concept of both, including their openness, lack of direction, and unspecified potentiality. Różewicz arranges this space by using the discours of memory that is non-linear, non-narrative, anti-teleological, non-explanatory, and definitely not goal oriented. Simply speaking, it is postmodern.

In terms of dramatic function, the intrusion of a public into a private sphere is engendered by the appropriation of the Hero's home by characters who redefine it into the space they want to inhabit. Thus while in *The Marriage* the instability and transformability of a home, the dynamics of inhabitation and eviction parallel a creative and cognitive process of the unstable, intersubjective self, in *The Card Index,* the repeated annexations of a home by a public sphere parallel our unwilled public performance of an intimate mnemonic process. Both plays manipulate time and space: Gombrowicz's by dramatizing an atemporal movement of a dream, Różewicz's by projecting outwards an internal process of remembering (a movement in time and space).

But unlike in *The Marriage,* which divorces the changing space from temporality, in *The Card Index* the unchanging space is marked by time in order to confront us with the historicity of humans. While in *The Marriage* the oneiric convention endows the eccentric experiments with the self with impunity, in *The Card Index* a similar convention, a crossbreeding of a dream and a memory play, becomes a vehicle for moral anxiety. The self in Różewicz's play emerges not from the struggle for its individuality, but from a series of evasions. In other words, if in Gombrowicz's play the exiled self wades through the subjectivity of others toward its own (and the home and family relationships epitomize this struggle), in Różewicz's the exhausted self evades asserting its subjectivity, and the transient bedroom is the figure of this fatigue. While staying in the most intimate of domestic and mental places, in his centrally located bed and in his memories that are central to the poetics of the play, the Hero is evicted from his privacy (and contextualized) and from the present (and historicized). However, as a subject he is not a source of his memories, he does not "own" them. They posses him.

It has been noted many times that in *The Card Index* memory plays a crucial role. On the simplest level it justifies the appearance of dramatic figures. They incorporate an uncertain, ontologically liminal status of objective dramatic agents (when involved in dramatic interaction), projections of memory (in view of the poetics of the play), and possible figments of the Hero's imagination (in their relationship to his life). The Hero's "web of interlocution," a Taylorian term particularly apt for this play (Taylor 1989, 36) is composed concentrically (in terms of relationships) and randomly (in terms of the order of the encounters) of his family members (dead and alive), friends and acquaintances, subordinates, strangers with whom the Hero has shared his public existence, and accidental passers-by. Time traverses these circles, and the Hero's past and present intersect, as do his public and intimate lives. These intersections create genealogical, biological, cultural, and historical spaces, which engage him in interpersonal encounters. But most important, memory justifies the intrusion of other characters into the Hero's home and turns this home into a traditional mnemonic locus.

But Różewicz both employs and subverts this trope. It is evident that in *The Card Index* the workings of memory and its theatrical rendering are deeply resented by the apathetic Hero. Remembering is not a deliberate effort, much less a hermeneutical effort, to reconstruct the teleological order of the past and its closure. When compared to such canonic modernist plays as *Death of a Salesman, The Glass Menagerie,* or *Dream Play, The Card Index* does not present a subject who relives his past for cognitive, psychological, or emotional reasons. Neither Bergson's *memoire pure* nor Proust's *memoire involontaire,* it is, rather, an almost accidental and certainly paradoxical consequence of the Hero's will to forget that engenders his persistent abulia. It does not explain the present but rather problematizes it. In this sense it is also the Hero's peculiar redemption, since it strips him of the power to totalize and to give a unified meaning to the past. The Hero's unwillingness to act, a source of important tensions in the play (not to mention its peculiar humor), is directly related to the functions of space and time. Unlike in traditional mnemotechnics, he does not deposit the images he wants to remember in a house in order to link them "to the past events which represent the substance or contents of the mnemonic effort" (Spieker 1996, 71). This process is reversed. It is time and space that deposit the images and past events in him. In the absence of the will to remember and of a reliable mnemonic locus, the Hero becomes a site of the impossible amnesia in which history deposits its fragmentary constructs.

However, even though the Hero refuses to participate, he cannot escape interaction. Because in a memory play interaction is defined primarily in subjective terms, the Hero is central to it (Szondi 1987, 25–26). Every major encounter engages him; every conversation requires the recognition of himself and his interlocutors and fosters the definition, even if it is deficient, of both self and relationships. This is a result of Różewicz's proclaimed compromise with the theater's demands that the Hero be actively involved in the play's action. Yet the playwright found a formula for such involvement in a paradox, in the activation of absence. The Hero's indolence in the present activates his past; his physical passivity triggers mental animation; his reluctance to give testimony to his life prompts the admission of witnesses to it. In short, the presence of the scenic reality results from the absence of the Hero's will to evoke and to maintain it. The Hero's adventure with memory proves his inablity to enjoy "the authentic spirit of modernity" which de Man sees captured, in his discussion of Nietzsche, in the philosopher's "ruthless forgetting, the blindness with which he throws himself into an action lightened of all previous experience" (1983, 147). The Hero's ineffectiveness in action is a direct result of his inablity to find himself in the disavowed modernity.

In a dramatic sense, the Hero gains access to his past through encounters that are undramatic, discontinuous, open-ended texts of unwilling memory, and that fail to order the past in response to the ambitions of rational thinking. On the contrary, they fragment what once might have had some order, now impossible to reconstruct. Remembering in *The Card Index* is paradoxical also because in remembrance, to paraphrase Walter Benjamin, we find crystallized the increasing self-alienation of humans, who inventory their past like so many lifeless possessions. That is to say, in *The Card Index,* the profusion of remembered experience is coupled with the atrophy of the self.[18] Despite forcing his character into relations with others and defining such interaction in subjective terms, Różewicz constantly undermines the centrality of the Hero's subjectivity. Against modernist inwardness, instead of probing the Hero's individual personality, his interest is in the workings and failures of cultural, historical, and ideological discourses that organize the experiences for the Hero and in the language in which the text of his life is written.[19] I will address both interests in the context of the Hero's familial relationships.

Despite the fragmentary nature of its dramatic action, it is not difficult to reconstruct the Hero's family history in *The Card Index.* This history involves attachment to individual and collective religious practices; close and permanent family ties; solid upbringing of and schooling for children; and middle-class social values and constraints. The Hero's encounters with family members, particularly with the Uncle, mark the spaces of loss and inadequacy of both the past and the present. The Uncle, who visits the Hero on his way from a pilgrimage, incarnates the cultural legacy of a devout, diligent, and robust soldier. This legacy, modeled on the traditions of the old Polish gentry entertaining the ideal of a premodern harmonious country life combined with military duties, was still alive in the interwar period. As the embodiment of lost authenticity—of being true to some kind of essence and of interiorized unquestionable ethical frameworks, to the clearly defined good and a fixed cultural code to which it refers—the Uncle represents the desired and unproblematic, but also historicized, unity of the self, a quality that the Hero cannot claim as his own. His notion of authenticity clearly feeds on gendered cultural stereotypes. The traditional paradigm of masculinity in Polish culture extols mobility (the trope of journey) and activity (the imperative of participation), whereas the paradigm of femininity venerates stasis (the trope of home) and passivity (the imperative of waiting, maintaining, and preserving). The Hero clearly associates authenticity with the masculine model, which he, incapacitated by his chronic abulia, no longer follows. That is, authenticity appeals to him primarily through cultural codes. But this appeal also owes much to his disappointments with the present realizations of the model itself, with his direct political involvement and public activism, which have brought him moral anxiety, a sense of superficiality, and persistent alienation from the self.

There is nothing nostalgic in this appeal, since the Hero in fact rejects the old-fashioned heroism by rejecting a cultural paradigm of masculinity, as often happens in postmodern texts.

Considering the importance of language and its manifold contextualizations, it becomes clear that the Hero's biography is as much rooted in the misconstrued texts of his memory as the "biography" of reality is rooted in conflicting discourses, both oral and written. The initial scene with his parents is revealing in this respect, because it demonstrates how the discourse of private, familial life intersects with the public discourse of ideology. In his confession, the Hero speaks three different dialects: the dialect of childhood, the dialect of religion, and the dialect of politics. In the first (simple syntax, diminutives, etc.) he admits to stealing sugar and eating sausage on a

Good Friday thirty years ago. These prewar transgressions against religious tenets intertwine linguistically with postwar political transgressions against ideological dogmas. Clearly, their meaning depends on historical and ideological contexts (in this case, the appropriation of Christian ethical vocabulary by the political discourse of the explicitly atheistic system). The Hero's plea: "Mom and Dad; after thirty years I have realized the enormity of my sins. . . . Mom, don't defend me. Renounce your son" (41), resembles in style, as critics have already noticed, the forced renunciations during Stalinist political trials, and brings into focus the religious nature of utopianism of which Stalinist terror was an indirect consequence.

Although his appeal initially matches the religious framework, the Hero grows increasingly insane in self-accusations, turning confession (an individualized gesture based on trust in divine mercy and absolution) into an act of political self-denial (a collectivized gesture based on fear of the state's vengeance and punishment). Furthermore, the allusion to Stalin's paranoid fear of assassination, and to his subsequent purges, clearly underlies the Hero's self-incrimination: "I also planned the removal of our dearest Granny . . . I now recollect with revulsion that I planned to remove Dad as well" (41). The idea of patricide further enhances the possibility of a political reading of these lines, since the rhetoric of defining Stalin included naming him the father of all the nations (and clearly copying the notion of God, the Father). What constitutes the relationship between subject and its textual representation in *The Card Index* is history.[20]

The Hero's position is paradoxical. Neither his individual choices nor the framework in which he makes them sufficiently validates his existence. That is to say, neither his disengaged privacy (directed against historical trappings of mandatory public activism), nor his withdrawal (directed against social and political coercion, ineffectiveness of action and literary conventions), neither his past nor his present gives his life unquestionable meaning. Różewicz's protagonist finds himself evicted from a discredited but still desired modernity, with its discourse of individualism, redemption through culture, with its conflicting strands of consumerism, instrumentalism, and the underlying longing for meaningful moral imperatives, not to mention its longing for clear referentiality of language. Instead, he inhabits, with resentment, the postmodern condition or what David Hirsch called recently the "post-Auschwitz" landscape (1991), which cuts loose the discourse of subjectivity from the notion of individualism and moors it in cultural artifacts and history. He inhabits a world that makes it clear that culture does not redeem modern life (Huyssen 1986, 210) and replaces modernist concern for the moral with the postmodern concern for the ideological. In other words, Różewicz's Hero is a "postmodernist subject [who] lives . . . in full knowledge both of the power of and desire for those humanist master narratives and also of their impossibility, except as they are acknowledged to be necessary (if illusory) consolations" (Hutcheon 1988, 191). The play repeats the Hero's plight in its relation to avant-garde poetics. It incorporates some of its major features (e.g., the technique of montage, the idea of the dissolution of the subject and the fragmentation of action), but invalidates its attack on memory and its dismantling of history. In its major characteristics it is a postmodern text, a postmodern memory-theater whose intent Jeanette R. Malkin defines as "to evoke erased memories of national past, to recontextualize, reopen canonized memory-'narratives,' rethink taboo discourses, intervene in the politics of memory and repression, and to engage (and occasionally enrage) the memoried consciousness of its audience" (1999, 3). It also conveys "the sense of a *conflicted and traumatized relation to the past*" (9).

While addressing the particular issues of Polish cultural, historical, and political experience, Różewicz's text engages itself in the most pressing conflicts of modernity: conflicts over the sources for constitutive goods, conflicts between the disengaged instrumentalism and the modernist protest against it, and conflicts between moral standards and the fulfillment of human life (Taylor 1989, 495–521). Such conflicts, not the playwright's confusion, explain the much-discussed inconsistencies of Różewicz's Hero. He longs for the time when there was still room for heroism and a clearly defined higher purpose in life but dreads the reality in which these ideals are put into action. He praises ordinary life but recognizes that ordinariness feeds boredom and insensitivity and results in the Nietzschean "pitiable comfort." His consumerist appetites acknowledge the dangers of a permanent deficiency of commodities. His revocable relationships (it is not a coincidence that people who visit the Hero have been betrayed, abandoned, or hurt by him) look back at possible affiliations with depth and commitment (his selfhood cannot be defined otherwise). Finally, his experience with the diminishing and fragmented self is undercut by his awareness that forces capable of totalizing the self ultimately cause its disappearance. If modernism prepares one kind of traps for the subject (its totalizing narratives, hierarchies, and structures), then postmodernism prepares others. In its double paradigms, as an emancipatory force and as a playful game of pastiche, it frees the subject but leaves the question of direction unanswered; it enjoys playful imagining but also makes history weightless.

In *The Marriage* and *The Card Index,* Gombrowicz and Różewicz, respectively, explore a new experience of the self in the postwar world in which metaphysics is in crisis and which is marked by unprecedented historical ordeals. Gombrowicz's subject tries to inhabit himself despite his evictions into the overwhelming convulsions of the intersubjective. The foundation for this inhabitable self is not fully formulated, except for its emancipatory, creative, and cognitive aspirations. It is a doubly encoded sylleptic I, placed at the intersection of modernist inward individualism and postmodern intersubjective, fragmentary, and contextualized subjectivity. Różewicz, on the other hand, diagnoses a self that lives, unwillingly and with great reluctance, a postmodern condition. The Hero longs for all the characteristics of "a distinctly modern self," from its notion of freedom (he wants to disengage himself from history and politics), a sense of uniqueness (his multiple selves pain him), the emphasis on authenticity and ethical imperatives (his admiration for the Uncle and his moral anxiety), the affirmation of ordinary life (the episode with his war bride), and the importance of dignity and respect (Abbey 2000, 79–80). He is reluctant to forsake modernity, even though he is aware of the impossibility of realizing himself as a modern self in the world that has intensified rather than solved modernity's conflicts and aporias. In other words, Różewicz's subject is exiled from desired and disgraced modernity but does not want to inhabit postmodernity either. That is why he would rather not act at all.

In both plays, a home (and a family) is a primary site and a trope of the self. In Gombrowicz's play a home is initially invoked by the protagonist, but its further transformability and liminality corresponds to his interactions with other characters as the space becomes a playground for the contesting forces of modern and postmodern experience of the sylleptic I. In Różewicz's play, a home is invaded by unpredictable guests from the Hero's past, as it becomes a playground for historical, cultural, and ideological contextualizations of his life. Both playwrights see the subject as a plural self, rather than as a unified, consolidated being. But Gombrowicz envisions such pluralism as a result of unavoidable intersubjectivity in human interactions, whereas Różewicz sees it as a result of unavoidable historical and civilizational changes. Such pluralization puts the subject in the precarious position of having to invent himself (thus acquiring various levels of fictionality) without being able to do so independently, but gaining the possibility of inventing others (*The Marriage*), or fragments him without acknowledging the cognitive liberty such fragmentation may provide (*The Card Index*). Whereas Gombrowicz's subject is enriched by such multiplication (despite its often painful consequences) and learns to celebrate it, Różewicz's subject is disempowered and disappointed. In both cases, the desired world, and the new definitions of subjectivity on which it is based, reveals its potential, but also the unexpected, violent, or reductive consequences of its realization. Once subjectivity has become problematic and has taken the form of intersubjectivity in human relations (in *The Marriage*), and of scattered, unwanted, and unreliable mnemonic encounters (in *The Card Index*) the subject's cognitive activity changes. In *The Marriage,* Henry tries to decipher the volatile text of his experience as his self cowrites it with others, but to whose logic he has to succumb and whose meaning he cannot grasp. In *The Card Index,* the Hero's passive and fragmented self in the present is defined by the activated fragmentary text of his past. In a battle between the celebrated subjectivity and epistemology of high modernism and the celebrated intersubjectivity and ontology of postmodernism, Gombrowicz is an explorer of Consciousness who distrusts Being, while Różewicz, as has been already noted by Kazimierz Wyka, is an explorer of Being, who does not trust Consciousness (Wyka 1994, 165).

Notes

1. Written in 1946, published in 1953 by Parisian émigré publisher Instytut Literacki and in Warsaw in 1957, *The Marriage* was first performed by a student theater in Gliwice in 1960. The play was directed by Jerzy Jarocki and designed by Krystyna Zachwatowicz. The same artistic team worked on its first professional staging in Warsaw's Teatr Dramatyczny in 1974. *The Card Index* was written between 1957 and 1959 and was published in 1960. It was performed the same year in Teatr Dramatyczny in Warsaw (directed by Wanda Laskowska; set design by Jan Kosiński).

2. Three generations of theater directors have been strongly influenced by these plays, among them Jerzy Grotowski, Jerzy Jarocki, Jerzy Grzegorzewski, and Grze-

gorz Jarzyna. Konstanty Puzyna, the best critic of that generation, claimed that Grotowski's *Apocalypsis cum figuris* would not have been created without Gombrowicz.

3. HENRY:

The curtain has risen . . . An obscure church . . .
An incongruous ceiling . . . A strange vault . . .
And the sign slips into the abyss of the abyss
Of the sphere of spheres, and stone and stone
Through an entrance that has never been entered
Stands a deformed altar of a foreign Psalter
Clasped shut by the absurdity of the chalice
That sinking into stillness gouges out the pastor . . .
A void. A desert. Nothing. I am alone here
Alone
Alone

(Gombrowicz 1969, 25)

The translation loses the meaning of an important line: "Tu wrota niemożliwe co wciąż przemyśliwam" by rendering it as "Through an entrance that has never been entered." The original implies a continuing preoccupation with the entrance to the church, a preoccupation that supports my thesis that God is exiled, not dead.

4. HENRY: But . . . are we? All the same I have the feeling . . . We're somewhere . . . There . . . There is something over there . . . *Part of a wall becomes visible, some furniture, the outline of a room.* I've seen all this before somewhere.

HENRY (dramatically):

We are somewhere
We are somewhere. But where?
What's that?
A room appears—the dining room of a county manor house in Poland that looks as though it has been transformed into a dive.

(Gombrowicz 1969, 27)

The home is linked to the concept of touching, the most important method of degradation in *The Marriage.* The Drunkard does not touch the Father because his face is like a home ("Mordę ma jak dom!") (Gombrowicz 1995, 123).

5. Johnny, Henry's alter ego, describes the space "z pewną trudnością" (with certain difficulty): "JOHNNY (hesitantly): I swear this room reminds me of something . . . It reminds me a little of your dining room in Małoszyce. It's similar and yet not similar . . . That clock. That chest of drawers. There's the room I slept in when I came to visit you during the holidays." And later he adds: "It would seem to be the same dining room, even though it does resemble a restaurant or a dive . . . or an inn . . . or a boardinghouse . . . or a tavern" (Gombrowicz 1969, 27–28).

6. "These curtains are impossible. I don't understand why this palace is so shabby and poorly kept. There are so many servants around here and still the dirt is everywhere" (Gombrowicz 1969, 128).

7. Henry's celebration of another man at the end of the play responds to Johnny's suggestion at its beginning: "What do you need God for when I am here? / Don't you see, friend, that I am the same as you? / Why let yourself get upset by ghosts / If you and I are of flesh and blood / If you are as I and I am as you!" (Gombrowicz 1969, 27).

8. For a summary of the critical approaches to the subjective structure of *The Marriage* as well as for criticism of Jan Błoński's psychoanalytical interpretation of the play, see Sugiera 1999, 36.

9. Thus, in a way, *The Marriage* uses the trope of homecoming in a traditional fashion, as Błoński asserts, by confronting the formative and the most tenacious experience of intersubjectivity (or of what socializes us) with Henry's sense of individuality (or of what separates, distinguishes us from others). Becoming a stranger to and estranging the familiar (and familial) makes room for this cognitive and creative encounter with the Other, also the Other in himself, and allows Henry to travel his own self through that multiplied Other. In Freudian terms, Henry's homecoming is a journey into the structure of the self. When seen in Bachelardian terms, his homecoming is both a return to the source of creativity and a quest for freedom from it. In our terms, his homecoming, both as an encounter between the subjective and the intersubjective and between the creative and the interpretative, realizes itself in the dynamic process of perpetual inhabitation of (consent, recognition, self-reflection) and eviction from (rejection, suppression, unawareness) the self, which multiplies, rather than solidifies, Henry's subjectivity (and his dramatic roles), and challenges his independence.

10. "If, however, there is a corpse, then there has to be a funeral, and if there has to be a funeral, then four of you must stand next to him so you can raise him up at a signal from me. . . . If, however, four of you are standing over there, next to him, then four of you must stand over here, next to me" (157).

11. HENRY: And you wouldn't feel any pangs of conscience afterwards?
JOHNNY: I would if I were alone, but not if there were the two of us, because one would imitate the other." (38)

12. Tischner explains: "The word *absolute* derives from *absolvere*—to dissolve. What is absolute dissolves our bonds with this world and ties us to the other world, in which this world finds its justification. What is absolute cannot be criticized and does not need to be justified. It is transcendent" (1990, 35).

13. Henry expresses his belief in his solitude many times. He acknowledges the sense of his selfhood, while recognizing that he is not the sole source of his behavior: "Our madness / is outside ourselves, out there . . . There, there, out / there. / Where I myself end, there begins / my wantonness . . . And even though I live in peace /

Within myself, still do I wander outside myself / And in dark, wild spaces and nocturnal places / Surrender myself to some unbounded chaos!" (79). Finally, at the end of the play, Henry expresses the sense of imprisonment in himself: "In vain do you struggle to get free of yourself in order / to reach me, and / In vain do I struggle to get free of myself to reach / all of you / Yes, I am imprisoned . . . / I am a prisoner / Even though I am innocent" (158).

14. The autobiographical elements and the subjective form of drama coincide in Różewicz's play as they did in Strindberg's. For the elaboration on the I dramaturgy, see Szondi (1987, 22–32). For a list of critical sources relating Różewicz's lyrical personae to the Hero, see Filipowicz (1991, 17–18).

15. The commentators find the most explicit proof of such reading in the Hero's old-fashioned monologue, a dramatic cry of a man who, having avoided death, lives in its shadow: "Hero: Everything dies under your hand because you don't believe. Where do you think you're crawling, you ass? You've been crawling for the last 38 years. To the sun? To truth? To the wall, I stand against the wall. My brothers, my generation, it's to you I am talking. They can't understand us, neither the young nor the old! (*Turns to the audience*) How did it happen? I can't understand it. There were so many things in me and I was so many different things and now there is nothing. Here. Here! There is no need! No need to cover up my eyes. (*Pause*) I want to see right to the end" (Różewicz 1969, 62).

16. The Hero frequently reacts to his own thoughts and nightmares. Those reactions imply air strikes, executions, and atrocities. In his conversation with a young German girl, the Hero compares the war to hunting, a primeval celebration of death. In his encounter with a peasant, whom the Hero killed in the underground army, he revisits the absurdity of a death order against one's fellow soldier.

17. The Hero feels morally responsible for his professional compromises and his uncritical approval of Stalinism. These doubts also haunt the Hero in the scene with the Miner, once the victim of his ideologically zealous reportages. The scene in the Budapest cafe, where beautiful young women relax in a holiday atmosphere, is more explicit. The Hero, who desperately avoids defining himself as a poet, and by extension a bearer of historical memory, sees death, not life, around him. When looking through the window, he mistakes a merry-go-round for the gallows that in 1956 claimed the lives of many Hungarians. This image reverberates strongly for readers of Polish poetry. In Miłosz's 1943 poem "Campo di Fiori," a merry-go-round outside the walls of the Warsaw Ghetto plays a central role in this poetic homage to the fate of the Jews (Majchrowski, in Różewicz 1997, 12).

18. The protagonist of Różewicz's play has many names. In dramatic terms, the abundance of personal identifications, used in various encounters by the same interlocutor, both multiplies and fragments the Hero's subjectivity in his interactions with others. A loss of a singular proper name signals the loss of essence and the sacral

dimension of human existence. Both result from the loss of God. Whereas in *The Marriage,* God is exiled in the name of the interhuman and its remaking of the world, which imitates (but also parodies) God's creative gestures and constitutes a new church, in *The Card Index,* he is lost in the fragmentation and the uncontrollable and chaotic multiplication of signifiers, which relieve us from teleological narratives but also challenge our epistemological potential. Knowing one's own name and being addressed with it by others creates what Tischner calls a "space of epistemological association with the other" (1990, 226). It is this space that forms the foundation for our knowledge about who a person is and extends beyond epistemology into axiology. This axiological dimension of existence suffers the most in *The Card Index.*

19. Zbigniew Majchrowski has noted Różewicz's interest in biography as language in his analysis of *The White Marriage* (1993, 110).

20. Other textual traces of the past and the present in the play include newspaper clips, old letters, and written notes. The first seem to evoke objective reality and to create the illusion of "pure referentiality" by giving voice to "naked facts" (Nycz 1995a, 229), only to prove that what turns events into "facts" is granting them meaning by choosing them among other events (see Hutcheon 1989, 75). Moreover, though they say nothing important, they can still become ideologically suspect when put in a different context. Old letters textualize the ordinary (but at one time important) events in people's lives, which are now available to us in manifestly insignificant, decontextualized fragments. Finally, the brief and contradictory autobiographies, which the two officials from the housing administration find in the Hero's hand, point either to political coercion or to the Hero's own manipulations of the "facts," possibly for the sake of different applications. In the *Card Index* the texts of the past and the present are equally subjective, arbitrary, fragmentary, and open-ended, as is the whole play.

Works Cited

Abbey, Ruth. 2000. *Charles Taylor.* Princeton and Oxford: Princeton University Press.

Bachelard, Gaston. 1969. *The Poetics of Space.* Trans. by Maria Jolas. Boston: Beacon Press.

Bertens, Hans. 1995. *The Idea of the Postmodern: History.* London and New York: Routledge.

Błoński, Jan. 1994. *Forma, śmiech i rzeczy ostateczne: Studia o Gombrowiczu.* Kraków: Wydawnictwo Znak.

Filipowicz, Halina. 1991. *A Laboratory of Impure Forms: The Plays of Tadeusz Różewicz.* New York: Greenwood Press.

Gombrowicz, Witold. 1969. *The Marriage.* Trans. Louis Iribarne. New York: Grove Press.

———. 1988. *Diary.* Trans. Lillian Vallee. Evanston, Ill.: Northwestern University Press.

———. 1995. *Iwona, księżniczka Burgunda; Ślub; Operetka; Historia.* Kraków: Wydawnictwo Literackie.

Hutcheon, Linda. 1988. *A Poetics of Postmodernism: History, Theory, Fiction.* New York: Routledge.

———. 1989. *The Politics of Postmodernism.* London: Routledge.

Huyssen, Andreas. 1986. *After the Great Divide: Modernism, Mass Culture, Postmodernism.* Bloomington: Indiana University Press.

Jarzębski, Jerzy. 1982. *Gra w Gombrowicza.* Warsaw: Państwowy Instytut Wydawniczy.

———. 1992. "Ucieczka z rodzinnego domu." In *W Polsce czyli wszędzie*, 19–37. Warsaw: Wydawnictwo PEN.

Kott, Jan. 1962. *Miarka za miarkę.* Warsaw: Państwowy Instytut Wydawniczy.

Krąpiec, Mieczysław Albert. 1974. *Ja - człowiek. Zarys antropologii filozoficznej* (I—Man: Sketching philosophical anthropology). Lublin, KUL.

Longinovic, Tomislav Z. 1988. "I, Witold Gombrowicz: Formal Abjection and the Power of Writing in *A Kind of Testament.*" In *Gombrowicz's Grimaces. Modernism, Gender, Nationality*, ed. Ewa Plonowska Ziarek. New York: State University of New York Press.

Luntley, Michael. 1995. *Reason, Truth, and Self.* London: Routledge.

Majchrowski, Zbigniew. 1993. *Poezja jak otwarta rana: Czytając Różewicza* (Poetry as an open wound: Reading Różewicz). Warsaw: Państwowy Instytut Wydawniczy.

Malkin, Jeanette R. 1999. *Memory-Theater and Postmodern Drama.* Ann Arbor: University of Michigan Press.

Man, Paul de. 1983. *Blindness and Insight.* Minneapolis: University of Minnesota Press.

McHale, Brian. 1987. *Postmodernist Fiction.* London: Methuen.

Nietzsche, Friedrich. 1989. *On the Genealogy of Morals and Ecce Homo.* Ed. and trans. Walter Kaufmann. New York: Vintage Books.

Nycz, Ryszard. 1995a. *Tekstowy świat: Poststrukturalizm a wiedza o literaturze* (Textual world: Post-structuralism and literary scholarship). Warsaw: IBL.

———. 1995b. "Traces of 'I': Concepts of Subjectivity in Polish Literature." *Canadian Slavonic Papers* 37, 3–4 (September-December): 373–92.

———. 1997. *Język modernizmu: prolegomena historycznoliterackie.* Wrocław: Fundacja na Rzecz Nauki Polskiej.

Ratajczakowa, Dobrochna. 1985. *Przestrzeń w dramacie i dramat w przestrzeni teatru* (Space in drama and drama in theater space). Poznań: UAM.

Różewicz, Tadeusz. 1969. *The Card Index.* Trans. Adam Czerniawski. London: Calder and Boyars.

———. 1997. *Kartoteka: Kartoteka rozrzucona.* Introduction by Zbigniew Majchrowski. Kraków: Wydawnictwo Literackie.

Spieker, Sven. 1996. *Figures of Memory and Forgetting in Andrej Bitov's Prose: Postmodernism and the Quest for History.* Frankfurt am Main: P. Lang.

Sugiera, Małgorzata. 1995. "Witold Gombrowicz's World without God." *Renascence* 47 (Spring): 229–41.

———. 1999. "'Cieniów marsz w oparach złudy': *Ślub* Witolda Gombrowicza" ("Shadows, marching in clouds of illusion": Witold Gombrowicz's *The Marriage*). In *Lektury polonistyczne,* ed. Ryszard Nycz. Kraków: Universitas.

Szondi, Peter. 1987. *Theory of the Modern Drama.* Minneapolis: University of Minnesota Press.

Taylor, Charles. 1989. *Sources of the Self: The Making of the Modern Identity.* Cambridge, Mass.: Harvard University Press.

Tischner, Józef. 1990. *Filozofia dramatu.* Paris: Editions du Dialogue.

Trojanowska, Tamara. 1996. "Behind the Open Doors: Havel's *Largo desolato.*" *Canadian Slavonic Papers* 3–4: 419–27.

Wyka, Kazimierz. 1994. *Baczyński i Różewicz.* Kraków: Wydawnictwo Literackie.

PART II

History, Politics, and the Home

5 ||| Home Loss in Wartime Literature

A Typology of Images

Madeline G. Levine

If the concept of home did not appear as a focal point for memories of better times, and the loss of home as an emblem of all the dislocations and losses experienced in wartime, that would be something to marvel at. Common sense leads us to expect that home will be present (if only through the conscious evocation of its absence) in much of the writing that emerged during and after World War II. And indeed that is the case. During the past half century a vast amount of writing dealing with World War II was produced in Poland. Since the mid-1980s, writing about the Holocaust, once a mere trickle in the stream of belles lettres devoted to all aspects of the war, has become a literary growth industry in Poland as, indeed, it has been elsewhere in Europe and North America since at least the 1970s.[1] What I have to say in this chapter about home and homelessness in Polish literature of the Holocaust and World War II is based on a good deal of reading, but of no more than a small fraction of the thousands of poems, memoirs, works of fiction, and contemporaneous and retroactively constructed diaries and journals of those terrible years. What I have attempted here is to construct a typology of the surprisingly limited number of ways in which the home and loss of home are conceptualized and represented in Polish-language literature about wartime Poland.[2] My arguments in this essay are based solely on evidence from poetry and prose fiction, broadly construed to include memoir literature that aims for aesthetic effect. I do not consider drama, "ordinary" memoirs, essays, documentary studies, or film, although a cursory exploration of relevant works in these genres suggests that they, too, make use of the same limited categories of imagery.

Varieties of Home Loss

In the works on which this essay is based, home—a true, stable, nurturing, and protective home, one that exists in the here and now and will continue to exist for the foreseeable future—is almost never depicted.[3] The homes that are conjured up are almost always defective, or provisional, or already reduced to an abstraction as idealized family homes, existing only in memory or imagination. Living in one's own home ought to be the most normal condition imaginable; to be at home, after all, suggests the very essence of normality and comfort. In these writings from out of and about the wartime experience, however, ordinary life at home is nonexistent and familiar patterns no longer hold sway. People may go on existing in *houses,* but they no longer live in *homes.* Homes are transformed from sheltering spaces into loci of mortal danger. A perverted form of domestic life, often reduced to a primal struggle for survival, is pursued in locations never before conceived of as dwelling places: cellars, pigsties, bunkers, secret chambers. And even these give way, as once sturdy structures are reduced to rubble and ash.

A home is both a material and a spiritual structure. Home may encompass both the life lived within a specific dwelling and the larger space or community within which a person is at home in the universe. Homelessness in this literature is always the loss of the home in the physical sense, and often its loss in the spiritual sense as well. In literature about the Jewish experience of the war, the loss of home always occurs on two levels—it always combines loss of physical shelter with painfully experienced deracination.[4]

Two types of destruction resulting in home loss have been posited by the geographer J. Douglas Porteous: *domicide,* which is the demolition of the dwelling place as such, and *topocide,* which is the ruination or obliteration of the larger area in which the home was situated, hence, the despoiling or destruction of an entire community.[5] I find these terms helpful for distinguishing among the various types of home loss representation in literature about World War II and the Holocaust. In appropriating them, however, I have enlarged the range of destruction they refer to far beyond Porteous's original use of them as signifiers of the comparatively benign violence of the urban middle-class drive for *Lebensraum:* slum clearance, gentrification, and the construction of major highways. Here, these terms will serve to denote the horrific physical and social destruction visited upon Poland by the occupying powers—both Germany and the Soviet Union.

Domicide as used in the present essay encompasses not just the demolition of a dwelling's outer shell (rarely the sole focus in the literature under consideration), but also the literal and symbolic forced displacement or extrusion of its intimate interior furnishings, the home turned inside out, the connection between house and home forever sundered. *Topocide* includes not just the destruction of a neighborhood but the disappearance of an entire city. Cities may cease to exist as a sheltering locale in two different ways: objectively, because they have been physically reduced to rubble (as happened to Warsaw during and after the 1944 uprising), or subjectively, because those who require its shelter have been banned from its environs (as was the case with every Polish city and town in which the Jews were forced into guarded ghettos). *Topocide* in this latter sense implies that the formerly sheltering city has been transformed from home place into enemy territory. Under each of these two broad categories there are numerous instances of home loss depicted in the most literal way, representing simply and powerfully the immediate tragedies befalling a family and a people. Other representations of home loss are freighted with symbolic meaning, the destruction of the home or city bringing into question the very nature of modern civilization and divine providence.

Symbolic Topocide

Symbolic topocide figures prominently in depictions of Jewish homelessness. "My country is my home," wrote Julian Tuwim in *Kwiaty polskie* (Polish flowers), his at once angry and nostalgic poem of exile:

> My country is my home. My country
> Is my home. A Polish home
> Was granted me. It is my fatherland
> And other countries are hotels.[6]

Having escaped abroad ahead of the invading armies and found refuge across the ocean—first in Rio de Janeiro, where he began his lengthy poem, and then in New York, where he completed it—Tuwim felt and could express only the exile's loss of home, no different for him as a Jew than for any other Pole. In contrast, Jewish writers who experienced the Holocaust in Poland evince a sense of isolation, of alienation from their Polish homeland just when they most need its support. The poet Władysław Szlengel, confined to the Warsaw Ghetto and well aware that an even worse catastrophe awaited his people, wrote a haunting poem about the beloved city beyond the ghetto walls, the city he gazed at yearningly, "stealing" its forbidden sights from his "window onto the other side," and waiting for some response:

> My eyes stare greedily,
> stuck like knives into the breast of the night,
> into the silent Warsaw evening, into my blacked-out city . . .
> I shut my eyes and whisper:
> "Warsaw . . . speak to me . . . I am waiting . . .[7]

That no response will come from the other side, that all ties with Polish Warsaw have been severed, is the painful theme of Szlengel's deceptively simple, ironic poem "Telefon." The speaker yearns for contact with someone from his former life; he wants, literally and symbolically, to be connected. He picks up the telephone receiver (strangely enough, the phone lines linking the ghetto with the rest of the city were not severed) and suddenly is struck by the realization that there is no one he can call:

> And suddenly I think: By God,
> I really have no one to call,
> in nineteen thirty-nine
> I went down a different road.
> Our paths have parted,
> friendships are mired in the deep
> and now, so help me, there's no one
> I can even call to the phone.[8]

And so, at once pathetically and bitterly, the speaker dials the recorded time operator, the *zegarynka,* to whom he attributes sentiments of compassion and solidarity that he can no longer imagine in a living human being:

> Now my heart will rest easier,
> for I know that when I call
> someone will hear me out calmly,

though she's on the other side of the wall.
That someone remembers so clearly,
we were bound by a common fate,
she does not fear speaking with me,
and she has such a soothing voice.[9]

Szlengel, deprived of contact with the city that nurtured him, yearns to be reconnected with it and bitterly grieves its loss. Other writers, too, confront the cruel truth that Warsaw is no longer what it once was: the city is not just forbidden territory but the locus of mortal danger for any Jew who would dare to reclaim his place in it. The figure of the Jew as twofold victim, marked for extermination by the Germans and deprived of a sheltering communal home by his Polish fellow citizens, has by now become a commonplace in Holocaust writing by both Jewish and non-Jewish writers. Jerzy Andrzejewski was probably the first Polish writer to pursue this theme in fiction. He began writing *Wielki tydzień* (Holy Week), his famous novella about Polish moral and political responses to the annihilation of Polish Jewry, in 1943 and rewrote it immediately after the war to dramatize his belief that Polish society had failed to meet its moral obligations to the Jews.[10] Andrzejewski explores the Jewish loss of home and homeland through the story of his heroine, a refined Jewish woman named Irena Lilien. Homeless in the literal sense, Irena has also lost the homeland that once gave her her identity. She brings death to those few Poles who dare to open their homes to her (and who have themselves lost the capacious, multiethnic homeland they once thought was theirs). Ultimately a victim of Polish cowardice and anti-Semitism that, consciously or unconsciously, supports the Nazi agenda of genocide, she has no choice but to accede to her own destruction, to go to her death in the burning ghetto.

Szlengel's lyrical persona and Andrzejewski's heroine never dwell on the loss of their physical home, their former place of residence. They know that they are doomed to die in the ghetto at the hands of the Nazis, but the bitterness that wells up inside them stems from their feeling betrayed by their compatriots, who have acquiesced in denying them the right to consider Poland as their home. (Irena accuses *all* Poles of delighting in the Nazis' solution to their "Jewish problem.") This feeling of abandonment constitutes a "compound loss" of home, as opposed to the "simple loss" expressed by most (non-Jewish) Polish writers. It appears repeatedly in the writings of

Jewish authors, but not only in works by Jews, as the reference to *Holy Week* demonstrates. Examples of many different tonalities are numerous. Ida Fink, for instance, renders the loss symbolically in this lyrical passage from her story "The Garden That Floated Away":

> Once I saw a garden float away. It was our neighbors' garden, just as beautiful and lush as ours, and there were fruit trees growing in it, just as in ours. I saw it float away, slowly and majestically, into the distance far beyond our reach. . . .
>
> Wojciech's garden, the garden of our childhood friend, suddenly shuddered, swayed, began to pitch and roll, and slowly, slowly, it started to float away, like a huge green ocean liner. It sailed away slowly but steadily; the distance between us grew quickly, the garden got smaller and disappeared. It had floated away to an inaccessible distance, far beyond our reach. (Fink 1995, 11, 13)[11]

I do not mean to suggest that Poles could not also experience a double loss. Every surviving inhabitant of Warsaw, after all, eventually lost both his place of residence and his city, as did the hundreds of thousands of Poles deported to remote and alien places in the Soviet Union, but what Polish survivors did not ever lose was the sense that their country, divided and occupied as it was, was still *theirs.* The Polish sense of political abandonment by the West, at Yalta, was never experienced *by individuals* as the personal indifference or hostility of their neighbors, as excommunication from the nation, and is thus only the palest reflection of the profound losses represented symbolically by the depictions of topocide cited here.

Physical Topocide

Loss of the city as home through its material destruction is the central theme of Miron Białoszewski's *Pamiętnik z powstania warszawskiego (A Memoir of the Warsaw Uprising),* the most important text recording the physical topocide of Warsaw. In his deliberately fragmented, jagged, antiheroic memoir of the calamitous uprising in 1944, Białoszewski mentions, but never once describes, the apartment he used to call home. His attachment to place, at least as he recalls it a quarter century later, is to the city itself—an attachment that only grows stronger as the city crumbles around him. Białoszewski rediscovers the beauty of his city as it is inexorably dismantled by shelling and bombing. Through weeks of panic and terror, of madly seeking shelter in a succession of cellars and ruins of houses as the city caves in around him, Białoszewski stops repeatedly to focus on distinctive architectural details, on monuments, churches, and ordinary buildings, on the disintegrating streetscape of his dying city:

> It was dry. Dusty. You could feel the soot in your teeth. Jagged fragments, earth, obstacles underfoot.
>
> It was right after a bombing. Right there. From a distance you could already note the absence of the three- or four-story stone house at the corner. No. Not from afar. . . . Because we were walking on Wilcza. And the corner of Wilcza and Mokotowska was bombed. Completely shattered. Precisely—shattered. Drily. Cracklingly. Into boards, laths, walls, bricks. The rest, badly scarred, stood there, hung there. The stone house was pouring out into the streets. (Białoszewski 1991, 189)[12]

Domicide

Topocide and domicide overlay each other in *A Memoir of the Warsaw Uprising.* The city reduced to ruins reveals the skeletons of former dwellings. Facades are blasted off buildings, outer walls fall away, and what was once concealed within them, the intimate artifacts of people's lives, are revealed for all to see.

A similar device of baring domestic interiors is used to different effect in Czesław Miłosz's much anthologized poem "Biedny chrześcijanin patrzy na getto" ("A Poor Christian Looks at the Ghetto"). Miłosz's poem records the horror felt by the survivor-witness and obliquely raises the question of Christian moral complicity in the Holocaust. Despite the strangeness of speaking about the poem without addressing the haunting image of the "guardian mole" (the "strażnik-kret") that dominates its second half, I direct the reader's attention only to the poem's opening stanzas. The speaker in the poem, the survivor who fears he is morally compromised, bears witness by averting his gaze from the still-living human beings silhouetted in the windows of the ghetto's burning buildings, proclaiming instead, in apocalyptic tones, the destruction and incineration of the very elements from which the buildings themselves, their interior furnishings, and their occupants were once composed:

> Bees build around red liver,
> Ants build around black bone.
> It has begun: the tearing, the trampling on silks,
> It has begun: the breaking of glass, wood, copper, nickel, silver, foam
> Of gypsum, iron sheets, violin strings, trumpets, leaves, balls, crystals.
> Poof! Phosphorescent fire from yellow walls
> Engulfs animal and human hair.
> Bees build around the honeycomb of lungs,
> Ants build around white bone.
> Torn is paper, rubber, linen, leather, flax,
> Fiber, fabrics, cellulose, snakeskin, wire.
> The roof and the wall collapse in flame and heat seizes the foundations.
> Now there is only the earth, sandy, trodden down,
> With one leafless tree. (1988, 64–65)[13]

Unlike Białoszewski's deliberate recording of only the *facts* of destruction (as best he could remember them), "Poor Christian" offers perhaps the bleakest vision of homelessness in the literature of the Holocaust, for what is felt to be lost here is the very possibility of a human community on our desecrated earth.

The Home Turned Inside Out

Four years later, and two years after the end of the war, Miłosz wrote a quite different poem about what had been lost in the war and in the political violence of the postwar peace. In "Piosenka o porcelanie" (Song on porcelain) he offers his tender lament for the loss of prewar innocence, of an entire way of life that had once seemed so permanent. All this loss is encapsulated in the poem's image of violated domesticity—porcelain dinnerware reduced to fragments in a public space:

> Rose-colored cup and saucer,
> Flowery demitasses:
> You lie beside the river
> Where an armored column passes.

Winds from across the meadow
Sprinkle the banks with down;
A torn apple tree's shadow
Falls on the muddy path;
The ground everywhere is strewn
With bits of brittle froth—
Of all things broken and lost
Porcelain troubles me most.

(Miłosz 1988, 83–84)[14]

Clearly, the exterior structures that encompass a home are not nearly as important as the things contained within them, laden as those possessions are with symbolic value. Like Miłosz's "Porcelain," numerous works by many authors speak of a variety of household artifacts—utilitarian objects necessary for nourishment and warmth, and beloved objects (often held only in memory) that offer vital spiritual sustenance. Both categories of household objects figure importantly in the representation of home loss, standing in synecdochal relationship to the home itself. When these intimate possessions are exposed to public view, the home is violated, literally and symbolically.

The forced removal of Jews from their homes on "Aryan" streets to the ghetto district is often depicted in literature as a removal of objects. In both poetry and prose, lists and inventories of these evicted possessions are common devices for representing the profound violence being done to normal life. In "Rzeczy" (Things), Władysław Szlengel portrays the forced resettlement into the ghetto as a procession of Jewish goods through the streets of Warsaw:

From Hoża and Wspólna Streets, and Marszałkowska
came the carts . . . the Jewish carts . . .
 furniture, tables and stools,
 suitcases and bundles,
 chests, boxes, and bedding,
 suits, portraits,
 linens, pots, carpets,
 and drapery from off the walls.[15]

In Bogdan Wojdowski's autobiographical novel *Chleb rzucony umarłym* (*Bread for the Departed*), there is a comparable depiction of the displaced objects making their way along the Warsaw streets. One of

Wojdowski's ambitions in this novel is to represent fully and truthfully the psychological as well as the physical traumas of the doomed Jews of Warsaw. In his resettlement scene, therefore, in addition to naming the many household items that have to be carted across the city, he also focuses the reader's attention on the emotional pain his sensitive child-hero feels when his family's intimate household items, normally concealed from public view, are shamelessly exposed to the stranger's gaze:

> Their household goods rested on a two-wheeled cart that they'd rented from Sura, the fruit seller; it had a shaft and a leather loop on a chain. . . . The wicker basket, tied with coarse cord, had popped open, and the red corner of their featherbed stuck out from underneath a blanket; the cast-iron pots on top of the load filled up with water and the flour-streaked breadboard on which Mother kneaded dough was wet. . . . David looked on with disgust as his mother fussed with the linens, smoothing and pressing them under the blanket, pulling the rope tighter in an effort to keep her belongings from getting soaked. He pretended he didn't see the way passersby looked at them. (Wojdowski 1997, 71)[16]

The Ersatz Home

After the loss of home, until death ends the struggle for survival, a substitute for home must be arranged if life is to be sustained. The ersatz home is a common theme in the prose fiction and memoirs of World War II, but seems to appear rarely, if ever, in poetry. Wojdowski's novel, with its focus on the reconstitution and ultimate erosion of family and community life in the ghetto, offers numerous examples of such homes: the wretched apartment David's family is allotted, the outbuildings and sidewalks teeming with refugees from provincial towns, the "communal" apartments invaded by hordes of impoverished people sick with typhus and dying of hunger. The ersatz home is the opposite of inviolate. It is a place of ever increasing misery, inseparable from the dangerous streets outside, and open to invasion by the even more desperate homeless and the marauding representatives of police power. In these circumstances those residents of the ghetto who, like David's parents, are not yet fatally demoralized struggle to construct a semblance of what home was once like. Ritual and habit are important in this undertaking: making sure the children still study, washing and ironing the few remaining pieces of clothing, observing the Jewish holidays and feasts with ersatz foods to complement the ersatz home.

Białoszewski, too, chronicles the primal human need to recreate home even in the most desperate of circumstances. Repeatedly in *A Memoir of the Warsaw Uprising* he shows us people struggling—without benefit of formal walls and other demarcations of living space, in crowded underground shelters and filthy ruins—to maintain some pitiful semblance of home life:

> So, on to Wilcza! . . . And thus we entered a new topographic-residential phase.
>
> The first thing we did on Wilcza, at Mrs. Rybkowska's, was to build a stove. A more solid one this time. Made of several bricks. Held together with clay. With a grate in the center. And a pan to catch the ashes. Zocha started cooking something right away. (Białoszewski 1991, 167)[17]

The most degraded form of the ersatz home is the hiding place. These hovels, bunkers, and corners of barns appear, of course, only in writings about Jewish experience. Not even the ruins described in *A Memoir of the Warsaw Uprising* come close to being comparable to the places that Jews hid in for months and even years:

> The man was hiding in a barn. He was no longer young, and he had been through a lot. He had been hiding behind a straw partition for two weeks. It wasn't much of a shelter. Nor was this his first hiding place. For weeks he had wandered in and out of attics, barns, cellars, even family graveyards. . . . It was stuffy in the hayloft; dust from the dry straw floated in the air of these few square meters. The man made a chink for himself in the outside wall of the barn; through this chink he could keep an eye on a scrap of the world. . . . There was one more attic, then a forest; he endured the last months of the war buried in a hole beneath a pigsty. (Fink, "The Pig," 1995, 79–82)[18]

This is how Ida Fink describes the indescribable in *A Scrap of Time,* leaving to the reader the impossible task of imagining having to live in such places. In another story from the same collection, Fink elaborates on what it was like to make one's home in hiding. A Jewish survivor is speaking:

> It was a bricked-in storage area in the cellar, so narrow it could scarcely hold two people. But we went down there only as a last resort, when a

> visitor came, or when there were Germans in the village. Otherwise, we sat in the small room during the day, and at night when the doors were locked, in the main room of the hut. Olek played cards with the husband, and we read books aloud.
>
> But towards the end of the war, when troops were quartered in the area, we didn't leave our shelter for two months. Those two months were very hard. I had pains in my joints; but being sick was the least of it. It was impossible to lie down. We had to sit all the time. . . . Sometimes Germans spent the night in the hut. We could hear their footsteps; they would go down to the cellar, they were right there on the other side of the thin wall with potatoes piled against it. (Fink, "Shelter," 1995, 127–32)[19]

As hiding place stories go, this one is relatively benign. The horror in "Shelter" derives not from the wartime experience of the speaker but from her rescuers' postwar act of kindness. The speaker and her husband were saved by a desperately poor peasant couple to whom they had promised money to build a new house if they survived the war. Five years after war's end they have made good on their promise and return to the village to see the home their money has made possible:

> The husband pushed aside a wardrobe and I looked—a white, blank wall . . .
>
> He lifted a red, waxed board and told us to look closely. "There, now, just in case something happens, you won't have to roost like chickens, a shelter as pretty as a picture, with all the comforts!"
>
> I leaned over and saw stairs leading down into a small, dark room, without any windows or doors. It had two beds, two chairs, and a table. (Fink 1995, 133–34)[20]

In the eyes of this well-meaning peasant, Fink suggests, the natural condition of Jews is a cyclical recurrence of victimization and homelessness. The compound loss of home and homeland stretches out into an endless future.

The Sheltering Home of Dreams

Is there really no positive image of home in this literature? No; at least, not in the narrated present. A truly sheltering home, a home that nurtures the spirit, appears only in memory, filtered through a child's innocence, and often attached to a beloved household object. Wojdowski conjures up such a home when David recalls his grandfather teaching him the Hebrew alphabet and telling him stories from the Bible, or when he remembers in loving detail every illustration on the silver platter decorated with the zodiac that graced the family's seder table.

Miłosz's cycle "Świat: Poema naiwne" ("The World") opens with an idyllic image of the sheltered world of the childhood home, with happy well-fed children experiencing only normal childhood fears. But even in this cycle, composed, as Miłosz has often stated, as a willed act of opposition to the despair he felt in 1943, darkness and terror lie just outside the charmed circle and it is hard to believe in the protective power of the father (both the earthly and the heavenly one):

> "Where are you, Father? The night has no end.
> From now on darkness will last forever.
> The travelers are homeless, they will die of hunger,
> Our bread is bitter and hard as stone.
>
> "The hot breath of the terrible beast
> Comes nearer and nearer, it belches its stench.
> Where have you gone, Father? Why do you not pity
> Your children lost in this murky wood?"
>
> (Miłosz, "Fear," 1988, 53)[21]

An idealized vision of home and family can be found, too, in a number of Tadeusz Różewicz's postwar poems. His happy homes contain innocent children, doting mothers, and sweet old grandmothers, but for that happiness to persist the household must be oblivious to the murderous reality experienced by its young men. In "Powrót" (The return), a poem written shortly after war's end, the innocence of childhood remains unblemished, but it has become an attribute of the lyric persona's parents, who have aged but not grown up. Just as in Miłosz's "naive poem," evil threatens this home too, but here the agent of evil is the child himself, now grown to manhood:

> Suddenly the window will open
> and Mother will call me
> it's time to return
> the wall will part
> I will enter heaven in muddy boots
> . . . .

Here in heaven mothers knit
little green scarves
flies buzz
Father dozes by the stove
after six days of work.
No—I cannot tell them
that men leap
at other men's throats.[22]

|||

THE TYPOLOGY PROPOSED in this essay provides a new way of perceiving the pervasive imagery of home loss in wartime literature and its poignant symbolic encoding of the greater losses of family and community bonds, of life itself. By deconstructing, as it were, the concept of the destroyed home, by focusing on different levels and layers of physical and spiritual destruction, down to the point at which no recognizable home remains, this approach permits us to see what unites and what separates the two great strands of Polish wartime literature—the one dealing with Polish suffering and the other with the experience of Jews during the Holocaust. Both strands have in common their understanding of the vulnerability of human structures, both architectural and social—a vulnerability that is represented persuasively by the figure of the destroyed home and its pitiful contents. The Jewish strand differs not so much in the type of imagery employed as in the emotional valence assigned to each set of images. Thus, shame, which is not depicted as part of the Polish experience of dispossession (Białoszewski) is an added element of the suffering inflicted on Jews when their homes are turned inside out for all to see (Szlengel and Wojdowski); Jewish citizens' sense of being at home in Poland disappears along with their places of residence when they are herded into the ghetto (Andrzejewski and Szlengel); when they are reduced to living in grotesque simulacra of homes, Jews must do so not as part of an entire suffering community in similar circumstances (as in Warsaw during the uprising, in Białoszewski's depiction), but apart from those who still live more or less normal lives inside intact, normal houses (Fink).

Those who write about World War II and the Holocaust know that man has been left homeless in the deepest, spiritual sense. And yet, although none of the imagery surveyed here offers hope that a new and sheltering home can ever be constructed for those who have survived their own dispossession, the very frequency with which references to home loss appear in the literature suggests a poignant reluctance to let go of the concept of home, to accept that loss.

Notes

Unless otherwise indicated, English translations of quoted works are mine and are unpublished.

1. The comparative study of national Holocaust industries may well tell us as much about the national psyches of the commemorators as about the Holocaust itself. Poland is a latecomer to Holocaust obsession in comparison with the United States. See Peter Novick's fascinating and provocative study of this phenomenon in American, and particularly American-Jewish, identity formation, *The Holocaust in American Life* (Boston: Houghton Mifflin, 1999). Sidra DeKoven Ezrahi documents the stages of Holocaust witnessing, forgetting, and rediscovery in various national literatures (not including Polish) in her seminal study *Not By Words Alone: The Holocaust in Literature* (Chicago: University of Chicago Press, 1980).

2. I use the term *Polish-language literature* to signal that I exclude from analysis the poetry and eyewitness accounts written in Yiddish by Polish Jews on Polish soil, as they belong to and describe a different cultural milieu.

3. Although I have a far broader range of texts in mind than those cited here, my examples will be taken from the following works: Jerzy Andrzejewski's novella *Holy Week* (1945); Miron Białoszewski's *A Memoir of the Warsaw Uprising* (1970); Ida Fink's stories collected under the title *A Scrap of Time* (1987); Bogdan Wojdowski's autobiographical novel about the Warsaw Ghetto, *Bread for the Departed* (1971); Władysław Szlengel's poetry, written in the Warsaw Ghetto between 1941 and 1943 and collected posthumously in the slim volume *What I Read to the Dead* (1979); and several poems by Tadeusz Różewicz and Czesław Miłosz.

4. The single exception to this rule appears to be the wartime writing of Polish Jews who spent the war years abroad and did not personally witness the establishment of the ghettos and the transports to the concentration and death camps. Julian Tuwim or Antoni Słonimski, for example, could know that the Jews of Poland and Europe were being slaughtered and the Jewish towns of Poland emptied out, and yet they could still imagine themselves and other Jews as fully at home in the far-flung community of Poles. Tuwim's defiant essay "My, Żydzi polscy . . ." (We, the Polish Jews; 1943), and several long passages in his narrative poem, *Kwiaty polskie* (Polish flowers, 1942–44), offer eloquent testimony to his desperate faith in a continuing Polish-Jewish social bond.

5. See Porteous's stimulating essay "Domicide: The Destruction of Home" (1996).

6. My country is my home. Ojczyzna
Jest moim domem. Mnie w udziele
Dom polski przypadł. To—ojczyzna,
A inne kraje są hotele.

(Tuwim 1967, 116)

7. Wbijają się oczy żarłocznie,
jak ostrza w pierś nocy utkwione,
w warszawski wieczór milczący,
w miasto me zaciemnione . . .
. . . .
zamykam oczy i szepcę:
—Warszawo . . . odezwij się . . . czekam . . .

(Szlengel, "Okno na tamtą stronę" [Window onto the other side], 1979, 60)

8. I nagle myślę: na Boga—
nie mam właściwie do kogo,
w roku trzydziestym dziewiątym
poszedłem inną drogą—
Rozeszły się nasze drogi,
przyjaźni ugrzęzły w toni
i teraz, no proszę—nie mam
nawet do kogo zadzwonić.

(Szlengel, "Telefon," 1979, 63)

9. Już lżej teraz sercu będzie,
gdy wiem, że kiedy zadzwonię,
ktoś mnie spokojnie wysłucha,
choć jest po tamtej stronie.
Że ktoś to wszystko pamięta,
Że wspólnie łączył nas los,
i mówić się ze mną nie boi,
a tak spokojny ma głos.

(Szlengel, "Telefon," 1979, 63)

10. See also Andrzejewski's essay in the volume he edited warning against anti-Semitism as a still-present problem in postwar Poland: *Martwa fala: Zbiór artykułów o antysemityzmie* (Dead wave: A collection of articles on anti-Semitism) (Warsaw: "Wiedza," 1947).

11. See Fink, "Odpływający ogród," 1987, 17–18.

12. See Białoszewski 1970, 174.

13 Pszczoły obudowują czerwoną wątrobę,
Mrówki obudowują czarną kość,

Rozpoczyna się rozdzieranie, deptanie jedwabi,
Rozpoczyna się tłuczenie szkła, drzewa, miedzi, niklu, srebra, pian
Gipsowych, blach, strun, trąbek, liści, kul, kryształów—
Pyk! Fosforyczny ogień z żółtych ścian
Pochłania ludzkie i zwierzęce włosie.
Pszczoły obudowują plaster płuc,
Mrówki obudowują białą kość,
Rozdzierany jest papier, kauczuk, płótno, skóra, len,
Włókna, materie, celuloza, włos, wężowa łuska, druty,
Wali się w ogniu dach, ściana i żar ogarnia fundament.
Jest już tylko piaszczysta, zdeptana, z jednym drzewem bez liści
Ziemia.

(Miłosz 1976, 100–101)

14. Różowe moje spodeczki,
Kwieciste filiżanki,
Leżące na brzegu rzeczki
Tam kądy przeszły tanki.
Wietrzyk nad wami polata,
Puchy z pierzyny roni,
Na czarny ślad opada
Złamanej cień jabłoni.
Ziemia, gdzie spojrzysz, zasłana
Bryzgami kruchej piany.
Niczego mi proszę pana
Tak nie żal jak porcelany.

(Miłosz 1976, 141–42)

15 Z Hożej i Wspólnej, i Marszałkowskiej
jechały wozy . . . wozy żydowskie . . .
meble, stoły i stołki,
walizeczki, tobołki,
kufry, skrzynki i bety,
garnitury, portrety,
pościel, garnki, dywany
i draperie ze ściany. . . .

(Szlengel 1979, 125–28)

16. See Wojdowski 1971, 76.
17. See Białoszewski 1970, 153.
18. See also Fink, "Świnia," 1987, 57–58.
19. See also Fink, "Schron," 1987, 90.
20. See also Fink 1995, 91.
21. Gdzie jesteś, ojcze! Noc nie ma granicy,

Odtąd już zawsze ciemność będzie trwała.
Bezdomni, z głodu umrą podróżnicy,
Chleb nasz jest gorzki, wyschnięty jak skała.

Gorący oddech straszliwego zwierza
Zbliża się, prosto w twarze smrodem zieje.
Dokąd odszedłeś, ojcze, jak ci nie żal
Dzieci, w te głuche zabłąkanych knieje."

(Miłosz, "Trwoga," 1976, 92)

22. Nagle otworzy się okno
i matka mnie zawoła
już czas wracać
rozstąpi się ściana
wejdę do nieba w zabłoconych butach
. . . .
Tu w niebie matki robią
zielone szaliki na drutach
brzęczą muchy
ojciec drzemie pod piecem
po sześciu dniach pracy.
Nie—przecież nie mogę im
powiedzieć że człowiek człowiekowi
skacze do gardła.

(Różewicz 1988, 2:76)

Works Cited

Andrzejewski, Jerzy. 1945. *Wielki tydzień* (Holy Week) In *Noc: opowiadania.* Warsaw: Czytelnik.

Białoszewski, Miron. 1970. *Pamiętnik z powstania warszawskiego.* Warsaw: PIW.

———. 1991. *A Memoir of the Warsaw Uprising.* Trans. Madeline G. Levine. Evanston: Northwestern University Press.

Fink, Ida. 1987. *Skrawek czasu.* London: Aneks.

———. 1995. *A Scrap of Time and Other Stories.* Trans. Madeline G. Levine and Francine Prose. Evanston: Northwestern University Press.

Miłosz, Czesław. 1976. *Utwory poetyckie.* Ann Arbor: Michigan Slavic Publications.

———. 1988. *The Collected Poems, 1931–1987.* Trans. Czesław Miłosz. New York: Ecco Press.

Porteous, J. Douglas. 1996. "Domicide: The Destruction of Home." In *The Home: Words, Interpretations, Meanings, and Environments,* ed. David N. Benjamin, 151–61. Aldershot, England: Avebury.

Różewicz, Tadeusz. 1988. "Powrót." In *Poezja,* 2:76. 2 vols. Kraków: Wydawnictwo Literackie.

Szlengel, Władysław. 1979. *Co czytałem umarłym: Wiersze getta warszawskiego.* Ed. Irena Maciejewska. Warsaw: PIW.

Tuwim, Julian. 1967. *Kwiaty polskie.* Warsaw: Czytelnik.

Wojdowski, Bogdan. 1971. *Chleb rzucony umarłym.* Warsaw: PIW.

———. 1997. *Bread for the Departed.* Trans. Madeline G. Levine. Evanston: Northwestern University Press.

6 The Archaeology of Occupation

Stefan Chwin's Writings on Danzig/Gdańsk

Bożena Shallcross

One of the peculiar characteristics in the twentieth-century European history of the house is the repeated pattern of its loss and acquisition due to changes in a country's political fortunes. This fluidity of ownership, a frequent occurrence during the course of a war, seems to be inscribed in the checks and balances of any wartime situation. But it is the postwar acquisition of someone else's house and its illegal appropriation that represents a disturbing fact in the Polish experience.

It was in Poland in particular that the immediate occupation of the country by the German army during the first months of World War II was followed by the forced resettlement of thousands of citizens. Middle-class Polish families had to leave their houses within a few hours, take only what belongings they could carry, and travel by any available means to other places or even cities and villages. Beginning in 1940, Polish-Jewish families were systematically pushed out from the "Aryan side" of the cities and made to resettle in designated ghettos. Thus, at Hitler's command, a sort of pecking order was established in Poland: the more desirable houses were given to German families and military personnel; those houses that were considered merely habitable were allotted to relocated Poles; and the cramped, deteriorating quarters of the ghettoes were assigned to the Polish-Jewish population. I should add that the displacement of Poles by the surrounding armies also occurred under the Soviet occupation.

A partially reversed process took place just after the war. With the German population fleeing to the West, the Poles—from what are today Ukrainian, Lithuanian, and Belarusian territories—were resettled in the so-called Recovered Territories of East Germany.[1] From Breslau/Wrocław to Danzig/

Gdańsk, the houses these refugees seized were abandoned by Germans, who, like those they previously displaced, often took only what they could carry—leaving behind what was characterized as their "tables, on which meals were left untouched" (Borodziej 1997, 18). Meanwhile, in other parts of war-ravaged Poland, a similar development occurred in which some of the Jewish survivors came home, only to find themselves stripped, once again, of the proverbial roof over their heads.[2]

To what extent this convoluted history continues to plague the memory of the older generations of Poles whose lives were so brutally disrupted would be hard, if not impossible, to estimate. Before 1989, because of the communist censorship and propaganda, this question, and the incorporation of the former German territories, has never been a subject of serious national debate in Poland, but rather has been presented as a historical fact.[3] Not surprisingly, the literary representations (to mention only Eugeniusz Paukszta and Stanisław Worcell) were limited to the official propagandist line. The only exception to this rule was—as far as I know—Leopold Tyrmand, who was not shy in his *Siedem długich rejsów* (The seven long voyages; written in 1952; published in 1959 abroad) about portraying one aspect of the transition: the theft of goods of material and visual culture, especially from German churches. This subject, however, has not escaped the attention of the younger Polish writers such as Olga Tokarczuk, Stefan Chwin, Kazimierz Brakoniecki, Andrzej Zawada, Pawel Huelle, and Marek Jastrzębiec-Mossakowski, all of whom entered the literary scene after 1989, and since then have explored in their fiction the former German cities, their cultural texture, and history.

With regard to Polish literature and literary studies, the emotional toll of a loss is dealt with sufficiently, albeit with various degrees of success.[4] However the dilemma that interests me, also rooted in the nation's past—that of acquiring (often under shady circumstances) material goods, particularly houses or the property on which they were built—seems not to concern the majority of contemporary Polish writers and critics to any great extent. What still awaits a chronicler is the rich field covering the entire war and postwar history of such cities as Wrocław and Szczecin, as well as the experiences of their German and Polish citizens. From this point of view, Stefan Chwin is the first Polish author who describes, step by step, how a Polish family moved into and lived in a German house.

Changing Hands

One of the narratives I have chosen to examine bears both the stamp of idealization and certain denial. Chwin's noteworthy novel *Hanemann*,[5] published in 1995, is in effect a tale of two cities; more precisely, it is the story of one port city with two names: Danzig, given by the Germans after its seizure in the fourteenth century, and Gdańsk, the Baltic city's original Polish name.[6] Chwin's novel represents a rare attempt among those few Polish works of fiction on the subject because the author evokes its complexity from both the Polish and German points of view. In fact, in his article "Literature of the Borderlands and the Central European Dilemmas," Chwin views this aspect of fictional writing as both one of its defining moments and its mission: "'The literature of the borderlands attempts to enter the point of view of the other and respects one's right for an ambiguous identity" (1997, 166).

The story itself, written in the first person, harks back to this period, that is, to the 1930s, when Danzig, which had acquired the status of a free city after World War I, was a German city in Polish territory with a sizable Polish minority. Specifically, the novel begins with the story of Hanemann, a German professor of medicine who experiences the tragic loss of his fiancée—an event that prompts his total withdrawal from life. This is but the logical conclusion for a man who had, even during the war, contemplated reality as if from afar; when his life is accidentally spared during the last stage of the battle of Danzig, he elects to stay behind while his compatriots flee to the West. His decision is motivated less by his topophilic sentimental attachment to the city than his silent existential despair.[7] From his window he observes the Poles as they pour in from the countryside to take over what was once designated an autonomous city. In this manner, Hanemann witnesses the total transformation of his reality. While the professor personifies the best qualities of the German intelligentsia and its culture, including his antifascist stand, his middle-class house embodies its material counterpart. This house, located in a picturesque part of Danzig, becomes one of the novel's focal points, as it withstands the moment of appropriation and the long process of polonization that follows. A dramatic transformation was about to unfold in the spring of 1945: the imposition of a new political and economic order, and the dire consequences wrought upon all those individuals caught in the midst of the changing of borders.

Chwin's novel develops several plots and offers several possible readings. For Jerzy Jarzębski, *Hanemann* is comprised of the history of objects; the "history of the Great Transformation, which replaced one culture with another" (Jarzębski 1997, 114); the story of the protagonist and his gradual adaptation to the Polish realities of Gdańsk; the assimilation that Poles underwent in this once German city and their subsequent acquisition of German houses; and, finally, a very personal struggle between life and death (115). While the fleeing German population is presented in the novel with limited historical verisimilitude, the image of the Polish population's settling in Gdańsk is determined by a different strategy. For Jarzębski, this entire process is inexplicably idyllic, and the critic finds the novel's more realistic vision to be subsumed by secondary considerations. Thus, according to him, the main problem has yet to be addressed, although "this passing of houses, apartments, objects from one hand to another was something drastic—as much as the emotions released by the interaction of the two nations, one of which committed an incredible crime against another" (115). The question of what causes the incompleteness and the absence of more realistic descriptions in *Hanemann* is conflated with another question just as timely: How does the novel capture the moment of inhabitation? What, according to the novel, constitutes and determines the deeper emotional conditions of appropriation? And how can we begin theorizing the literary representation of such a process?

Rare as this novel is in Polish postwar literature, Chwin's vision *does not contest* the widely accepted notion among Poles that there was nothing morally wrong in moving into abodes that were abandoned. On the contrary, they had a right, the author implies, for when at last the guns fell silent, the Polish nation was by-and-large homeless. And, indeed, every episode in *Hanemann* conspires to confirm and support this claim. This is presented most clearly by the proponents of his second tale, a young Polish couple, who, like so many others, have been left homeless. The narrator follows the couple, survivors from the ruins of Warsaw, in their meanderings throughout Danzig. The couple is poor, but innocent at heart and in love. Because the young woman is pregnant, their flight from central Poland possesses a biblical dignity, with allusions of Joseph and Mary seeking shelter in Bethlehem. Indeed, we soon learn that the Father's name is Joe (Józieczek). The fact that the narrative is told by the unborn son encourages certain imaginative shifts away from reality.

It is winter, the war zone has been pushed further to the West, the city's streets are empty and so are its houses. With the exception of the center of the city, which has been almost totally destroyed, the houses in what turns out to be Hanemann's neighborhood are intact and filled with material goods that attest to the richness of the German bourgeois legacy. Chwin's novel glorifies this aspect of a complacent, even smug, lifestyle "as it always takes the side of bourgeois culture, which appreciates rootedness, the taking care of the immediate environment, and the identification with a local community" (Jarzębski 1997, 113).

As the homeless couple saunters through the desolate neighborhood of Jaschkentaler Weg (Jaśkowa Dolina), their "pickiness" in their search for shelter after such an arduous journey reminds the reader almost comically of the ritual one undertakes during the course of a shopping spree:

> They were passing from one gate to another, when they stopped under the overhanging Virginia creeper in front of a gate numbered either 6 or 14; here they stood on the path that lead to a dark villa with a round mansard, but when the Father, adjusting the rucksack on his back, was about to cross the stony threshold of the yard, the Mother held him by his sleeve and said: "Wait, let's see what's further ahead," so they walked on. (60)

Their search for suitable lodgings occurs not without grave misgivings, as when they desist in their inspection of one house only because the German names on the doors make the Mother squeamish and uncomfortable. Finally, the two outsiders find an abode to their liking, but are driven to scrutinize the outer structure more carefully. With so many vacant houses to choose from, the couple is concerned primarily with certain practicalities that otherwise would have been overlooked: it is important that the roof is stable and made of good quality material, that there are convenient walkways to and from the house, and that the height of the railing on the stairs be to their liking. Their initial topophilic attitude, as Yi-Fu Tuan, theoretician of space and domestic environment, would have it, turns the couple into selective birds examining the worthiness of their future nest before deciding to settle in.

The fact that the house they like is left undisturbed seems an oddity to the Varsovian couple. And surely it is, for they are mistaken in their belief that the house had been recently vacated; having reached the top of the stairs, they, instead, walk into a robbery in progress. The victim is Hanemann, who in that instant has been set upon by two Polish thieves. The Father comes to the professor's rescue and successfully defends him. The Father has symbolically vanquished, and the narrator—his unborn child—likens him to the Archangel Michael from Hans Memling's famous painting *Last Judgement.*[8] Although the least convincing part of the novel, this aggrandizing incident is nevertheless closer to historical fact, for it can be buttressed by numerous accounts of the so-called *szabrownictwo* (looting). *Szaber,* ironically a word derived from German, became popular in Polish after the war, a popularity prompted by the systematic plundering of properties that had belonged to the Germans, plundering that had become so widespread that the law was helpless to curb it. But Chwin's strategy avoids the massive scale of looting and what it connotes for the sake of a different strategy meant to build an archaeology of occupation with its layers of emotional and material significance. In his representation of the process of repossession, however, there appear blank spots or "places of indeterminacy" (miejsca niedookreślenia), to use Roman Ingarden's phenomenological category.

After protecting Hanemann, the Father feels he has earned the right to stay at least overnight in the house, and he and his wife move to the empty apartment on the ground floor. The place had once been occupied by its rightful owners, the Walmanns and their two daughters, who were "conveniently" killed while the ship on which they were escaping was torpedoed by the Soviets. Thus, the task of establishing the characters' ethics with respect to how they acquired their lodgings as beyond reproach is realized, because the couple is not taking the dwelling simply as booty by intimidating and forcing the German family to leave. By inserting this crucial information in the narrative, Chwin avoids any controversial implications. For it is not enough to convince us that the couple deserve these lodgings as their just reward, and out of sheer necessity; we have to accept the notion that the flat's very emptiness is the main requirement for immediate appropriation. In this, the author is merely following precedent.

Throughout history, settlers and conquerors have invented strategies that justify their encroachment. One such rationale is centered on the premise that a place or a territory can be inhabited only if the previous occupants or colonizers have withdrawn, or if the space is otherwise regarded as empty. This is an important postulate. To recall an instance from the history of the same part of Europe, the German medieval expansion in Greater Poland was rationalized as the settling of empty lands (*deserta*), as if those who lived there were inferior and thus did not count (Gorecki 1992, 262).[9] Although German infiltration essentially targeted public areas, the distinction between public and private space is less critical for my discussion of appropriated houses. Accordingly, it is the phenomenon of invented emptiness that in Chwin's narrative justifies settlement. In this regard, the author employs an archetypal argument in his representation of the cycle of change.

Imbued by the presence of the Other, the essence of this abode remains distinctly different for the Polish sensibility. Not regarded as merely shelter from the elements, the apartment represents a construct with its own identity. Though deprived of human presence, the flat still seems to the couple to be inhabited by the German family. Evidence of their ownership, their ethnicity, and their taste—all the intimate details that were a part of their life—are too pervasive to be ignored. In the bathroom, for instance, the Mother's gaze first falls on a former inhabitant's initials on a towel; when she proceeds to clean the bathtub, other minute traces of the Germans' presence are brought to her attention. Determined to rid the house of the last vestiges left by the owners, and deeply uncomfortable with them, she scours what is already clean. If like St. Joseph, burdened with pragmatic responsibilities, the Father sees his duty as protector and provider, then the Mother possesses the attribute of "a vessel most clean," ascribed to the Virgin Mary. Significantly, in medieval iconography Mary's other attributes consisted of a linen towel and a pristine water basin. By displaying these items in the bathroom, the author takes pains to employ the disguised symbolism that makes the reader aware of the fact at that moment also one religion is being replaced by another.

Thus, if an empty space represents the first condition for habitation, the second condition requires its purification. Correspondingly, performing the ritual of cleansing, of sanitizing one's new surroundings, implies a degree of contamination of the space by the Other; in *Hanemann* this indicates a whole range of meaning, from the intimate to the ideological. Before the Father and Mother go to bed, they wash all the sheets, which like the bathtub, are perfectly clean: yet, the fresh aroma of rose petals—Mrs. Walmann's aesthetic touch—still remains on the sheets and keeps the couple awake. Indeed, the scent of someone else's household is tantamount to the scent of the person who resides there, which together constitute, in Gaston Bachelard's phrase, the house's "psychology,"[10] its essence.

The subconscious sense of trespassing on other people's property that the couple experiences is further demonstrated by their ablution. Still dissatisfied with their efforts to cope, the couple rises from the bed at midnight and takes a bath. This ablution has an immediate effect and the German household slowly makes its transition to a Polish one, as the Polish family inevitably imposes its own identity on this space.

The paradox is that despite acceptance of the widespread practice of appropriating houses, the act of inventing emptiness, followed by the ritual of cleansing the interior space, indicates that there is something slightly immoral in such acquisition.[11] To put it simply, the Walmanns' place is a living entity that is left defenseless. Therefore, there exists a certain sense of guilt that is not directly addressed by the author.[12] Probing the morality of this accrual seems not to be a challenge for Chwin, who tends to solve the moral dilemmas by employing those symbolic and theological means that soften disturbing historical facts. The author offers his characters ethical comfort by soothing tensions and mitigating more controversial aspects of their situation. Precisely this sort of authorial emendation preoccupied Chwin in his acclaimed 1993 study *Literatura i zdrada: Od Konrada Wallenroda do Małej Apokalipsy* (Literature and treason: From Konrad Wallenrod to Minor Apocalypse). Discussing Adam Mickiewicz's *Konrad Wallenrod,* he followed the Romantic poet's "places of indeterminacy" to observe his strategy of "avoiding difficult questions" and of committing "philosophical simplifications."[13] Why do we see refractions of the same corrective approach in his own fiction, in the works written, after all, by a writer of such high awareness? I shall return to this question later.

Objects of Change

> The authenticity of a thing is the essence of all that is transmissible from its beginning, ranging from its substantive duration to its testimony to the history which it has experienced.
>
> —Walter Benjamin

In Chwin's narrative, the totality of the loss and acquisition of the house, along with the cultural identity it bears,[14] is conditioned by the moving boundaries of the land, on the one hand, and by the representation of movable objects, on the other. But the political and the intimate aspects are not seen merely as cause and effect. Rather, they are intertwined: while the changed boundaries have a destructive impact on the house, the house—in particular, what remains within its walls—suggests a broader political dimension, although illustrating it on a minute scale.

Empty of its former inhabitants, the microcosm of the Walmanns' apartment is resplendent with furnishings. The familiar domestic objects that surround the Polish "holy family" are all of German manufacture. The narrative at this point captures the moment when those articles become "post-German" ("poniemieckie," as the Polish adjective connotes their origin) and the whole abode acquires a new cultural identity.[15] The representation of objects in the novel, while rendered in smoothly elegant prose, nevertheless demonstrates the strength of the material that went into their making. Chwin's respect for a well-crafted object is connected to his interest in German culture in general and in its deeply ingrained notion of objecthood. The aesthetic, antiaesthetic, and existential manipulations of objects promote their visibility and growth as the novel's primary poetic material. The enormous appeal that objects enjoy in the narrator's eye, the tension between their material status and, especially, their very impermanence constitute *Hanemann*'s object lessons. The mechanics of objecthood represents the third and final stage of appropriating the house of the Other.

In *Hanemann* the author excels at reconstructing interiors within interiors: special attention is paid to various rooms, closets, and the odd nook and cranny. The narrator's eye penetrates the intimate space of drawers, armoires, and china cabinets, all accommodating an assortment of domestic knickknacks. The tiniest details are rendered, be it the glint of a key ring, the feel of linoleum underfoot, or the colors of glass viewed against the light. Entire passages are dedicated to the description of this world of objects produced and venerated by Germans. Appearing in series and categories, things are classified according to their wartime usefulness or the lack thereof. The paraphernalia the narrator masterfully presents in his prose matters for several reasons. Jarzębski speculates that this solid foundation of human existence opposes—within the dynamics of the novel—the destructive influence of ideologies (Jarzębski 1997, 113). In other words, the more furnishings one acquires, the less prone to the ideological vagaries of the mind one's life becomes—a premise that Chwin's novel seems to question.

For the Walmanns, once comfortably ensconced in their apartment, what mattered most was solid furniture purchased at a reasonable price, a linen closet brimming with brocaded toweling, family photographs displayed in gilded frames on the mantelpiece and side tables, and the tender memories and associations that enveloped these objects. As Madeline G. Levine points out, this representational method fundamentally affects the notion of the home: "It turns out that the exterior structures that encompass a home are not nearly as important as the things contained within them, laden as those possessions are with symbolic value. Numerous works speak of a variety of household artifacts—utilitarian objects necessary for nourishment and warmth, and beloved objects (often held only in memory) that offer vital spiritual sustenance" (13–14).[16]

Gradually, the German house that was first reduced to its primary function as a safe haven takes on the identity of its new inhabitants, marking an end to everything German that had filled it. Images of the furniture's gradual decay, along with its attending paraphernalia, abound in the novel as each object is incrementally replaced by its Polish counterpart in its communist variation, which is, by contrast and in all respects, inferior. Objects made by German hands either must retain their function or vanish completely.

> Every morning, in the kitchen, our eyes cherished a blue inscription in Goethe's tongue: "Welcome, New Day. Bring Happiness to the Family and Neighbors," which was embroidered in Gothic type on white fabric. But time was touching the whiteness with rusty little stains from apple and carrot juice, until finally, one day, the white linen slid down to the green linoleum, and ever since has been used to scrub the floor. (123)

The status of this single "post-German" object changes from an item adorned with an edifying message to discarded matter. Only now, the appropriation is complete and the German house becomes a Polish home. With this stage finished, the German city of Danzig ceases to exist. The finality of this fact changes entirely the reason for which the long descriptive parts were embedded in the narrative: through them, *Hanemann* rebuilds and *preserves* in words the lost city and the multitude of its objects.

Danzig provided the perfect conduit for such propensities, for the port city was known throughout Europe especially for the heavy, dark, wooden furniture it produced. The furnishings that made up Walmann's flat were no different from many other well-to-do German households. But it is the depiction of porcelain vases, terra cotta figurines, and ornate silverware—light and delicate objects—that best illustrates the bourgeois mentality in the novel. Because of the novel's pronounced link with German Romanticism, one can view this panorama of objects in *Hanemann* as close to Biedermeier, typical of the German bourgeois style that prevailed between 1815 and 1848 and connoted a kind of practical comfort at moderate cost, but was permeated with a Romantic aura.

It is not by accident that a demitasse, a domestic utensil that possesses a kind of fragile beauty, placed among "white dishes shaped like swans and pelicans" (122), should also represent a well-balanced pre-Kantian combination of beauty and purposefulness. In addition, as a recurring image in *Hanemann,* the demitasse as a symbol has its precedents in other literary works. An incorporation of the correspondence between the German Romantic poet Heinrich von Kleist and his lover, Henrietta Vogel, in which a demitasse is a posthumous gift from Henrietta to her husband, is but one example. However, a more aesthetic appreciation of such delicate objects is given in Czesław Miłosz's poem "The Song on Porcelain," which laments the devastation of fragile objects that passes without notice amid the war's devastation. It is precisely from this source that Chwin derives his conception of a subtle and short-lived beauty, which in his treatment evolves into a parallel between porcelain and young women.

Within this constellation of intertexts, *Hanemann* as a philosophical treatise on objects in German culture has an important preamble in *Krótka historia pewnego żartu* (A short history of a certain joke, 1993a), Chwin's volume of short stories based on his childhood recollections. As in *Hanemann,* entire passages of this book obsessively glorify the German sense of objecthood and utilitarian design. *A Short History*—conceived more as autobiographical sketch than the elaborate prose of *Hanemann*—describes a modest neighborhood, one of Danzig's working-class districts, several of which were built between the two wars. Despite their relatively simple, low-cost design, these structures inspire a more dignified attitude than the stolid, stocky silhouettes of Stalinist apartment buildings. The difference between them, albeit fundamental, lies in details. Chwin, a passionate collector of details endowed with the eye of a Flemish painter (the Master of Flemalle and his Merode Altarpiece comes immediately to mind), indexes everything: "embrasures, frames, thresholds, doorknobs, stoppers" (1993a, 116).[17]

What is the inner logic of creating a list of the individual shapes of countless tiny objects that characterizes all Chwin's works of fiction? Besides a certain *horror vacui* complex (which, by the way, results in the best pages of Chwin's prose), this strategy on the one hand does enhance to the maximum the concreteness of the quotidian, while, on the other, it captures more accurately the difference between Polish and German material culture and shows the depth of the postwar transformation from one to the other.

As I already mentioned, Chwin's object-oriented descriptive strategies effectively recreate the lost domestic culture of Danzig. For a very precise and complete ekphrastic performance equals, as phenomenology instructs us, the actual existence of an object. According to Husserl, this method allows us to view a writer as a phenomenologist, as someone who is actually capable of recreating in words the lost city.[18] In Chwin's case, however, his philosophy of objects is also endowed with a certain existential bent since his textual rebuilding and preserving of the lost culture evolves into a reflection on the nature of dwelling, on the effort dwelling takes, and on its plight, as Heidegger describes it (Heidegger 1975, esp. 161).

Germans built houses and made furniture, tools, and trinkets that were, in each and every trifling aspect, user friendly, that addressed what Heidegger categorized as *Dienlichkeit.* These objects become a site of peculiar illumination for the narrator as he reveals his discriminating sensitivity for their "facilitating and caressed detail, a polished finish, . . . the sphere of pleasures addressed to all the fingers: the index, the pinky, the middle, the ring finger, and the thumb" (*A Short History,* 116). The purposefulness, *Dienlichkeit,* and practical inventiveness that characterize apartments, furniture, and utensils testify to a special sort of interaction—to the nearly tender reciprocity between objects and their owners-users viewed in *Hanemann* and *A Short History* as the main feature of German material culture.

Chwin also reminds us that objects are vulnerable. Therefore, the phenomenological pendulum of his prose swings in the opposite direction to evoke peculiar processes of aesthetic deterioration and shabby banality combined. Whereas the sudden destruction of material goods may speak more of the forces that caused their breakage, the slow reclaiming of objects by time and neglect ultimately exposes the weakness of the communist economy and its lack of any sense of beauty. To say the least, the care and restoration of things German did not belong to the communist system's vocabulary, therefore objects—witnesses of the long intimate history of Danzig/Gdańsk households—speak the language of their past splendor and neglect.

I should emphasize, however, that although Chwin glorifies German material culture and considers it superior to the communist version of its Polish counterpart, he does not describe it only in positive terms. Rather he reaches for the traditional aesthetic notions of the good and beautiful and of the useful and beautiful to pursue a more nuanced distinction than the rigid opposition between superiority and inferiority. This shift makes the foundation of his philosophy of objects paradoxical. The practical results of the utilitarian German mind cannot be separated—contrary to Jarzębski's claim—from its roots, from the aggressive nationalist ideology. Things German, although superior in every respect, are products of the most destructive political system known to mankind; by contrast, the great utopianism of communism resulted in universal shabbiness and a mediocre (derivative at best) design. Hitler and Stalin—the antiheroes of a childhood represented in *A Short History*—whose grotesque hovering spirits seem to be incompatible with the essence of things, nevertheless are quite connected with the things' destruction, either sudden or gradual.

In conclusion, Chwin's account of acquiring someone else's property, even under circumstances that absolve such a deed, is determined by three interrelated processes, the details of which I examined above: the emptiness of the abode, its purification along with the ablution of those involved in the process, and the gradual obliteration of material vestiges that tangibly represent the cultural Other.

Getting back to the question concerning Chwin's corrective approach to history, I would argue that it stems from several sources. His focus, narrowed down to only one family and one household, reconciles the complexities inherent in any wider perspective. Moreover, the world Chwin describes is gone forever, half a century dividing the author from his novel's events also affects his idealizing distance and molds his generational experience. Born in 1949, the author did not experience World War II directly, nor did he perceive its aftermath, including the Polish repossession of German real estate, as a completely closed chapter. He learned about the past from the still fresh and sometimes mesmerizing traces left in the span of his childhood. His parents' post-German flat, the abandoned bunkers and burned-out tanks on the beaches of the Baltic Sea; the shells and helmets found in the woods; half-obliterated German inscriptions on never repainted facades—they all defined his identity, his historical consciousness, and memory. They were his childhood's toys, his playground, and history lessons, for as Jan Błoński observes, "one can be deeply touched by history if only playing with his neighbors in the yard" (Błoński 1993, 4).

Chwin applied the pervasive language of vestiges—another Romantic characteristic of his prose—first in *A Short History* and later in *Hanemann.* His writings on Danzig/Gdańsk became a territory of his confrontations with both World War II and postwar history as fused with the material and cultural Otherness. This multilevel territory, or a palimpsest if you will, marked by the author's descriptive precision, is also used for a textual confrontation controlled by a rich system of rhetorical, religious, and stylistic means. Therefore, these two spheres—historical and textual—interpenetrate, reinforce, and create each other in both *Hanemann* and *A Short History.* Their coexistence is facilitated by an aesthetic effect of idealization, of a gentle, almost nostalgic, correction of history's brutal course. Chwin transforms the history of Polish repossession of German homes into an *art of occupation,* into a metonymy evoking the whole nation's transition to normalcy after a historical eruption. Because of this, otherwise noble, conciliatory spirit, the gap between verisimilitude and idealization increases in his writings as history takes on the proportions of myth and the trivial aspects of domesticity acquire a measure of both primordial and historical significance.

Notes

This chapter is dedicated to Jadwiga Maurer.

1. Ziemie Odzyskane was the official term given by the communist authorities to the incorporated regions for propaganda purposes.

For the autobiographical account of the loss of Polish home in the prewar Polish territories, see Marsden 1995. Marsden describes the case of the Polish émigré poet Zofia Ilnicka and the acceptance of the loss during her travel to the family manor located near a Belarusian village.

2. This circulation of private possessions and houses abruptly ended with the communist regime's de-privatization of flats and other domiciles, including manors and palaces that formerly belonged to the Polish gentry and aristocracy. Once more,

as night follows day, thousands of people lost their homes. Nearly fifty years later, in yet another reversal—this time as a result of the fall of communism in 1989—reprivatization was introduced as government policy. But for many of those dispossessed who would claim ownership, it was too late: an era had passed, and only a very few of these estates have retained any semblance of their original grandeur.

3. For further bibliographical references regarding the expelled Germans, see Traba 1997.

4. It can be observed, for instance, in the so-called *literatura kresowa* (literature of the borderlands). The problem is most apparent in Józef Mackiewicz's novels *Droga do nikąd* (The road to nowhere) and *Sprawa pułkownika Miasojedowa* (Colonel Miasojedow's case). For a recent survey of this phenomenon, see Czaplejewicz and Kasperski 1996.

5. At this date, Chwin's novel has received two major literary prizes: the Koscielskis Award and the Andreas Gryphius Prize (the latter is a German award that recognizes efforts of reconciliation between European nations).

6. Günther Grass's novels, most notably *The Tin Drum,* portray the interaction between German Danzig and Polish Gdańsk. His *The Call of the Toad* describes the Danzigers' postwar return to the city of their birth as a return to the place of their eternal rest.

7. For a systematic survey of the topophilic attitudes, see Yi-Fu Tuan 1974.

8. Owned, incidentally, by the National Museum in Gdańsk.

9. See also Irena Grudzinska Gross's comments (1991, 153) on the pioneers' vision of North America.

10. Gaston Bachelard (1969) uses this term in his ruminations on the individual character and psychology of the house; see esp. the introduction and chapters 1 and 2.

11. A similar reaction to the same dilemma is described in a nonfictional account, Sikorski 1997. The author, who purchased a manor house from the state in 1989, encounters a number of tasks, from ridding himself of squatters to negotiating with the rightful prewar owner, who was expelled from his estate by the communist authorities. He succeeds in both instances: after providing shelter for the squatters, he discovers that the old owner had died and his daughter has given up all claim to the estate. Thus, the initial phase, emptying the appropriated house, is completed. The second stage of appropriating the house requires its purification. Eagerly, Sikorski sets out to restore the manor; he rebuilds the destroyed walls, restores the plumbing and electricity, cleans out the accumulated rubble, and generally revamps both the interior and the surrounding park. "Half a century's filth is gone" (243), he writes with pride and relief. The slate, as it were, is wiped clean.

12. One minor exception is implied in reference to Mother's childhood recollection, when she entered her neighbors' flat and was greeted with a reprimand: "And what are you doing here? Is it nice to come in without knocking?" ("A cóż to ty robisz tutaj? A ładnie to tak wchodzić bez pukania?") (Chwin 1995, 68).

13. In particular, see the chapter "O czym wołał nie pisać Mickiewicz w *Konradzie Wallenrodzie?*" (What did Mickiewicz prefer not to write about in *Konrad Wallenrod?*) in Chwin 1993b, 422–48.

14. A person who like myself, was born in the fifties and grew up in a German historical palace, surrounded by German furniture and other objects, could not have any awareness of their Germanity, nor of any distinction between things that were either Polish or German. This realization, along with the cultural semantics it implied, came later in my childhood.

15. In one instance, the narrator is asking, "When did the post-German chairs disappear from 17 Grottger Street?" (*Hanemann,* 121).

16. See Madeline Levine's chapter in the present volume, "Home Loss in Wartime Literature: A Typology of Images." For Hanemann, who is a German bourgeois only by origin, spiritual sustenance is provided solely by a reproduction of Caspar David Friedrich's painting.

17. I do not include in my discussion Chwin's last novel, *Esther* (1999), because its representation of Danzig and its environs deals mostly with prewar history.

18. For an elaboration of the parallel between an artist and a phenomenologist, see Hirsh 1968, 113.

Works Cited

Bachelard, Gaston. 1969. *The Poetics of Space.* Trans. Maria Jolas. Boston: Beacon.

Błoński, Jan. 1993. "Słów parę . . ." Introduction to *Krótka historia pewnego żartu: Sceny z Europy Środkowowschodniej,* by Stefan Chwin, 2–6. Kraków: Oficyna Literacka.

Borodziej, Włodzimierz. 1997. "Wojna i jej skutki w świadomości zbiorowej Polaków i Niemców—w pół wieku po wojnie" (War and its aftermath in the Polish and German collective consciousness—half a century after the war). In *Tematy polsko-niemieckie,* ed. Elżbieta Traba and Robert Traba, with the assistance of Jorg Hackmann, 15–25. Olsztyn: Wspólnota Kulturowa Borussia.

Chwin, Stefan. 1993a. *Krótka historia pewnego żartu: Sceny z Europy Środkowowschodniej.* Kraków: Oficyna Literacka.

———. 1993b. *Literatura i zdrada: Od Konrada Wallenroda do Małej Apokalipsy.* Kraków: Oficyna Literacka.

———. 1995. *Hanemann.* Gdańsk: Wydawnictwo Marabut.

———. 1997. "'Literatura pogranicza' a dylematy Europy Środkowej" (Literature of the borderlands and the Central European dilemmas). In *Tematy polsko-niemieckie,* ed. Elżbieta Traba and Robert Traba, with the assistance of Jörg Hackmann, 161–71. Olsztyn: Wspólnota Kulturowa Borussia.

Czaplejewicz, Eugeniusz, and Edward Kasperski, eds. 1996. *Kresy w literaturze: Twórcy dwudziestowieczni* (The borderlands in literature: The twentieth-century writers). Warsaw: Wiedza Powszechna.

Gorecki, Piotr. 1992. *Economy, Society, and Lordship in Medieval Poland: 1100–1250.* New York: Holmes and Meier.

Gross, Grudzinska Irena. 1991. *The Scar of Revolution: Custine, Tocqueville, and the Romantic Imagination.* Berkeley: University of California Press.

Heidegger, Martin. 1975. "Building Dwelling Thinking." In *Poetry, Language, Thought.* Trans. and introd. Albert Hofstadter. New York: Harper and Row.

Hirsh, Rudolf. 1968. "Edmund Husserl und Hugo von Hofmannstahl: Eine Begegnung und ein Brief" (A meeting and a letter). In *Sprache und Politik: Festgabe für Dolf Sternberg* (Language and politics: A presentation for Dolf Sternberg), ed. Carl-Joachim Friedrich and Benno Reifenberg. Heidelberg: L. Schneider.

Jarzębski, Jerzy. 1997. *Apetyt na przemianę: Notatki o prozie współczesnej* (Appetite for change: Notes on contemporary prose). Kraków: Znak.

Marsden, Philip. 1995. *The Bronski House: A Journey Back.* New York: Arcade Publishing.

Sikorski, Radek. 1997. *The Polish House: The Intimate History of Poland.* New York: Simon and Schuster.

Traba, Robert. 1997. "Wysiedlenia Niemców z Polski—refleksje na marginesie literatury najnowszej" (Expulsion of the Germans from Poland: Reflections on the latest literature). In *Tematy polsko-niemieckie,* ed. Elżbieta Traba and Robert Traba with the assistance of Jörg Hackmann. Olsztyn: Wspólnota Kulturowa Borussia, 26–33.

Yi-Fu Tuan. 1974. *Topohilia: A Study of Environmental Perception, Attitudes, and Values.* Englewood Cliffs, N.J.: Prentice Hall.

7 ||| Homeland without a Home

Tadeusz Konwicki's Experience of Home

Katarzyna Zechenter

If the home of a Romantic poet was supposed to project the poet's unique "I" to the outside world, the home of the political opposition writer in communist Poland of the 1970s and 1980s suffers from the exact opposite projection: it is invaded and defined by the outside. The disintegrating political system is reflected by the dilapidated and neglected apartment, its dirty windows, and its perverse feeling of utter resignation. Tadeusz Konwicki (b. 1926) is a writer whose famous image of a run-down apartment in a gray and decaying Warsaw came to symbolize the state of Polish society of the late seventies and eighties. However, the roots of Konwicki's presentation of home and domesticity as a reflection of historical and political space began much earlier, with his first novel, *Rojsty* (Marshes; written 1948, published 1956).

Konwicki belongs to a generation that lost its home in both the spiritual and literal senses of the word. This loss was expressed in the works of many writers and poets from the Polish Borderlands, such as Czesław Miłosz or Józef Mackiewicz. This loss and the resulting search for the past have since become a major part of Polish contemporary literature. As Stanisław Vincenz once remarked, every writer repeats the fate of Odysseus, searching for her or his Ithaca. For Tadeusz Konwicki, even in his early fiction, the loss of the first home turned into an unsuccessful search for a new home and affected his understanding of history, politics and domesticity. His first novel deconstructs the traditional patriotic Polish home of the era. Home denotes a space where the discrepancy between popular Romantic values on which the protagonist was raised and the reality of guerrilla warfare is realized. For Konwicki's protagonist, "the patriotic home" of the Borderlands exemplifies the essential part of Romantic ideology that led his generation to political disaster in 1944 because the literary patterns of nineteenth-century freedom fighters could not find their actualization in the reality of twentieth-century warfare. Consequently, Konwicki's descriptions of home contain elements of pastiche and parody while its inhabitants are presented in a satirical light because, as Maria Janion notes, *Marshes* should be read as "a typically anti-Romantic reaction encountered often in the psychic life of Poland" (1994, 157).

The protagonist's home, which at first sight appears to be a representation of the popular concept of "bastion of Polishness" ("ostoja polskości"), is initially described in a manner typical for popular patriotic literature of that period: home is a place furnished with memorabilia and keepsakes that belonged to previous generations fighting for freedom. His mother is described in accordance with the image of the suffering "Polish Mother" ("Matka Polka"): "the beloved heroine of the insurrectionist poetry of the gentry and nineteenth-century novels" (Janion 1994, 159)—an aged woman who blesses her son as he leaves to fight the Russians and who prefers to remember her deceased husband as a hero fighting for freedom rather than what he actually was. Learning that her son wants to enlist, she reacts as custom dictates: "I will not stop you," she replies. "Your father gave his life for this country. Just look out for yourself" (*M* 24). Eventually, it becomes evident that the description of home also contains a conscious deception to preserve the idealized image of Polish patriotic domesticity. The protagonist's father, for instance, first introduced as a hero whose death resulted from his military service during World War I, is revealed to be a man of loose moral character whose premature death in fact resulted from his drinking, gambling, and womanizing (*M* 17). Books that belonged to the protagonist's father are covered with dust and his medals are rusted (*M* 17). The protagonist himself seems not to have much respect for his "daddy's huge portrait" (*M* 16).

The interpretation of Konwicki's ironic treatment of the Polish patriotic home and domesticity in *Marshes* was hindered by the delayed appearance of the novel in 1956. That year, when the political thaw in Poland was "swelling into a flood" (Davies 1986, 9), Konwicki's book seemed to belong to a bygone political era that required from writers an unequivocal condemnation of anything connected with the Home Army. For years the critical reception of *Marshes* remained preoccupied with the political implications of the delay, suggesting that Konwicki's portrayal of the Polish patriotic home and the Home Army was influenced by his communist sympathies. However, the anger permeating *Marshes* and the resulting ironic presentation of the patriotic home of the Borderlands was not connected with Konwicki's conversion to communism but was rather the result of his rebellion against the tyranny of literary models. Konwicki's generation grew up on Romantic literature, which heavily influenced its understanding of patriotic obligations and duty. This upbringing on books required an adherence to literary patterns, and Konwicki once said that his "generation read itself to death" (*CaH* 66). In another interview, Konwicki stated that the outlook on the world for him and his colleagues "was heavily influenced by literary traditions, especially Żeromski. . . . Pausing on page 344 of Żeromski, we headed off into the woods" (Konwicki 1971, 8–9). *Marshes* also reveals the disappointment and anger of a young man whose literary upbringing was not able to balance the wartime reality and the "anger of a boy who not only lost the war but was also chased away from home. And the fellows who predicted victory have disappeared" (Konwicki 1990, 79–80).

In Konwicki's novels written during the period of socialist realism (1950–56)—*Przy budowie* (At the construction site), *Władza* (Power), *Godzina smutku* (Hour of sadness), and *Z oblężonego miasta* (From the besieged city)—home is again presented as a product of history but also as an exemplification of specific political arguments rather than a private dwelling of the 1950s. Consequently, the home of Mikołaj Gałecki, a young communist from *Power,* is reduced to a space that copies the public sphere: pictures of Stalin and books by leading Marxists fill his small room. Gałecki is a devoted communist whose library is filled with party journals and books written by "the comrades, Lenin and Stalin, books in which one can find the answers" (*P* 37). As the Party constitutes for Gałecki the larger home, the role of an actual home is reduced and Gałecki's home is rarely recalled during the novel: "since childhood I have been learning life from my comrades. The Party was for me a substitute for home and family" (*P* 272). Gałecki's family home, which is actually a shed without even a proper floor, serves as an example of capitalist exploitation, since his family lives in utter poverty, as well as a meeting place for his father's comrades.

The homes, or rather humble apartments, portrayed in Konwicki's novels of the 1950s are neatly divided along the lines of political correctness of the era: there are the apartments of those who accept political changes and there are the apartments of those who adhere to the old principles. This division is reflected in the description of dwellings and objects filling these houses; they belong to the supporters of the old system and are too warm, stuffy, almost suffocating. Windows in those houses do not face new construction sites, and these houses lack simplicity, their walls covered with thick, dark wallpaper. Their description resembles descriptions of typical bourgeois apartments common in literature of Young Poland, as, for example, Mrs. Dulska's apartment, which became a symbol of vulgarity, narrow-mindedness, and dishonesty. Those stuffy apartments, such as Korejwa's apartment in *Power,* are presented not only as the remains of prewar bourgeois taste, which delights in tasteless and vulgar art but, most important, as the refuge of the class enemy, someone who refuses to accept social changes. In *Power,* for instance, the celebration of the third anniversary of the People's Republic takes place in a guild hall decorated with a "repulsive painting" that "shook the tender soul of the bourgeois" (*P* 131). The aesthetic uneasiness of the narrator strengthens the aura of suspicion surrounding those who do not agree with the new system, just as the aesthetic ugliness of the apartments corresponds with political narrow-mindedness: it is precisely Korejwa, later denounced as the bearer of "national-rightist deviation," who knows how to deal with the "relics of prewar bourgeois." As Michał Głowiński summarizes it: "The little world in which [the enemy] lives is horribly ugly; it violates good taste. . . . The enemy also has to be condemned on aesthetic grounds" (1992, 77).

On the other hand, there are the new small studio apartments or single rooms rented by communists. These homes are clean, simple, and filled with fresh air, although their furnishings are rather humble: a bed, some books and Party magazines, a white washbasin, a towel, a table with a few glasses, and a teapot on the window. Their simplicity and purity of space resembles that of a monastic cell. This comparison is strengthened when engineer Lisowski emphasizes the cleanliness of the new communist home and its effect on the private lives of devoted communists: "People today live better and purer. . . . Eroticism to a large extent has disappeared, as well as exhibitionism" (*HoS* 22). Lisowski, a hero of socialist work in *Hour of Sadness,* has in his simple apartment only scientific books on agriculture, not even one novel that could divert his attention from his work or shake his image as a man devoted to his principles. In other words, his home is an extension of his work while his work suggests absolute devotion to the Cause (*HoS* 8).

With the changing role of the home in socialist-realist novels, the role of the builder of a new home is presented in a new light as well. Since the new home no longer constitutes a private sphere, the builder becomes the creator of the new ideology rather than the builder of a dwelling. He feels responsible not only for the actual construction but also for the social consequences of his work. The importance of changing people through the way they live and through their homes is emphasized especially in Konwicki's short novel *From the Besieged City* (1956), where the protagonist, Porejko, and his young communist friend, Mikołaj Gałecki, become architects. Porejko is not a devoted communist; in fact, he eventually "escapes" from Poland, but he agrees with Gałecki's notion of designing not just buildings but the future as well: "for the first time we will design everything: movie theaters and kindergartens and stands with newspapers. The *whole lifestyle* [my emphasis] of ten thousand people depends on us" (*FBC* 136). The visionary and futuristic aspect of Porejko's and Gałecki's dreams was in agreement with socialist-realist poetics, which relied heavily on the future tense because the actual accomplishments of changing people's lives were still not discernible, and it was easier to concentrate on the future: the new and better homes that would be built along with new lives. I use the term "to build lives" because many socialist-realist novels, including Konwicki's *At the Construction Site,* were interpreted as a sort of instruction book for building "large highways, railroads and industrial construction projects" (Lasota 1950, 119) and thus, of course, for building the new people building these highways and projects.

The period of socialist realism in Konwicki's works ended rather abruptly and was followed by a new understanding of the concept of home and domesticity. Although Konwicki remained skeptical about the events of October 1956 and did not abandon his sympathies for the old system immediately, he stopped writing and began making films. As a result, his next novel, *The Hole in the Sky,* appeared in 1959.

The Hole in the Sky is the first novel that creates the phenomenon I call a homeland without a home because it presents a small geographical region, the valley of the Wilejka River, as the true home of the protagonist, while the protagonist's house, its furnishings, and the family living there become secondary. The essential aspect of a homeland without a home is the division between on the one hand the sacredness and centrality of the land where the oneiric home of the past is located and on the other the desacralization of the contemporary home. The oneiric home is always located in the Wilejka valley, which is presented as the original and ethical center of the world—in other words, the Sacred. The contemporary home, on the other hand, is located in today's Warsaw; but as Warsaw "isn't my city" (*AM* 67), the contemporary home represents temporariness ("tymczasowość"), being lost ("zagubienie"), and above all the desacralized existence of the contemporary world.

Although the Wilejka valley did not entirely disappear from Konwicki's works, even during the years of socialist realism, and is mentioned, incognito, in *Hour of Sadness* when the protagonist finds a little plate from the time of the January 1863 uprising, it is *The Hole in the Sky* that openly brings the Wilno region back into Konwicki's world. This novel freely returns to the valley of the protagonist's youth and fully develops the concept of homeland without a home as Konwicki begins the process of mythologization of his homeland and of presenting two parallel yet opposite homes—the oneiric home rooted in his childhood in the Wilno region and the contemporary home in the shadow of Stalin's Palace of Culture, rooted in the gloomy reality of the Polish republic. With every consecutive novel, "*Homo convicien-sis*" (Błoński 1993, 8) finds himself in the valley of Wilejka—either in his dreams, his subconscious, or his memories. What is important, however, is that beginning with *The Hole in the Sky,* the vehicle for bringing back the Borderlands is not anger or disappointment, as was the case with Konwicki's earlier works, nor even nostalgia for an ideal "paradise lost," but rather the gradual rediscovery of the Center, the Sacred. The stronger the desacralized aspect of contemporary space, the stronger the need for rediscovery of the Sacred since "even the most desacralized existence still preserves traces of a religious valorization of the world" (Eliade 1987, 23).

As I said earlier, Konwicki's experience of oneirically defined home is rooted in a particular "small and personal history" of a "private home-land"[1]—the role of home, however, is largely replaced by the role given to the whole Wilejka valley, which becomes the symbolic home of the protagonist, as well as the symbolic "center of the inner world, in which all roads later traveled have their beginning" (Zaworska 1970, 115). The oneiric home remains vague and eludes precise description: it is sometimes called the Golden House, which suggests its preciousness, but it is not precisely defined. The narrator's strategy is not so much to describe it but rather to suggest the depth of longing for the home:

> As I watched, I suddenly began to yearn for the green valley with murmuring river, the big house that I called the Golden House . . . and I understood for the first time in my life what longing really is. For until then I had never had reason to feel it. (*ASB* 54)

This longing for the home of the past parallels the protagonist's ambivalent feelings—of reluctance and hesitation—about his contemporary home.

The oneiric home of the narrator is a vital part of the eternity of its entire surroundings: opening oneself to it and transgressing the borders of the house elevates the surroundings, the valley, to the status of the home in a manner similar to Soplicowo, where the whole area, not just a manor house, is incorporated as home (Graczyk 1993, 64). The home of the protagonist opens into the Borderlands, which become his true home, and in this way everything connected with the Borderlands becomes a part of the protagonist's past: the land, its trees, the Wilejka River, and the people. And so Helena in *Bohin Manor* can say that "this forest is our home" (*BM* 81), indirectly suggesting a link to the forest as the last home of the 1863 insurgents. And although there is no peace inside the house (in *Bohin Manor* the father murders his daughter's lover, and in *The Anthropos-Specter-Beast,* Retep holds a girl hostage in the manor house), the Borderlands offer some peace: the white church stands next to a "little Muslim mosque" and next to the "double crosses of the Orthodox Church" (*ASB* 33–34), while the river offers purifying and regenerating symbolism to everyone.

Although the narrator remains vague as to details of the oneiric home, descriptions of the valley are specific and numerous. Slightly altered descriptions of the valley appear in each novel, while certain aspects of the surroundings, such as the river and its steep banks, Puszkarnia, the old paper mill or the railway embankment, remain mostly unchanged even when the story is set in central Poland, as in *Power* or *Hour of Sadness.* The valley, in other words, always remains the same, allowing the reader to recognize its fictional configurations by heart so that "it is literally possible to sketch a map of the valley" (Zaworska 1970, 115). This approach is another essential part of Konwicki's poetics, which requires each of his novels to be an interpretation of the previous one, as well as a continuation of his earlier work.

The Borderlands, or to be precise, the Wilejka valley, possesses special meaning for Konwicki's protagonist. It serves three major functions: first, as the Sacred, second, as a sacred graveyard, and third, as the place where the protagonist's home was actually located. These three roles are tightly intertwined and to some degree cannot exist independently since each of the levels entails the other two: the graveyard is always near the home and the home is always in the middle of the Sacred. The Borderlands are presented as the protagonist's ethical and mythical center, in agreement with Mircea Eliade's observation that "the true world is always in the middle, at the Center" (Eliade 1987, 42). In *Bohin Manor,* Konwicki's most open novel about the Borderlands, the land is presented as the "paradise mentioned by the Bible" (*BM* 181), but in his earlier novels this paradise is often suggested indirectly. In *The Anthropos-Specter-Beast,* for example, the valley as paradise is suggested by the lavishness of nature in "the very green valley," the beauty of the trees, and "flowers of every color" (*ASB* 13).

If the Borderlands are presented as the Sacred, then the Wilejka River, the indispensable aspect of the valley, is presented as a hierophany—a manifestation of the Sacred. The Wilejka River also has its roots in the garden paradise of the beginning of the world and is a witness to the suffering of the first people, who attempted, unsuccessfully, to escape their fate: "the first people walked along this river, until they reached the Niemen river" (*BM* 181). The river is present in almost every one of Konwicki's novels, and most often it is the river that saves the life of a protagonist. Most important, the river is both the depository of memory and a saving force, as when, in *The Dreambook for Our Time,* the protagonist's life is spared when his attackers see that he is wearing a cross from the 1863 uprising, which he fished out of the river a few days earlier.

The second function of the Wilejka valley is to serve as a sacred graveyard: here are buried the tragic heroes of the 1863 uprising. Death does not lose its ritual character in Konwicki's work; in some ways death is the beginning of new spiritual existence, as the dead are an essential part of the new life. The graveyard is always present, either as the grave of an unknown insurrectionist or a cross erected in memory of those who died in the 1863 uprising. This motif can be found in almost all of Konwicki's novels, beginning with *Marshes,* where the partisans of 1944 stumble upon a gravesite of 1863 partisans. Death, however, is never restricted to the public sphere of life. In *Bohin Manor* death closely surrounds the family: Helena Konwicka lost her fiancé in the uprising of 1863. She herself is an orphan—her mother died while giving birth to her and was buried, for unknown reasons, near a country road, like a beggar. The man she loves, a Jew from Bujwidze, Eliasz Szyra, will be killed by her father when he learns that she is pregnant. Helena's father often talks to his dead wife, for the dead are always somewhat present.

Finally, the Borderlands are also presented as the location of the protagonist's home. In *Bohin Manor,* this home appears at first sight to be a typical Polish manor house. It is white like the archetypal Soplicowo in *Pan Tadeusz* ("There stood a manor house, wood-built on stone; / From far away the walls with whitewash shone, / The whiter as relieved by the dark green / Of poplars . . .") (1998, 2), and it is surrounded by old trees and located near a river in the manner in which noble houses were built in Poland.[2] Such description invites nostalgia for the tranquillity of domestic paradise. This tranquillity, however, is only an illusion as the house does not belong to Helena's father: his family home was taken from him by the czar's decree as a punishment for his participation in the uprising. Bohin Manor is thus referred to as "foreign" (*BM* 123), and although well lived in, it is still "the stranger's house" (*BM* 40). In other words, this home, which initially seems to suggest "protected intimacy" (Bachelard 1964, 3), paradoxically reveals the homelessness of those who live there. If not for the help of their neighbor, the dubious Mr. Plater, Helena and her father would not have a place to live; they would be homeless. The break in the ownership of the house parallels the ruptures in the family history of the narrator. Helena, the narrator's grandmother, constantly "searches for her mother." Not only does she feel alone and have no one to confide in, but she is also troubled by the mysterious burial of her mother, who, though she was the mistress of a large manor house, Miłowidy, was buried like a beggar. The narrator himself searches for his father, whom he remembers only from his deathbed (*BM* 125).

The oneiric home of the Borderlands is contrasted with the desacralized existence of contemporary Warsaw and the narrator's life in a communal building. Unlike the oneiric home, which is always located in the Wilejka valley, the contemporary home is located in Warsaw, with the exception of the novel *From the Besieged City,* which is partially set in Kraków. The city, however, is not the place where the protagonist belongs. He constantly feels alienated from it, although he feels a certain compassion for the disintegrating city. Such an approach might be partially the result of Konwicki's romantic roots—like most Polish Romantics, Konwicki exhibits a certain dislike for and distrust of cities.

Konwicki's Warsaw, however, is also a representation of the profane, which manifests itself in two major ways: through the mechanization of life and through the destruction of nature, which for Konwicki's protagonist always carries strong religious connotation. If we agree with Le Corbusier's famous formula that the house is "a machine to live in," Konwicki presents a machine that is constantly breaking and falling apart, and, most of all, a machine that is the result of the desacralization of the contemporary world. The narrator's new home in *The Polish Complex* or *A Minor Apocalypse* is located in the dilapidated Warsaw of the 1970s, which Konwicki compares to a gigantic machine: "the city was beginning to hum like a drive belt" (*MA* 7). He characterizes the building in which the protagonist lives as another "great engine mov[ing] slowly into daily life" (*MA* 5). The behavior of the protagonist suggests mechanization as well: "an accretion of automatic habits" fills his lonely life (*MA* 7). The communal apartments are the result of mass production, and as such they offer none of the domestic well-being that a home is supposed to possess. They offer no individuality, either, as they are presented as "an integral part of the gigantic transformation of the world undertaken by the industrial societies, a transformation made possible by the desacralization of the cosmos" (Eliade 1987, 51).

One of the most important symbols of the new desacralized existence is the omnipresent television—the only element of the contemporary home that can be found in all of Konwicki's Warsaw novels. Positioning an indifferent machine, a television set, as the home's most important object, Konwicki emphasizes more than just the hidden power of indoctrination or television's numbing abilities. The omnipresence of television implies the passivity of the younger generations as people mindlessly watch and accept a deformed and simplified version of reality. It also suggests the loss of collective memory in contemporary Poland as Poles in *A Minor Apocalypse* do not notice the changes in their national anthem or national flag. In *The Anthropos-Specter-Beast,* written in 1969, when television was slowly becoming popular in Poland, it is presented as the main source of knowledge for the young protagonist and a deadening force for his unhappy and unemployed father.

Television plays an even more telling role in Konwicki's vision of the contemporary home after 1970, when home represents a fully depersonalized and emotionally abandoned space. The television, always on, insures that the state is always present in the home. Unlike the characters in Orwell's dystopic *1984,* Poles in *A Minor Apocalypse* have the ability to turn the screen off, yet they choose to watch television constantly. Ironically, television provides evidence of a feeble political opposition in Poland during the late 1970s for viewers because television sometimes shows, by chance of course, rare instances of resistance as in the surrealistic scene in *A Minor Apocalypse* in which party members undress in front of the Party Committee. Television is watched by everybody, even by the secret police busy torturing the protagonist and by people in poor and dirty fast food restaurants. In some ways, television is also omnipotent since, in Konwicki's novels at least, it can run without electricity. In *The Polish Complex,* the blackout does not shut down the television set and, in one of the most beautiful examples of Konwicki's ironic genius, the program about learning Russian can go on. Nonetheless, television in the shabby Polish reality of the 1970s does not possess the power of dexterous manipulation, as in *1984.*

Eliade suggests that one of the most widely disseminated cosmological images is "the cosmic pillar that supports heaven and at the same time opens the road to the world of the gods" (Eliade 1987, 34–35). In the desacralized world of Konwicki's Warsaw novels, the role of *axis mundi* is fulfilled in reverse—Stalin's hated Palace of Culture and Science fulfills the role of a ceremonial pillar that opens not to the world of the gods but to the underworld. The Palace of Culture is present in most of Konwicki's later novels—his novel *Ascension,* for instance, presents a journey to the top of the palace. Yet it is not the world of the gods that Konwicki's protagonist explores but the large underground world lying directly beneath the palace and constituting its essential secret part, which is not known to the majority of the people but is only sensed by them. The palace's enormous labyrinthine rooms and secret tunnels are as difficult to navigate mentally as the world above. In *A Minor Apocalypse,* entering the underground is presented as an "excursion to hell" by the protagonist, who is going to see the preparation for the Party's feast celebrating Poland's loss of independence to Russia. In *Ascension,* the very ascension to the top of the palace results in inexplicable fear and the desire to come back, to "simply come back" (*A* 249). The constant presence of the Palace of Culture, which on the most basic level represents Soviet domination over Poland, can be deconstructed as a sort of antihierophany; not a manifestation of the Sacred but rather a manifestation of the desacralized. The Palace of Culture is the most hated object in Konwicki's world—"an old chalet" (*MA* 4), an "architectural cadaver" (*Pu* 9); and yet it is an indispensable part of contemporary desacralized space. Its domineering existence is assured even in Konwicki's latest novel, *Czytadło* (Pulp fiction), written in 1992, in post-communist Poland. The symbolism of sovietization is no longer considered valid, yet its power to desacralize is still there.

If the mechanization of life is one of two major aspects of the desacralization of the contemporary world, the death of nature is no less important. Nature plays an essential part in the borderlands, linking them metaphorically to paradise and the Garden of Eden. The home in Warsaw, however, is located in a place deprived of nature, a place constantly desacralized. Two aspects of nature are common in Konwicki's work: trees and the river. The image of a tree is especially telling as it symbolizes life, youth, and immortality: the forest, as in *Bohin Manor,* is occasionally presented as home. Sometimes the protagonist fixates on a tree because of its beauty, stability, security, or because of its connection to his past. Yet in contemporary Warsaw the protagonist is attached to a single and sickly tree that he can see from his windows (*ASB* 8), which, by comparison, brings to mind the old and powerful trees surrounding the oneiric house in the Borderlands. The destruction of nature is one of the major aspects of the destruction of the world: the narrator lamented the death of rivers and trees as early as 1969, in his tragic novel *Ascension.*

Devoid of memory, eternally incomplete and fragmented, the contemporary home of the late seventies and eighties is a faithful reflection of the political situation and neither radiates energy nor projects any positive image to the outside. In short, the contemporary home is a random collection of broken, old, and useless objects accumulated over time; damaged pieces of furniture, old coats, shoes and slippers, and "junk strewn about the floor" (*MA* 22), piled in the corridor, and in the "cluttered rooms" (*MA* 12). Depersonalization is visible in eternally dirty windows and annoying sounds coming from unknown places: "a sound that would be good for killing rats, made its first appearance in our building a few months ago. . . . It would start up suddenly and then suddenly die down after forty minutes or so. During the day, at night, too. It kept the tenants in a state of constant, hysterical anticipation" (*MA* 22). I mentioned earlier that the contemporary home does not provide shelter, unlike the home of the past, which, at least partially, was able to protect some of its inhabitants. The difference lies not so much in the ability to protect, because Konwicki's home is always destroyed by history, but rather in the fact that the home of the past suggests the possibility of protection. In *Bohin*

Manor, for instance, Konwicki's grandmother escapes the world (especially her Russian neighbor) by staying in her home to give birth to her illegitimate son—there she is protected by heavy window shutters and doors. The doors of the contemporary home, however, open to let in the secret police or friends from the political opposition who bring the protagonist only a death sentence:

> Suddenly my doorbell rang. . . . My heart began beating rapidly, and not without cause, for they came to see me only about twice a year and each of their visits had marked a radical change in my life. (*MA* 10)

The contemporary home never suggests intimacy, much less security.

The home of the 1970s denotes a place that is fully desacralized, fully depersonalized, emotionally abandoned, devoid of history and, most of all, intimacy. Traditionally, Polish homes were adorned with memories of wars and uprisings, with pictures of men who died during those wars. In the apartments of the seventies, a break from the past is suggested in two ways: openly, by the narrator, who cannot remember the past, even World War II, in which he took part, and indirectly, by lack of any family tokens of remembrance. It is also significant that Konwicki's home constitutes protection neither against the world nor against history. It does not reflect the inhabitants' individuality, as there is no separation between the private and public sphere since history invades and destroys homes leaving *Homo conviciensis* constantly longing for the oneiric home. Yet, the home of the seventies now represents space that is not only fully depersonalized and estranged, but that even seems to mock its owner: the little jade plant, the "drzewko szczęścia," popular in Poland in the seventies as a good luck charm, begins to grow well in the protagonist's apartment either right before he is told he should set himself on fire in front of the Party Central Committee building to protest the sovietization of Poland or when he is accused of committing a murder (*Pu* 7): "my jade plant has been sickly for many years and now suddenly, without any external cause, it has surged upward, sending out a large number of powerful, knotty branches" (*MA* 15).

Tadeusz Konwicki's concept of home and domesticity is complex. Generally speaking, home represents for him a space that is continuously shaped and destroyed by history. It is never truly formed by its inhabitants, who do not concern themselves with issues such as aesthetics or intimacy. Beginning with *The Hole in the Sky,* Konwicki divides the home into two equally important homes. The oneiric home plays the role of a moral and ethical center, the Sacred, where the protagonist truly belongs. The second home, the contemporary home, constitutes a desacralized, fragmented, and emotionally abandoned space reflecting the political history of contemporary Poland. The home of the past, however, is not so much a specific space but rather the surroundings of the home. Since the Wilejka valley is presented as a more domestic space than the protagonist's home, Konwicki's protagonist lives in a homeland without a home.

Notes

All translations from Polish, unless mentioned otherwise, are my own. The following abbreviations for Konwicki's novels are used:

A	*Ascension*
ACS	*At the Construction Site*
ASB	*The Anthropos-Specter-Beast*
BM	*Bohin Manor*
CaH	*Calendar and the Hourglass*
FBC	*From the Besieged City*
HiS	*The Hole in the Sky*
HoS	*Hour of Sadness*
M	*Marshes*
MA	*A Minor Apocalypse*
P	*Power*
Pu	*Pulp Fiction*

1. In agreement with Stanisław Ossowski's definition (1967, 210), the "private homeland" denotes the region with which an individual has a personal relationship based on direct experiences; such a relationship is based neither on ideology nor beliefs.

2. The typical Polish manor house was a one-story structure, built of larch or fir, and located "near the village, on a hill, near water"; see Mickiewicz 1967, 6 (note to line 25). For further references on the subject, see Gloger 1972.

Works Cited

Bachelard, Gaston. 1964. *The Poetics of Space.* Trans. Maria Jolas. Foreword by Etienne Gilson. New York: Orion Press.

Barańczak, Stanisław. 1992. *Breathing under Water and Other East European Essays.* Cambridge, Mass.: Harvard University Press.

Bereś, Stanisław. 1994. "Bohin Manor: Romance with Nothingness." *Review of Contemporary Fiction* 14, 3: 189–96.

Błoński, Jan. 1993. "Kiedy pęknięte zwierciadło mówi prawdę" (When a broken mirror tells the truth). *Tygodnik Powszechny,* July 20.

Bross, Addison. 1994. "Tadeusz Konwicki's *A Dreambook for Our Time:* A Polish Classic." *Review of Contemporary Fiction* 14, 3: 172–79.

Chwin, Stefan. 1989. *Romantyczna przestrzeń wyobraźni* (Romantic space of imagination). Bydgoszcz: Pomorze.

Davies, Norman. 1986. *Heart of Europe: A Short History of Poland.* Oxford: Oxford University Press.

Eliade, Mircea. 1987. *The Sacred and the Profane: The Nature of Religion.* Trans. Willard R. Trask. San Diego: Harcourt Brace.

Gloger, Zygmunt. 1972. *Encyklopedia staropolska.* 4 vols. Warsaw: Wiedza Powszechna.

Głowiński, Michał. 1992. *Rytuał i demagogia: Trzynaście szkiców o sztuce zdegradowanej* (Ritual and demagogy. Thirteen essays on degraded art). Warsaw: Open.

Graczyk, Ewa. 1993. "Szczęście Pana Tadeusza" (Pan Tadeusz's happiness). In *Balsam i trucizna: 13 tekstów o Mickiewiczu* (Balm and poison. 13 texts about Mickiewicz), ed. Ewa Graczyk and Jacek Majchrowski, 9–76. Gdańsk: Atext.

Janion, Maria. 1969. *Romantyzm: Studia o ideach i stylu* (Romanticism: Studies of ideals and style). Warsaw: PIW.

———. 1990. *Życie pośmiertne Konrada Wallenroda* (Afterlife of Konrad Wallenrod). Warsaw: PIW.

———. 1994. "Where the Marshes Are: Romantic Mediumism in the Novels of Tadeusz Konwicki." *Review of Contemporary Fiction* 14, 3: 156–71.

Konwicki, Tadeusz. 1954. *Godzina smutku* (Hour of sadness). Warsaw: Czytelnik.

———. 1955. *Władza* (Power). Warsaw: Czytelnik.

———. 1956. *Z oblężonego miasta* (From the besieged city). Warsaw: Iskry.

———. 1959. *Dziura w niebie* (The hole in the sky). Warsaw: Iskry.

———. 1971. "Współautorstwo czytelnika. Z Tadeuszem Konwickim rozmawia Zbigniew Taranienko" (The coauthorship of the reader: Zbigniew Taranienko talks with Tadeusz Konwicki). *Argumenty* 44: 8–9.

———. 1976. *Kalendarz i klepsydra* (Calendar and the hourglass). Warsaw: Czytelnik.

———. 1977. *The Anthropos-Specter-Beast.* Trans. George and Audrey Korwin-Rodziszewski. New York: S. Phillips.

———. 1982. *The Polish Complex.* Trans. Richard Lourie. New York: Farrar, Straus and Giroux.

———. 1984. *A Minor Apocalypse.* Trans. Richard Lourie. New York: Vintage Books.

———. 1990. *Pół wieku czyśćca. Rozmowy z Tadeuszem Konwickim* (Half a century of purgatory: Conversations with Tadeusz Konwicki). Interviews by Stanisław Nowicki (Stanisław Bereś). Warsaw: Oficyna Wydawnicza.

———. 1992a. *Bohin* (Bohin Manor). Wrocław: Siedmioróg.

———. 1992b. *Czytadło* (Pulp fiction). Warsaw: Niezależna Oficyna Wydawnicza.

———. 1992c. *Rojsty* (Marshes). Warsaw: Niezależna Oficyna Wydawnicza.

Lasota, Grzegorz. 1950. "Przy budowie" (At the construction site). *Twórczość* 10.

Lubelski, Tadeusz. 1984. *Poetyka powieści i filmów Tadeusza Konwickiego: Na podstawie analiz utworów z lat 1947–1965* (Poetics of Tadeusz Konwicki's novels and film based on the analysis of his works from 1947 to 1965). Wrocław: Wydawnictwo UW.

Mickiewicz, Adam. 1967. *Pan Tadeusz.* Ed. S. Pigoń. Wrocław: Ossolineum (BNI 83).

———. 1998. *Pan Tadeusz.* Trans. Kenneth R. Mackenzie. New York: Hippocrene Books.

Miłosz, Czesław. 1992. *Szukanie ojczyzny* (Searching for homeland). Kraków: Znak.

Możejko, Edward. 1994. "Beyond Ideology: The Prose of Tadeusz Konwicki." *Review of Contemporary Fiction* 14, 3: 139–55.

Ossowski, Stanisław. 1967. *Z zagadnień psychologii społecznej* (On problems of social psychology). Warsaw: PWN.

Rybczynski, Witold. 1987. *Home: A Short History of an Idea.* New York: Penguin Books.

Zaleski, Marek. 1990. *Mądremu biada: Szkice literackie* (Woe from wit: Literary sketches). Paris: Libella.

Zaworska, Helena. 1970. "Dolina" (The valley). *Twórczość* 1.

PART III

Urban Home/lessness

8 ||| Place of Estrangement

Homelessness at Home in the Works of Three Postwar Polish Writers

Henryk Dasko

DURING THE YEARS of severe censorship in Poland, between the late 1940s and the late 1960s, contemporary Polish literature was frequently able to offer its readers a glimpse of life different from the lacquered reality preferred by official propaganda. Given a little creativity by an author, subjects restricted by administrative taboos could find their way into a short story or a novel. Corruption by state officials could not be discussed at any public forum, but it could serve as material for a local murder mystery (Toeplitz 1970, 151).[1] The story of the anti-Soviet underground in the Eastern Borderlands in the mid-forties was not a part of any history course taught in Poland, but was repeatedly if fragmentarily told by Tadeusz Konwicki in his novels and films.[2]

Realism was the prevalent method of the period and the reality of Stalinist and post-Stalinist Poland was seldom cheerful. The dark colors of everyday existence found their way into fiction regardless of a writer's own style, and even the most optimistic works of that period frequently contain an element of bitterness or despair. Authors of the younger generation, who could not fall back on memories of their prewar lives, seem particularly susceptible to that. Remarkably, the grimness of perceived reality is particularly acute in literary descriptions of home.

Aleksander Ścibor-Rylski published his first novel, *Węgiel* (Coal), at the end of 1950. He was just twenty-two years old and had yet to finish university. The war, which broke out when Ścibor-Rylski was only eleven, had compressed his adolescence: by the age of sixteen he was already an officer in the underground Home Army during the Warsaw uprising of 1944. At seventeen, he published his first poems in a fledgling Warsaw journal; at nineteen, already a reporter for the Polish military press agency, he crisscrossed the country by train for weeks on end. It was during those travels that *Coal* was written.

Coal was a hit. By 1948 the final false front of pluralism had been erased from Polish political and cultural life. The country, like all other Soviet satellites, entered the grim, monophonic era of Stalinism. In literature, the Zhdanovian doctrine of socialist realism, gradually gaining ground since the early postwar years, was officially proclaimed in January 1949 at the Writers' Congress in Szczecin. *Coal* was to epitomize the genre—a prototypical, formulaic "production novel," as they were then called. Set at a Silesian coal mine, the book told a rather predictable story of a struggle to achieve production goals. Although Ścibor-Rylski started writing before the tenets of the socialist-realist doctrine were codified or even fully articulated, the novel contained them all: there were productivity leaders and shirkers, activists and saboteurs, a life-threatening crisis and a struggle, and, finally, a glorious victory of the new. Coal mining was at that time Poland's largest and most important industry, which automatically gave Ścibor-Rylski's novel the weight of national relevance. Despite its formulaic plot, the book was an unqualified success: praised by critics, enshrined in a list of compulsory high school reading, within three years it ran through six separate editions, and in July 1951 young Ścibor-Rylski was awarded a state prize for literature.

It would, however, be wrong to attribute the novel's success solely to the well-oiled *agitprop* machine, pushing another hack novel. Unlike many of his contemporaries, whose names have been largely and mercifully forgotten, Ścibor-Rylski was a talented writer: the critic Tadeusz Drewnowski, no friend of socialist realism, forty years later noted Ścibor-Rylski's excellent narrative and observational skills, apparent in his debut novel (Drewnowski 1991, 349). Zbigniew Jarosiński (1999, 80), the author of a recent book on Poland's Stalinist literature, admired his talent.

Ścibor-Rylski's craftsmanship was solid. The story, despite the predictability of the final outcome, had enough twists and turns to keep readers on the edge of their seats. The dialogue, laced with the convincingly reproduced argot of the Silesians—Ścibor had a great ear for language—positively sparkled. Relative to other proletarian novelists of the time—from the Soviets Vassily Azhayev and Syemyon Babayevsky to the American Upton Sinclair—Ścibor-Rylski was rather easy on ideological rhetoric. There was sex, of the extramarital and illicit variety. There were exciting technical details about coal mining, and even motorcycle racing.

And yet, there was something within that novel that evoked a feeling of profound sadness. Beneath its optimistic facade, its sham realism, *Coal* was a novel about literal and physical homelessness, present, past, or threatening. A secondary plot, expressed at a more intense emotional and artistic level than the struggle for exceeding production quotas, ran through the book. It described, with a maturity and sophistication belying Ścibor-Rylski's tender age and his lack of experience, a human condition. If a socialist-realist novel is to be seen as a representative example of literary kitsch (Jarosiński 1999, 73)—and *Coal* is certainly no exception—then Ścibor-Rylski's description of the living conditions of his protagonists breaks out from that classification.

Wojciech Tomasik, in his comprehensive study of the Polish production novel, writes that the characters "inevitably complain about the tightness of their living quarters, but bear it patiently" (1988, 94). Ścibor-Rylski paints a much different and much bleaker picture, unusual in its candor, placing his protagonists within a truly Dickensian environment. Examples abound: a widowed miner and his three young children are forced to live in a corner of a single room, occupied by the miner's alcoholic father. Almost every night, drunken orgies take place in the apartment as the father brings prostitutes home and assaults his family in a drunken stupor.

Another worker's home is a converted chicken coop. He shares it with his old mother and his three little children. There is no bed for him—an earthen floor with a handful of straw serves as his place of rest. A workers' hostel, managed by the mine, is described by a party secretary as being suitable for pigs, but not for humans. A schoolchild has no place to do homework. For an unmarried miner, no shelter is available, unless he is lucky enough to be taken in by another worker's family, itself struggling with grossly inadequate living space.

None of this seems to be caused directly or indirectly by the ravages of the recent war. Although Poland had suffered enormous material losses, the Silesian lands had not. Homelessness, or, at a more literal level, inhuman living conditions, are not the result of the recent catastrophe. Remarkably, with the exception of one case, Ścibor-Rylski does not attribute the problem to imperialist plotting, sabotage, the so-called wrecking, or other causes used as a standard plot element in other socialist-realist novels. While remedies are found for most of the protagonists—in the obligatory happy ending, a new apartment building is built, the miner's hostel receives new bedding, and miners are lodged in a villa belonging to the counterrevolutionary mine manager—the emotional intensity with which Ścibor-Rylski treats the issue of near or complete homelessness differs markedly from other elements of the novel.

This picture is not, by any standard, a tear sheet from an optimistic and propagandist handbook. It is a dark, remarkably cohesive vision of a tough reality, with no manipulation in sight. It is perhaps the only aspect of *Coal* contradicting the words of the critic and literary historian Piotr Kuncewicz, who in his essay on the socialist-realist novel observed that "the entire world as described by Ścibor-Rylski simply does not exist" (1993, 2:450).[3]

Like Ścibor-Rylski, Marek Hłasko too debuted at a young age. Born in 1934, he broke onto the Polish literary scene in 1954, and his short stories, collected in a volume and published in the summer of 1956, demolished the traditional hierarchy of literary judgments in Poland in the mid-fifties.

Hłasko was a product of the Stalinist era and his early, prepublication efforts bore all the classic marks of the socialist realism genre. However, by the time his works appeared in print the first signs of a political thaw could be detected in Poland and Hłasko moved quickly to the forefront of change. By mid-1955, as Poland gradually shed the restrictions of Stalinism, Hłasko and his works became the ultimate, transgenerational and transsocietal symbol of political and cultural renewal, extending far beyond the boundaries of literature. By mid-1956, he had achieved astonishing personal and artistic popularity, both as a writer and as the personification of new national hopes. He wrote quickly and his short stories and novellas were awaited eagerly by the public; upon appearing in a Polish periodical, his piece would be immediately reprinted by other magazines—an unprecedented practice.

Ósmy dzień tygodnia (The eighth day of the week) was written in May 1956. In its day it was an important work and a classic of Hłasko's anti-Stalinist period. The author himself felt that it included important moral statements that needed to be expressed quickly, lest the period of political liberalization end soon (Stankiewicz-Podhorecka 1994, 75). The story of two lovers, unable to physically consummate their relationship and surrounded by unexorcised demons of the Stalinist past, *The Eighth Day of the Week* takes place in Warsaw during four days in May of 1956. Hłasko, who often set his stories in a real and identifiable geography, was even more specific this time, providing important intertextual clues to his literary style and his *Weltanschauung* during the period of political and social turmoil in Poland.

In the opening scene of the story, a radio blares out the results of an international bicycle race, the most widely recognized annual sporting event in Poland at that time. In the text the action takes place on a Thursday, when "the Polish team suffered a setback. The stage was won by the Rumanian Dumitrescu" (Hłasko 1973, 9). In actuality, the International Race of Peace took place between May 2 and May 15 of that year, a period that contains two Thursdays, on both of which the Polish team performed superbly; they shared the top spot in the overall team classification and, on the second Thursday, the Polish racer Królak actually won the leader's yellow jersey, which he kept until the end of the race. The Rumanian Dumitrescu, though a dangerous competitor, never won a stage that year (Tuszyński 1989, 135). Moreover, Królak's victory in the race, the first ever for a Pole, was perceived in Poland as a major national triumph, one of the greatest in Polish sport after the war.

None of that appears in Hłasko's story. On the contrary, a major success has been turned into a defeat. This is characteristic of Hłasko's style during that period, marked by disclosures of political crimes and the failure of the economic and social experiment. That, more than anything else, is responsible for Hłasko's bleak vision of the surrounding world.[4] To the extent that Ścibor-Rylski manipulated reality to suit his ideological needs, Hłasko did too, albeit to a reverse purpose. Indeed, the starkness of Hłasko's landscape is so pervasive that critics have frequently viewed his work as being a mirror image of the socialist-realist, rose-colored vision of society.[5]

If Ścibor-Rylski represents one extreme of literary realism, Hłasko can only be placed at the opposite end of the spectrum. And yet there is a point at which both *Coal* and *The Eighth Day of the Week* intersect, or rather run parallel. While none of Hłasko's reality can be perceived as cheerful or optimistic, some of his darkest hues are reserved for descriptions of domestic life.

First, there are the premises where the protagonists reside—a single, sordid room with a kitchen, occupied by five people in Warsaw's least desirable area. Then comes the dysfunctional family: a permanently depressed father; a hypochondriac, whining mother; an alcoholic, embittered brother, all of whom are prematurely worn out. In order to study, the heroine Agnieszka must seek refuge in the kitchen; there, among unmade beds, a cheerfully dumb lodger resides. Apparently there is no bathroom in the apartment, because that is where the lodger washes up. In the only room, the father stares out a window for hours on end, daydreaming about a sunny weekend that never comes. He performs an exercise routine, offensive to his cohabitants. Vertical family ties have long disappeared; there is neither a spiritual nor emotional connection between the older and the younger generation. The despair of family life and its physical surroundings in *The Eighth Day* are indeed strikingly similar to the gloomy, monochromatic reality of domestic life in *Coal.*

In his later works, situated in Israel or California, Hłasko frequently depicts the nightmarish living conditions of his main protagonist. It is a fitting illustration in the context of an autobiographical, émigré hero, whose very condition epitomizes homelessness. But *The Eighth Day* was written during the peak of Hłasko's popular success, which coincided with the political liberalization of Poland. Liberated from the confinement of socialist realism, Hłasko could write freely, without restrictions, able to select at will his literary tools in the spring of 1956 (Galant 1996, 23). It is no coincidence that, like for many other writers of his generation, he sought to employ the darkest pessimism as his primary artistic voice.

A decade younger than Ścibor-Rylski and four years Marek Hłasko's junior, Janusz Głowacki is known today predominantly as a playwright, but his beginnings were different. He got his start writing bitterly ironic short stories, most of them published in the Warsaw weekly *Kultura.* Part social satire, part grotesque, they quickly demonstrated Głowacki's sharp eye and remarkable sense of parody. His literary tools were acute and finely tuned, his satire biting enough to be unmistakably political yet tame enough to allow publication of his works. His style was uniquely suited to the Polish reality of the mid-sixties, when the relatively short period of political and cultural liberalization in Poland was replaced by the dour restrictions of Cold War communism.

One of his early successes was a short story, *Polowanie na muchy* (Hunting flies). First published in 1968, at a time of rapidly growing political repression in Poland, it soon made Głowacki a household name: Andrzej Wajda, at that time the unchallenged monarch of Polish filmmaking, made it into a popular and well-received film.

Hunting Flies is a story of Włodek, a prototypical Polish everyman of his era. In his early thirties, Włodek is locked into a predictable, drab, middle-class existence, typical of Poland's middle class in the late sixties. A chance encounter with a young and attractive woman leads him to a half-hearted and sad attempt to create a new life among the intellectual and artistic bohemians. This, too, is a story set in Warsaw, and it offers a detailed image of a Polish home and family life.

As in *The Eighth Day of the Week,* here too there is a multigenerational family, confined to a crowded apartment too small for its needs. The thirty-one-year-old protagonist, Włodek, his wife, and their six-year-old son share the place with the wife's parents, to whom the apartment belongs. In the story's opening scene, Głowacki offers a theatrical setting of the family's living room: Włodek, bent over a typewriter, finishing menial work he brings from the office; his gluttonous wife, sprawled on the couch; on the carpet, their disagreeable child. Włodek's father-in-law is there, permanently glued to the TV set, in a scene reminiscent of Agnieszka's father's incessant daydreaming in *The Eighth Day.* There even is a similarly absurd exercise routine: in Hłasko's novella, to keep fit, Agnieszka's father does handstands around the apartment; in *Hunting Flies,* Włodek's mother-in-law slaps herself obscenely about the hips, an activity designed to shift her cellulite around.

Włodek is not quite at home in those surroundings. He lives there, yet he exhibits constant duality of behavior, trying desperately and unsuccessfully to fit in, only to take every opportunity to attempt an escape. The largely symbolic apartment and the family within are his prison, sapping him of all energy. He sees his wife as someone "with whom he is to spend the rest of his life. To resemble her, to get fatter, to shrink—and then, the end" (Głowacki 1977,). Unable to make a decision to depart, permanently suspended in an in-between world, Włodek is sentenced to a life of pretense and duplicity within a place he must call home.

In the three works discussed here, each author chooses to resolve the plot in accordance with the rules of the appropriate literary convention. In *Coal,* there is the inevitable positive resolution: the needy workers are given new, spacious housing through the efforts of the Party, after the saboteurs have been exposed and duly punished. Existentialist novels offer no happy endings, and there can be no hope in *The Eighth Day of the Week.* In *Hunting Flies,* Głowacki offers a characteristically mocking finale: Włodek himself backs away from the distant rainbow and voluntarily returns to the duality of his everyday existence, at once oppressive and safe. Yet, except for the story's ending, all three works offer indisputably consistent settings, where one's home is the ultimate place of estrangement.

In all of them, there is the rare image of an urban home in postwar Poland—two located in Warsaw, the third in an industrial, urban landscape of Silesia. In all three cases, the characteristics of such a home are predominantly negative: lack of privacy, feeling of physical and psychological confinement, of emotional, and even physical, violence. The protagonists' lives are dominated by feelings of alienation and estrangement. The notion of a family in the traditional sense is nonexistent; emotional ties between family members have disintegrated. The most common and rudimentary concept associated with home and family—in English expressed by the adjective *homey,* in German as *Gemütlichkeit,* and in Polish as *ciepło rodzinne*—cannot be found in any of the settings.

Polish prose after World War II and before the 1980s offers surprisingly few images of a contemporary urban family home. While the pre–World War II home has been frequently revisited by writers such as Stanisław Dygat or Tadeusz Konwicki, the same cannot be said of the postwar Polish home . Images of such a setting are uncommon, and those presented by other writers of Hłasko's or Głowacki's generation (e.g., Andrzej Brycht, Marek Nowakowski) tend to be painted with a similarly dark brush. This in itself is unusual, for a family home represents one of the most common and transperiodic subjects in literature. Yet postwar Poland is clearly different.

Ścibor-Rylski and Hłasko are no longer alive and they never commented much on their own work. Głowacki, when asked about *Hunting Flies,* said the home setting seemed to him the perfect metaphor for the condition of Poland's intelligentsia in the sixties.[6] Viewed in a broader sense, the literary representation of a home can be seen not just as a literary vehicle, but rather as a reflection of the author's own vision of Poland.

When viewed through such a lens, the paucity of postwar description of an urban home in communist Poland reflects and typifies the enormity of social and psychological changes brought on by World War II and the loss of true national independence. As neighborhoods disappeared in ravaged cities and the continuity of life was interrupted, tradition, the core element of any home life, was lost. The Polish village experienced such disruptions to a lesser degree, as exemplified by the remarkable resilience of nonurban literature in postwar Poland (e.g., Tadeusz Nowak, Wiesław Myśliwski, Edward Redliński). In many cities, however, and particularly in Warsaw, the cultural code of tradition and continuity could no longer be reassembled. Unlike Konwicki or Kazimierz Brandys, Hłasko, Głowacki and the entire generation born in the mid- and late thirties had very few memories of an individual home.

Within the framework of such an interpretation, Ścibor-Rylski's unconventionally dark depiction of the home would translate into his own, internalized ambiguity toward communist power, which he ostentatiously and enthusiastically embraced. Ścibor-Rylski was born to a prosperous middle-class family, and his social, cultural, and political origins were, by definition, at odds with all aspects of Polish communism. Like many of his background, he too initially became a communist zealot. Yet, a careful reading of his later works in which autobiographical elements are present points to a different persona far less certain of his ideological choices.

Marcin, the protagonist of Ścibor-Rylski's novel *Pierścionek z końskiego włosia* (A horsehair ring) is closely modeled on the author's own experiences during the Warsaw Uprising and in the period immediately following the end of World War II. Marcin's decision to join the communists, riddled with self-doubt, is clearly and extensively identified as a choice born out of pragmatism and not ideological enchantment. Marcin was important: *A Horsehair Ring,* written in the sixties, could not be published during communist rule, for Ścibor-Rylski, notorious for his usual willingness to compromise with publishers and censors alike, refused to bend and make changes in the book. His earlier novella "Czarne ściany" (Black walls, 1958), which takes place immediately after the war, also includes a character with apparently autobiographical traits who remains torn between his old loyalties and the desire to lead a normal life. These were, without a doubt, Ścibor-Rylski's own emotions—shortly before he set out to write *Coal,* which was to become a classic of Poland's servilistic literature.

Marek Hłasko, it has often been said, felt betrayed. Throughout his life, he complained of being betrayed by all: his mother, his women, his friends. Stanisław Stabro traces this sense of betrayal to Hłasko's overwhelming and self-destructive sense of disappointment with the rhetoric and the practice of Polish communism. Hłasko, writes Stabro (1986, 75), had accepted the New Faith without restrictions, as evidenced by his early works, with their frequent expressions of unconditional fealty to communist dogma. His subsequent rebellion against the failed doctrine was similarly intense: within Hłasko's scheme of things, there was little room for ambiguity or relativism. Thus, every character in Hłasko's story expresses, at least to a certain degree, his own tragically personal emotions and resentments. The morbid, hopeless home of *The Eighth Day of the Week* is in reality a literary image of Hłasko's own dark universe. In May 1956, at the height of his own artistic success and the country's period of liberalization, he wrote to his mother that he felt "tormented and harried" (Stankiewicz-Podhorecka 1994, 75). He was in a depression, which he tried to mask with excessive drinking. Politically, he believed Poland would soon revert to the time of oppression and "the screw will be tightened." With remarkable accuracy, Agnieszka's home in *The Eighth Day of the Week* reflects Hłasko's vision of the country he was soon to leave.

Janusz Głowacki does not belong. An ultimate individualist, he has always shunned the collective path, as he frequently emphasizes in press interviews.[7] His protagonists, on occasion seemingly typical, upon closer examination turn out to be of their own, unique worlds. Głowacki's artistic vision, notes critic Henryk Bereza (1973, 6), is based on the premise that mockery and tragedy are not mutually exclusive. Within the limited range of Poland's moral and artistic choices of the sixties and seventies, Głowacki managed to carve out his own, rather solitary place. Never fully for, never fully against, frequently resorting to literary mimicry and masquerade, he, like his characters, appeared suspended between the scornful and the dramatic. Like Włodek in *Hunting Flies,* Głowacki himself led a life of make-believe within the confused reality of Polish communism of the sixties and the seventies. Like Włodek, he too concealed his true emotions and his true beliefs behind a mask—in his case, the mask of his characters. He pretended; he made the best of the situation, until at the end, fate took matters into its own, unpredictable hands. The most important decision of Głowacki's adult life was made for him, rather than by him: the introduction of martial law in Poland in December of 1981, when he was attending the premiere of his play in London, gave him no other choice but to remain in the West.

Was there a home? As memories fade, literature frequently takes on the role of a witness, a live corollary to the dry narrative of history. It is an illustration of Poland's sad and confused postwar reality that an entire generation of writers created a literary home as the ultimate symbol of homelessness.

Notes

1. Toeplitz attributes the great popularity of Polish thrillers in the fifties and sixties to the genre's high degree of realism.

2. The novels are *Rojsty* (Marshes) (Warsaw: Czytelnik, 1959) and *Sennik współczesny* (A dreambook for our time) (Warsaw: Czytelnik, 1963). Discussing the latter novel in the mid-eighties, Konwicki told the critic Stanisław Nowicki (Stanisław Bereś) that while certain things could not have been said directly, he used the mood and the setting of the story to illustrate devious tactics used by the Soviets. See Konwicki 1986, 36.

3. The postcommunist equivalent of political correctness requires that all socialist-realist literary output be lumped together as utterly worthless. In reality, several books of that era remain quite readable despite their obvious subjugation to the party line. This includes *Samson* and *Antygona* (Antigone), two early novels by Kazimierz Brandys; Igor Newerly's excellent *Pamiątka z Celulozy* (Memento from the cellulose plant); and, at a more popular level, *Coal.*

4. In February 1956 Hłasko wrote to the writer Jerzy Andrzejewski, "Communism turned out to be a stream of crimes and everything else was nothing but lies and disgrace" (in Stankiewicz-Podhorecka 1994, 140).

5. See, for example, Stabro 1986, 75; Komar 1972, 96.

6. Telephone conversation with Janusz Głowacki, November 13, 1998. Home or lack of it is a pervasive and frequently used metaphor in Głowacki's work, including his plays *Kopciuch* (Cinders), *Polowanie na karaluchy* (Hunting cockroaches), and *Antygona w Nowym Jorku* (Antigone in New York). In his American plays, Głowacki employs homelessness to illustrate the spiritual condition of émigrés who, in George Mikes's words, "have lost everything except their accent" (source unknown).

7. See, for example, *Tygodnik Powszechny* 19 (1993) and *Gazeta Wyborcza* 9, 10 (1998).

Works Cited

Bereza, Henryk. 1973. "Akt samookreślenia." *Kultura* 48: 6.

Drewnowski, Tadeusz. 1991. "Posłowie" (Afterword). In *Pierścionek z końskiego włosia* (A horsehair ring) by Aleksander Ścibor-Rylski, 348–54. Warsaw: Fundacja "Kultura."

Galant, Jan. 1996. *Marek Hłasko.* Poznań: Rebis.

Głowacki, Janusz. 1977. *Polowanie na muchy* (Hunting flies). Warsaw: PIW.

Hłasko, Marek. 1973. *Opowiadania.* Paris: Instytut Literacki.

Jarosiński, Zbigniew. 1999. *Nadwiślański socrealizm* (Polish Socialist Realism short stories). Warsaw: IBL.

Komar, Michał. 1972. "Hłasko." *Twórczość* 11:96–103.

Konwicki, Tadeusz. 1986. *Pół wieku czyśćca: Rozmowy z Tadeuszem Konwickim* (Half a century of purgatory: Conversations with Tadeusz Konwicki). Interviews by Stanislaw Nowicki. London: Aneks.

Kuncewicz, Piotr. 1993. "Poetyka powieści produkcyjnej" (The poetics of the novel of production). In *Agonia i nadzieja* (Agony and hope). 2 vols. Warsaw: BGW.

Ścibor-Rylski, Aleksander. 1950. *Węgiel* (Coal). Warsaw: Książka i Wiedza.

———. 1958. "Czarne ściany" (Black walls). *Twórczość* 2:8–66.

———. 1991. *Pierścionek z końskiego włosia* (A horsehair ring). Warsaw: Fundacja "Kultura" 90.

Stabro, Stanisław. 1986. "W bursztynowej kuli" (Within an amber sphere). In *Kaskaderzy literatury* (Stuntmen of literature). Łódź: Wydawnictwo Łódzkie.

Stankiewicz-Podhorecka, Temida. 1994. *Listy Marka Hłaski.* Warsaw: Ypsylon.

Toeplitz, Krzysztof Teodor. 1970. "Zbrodnia po polsku" (Crime, Polish style). In *Mieszkańcy masowej wyobraźni* (Inhabitants of mass imagination). Warsaw: PIW.

Tomasik, Wojciech. 1988. *Polska powieść tendencyjna 1949–1955* (The Polish tendentious novel). Wrocław: PAN.

Tuszyński, Bogdan. 1989. *Wyścig Pokoju* (International race of peace). Warsaw: Wydawnictwo Sportowe.

9 ||| The Destruction of the Center

Jerzy Jarzębski

Two cities: the former and the current capitals of Poland. One a medieval walled town with a hilltop castle and a hundred churches, the other an industrial and bureaucratic urban center, built mainly during the last three centuries and always looking toward the future rather than the past. The layouts of the cities are also hugely dissimilar: Kraków grew concentrically around its old main square; Warsaw pushed its historic old town aside, developing an American-style grid in its place. And finally, while Kraków was spared the calamities of twentieth-century history, leaving its core almost untouched, Warsaw, laid waste by the systemic destruction of World War II, is still being rebuilt according to evolving ideological and aesthetic concepts.

To live in Kraków and to live in Warsaw always meant two different things, especially in our century, when these differences were brought into sharp relief. Kraków was a "home," giving shelter from the ravages of history; it was a mythical dwelling, the national sanctuary, the Polish Akropolis, the sacred abode, every element deeply rooted in time and tradition. Warsaw, on the other hand, gave the feeling of being in the midst of life, in the center of political and economic goings on, thus underlining the fragility of the abode offered to human beings on this earth, the abode's vulnerability to disasters and cataclysms. The Warsaw house is more like the house from *A Memoir of the Warsaw Uprising* by Miron Białoszewski: bullet ridden, turned into a heap of rubble, reduced to the basement in which people on the run from massacre find a temporary shelter.[1] In my Kraków flat, I have—miraculously saved from the Warsaw Uprising—a small dresser encrusted with shrapnel and family albums from before the war, with bullet holes. Warsaw, more often exposed to the inclemencies of history, entrusted these objects to the custody of the safer city.

In these cities, we even find different things to laugh about. As the capital of a conservative middle class, inhabited by the dusty, hypocritical characters from *Moralność pani Dulskiej* (Mrs. Dulska's morality) by Gabriela Zapolska or the satires by Tadeusz Boy-Żeleński, Kraków becomes an object of ridicule. Warsaw, on the other hand, seems absurd as the place where the social utopias of the intelligentsia were taking shape, be it the versions from Stefan Żeromski and Wacław Berent or those conjured up by the Youthfuls in Witold Gombrowicz's *Ferdydurke.* And so these cities were different even in their lack of authenticity or preposterousness: each clings to a different paradigm and a tradition all its own.

The communist era dealt with Kraków and Warsaw in different ways, but it mythologized both. In the literary images from the postwar period, Kraków is predominantly described as old, traditional, conservative, while Warsaw is presented as new, modern, but also, and inevitably, tawdry and phony. Both cities, dissimilar before, drifted yet further from each other, and only in the standardized ugliness of their suburban housing developments do they seem the same. Nevertheless, the new regime and the new ideology made a general assault on the urban structure of both these cities, trying to refashion them according to new concepts. But although the ideology was the same, the assault took different forms and yielded different results.

A traditional city is a highly nonhomogeneous and hierarchical space. It builds itself, like the primitive settlement discussed by Mircea Eliade, around the sacred place, the center of the world, its axis, which function can be served by the totem pole, but equally well by the church tower.[2] The distance from this center determines the social importance of particular places within the space. A classic example of a city focused on the center is Kraków, where the oldest, the richest, and the most distinguished families owned houses around the main square and close to it; clerks and middle-income families lived between the circle of fortifications and the so-called second ring, while beyond stretched the area occupied mostly by workers, craftsmen, shopkeepers, and the like. Of course, this pattern was only of a general, statistical character; nevertheless, Kraków could be viewed as a city where social structure found its reflection in demographic mapping. In prewar Warsaw the spatial layout was less centralized, but one spoke of the working-class districts of Wola and Powiśle. Żoliborz and Saska Kępa were known as the provinces of clerks and the intelligentsia, while the central districts were inhabited by the upper-middle and middle classes.

The communist attack on the very structure of the city was purely ideological. One of the chief aims of the project was to "open the city center to the common people"—a slogan borrowed from the title of a poem by Adam Ważyk, *Lud wejdzie do śródmieścia* (People will enter the downtown), published in the 1950 collection *Nowy wybór wierszy* (New selected poems). But the process of opening the city center in Kraków, which had been inhabited for centuries, took a different form than in Warsaw, where the central parts had been bombed into a wasteland. In Kraków, the communist authorities decided to demolish the traditional social structure by administrative means. The authorities introduced a regulation limiting the maximum living space to ten, and later seven, square meters per household member. This meant that people living in large apartments in the city center had to share them with complete strangers who received special allocation papers. The "excess space" was assigned to them in a way reminiscent of postrevolutionary Soviet practices, as described by Mikhail Bulgakov or Alexei Tolstoy.[3] The regulations, which the authorities explained as necessitated by the difficult housing situation, in reality became an instrument of ruthless terror, depriving people of their privacy and often exposing them to political surveillance.[4] Another instrument used to similar ends by the government was rent control, which was aimed at the much-maligned "landlords," but in effect undermined the physical substance of the city. Owning an apartment house suddenly ceased to be a reliable source of income and became instead a burden. The rent collected from tenants was insufficient as a living and seldom covered basic repairs and maintenance. What is more, the landlord was required to obtain an official permit to live in his own house!

As a consequence of this policy, the houses in the city center, many among them of historic value, rapidly fell into ruin, while their owners and inhabitants moved to the new concrete housing developments, where the apartments were smaller and shoddily built, but unshared and equipped with modern conveniences. As the years went by, those remaining in the center were mostly newcomers to the city—the poorest, often criminal, element. This debasement, both physical and social, of Kraków's old town struck visitors to the city in the dying years of communism.

Postwar Warsaw stood apart from Kraków both in its physical and legal situations. Nationalization of land and what was left of real estate made the "war against landlords" unnecessary. The hecatomb of the 1944 Uprising and the mass exodus of older Varsovians made room for the migrants, which meant that the "common people" could take possession of the city center without major conflicts. In the first years after the war, the most important task was to rebuild as much as possible what had been destroyed—a grand project that united not only Varsovians, but the entire nation. Toward the end of 1948, when the Stalinists gained prominence in the higher echelons of power, Warsaw as a living space became the testing ground for a huge ideological experiment. A monumental volume called *Sześcioletni plan odbudowy Warszawy* (The six-year plan for rebuilding Warsaw) (Bierut 1950), a richly illustrated version of President Bierut's paper, delivered during the Party meeting, gives a good idea of the scale of the experiment. The book presented a vision of a city based on Soviet models, a city where the center-creating functions were removed from trade and business in favor of an immensely expanded bureaucratic and political apparatus. In the middle of this new Warsaw proudly rose the Palace of Culture and Science, named after Joseph Stalin. At 234 meters, for many years it was the second tallest building in Europe (after the Lomonosov University in Moscow), only recently overtaken by skyscrapers in Frankfurt and London. It was several times taller than the sixteen-story Prudential building, the highest in prewar Warsaw, and became the totem placed by the new regime in the center of the capital they appropriated for themselves.

But did this symbolic act of the communists establish a new focal point—either of the cosmos or the city? Not quite. The vision of the special functions of the city's center was rather simple: it was to be occupied by government offices and some department stores, to be slightly better supplied than shops elsewhere, and to provide suitable space for stage-managed demonstrations. People dancing on the main square of Mariensztat or marching in an endless parade before the podium on the Plac Defilad (Plaza of Parades)—such was the center's ideal fulfillment, and these were the images documented with delight by the films, newsreels, novels, and editorials of the period. People spilling from the steps of overcrowded trams (private autos were virtually nonexistent), long queues for even the most basic products, clandestine trade in back-alley doorways and street markets—all the things that constituted daily reality for most Varsovians—rarely found their way into official records.

The prices of land were not regulated by the market, which allowed on the one hand an often extremely wasteful use of space, and, on the other, made it possible to develop some completely unsuited sites for building purposes. An excellent example of both is the housing complex Za Żelazną Bramą (Behind the Iron Gate), a group of huge, shoddy apartment buildings separated by large spaces, occupying the potentially most expensive area in the center of the capital and at the same time demolishing, perhaps permanently, the traditional street pattern in this formerly Jewish section of the city.

If we agree with Algirdas Greimas that a city is a message to be decoded, then Kraków, by its appearance, communicated the impoverishment of the real estate owners. In Warsaw the message was different: the omnipotence of the huge state investor, who followed its own agenda without regard for tradition, aesthetics, or rational (i.e., capitalist) economic calculation, produced such ideas as the unsightly "longest building in Europe," erected opposite the Warsaw East Railway Station. It seems that the inordinate length of the building was due to purely practical considerations—the construction could be completed using only one crane, moving on rails. The same omnipotence gave rise to the idea of gigantic housing developments on city outskirts, where tens of thousands of inhabitants lived in rows of identical apartment buildings, monotonous landscapes with no guideposts for nonresidents.

The urban landscape of postwar Warsaw was jointly determined by the destruction perpetrated by the Nazis, the demands of communist ideology, the housing shortage (which made it necessary to build large apartment buildings in the city centers), the privileged position of the investor among the participants in the construction process, and finally, changing demographic conditions. The resulting metropolis, lauded in popular songs and propaganda as the model city, in reality was an odd hybrid where tradition clashed with modernity and the center was (and still remains) disfigured fragments of unfinished urban projects, giving an overwhelming impression of an architectural confusion. And what happened to the "common people," typified by the peasant migrants with a goat on the balcony and rabbits in the bathtub, which they have no other use for? Their assimilation into the urban civilization and the process of acquiring a new identity is no doubt an exciting subject of study for the sociologist. But before it came to that, before the pressures of the new, postcommunist economic reality in Warsaw and in Kraków removed the lower classes from the city center and reintroduced such urban attractions as luxury stores, art galleries, and good restaurants:

both cities endured a kind of disease, probably characteristic for many towns in this part of the world, that found its reflection in literature. The symptoms of this disease are dissolution of definite spatial structure, the center's loss of its specific qualities and functions, which resulted in disorientation, and a sense of confusion and unreality.

This feeling of confusion and destruction took quite long to find its way into fiction because for several years it was muted by the programmatic optimism of socialist-realist writing. Probably the first mainstream literary text that presented an unorthodox portrait of the new Warsaw was Leopold Tyrmand's quasi-detective story *Zły* (The bad one, 1955). This controversial novel, unashamedly using all the tricks of pulp fiction, smuggled in a vision of the city that stood so much apart from the varnished images painted in the socialist-realist vein that it could not have found favor with the Party and the critics. Jan Walc (1992, 175) was probably the first to notice the peculiar quality of Tyrmand's portrait. Characters in the novel refuse to accept the new development projects in the city center, meant as a showcase of the new regime. They roam the neighborhood of the Party building, but never actually enter it. The Palace of Culture is for them only "the skyscraper" looming indistinctly in the distance on the "biggest square in Europe," a building whose construction required the demolition of a whole district.[5] But the writing becomes much more vigorous when the author describes the Warsaw flea markets, which in those years occupied the ground floors and courtyards of ruined houses in the very center of the city. They are a seat of depravity, the haunt of drunks, tramps, and petty criminals, but it is also there that the true heart of this city is beating, because we see there those people who, notwithstanding the government's repression, have decided to take their fate in their own hands and make sovereign choices about their lives. Thus Tyrmand's novel sharply foregrounds the conflict created by the Stalinist reconstruction scheme: the architects erect new buildings and lay out new squares according to the dictates of ideologues,[6] but the old-time Varsovians will never completely accept them, choosing those places that are buzzing with life, places where one can buy and sell things and do business—even if those places are an insult to the aesthetic sense and the politically acceptable conceptions about how the center of the capital city should look.

Marek Hłasko, Tyrmand's junior by several years, started his writing career in the same period and shows the same Warsaw in his early short stories, but without the sentimentality and pathos that sometimes crept into Tyrmand's narratives about his city. Hłasko's Warsaw is a dirty, devastated city full of debased people worn out by a life of oppression and therefore often deprived of a higher moral sense. But perhaps a more significant element in Hłasko's picture of the city is its lack of structure: his Warsaw is desperately lacking "beautiful places" and "elegant society"; it is just an immense expanse of space cluttered with ugly, grimy houses and teeming with people animated only by the spirit of cynicism and aggression. In this mob it is impossible to tell petty criminals from artists or university professors. They all meet in the same dingy bar to drown their common sense of failure in a shot of the same lousy vodka with a "red label." The last preserve of the sublime in this world is love, but love requires for itself a special place, separated from public space, untainted by the city's overwhelming vulgarity and bad manners. The characters in *Ósmy dzień tygodnia* (The eighth day of the week) desperately strive for a stretch of "sublime space" for themselves, but it is impossible to find it, and their love founders.

Aleksander Ford, who adapted the short story for the screen, set it in the reconstructed old town of Warsaw, which then functioned as a sort of officially approved, propagandistic make-believe sublime space.[7] This alteration so contradicted the very idea of Hłasko's work that the enraged author withdrew his name from the credits.

The most striking images of Warsaw in the communist era were painted either from "below" or from "above." Marek Nowakowski, in a whole series of short stories, looks at Warsaw from below, showing the community of petty criminals, frauds, drunks, tramps, and the like. The authors who take the view from above—that is, from the perspective of the artistic and political elites—are Leopold Tyrmand in *Życie towarzyskie i uczuciowe* (Social and emotional life), Tomasz Staliński (Stefan Kisielewski) in the novel conveniently for us called *Widziane z góry* (Seen from the top), or Jerzy Andrzejewski in *Miazga* (Pulp). But all three of these novels question the legitimacy of the Warsaw "aristocracy"—in literature, art, or politics. The social "center," with few exceptions, is not far removed from the "periphery" of the lower classes; it also lacks good taste, and its splendors and material affluence seem pathetic when contrasted with the true beau monde, which is always elsewhere—in Paris, London, or New York. Tadeusz Konwicki looks at the city both from above and from below in all his Warsaw texts: *Wniebowstąpienie* (The ascension), *Kompleks polski* (The Polish complex), *Mała apokalipsa* (Minor apocalypse), not to mention the "mock diaries." And it is perhaps in the works of this author that one can best perceive the disappearance of social structure. In *The Polish Complex,* Konwicki makes his characters stand in a queue for the last commodity that has not been debased in the communist state: gold. But a society spending its life in queues has lost its ability to communicate normally (a point first made by critic Stanisław Barańczak), and what is more, the unequal starting positions provoke the conflict that must arise in situations where everyone is competing for rationed goods. A member of the queuing society has no distinct identity, or, to put it differently, always wears a mask and conceals his background; moreover, he does not have a normal home: Konwicki's characters are camping in the staircase, celebrating there the most homely of all Polish holidays, Christmas Eve. Waiting for the Savior replaces the futile and absurd waiting for the supply of goods. Similarly homeless is the hero of *Minor Apocalypse,* rambling through the labyrinth of the city on the way to his own Golgotha, or the dissident from *Rzeka podziemna, podziemne ptaki* (Underground river, underground birds). Equally homeless is the main character of *The Ascension,* an immigrant from the countryside. The reasons for this universal homelessness seem obvious: for Konwicki, a home in Warsaw, even if it does exist, must be unreal and suspect because the true home was to be found close to Vilna, the province of the writer's childhood and youth.

The characters created by Konwicki and Nowakowski like to visit the unofficial precincts of the city, its most seedy places, or even the system of cellars under the city center which (especially in *Minor Apocalypse*) bring to the same level of importance the places of differing status: the drinking joint and the Party Central Committee building. In the works of Konwicki and Nowakowski, the underground cellars are where the characters' lives become more authentic—that is, they are closer to each other and farther from the official hierarchies. But this labyrinthine structure has no true center, no sacred place one can strive for. And even if such a place does exist, it is debased and absurd. In *Minor Apocalypse,* for example, the last storehouse of luxury foods in Poland has been stockpiled by the communist rulers under the Party building for a feast celebrating the final loss of independence.

The most repulsive, most ominous images of the city, especially of Warsaw, are contained in works written in the 1970s. But the most original vision was created by Janusz Anderman in *Gra na zwłokę* (Playing for time) a novel set in Kraków. Its main character is also homeless and roams the streets, finding temporary places to sleep at night. But the author has created a schizophrenic character: at each moment he sees himself through the eyes of a hypothetical secret police informer and "writes a report on himself." This means that not even in the most "off-limits" places into which he strays can he find true privacy and a sense of security. As for the report, it is as stupid and vulgar as that of a typical sleuth would be. One could say that Anderman's character conjures up a kind of providential guiding spirit, but this Providence becomes thoroughly corrupt.[8]

The disease that ravaged urban space in Poland's communist era was firmly rooted in the ideologically based laws and in the ideological visions of urban development, but its effects could be seen in the society's state of mind; it produced collective neurosis and a sense of confusion and unreality of the urban world. Living a relatively normal life in this world meant either believing in all the sham symbols of State and Party control over living space, or maintaining a will strong and independent enough to create its own hierarchies and structures in a chaotic world. This was the way of Miron Białoszewski, who built around each of his new addresses a kind of private map and system of guideposts.[9] But Białoszewski approached his own space in a special way: for him it was by definition peripheral, whether the poet lived in the very center of Warsaw, three hundred meters from the Palace of Culture, or in the outlying district of Grochów. In the period when the old "center"—that is, the hierarchy of social and cultural values embodied in the structure of space—had been destroyed, and when believing in the new center, or even worse, wanting to get there, meant being seduced by a phony ideologized culture, "peripheral life" seemed the only mode of being for an intellectual or an artist. If we take a closer look at the spatial motifs in literature, we will notice that such motifs were based on a strong sense of the periphery and on play with physical distances. Examples are abundant: the stress on the parochial character of Polish culture and of the Polish condition, highly marked in Mrożek, Różewicz, Głowacki, and others; locating the point of reference and the ideal measure for valuing home-based literature in the works of émigré writers, namely Gombrowicz and Miłosz; the immense popularity of the borderlands motif in postwar literature, as well as the high status accorded to peasant writing or to fiction by authors from the lower strata of society. The most common subject for Polish literature after the war seems to be the lack of roots, which is rather natural in a country that has been "moved" several hundred kilometers westward as a result of international treaties, a shift that brought about profound changes in the composition and structure of the society. Small wonder then that for postwar Polish writers the archetypal "true home," the home from the time of childhood, was located beyond the eastern border, in the countryside or in a nobleman's manor—that is, "elsewhere," outside the realm of experience available here and now. But the sense of confusion and uncertainty probably did not arise from writers' having been sundered from their native places. The reason was that expropriated or abandoned space was not replaced by new space endowed with meaning and structure. To put it more precisely, this space, debased and featureless, did not offer prospects for establishing new roots, because it did not possess an authentic center, one created by centuries of tradition accumulating in the architecture and the people, as well as by free, spontaneous, competitive, and community-forging economic activity.

I have based this chapter on the two extreme examples of Kraków and Warsaw in order to show that the postwar destruction of the center occurred both in cities preserving their historic central part and in those where the center was newly created on the basis of an ideological plan; for even where, as was the case in Kraków, the center survived almost intact, other factors intervened, such as demographic changes, physical deterioration of housing stock, and economic stagnation, reducing everything to gray uniformity, jointly depriving central urban areas of their attraction and exclusivity, without which no authentic center can exist and function properly.

But more interesting than the direct effects of legislation and architectural projects is the universal character of these phenomena and the close interconnection of processes occurring in the spheres of politics, urban planning, culture, literature, and society's outlook. Ironically, in the deliberately centralized world of the communist state there occurred a massive erosion of the center, a rejection of its new form by the people, an escape to the periphery, and lastly, the removal of what had still functioned within the center, namely literary life, to the underground world of unofficial publishing, which by definition recognizes no central control.

What has remained of all this today, when the political situation has changed? Unquestionably, the new economic reality rapidly transformed the centers of large cities: they acquired a new, different kind of attractiveness, and the influx of investment capital radically altered their appearance, the social composition of the population, and the facilities that are available to the visitor. But if in cities like Kraków, with old central parts confined to small areas, the process of healing can advance rapidly, the center of Warsaw is still unhealthy, and the ills that are wearing it down faithfully reflect the problems of the Polish transition.

One of the first symptoms of the transformations that swept the country after the collapse of communism was the return of the flea market to the city center—an almost symbolic act, a postmortem triumph of Tyrmand and his fascinations, the process in a sense signified a return to the primitive accumulation phase of capitalism (similar to the short-lived period after the war, which ended when the communists snatched the still meager, nascent Polish capital assets). But what promised to be the beginning of the healing process, after these few years, looks more like another form of the disease. The lively and expansive flea market on the Plaza of Parades) today seems a symbol of chaos and a fresh debasement. New high-rise buildings spring up haphazardly around it. This convergence of economic activity in the center seems to be a positive sign for the restoration of its central character. But the flea market has acquired a strongly symbolic role; it epitomizes everything that is the least desirable in the expansion of capitalism: ruthlessness, greed, contempt for the weak and the destitute, erosion of traditional values by tawdry taste. As a result, the most recent Polish literature could be said to present the new social and political order through the prism of the flea market and its mores, and the nouveaux riches of politics and economy are never seen as anything other than grotesques. This means that literature of the nineties still focuses on peripheral areas, with a highly distrustful attitude toward the center. Cities like Gdańsk are found to be attractive due to the complexity and ambiguity of their history and culture, which means that they draw attention toward borderland areas and away from the discredited capital. "Don't move the capital back to Kraków!" plead well-known singers Andrzej Sikorowski and Grzegorz Turnau; this very popular song reflects the average person's sense of the crisis of the center.

It is not likely that we are going to see the rise of Polish cities lacking a deliberately center-oriented structure—cities like greater Los Angeles,[10] an agglomeration of townships spread out over a large area and connected by freeways. The tradition of creating complex and densely built-up urban units, combining economic, political, and cultural functions and imbued with the sense of history and loyalty, is very strong in Poland, as it is in the whole of Europe. For this reason everything that is going on in Warsaw, conceived both as a type of urban space and as a symbolic place, as a focal point for a system of cultural references, remains and probably will remain an important matter for the Polish nation, to a major extent determining its outlook and its attitude toward the country's past and present.

What we see in Warsaw today is undoubtedly the process of "producing space," capitalist style.[11] A new kind of center—for commerce, business, and finance—is emerging. The city has not yet come anywhere near restoring the authority of the center; such authority is the product of the entire culture and, once destroyed, it can be rebuilt neither easily nor quickly. At the same time, Warsaw remains one of those significant places where a certain experiment came to an abortive end. The experiment consisted of enforced remodeling of social structure and habitation patterns in the central urban area, combined with a profound change in the role to be played by the center in the new structure of the city. The experiment failed for several reasons: first, the new symbols of the center were rejected—the majority of the population associated them with the political regime imposed by a foreign power. Second, a structure of habitation based on tradition and social hierarchy was destroyed in the transformation process. "The common people enter the city center" in a manner similar to that of the farm boys in Mrożek's *The Party* entering the empty barn: vainly expecting that the new world will provide a more classy entertainment and, which is more improbable, endow life with some meaning. Unfortunately, these expectations are not fulfilled, and that gives rise to frustration and lack of self-confidence. Moreover, during the great migration from the periphery to the center and the other way round, the sense of possessing roots in space and historical time is lost.

The third reason why the experiment failed is socioeconomic. As Czesław Bielecki aptly remarks, the city "emerged as the meeting place and the realm of liberty," and it has been shaped for centuries by the "phenomenon of concentration." Therefore, the city center must be a fascinating place that draws large numbers of people, a place of special attraction, where pedestrian and car traffic is highly concentrated and intermingling. "If we look at the city as a phenomenon of concentration," writes Bielecki, "we will avoid the pitfalls that awaited all those who tried to heal the urban fabric without having that in mind. Many if not most of the twentieth-century cities combine the negative qualities of the rural village and the city only because their designers and administrators forgot that it is the density, the intensity, of human contact that generates progress. It is quite possible to build a high-rise housing development without a single meeting place, so that it would resemble a monstrous rural village. But it is equally possible to create an urban feel at the crossing of two streets built-up with low-rise but dense housing" (Bielecki 1996, 17).

We may add that a city thus understood is the product of democracy, since it is the *demos* that spontaneously decides, both in the Greek polis and in the modern metropolis, which areas of the urban space to fill with its gentle hubbub. The architect and the investor may only rationally participate in these processes if they do not attempt to "organize life" for the demos and to order space in an excessively arbitrary or doctrinaire manner. This always leads to dire results, as attested by the gigantic modernist urban planning projects, such as La Défense in Paris with its huge, always too empty forum for pedestrians, or, even more dramatically, by Brasília, which, by adhering to the principle of strict separation of various urban functions, became a dead embodiment of an aesthetic and social utopia.

But the creation of La Défense and Brasília in no way detracted from the charms of central Paris or Rio de Janeiro. In Warsaw the ruling utopia became aggressive, destroying in effect the very identity of the city and everything that had made Varsovians what they were. One can often hear today that true Varsovians are an extinct species. The literature of the last decades, although not that categorical in this respect, usually locates them on the periphery—even those who, like Białoszewski, lived in the very center. So what does "being on the periphery" mean in this perspective? It means the rejection of the center as concocted by the new times and the new regime. It means seeing in it a quasi-village, where only private contacts matter, and where there is none of that thrill that comes from participating in a dense crowd of people going about their various transactions and fascinations in a relatively congested space. A living city center complements and is an extension of the home, an enclosed and richly organized space creating a higher order of habitation. It needs to be something more than just a frail fortress protecting one's privacy. One must be willing to leave it in order to mingle with other people.

No such extended home is offered by the monstrous high-rise apartments, nominally in the center of Warsaw, such as the Behind the Iron Gate district. If in Kraków the process of destruction of the social fabric has not gone as far as in Warsaw, it is probably because the old center, although rundown and unattractive as a residential area, still remained an agora where Krakovians have always met. Postwar Warsaw lacked such an agora; it could be provided neither by the bombastic and ugly buildings that housed the state offices and ministries, nor by the shabby and tawdry space of the department stores in the center, which only shoppers from the countryside could find fascinating. The Warsaw crowd from the last years of communism, as is best shown in Anderman's *Kraj świata* (The edge of the world), "has nowhere to go," it is orphaned and lost. The crowd of today, that of Piotr Wojciechowski's *Szkoła wdzięku i przetrwania* (School of gracefulness and survival), is busy and preoccupied, but busy and preoccupied by little more than a small-time fraud that in the future will perhaps produce real capital and large-scale business.

My aim here has been to highlight certain processes that occur simultaneously on various levels of societal life and find their reflection in literature. I cannot agree with claims that the literary fascination with rural and small-town settings, and the location of narratives outside Poland—a tendency highly visible in the fiction of Andrzej Stasiuk, Olga Tokarczuk, Paweł Huelle, Stefan Chwin, Anna Bolecka, Natasza Goerke, or Zyta Rudzka—boils down to a passing literary fad. Looking for meaningful and inhabitable space outside the center (of the city or the country) reflects the center's malady and will go on until the center recovers its attractiveness as a rich space imbued with authentic values, economic and cultural. Those who want to learn something important about the condition in which our society finds itself should read closely both the signs produced by its literature and the ones created by its cities. In those two spheres one can see the processes that drive society, its collective mind, its architecture and culture, toward the state described by Andrzejewski as pulp, as well as those processes that reflect the laborious task of restoring and reerecting the structures of values, even if in the postmodernist, always evanescent and ill-defined, version. The history of the architecture of our collective home and the history of life and thought encapsulated in our literature are becoming for us what they really are: variants of the same history—a history lived out on many levels by the human community.

Translated by Tomasz Bieroń

Notes

1. After writing this chapter, I came across a very interesting book by Marta Zielińska entitled *Warszawa—dziwne miasto* (Warsaw—a strange city) (Warsaw: IBL, 1995); the author dedicates her attention especially to the city's physical frailty as affected by recurrent waves of destruction.

2. See Eliade 1961 ("Symbolism of the 'Centre'"), 27–56. See also Porębski 1978.

3. See Mikhail Bulgakov's *Zojka's Apartment* (written in 1925, world premiere 1926) and Alexei Tolstoy's *The Road to Calvary* (1922–41).

4. An excellent work on the subject is Boym 1994.

5. Walc points to the wonderfully oxymoronic phrase by Tyrmand from an interview with *Express Wieczorny*, about Warsaw "collapsing under the sledgehammer of reconstruction" (175). Walc is mistaken that the heroes of *The Bad One* never go to Constitution Plaza; in fact, they do go a few times. With perfect intuition about Warsaw, Tyrmand guessed that this investment, although tainted by ideology, creates a valuable big-city "interior."

6. One may recall here the ridiculous debate among the party bosses as to the ideological meaning of the statues crowning the rows of columns around the Palace of Culture or the equally bizarre directives regarding the plans for the Central Railway Station, which delayed construction for many years.

7. Bielecki writes: "The Old Town of Warsaw used to be a slum before the war. Rebuilt as a residential area for workers, intelligentsia, and artists, it changed its social structure and function. . . . The urban fabric became a kind of forgery, an architect's model of a historic city" (1996, 38).

8. For more about Anderman's novel, see Jarzębski 1984.

9. On Białoszewski's domestication of space, see Legieżyńska 1993.

10. On the Los Angeles phenomenon, see "It All Comes Together in Los Angeles," and "Taking Los Angeles Apart: Towards a Postmodern Geography," in Soja 1995.

11. On producing space, see Lefebvre 1991.

Works Cited

Bielecki, Czesław. 1996. *Gra w miasto* (Game of the city). Warsaw: Fundacja Dom Dostępny.

Bierut, Bolesław. 1950. *Sześcioletni plan odbudowy Warszawy* (The six-year plan for rebuilding Warsaw). Ed. S. Yenkewski et al. Warsaw: Książka i Wiedza.

Boym, Svetlana. 1994. *Common Places: Mythologies of Everyday Life in Russia.* Cambridge, Mass.: Harvard University Press.

Eliade, Mircea. 1961. *Images and Symbols: Studies in Religious Symbolism.* Trans. Philip Mairet. New York: Sheed and Ward.

Jarzębski, Jerzy. 1984. "Co się zdarzyło w teatrze mowy?" (What has happened in the theater of speech?"). In *Powieść jako autokreacja* (The novel as self-creation), 390–96. Kraków: Wydawnictwo Literackie.

Lefebvre, Henri. 1991. *The Production of Space,* trans. Donald Nicholson-Smith (Oxford: Basil Blackwell. Original ed., *La production de l'espace.* Paris: Anthropos, 1974.

Legieżyńska, Anna. 1993. "Dom Mirona Białoszewskiego" (Miron Białoszewski's home). In *Pisanie Białoszewskiego* (Białoszewski's writing), ed. Michał Głowiński and Zdzisław Łapiński, 62–80. Warsaw: Wydawnictwo IBL.

Porębski, Mieczysław. 1978. "O wielości przestrzeni" (On the plurality of space). In *Przestrzeń i literatura* (Space and literature). Ed. Michał Głowiński and Aleksandra Okopień-Sławińska. Wrocław: Ossolineum.

Soja, Edward W. 1995. *Postmodern Geographies: The Reassertion of Space in Critical Social Theory.* London: Verso.

Walc, Jan. 1992. "Fotografia Atlantydy" (A picture of Atlantis). In *Wielka choroba* (Serious illness), 170–81. Warsaw: Wydawnictwa Szkolne i Pedagogiczne.

10 The Best View Is from the Top

Autobiographical Snapshots, Communist Monuments, and (Post)Totalitarian Homelessness

Magdalena J. Zaborowska

> It is often said that writers of color . . . are condemned to write only autobiographical works. Living in a double exile—far from the native land and far from their mother tongue—they are thought to write by memory and to depend to a large extent on hearsay. . . . The autobiography can thus be said to be an abode in which . . . [they] necessarily take refuge. But to preserve this abode, they would have to open it up and pass it on. . . . When they open the doors of the abode and step out of it, they have, in a sense, freed themselves again from "home." They become a passage, start the travel anew, and pull themselves at once closer and further away from it by telling stories.
>
> —Trinh T. Minh-ha

Inspired by Trinh T. Minh-ha, who links the poetics of home to perils of intercultural passage and yearning for escape through narrative making, I would like to suggest that all (im)migrant artists have to wrestle with various expressions of autobiography.[1] Once we leave our homeland for an extended stay in another country, once we make a home, even a temporary one, elsewhere, no true return is ever possible. As Sidonie Smith (1993, 20–23) suggests, however, autobiography can become a means of textual reentry, of "talking back" and reconstructing identity. Words and temporary homes provide spaces for self-expression and dwelling that help anchor transitive identities, although they may never fully contain the selves produced by migration, diaspora, and exile. Meena Alexander stresses, "The act of writing . . . makes up a [piecemeal] shelter, allows space to what would otherwise be hidden, crossed out, mutilated. Sometimes writing can work toward a reparation, making a sheltering space for the mind" (1996, 3).

Writing about her immigration from Poland to England and the United States, Maria Kuncewicz (1895–1989) recalls her collection of reportages and vignettes about Warsaw, *Dyliżans Warszawski* (The Warsaw stagecoach). She had not seen that book about her beloved city since her hurried departure from her apartment, which was bombed and burnt in the Nazi attack on the Polish capital in September 1939. Years later, in lieu of the familiar building and city that both have ceased to exist, her reissued volume of stories becomes a mnemonic—"an atom of the burnt city"—and allows a certain way of seeing her home in the past, "as if an old piece of furniture could suddenly emerge from the ashes, at once very familiar and yet partially erased from memory" (Kuncewicz 1997, 5). But such written-up homeland becomes one's possession, an authorized story only from a distance imposed by exile. Kuncewicz emphasizes, "only having learned different floor plans, different warmth, a different sense of homes [abroad], did I appreciate and register the details of my past life" (7).

Such need to remember or recreate objects, structures, and spaces that are synecdochical representations of lost home has partially inspired this chapter. The evocative art of Beata Wehr has been another inspiration, in addition to the author's own (im)migrations from what she has been referring to as her "original" home in Poland. Wehr's work, more than a written account could ever do, emphasizes and embodies the palpable instability and elusiveness of dwelling understood as both location and process. Her paintings and mixed media travelogues are suspended between Poland and Tucson, Arizona, where Wehr currently lives and works. I have chosen *In Transit*,[2] a mixed-media book, to serve as a spatial commentary on the ideas expressed by my literary inspirations—Minh-ha, Alexander, and Kuncewicz—and to provide a visual motto for this transitionally autobiographical chapter.

Wehr's book on wheels is a textured narrative, a volume in motion that documents the artist's search for home and sense of place between two cultures and languages, as well as her movement through many different dwellings. It illustrates the interconnectedness of story and architecture, as well as autobiography, geography, and visual culture that contextualizes any experience of place and especially of home, homelessness, and exile.

As a dynamic account of transitions between various home locations in

Fig. 1: Beata Wehr, *In Transit,* book no. 23 (mixed-media, 21 × 21 × 4 cm)

Warsaw and the United States, Wehr's volume on the move is at the same time a material representation and a metaphoric, spatial articulation of her changing identity. As such, it reflects the narrative and kinesthetic[3] quality of the complex processes of self-representation between cultures. In these processes temporal, political, cultural, spatial, linguistic, and autobiographical elements blend much in the same way that the interdisciplinary approach required to assess them compels a set of what Minh-ha suggests are hybrid theoretical tools (1994, 24).[4] Much like the epigraph from Minh-ha opening this chapter, Wehr's hybridizing image helps envisage such dynamic theoretical hybridity. Necessarily ethnic and autobiographic to both artists, the notion of home implies identity understood as difference, passage, and temporary dwelling. Like Minh-ha's text, Wehr's book on wheels links spatial design and movement with story building—homes, identities, and narratives. In such a context, my discursive interpretation arises from shifting textures of reading and critical movements through time and space, where space is the underlying aspect of all social relations, including the production of art and academic discourse, as demonstrated by Henri Lefebvre (1995, esp. 31–36).

Wehr's book/form on wheels also helps to locate my readings of various meanings of *home* and *homelessness* in a dynamic relation to spaces between and within several academic disciplines: architecture, feminist theory, American studies, and literary and cultural studies. After all, books and built forms, language and design, narrative expression and architectural articulation are not that far apart, as Gaston Bachelard (1964), Fredric Jamieson (1991), Mary Ann Caws (1981), Jennifer Bloomer (1993), and Leslie Kanes Weisman (1992) have ably shown.[5] As with a book, so with a building: one should not judge a structure/story by its cover/facade, but read *between* the lines, look *within* and *enter* it to get the whole picture/story.[6]

Wehr's text/book in transit will also serve as a concentrated iconographic companion to my interdisciplinary reading of multiple perspectives on gendered and national identity as linked to home and homelessness in immigrant, expatriate, and variously exiled Polish and Polish-American women artists. Presence, absence, or ambivalent displacement of home as a literal or metaphorical geographic location, as well as a haunting discursive and architectural construct are central to the writings of such (im)migrant authors in the United States as Polish-Jewish Andzia Yezierska and Polish-Russian-Jewish Mary Antin, and more recently, Eva Hoffman.[7] Like these writers, Maria Kuncewicz, who was a World War II refugee in Western Europe and North America, explores her migrant identity of a "displaced person" as a function of geographic movement and an interpretive and creative mode of dwelling in specifically female, transcultural authorship. As Wehr's book on wheels helps to envisage, and Kuncewicz's painful reconstruction of the memory of her burnt home illustrates on the textual level, homemaking in exile compels its own kind of material and imaginary, but always autobiographic, labor of visualization.[8]

Below I discuss Kuncewicz's short story "Dom: Wizja przyszłego fin de siècle'u" (Home: A vision of a future fin de siècle), which sets up the rhetoric of home in the literal and metaphorical climate of the Cold War. Out of this climate arises the art of Zofia Kulik, whom I discuss following my autobiographical reading of the Palace of Culture and Science in Warsaw. The authorial intrusion between my discussion of these two artists is not designed as a narcissistic indulgence but serves as an introduction to some of the urban spaces and cultural and historic contexts that inform Kulik's art. Working with photography, semiotics, and socialist-realist architecture, Kulik maps out male and female bodies as fissures disrupting the proliferation of monumental religious, political, and gendered symbols and narratives that represent and proscribe Polish national identity during and after the Cold War.[9] She represents the generation of artists who followed in Kuncewicz's footsteps but had to contend with internal exile—the only uncensored dwelling space for artists and intellectuals during the height of socialism in Poland.

I end the chapter with a glimpse of cultural work performed by Hanna Szczubełek, who since the 1960s has been the chronicler of the Palace of Culture and Science in Warsaw, formerly named after Joseph Stalin. This socialist-realist high-rise figures prominently in Kulik's work too, and has been a notorious symbol of political homelessness that the Poles living "at home" rather than abroad endured under Soviet domination. An integral spatial embodiment of various historic and cultural contexts of the Cold War and its aftermath, as well as an irresistible magnet for autobiographic references by the author, the Palace emerges as a central architectural referent in this chapter. As such, along with Wehr's art, it helps to interweave various cultural artifacts, literary genres, and academic disciplines employed here. Located in the heart of the Other Europe, which is yet to be discovered by critics of postcoloniality and Western feminist theory, it is a repository of changing gendered national identities and histories. It endows with new meaning Homi Bhabha's claim that "the present can no longer be simply envisaged as a break or a bonding with the past and the future, no longer a synchronic presence: our proximate self-presence, our public image, comes to be revealed for its discontinuities, its inequalities, its minorities" (1994, 4).

Focusing on a few select examples, I aim to explore and signal some of the ways in which visually and spatially contingent "minority"—female gendered, undervalued, marginalized—representations of Polishness emerge from and construct multivalent discourses on national home and homelessness.[10] Looking back at my subject from within my current home in American academe and American studies, I locate my methodology on the borders, or in Bhabha's "in-between space[s]" of transcultural discourse. My argument plays on the blurry edges among disciplines, on the overlapping terrains where autobiography, feminist theory, postcolonial and posttotalitarian studies,[11] as well as architectural and literary theory meet, collide, and intersect. My readings of literature, Cold War architecture, and posttotalitarian art are deliberately dislocated and migratory, for I want to demonstrate not only

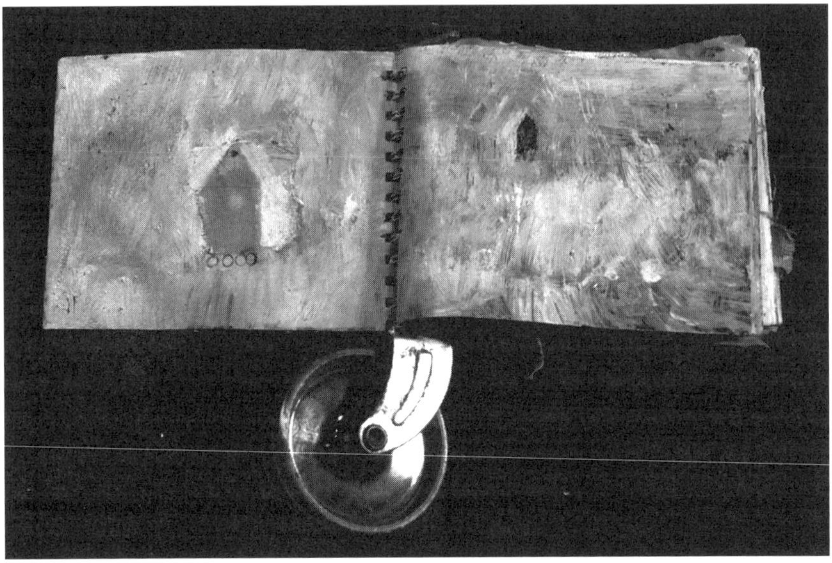

Fig. 2: Beata Wehr, *In Transit*

the blurring of interdisciplinary boundaries, but also of those delineating the subject and narrative genres of cultural critique. Like Wehr's book on wheels, this too is a work in transit.

The Location of Change

> And so the shelters the mind makes are crisscrossed by borders, weighted down as a tent might be by multiple anchorages, ethnic solidarities, unselvings.
>
> —Meena Alexander

The complexities of Eastern European history and culture are hard to articulate in this postcommunist, transitional moment, and that may be why relatively few compelling studies of that region have appeared in Anglo-American academe ever since the end of the Cold War.[12] As is well known, Eastern and Central Europe certainly have a past, perhaps too much of it, as some critics claim (e.g., Stern 1995, 13). The region also faces a more or less predictable future as an aspiring member of the European Union, which has promised to welcome different postcommunist countries once they have become more, well, European. Unlike the past and future, the present of the posttotalitarian East is often defined in discursive terms whose semantics emphasize passage, process, and incompleteness. It is "in transition between political and economic systems" and is undergoing the "changes" that lend it a curious "hormonal" flush and menopausal vulnerability; it is recovering from the "fall," entering a new democratic era; it is being "modernized" at a time when postmodernism is becoming passé in the West. These terms come from external descriptions of the East as a somewhat exotic semiotic location livid with ethnic strife, economic hardship, and tribalism, but one that also offers business opportunities as a source of cheap labor and a tempting new market for Western goods.

Although free from Soviet occupation since the memorable events of 1989–91, countries like Romania, Bulgaria and Poland can still be seen as locked in a cultural *terra incognita* and relatively invisible as producers of their own cultural meanings. For when represented, visualized, and defined from the *outside,* where and how do they fit on the so-called New European map? Are they Central? Eastern? Other? Postcolonial? Feminine? Aspiring Europeans? Former communists? Precapitalists?

José Rabasa stresses that Europe has been defined as a "privileged source of meaning for the rest of the world," in which "geography [can be seen] as a series of erasures and overwritings."[13] Like the map,[14] which "mirrors the course of history" (Rabasa 1995, 360)[15] rather than those who live it, most discussions about the "New Europe," "New World Order" or postcommunism/-socialism tend to reiterate the familiar "Soviet bloc" clichés so tirelessly reproduced by Western media. As the emerging Second World, struggling for a foothold between the First and the Third Worlds, Eastern Europe thus finds itself homeless, or nowhere, in that absurd, liminal nolocation that Alfred Jarry assigned to Poland so poignantly in *Ubu Roi.* Perhaps, as suggested by Milan Kundera, such dis-locations tell us more about the West, and why it still claims the prerogative of binary definition making, than about its marginalized, if not feminized, as Doina Petrescu stresses, "others."[16]

Of course, in Romania, Poland, the Czech Republic, Bulgaria, Belarus, or Ukraine, posttotalitarian cultural identities had been contested, deconstructed, reinvented, and performed long before the fall of the Berlin Wall captured the spectacle-hungry Western gaze (Goldfarb 1989). As conglomerates of paradoxes that challenge the scholars of postcoloniality, race, ethnicity, and gender—these identities do not lend themselves to easy applications of Western theory.[17] But precisely for that reason, they open up new, complex, in-between, interpretive spaces for locational feminist and postcolonial inquiry. They compel a deconstruction of the reductive juxtapositions that impact our discursive and methodological approaches: the First World versus the Third World, capitalism and communism, colonizer and colonized, home and exile, East and West, self and other, public and private, masculine and feminine, Western and Eastern ("Oriental").[18]

Home Is Nowhere: Maria Kuncewicz and the Global Republic

Written in 1944 in England, on the brink of the Cold War, Maria Kuncewicz's dystopic, futuristic short story "Home: A Vision of a Future Fin de Siècle" explores feminine otherness as a metaphor for "globalized" migration, while anticipating with unusual insight our present condition as a transitory, increasingly migrant Information Age society. Elizabeth Wilson (1992), Mary McLeod (1996b), Julia Kristeva (1995), Beatriz Colomina (1992), and Joan Ockman (1996) have demonstrated that women's presence in and movements through urban landscapes and public spaces signify otherness, disorder, outlawed sexuality, and breakdown of symbolic language, but can also generate alternative sites of renewal. As literature is often bound to do, Kuncewicz's piece, written more than half a century ago, anticipates this theoretical discourse. Its emphasis on the totalitarian underpinnings of postwar spatial arrangements and peculiar gendering of individual and collective identities reaffirms the importance of World War II and the Cold War as contexts for representations of the "woman's place."

In Kuncewicz's story, the utopian society of the "Global Republic" that springs up after World War III has "everybody liv[ing] everywhere." Transcultural migration, in the form of annual compulsory moves from place to place, from job to job, and from one sexual partner to another, has eradicated the concept of home and any traditional family life. In a confrontation between two women, who ostensibly meet to talk about novels but who in fact only talk about themselves, two aspects of home as exile come into conflict. Wanda, the so-called Old European, who remembers traditional life in a prewar society based on heterosexual family structure and the division of spheres, advocates forgetfulness of home as a space where pain, suffering, anxiety, and betrayal permeate any moment of happiness. Priscilla, the new "global" woman and an "interpreter of texts," who feels estranged and alienated in her uprooted culture, sees in Wanda's old-fashioned nostalgia a promise of refuge from the transigent, technology-laden world. To the younger woman, this imagined, idealized home, based on woman's otherness, glimpses the pleasures of internal exile and the homoerotic and artistic freedom that signify fulfillment of the self and subjectivity outside the nearly totalitarian, preprogrammed, computerized culture around her.

The story concludes with an ambivalent passage of the two women, who move together into a liminal space of their own making—Wanda's old house, which the Global Republic has preserved as a museum and example of how *not* to live. Priscilla initiates their double migration there: first, *into a revised past* from the homeless present of geographic rootlessness and transcultural flux; second, *into an alternative future,* in which women remain exiles, but in which they form familial ties based on creativity, freedom, and independent production of knowledge. Their stepping over the threshold into such redefined and reclaimed domestic space is presented as a reenactment of the original sin, but sans Adam. Anticipating some of Kristeva's work (1994) on women as strangers in the house of the father's symbolic language, Kuncewicz's narrative (1985, 303–5) identifies Wanda as Eve—"the oldest of the earthly refugees"—and Priscilla as her youthful alter ego, perhaps a metaphorical daughter or sister, certainly a willing partner in transgressive, alternative space making.

The story's reliance on passage, movement, and spatially engendered and contingent identity points to links among narrative, reading, authorship, and architecture. As Leslie Kanes Weisman claims, "space, like language, is socially constructed; and like the syntax of language, the spatial arrangements of our buildings and communities reflect and reinforce the nature of gender, race, and class relations in society" (1992, 2). The ambivalent conclusion of Kuncewicz's story constructs home as an "architextual" location—a meeting space for gendered collective and individual narratives of postnationalistic, cross-cultural memory and identity. As Mary Ann Caws defines it in her work on surrealism and poetics, the term "architexture" means to "call attention to the surface texture of the construction made by reading." She emphasizes that the interplay between the "concept of origin and that of the building process"—so vital in architecture—is crucial to the reader's passages through texts, which, like buildings, are always placed and constructed in the context of other structures/texts. Caws claims that reading itself functions as "performance and as passage . . . in relation to texts of exchange and city-scapes of passage" (1981, xiv–xv). Hence it is possible to claim that cultural meanings and narratives of gendered identity attach themselves to physical forms, such as Wanda's *house* in Kuncewicz's story, while these forms arise as encrypted with the changing relationships of power and ideologies that erected them and assigned or banned their dwellers.

But when considered on the level of national identity, woman's home is a questionable architextual location. Virginia Woolf famously wrote in *Three Guineas,* "As a woman I have no country. As a woman I want no country. As a woman my country is the whole world" (1966, 109). Like Woolf, postcolonial critic Madan Sarup links the notions of home, nation, and identity to those of forced and willful exile and migration and emphasizes their narrative aspect: "the story we tell of ourselves . . . is also the story others tell of us" (1994, 95). But are these two telling the same story? Perhaps who we are and where our true home is cannot be so easily articulated, even to ourselves because, as Kristeva (1994, 286) reminds us, we are all strangers in our own house. To Sarup, in addition to being the stuff of narrative, "identities are not free-floating, they are limited by borders and boundaries" (1994, 95). What is more, "[h]ome and language tend to be taken for granted; like Mother or Woman, they are often naturalized and homogenized" (Minh-ha 1994, 14).[19]

Minh-ha also claims that "figuratively but also literally speaking, traveling back and forth between home and abroad becomes a mode of dwelling" (1994, 15). This arises from the discursive notion of identity, that "product of articulation . . . [a] politics rather than an inherent marking" (14). And if, as in Kuncewicz's story, metaphors of place and movement help to explain identity as a dynamic, discursive process, then maybe the best location of one's home can be found *inside* that process of constant, traveling self (re)making. Perhaps it can be glimpsed as one of the points of reference by which one can gauge one's passage toward one's home-in-the-self.

Fig. 3. Beata Wehr, *Nomadic Life* (mixed media on board, 24 × 24 cm)

From Home for the Masses to Autobiography in Motion

Maria Kuncewicz wrote about home and Poland from within that peculiar condition of Cold War exile in the West. Those writers who remained behind the Iron Curtain had to contend with state-made definitions of dwelling and identity, not to mention the dictates of the ruling ideology. Adam Ważyk's once widely publicized and now forgotten socialist-realist poem about the Palace of Culture and Science in Warsaw centers on the monumental, "wedding cake" building that was a "gift" to People's Poland from Joseph Stalin and the Soviet Union in 1955.[20] Ważyk's strained paean illustrates how the overawed gaze of the beholder transforms Stalin's skyscraper into an architectural hybrid of the past, present, and future:

> Not ours were the walls
> of our architecture,
> palaces mortared with blood
> those poor man's efforts . . .
> without heart and beauty . . .
> And so differently from the rubble
> is now growing, to grow into socialism,
> with common rooms and libraries—
> our old town's gothic,
> our renaissance and baroque,
> our stern monument,
> our lacy pediment,
> like by seamstress's needle embroidered,
> and so differently over it flashes
> the roof tile that our heart touches.[21]

The roof tile flashing as bright as hope for a better future in the socialist country—which has survived centuries of feudal and more recently, interwar capitalist oppression—symbolizes a mass-oriented, collective homeland. It is a beacon calling to the onlooker and touching his or her heart like a quasi-religious vision.[22] The poem brings together three important ideological elements: proletarian anger at past class injustices embodied in traditional architecture and urban spaces, individual longing for the comforts and spirituality of the mythic home, and dreams about the idealized, utopian home-nation that is being constructed for the New Man and the proletarian masses. Like the political system that created it, this socialist home/palace is a process rather than a fixed concept, a dialectic progression toward a distant horizon—a construction site, rather than a romantic contemplation from within.[23]

Positioned on the dubiously famous largest square in Europe, Stalin's Palace is an architextual form that may best represent the post-1989 paradoxes of home and homelessness in Poland and Eastern Europe. As one of the most ideologically charged buildings in Polish national memory, it is not only an architectural form but also a repository, if not a textbook, of diverse collective and individual narratives of national identity. At the same time, it has

Fig. 4. Palace of Culture and Science in Warsaw under construction

always been a symbol of Poland's political homelessness during the Cold War. As Wojciech Tomasik argues, Warsaw is the "central focus in Polish symbolic space" (1999, 67), which makes it possible to see the centrally located Palace, no matter how controversial in its origin, as the main architectural representation through which the Polish capital and the whole culture continually (re)define and (re)imagine themselves.[24] As Marta Zielińska remarks, it is a locus of complex paradoxes that reflect those of Polish culture. It is a communist monument derisively nicknamed Peking, but also the consecrated space where Pope John Paul II held the first publicly broadcast mass in a communist country. As a cultural center that housed theaters, cinemas, museums, lecture halls, and the famous Congress Hall with the largest stage in the capital, the Palace also provided space for lofty intellectual pursuits and mass entertainment during the Cold War. It symbolized the Soviet domination and socialist "cultural politics" until 1989, only to have become an international trade headquarters for postcommunist Eastern Europe. Stalin's Palace now houses Coca-Cola Poland, expensive department stores, and "Queen's," a casino (Zielińska 1995, 26–27, 9–10).

Like many others in Poland, I grew up both hating and somehow liking the Palace. The latter sentiment is hard to acknowledge, as it is not very popular among some "native" Varsovians, who regard the rest of Poland as the provinces, and who used to make fun of country bumpkins herded through the Palace on compulsory school, factory, or farmers' collective trips. But by the time I was born, Stalin's high-rise was a fixed landmark, and I cannot imagine Warsaw and Poland without it. It was "our only skyscraper," as some other Varsovians and many Poles shyly-proudly proclaimed, no matter the mandatory May Day parades in front of it that were broadcast ad nauseam on both Polish TV channels every year. After all, as the highest building in the country, it was a spectacle to behold and its American-derived architectural form gave one a foretaste of those other metropolises beyond the Atlantic known only from the movies—New York, Chicago, Los Angeles, San Francisco.

As a historic landmark, the form was an abhorrent, haunting, Soviet-made eyesore, an evil growth on the body of the city that we loved. In the context of the Cold War geopolitical divisions of power, it symbolized a profound sense of homelessness and alienation that was part of the everyday experience of living in colonized Poland.[25] Its phallic grandiosity often matched the extent to which many Poles, and especially women, often felt beaten down, exploited, and inferior, for how dislocated many artists felt in their own country, in which the only intellectual refuge was offered by ambivalent internal exile.

Its construction compelled a brutal erasure of a prominent residential district that before the war marked the coming together of Warsaw's two distinct worlds: Jewish and Catholic (Zielińska 1995, 11). Indeed, its location where a part of the Warsaw Ghetto used to be seems to emphasize that the Jewish Warsaw—once the second-largest Jewish city in the world, after New York—has been erased beyond reconstruction not only by the Holocaust, but also by ideologically charged postwar urbanism.[26] The Palace's erection forced the resettlement of hundreds of families from the area that had to be demolished, and cost the lives of many workers due to the breakneck pace of its construction. And as much as the Palace is currently adapting to the brave new world of free-market economy, its chameleonlike presence continues to impart a poignant lesson on renewed homelessness to some Poles, who feel that its new corporate tenants symbolize yet another form of colonization.

However, beyond the tragedies of national history and politics, to me the Palace also signified possibilities for alternative modes of dwelling and self-realization in the culture of Cold War Poland. Bożena Mądra-Shallcross emphasizes, "the situation of 'dwelling in' is an existential necessity that grows out of the need for shelter or even camouflage for newly emerging intimacy and its secrets, which allow the budding of the first marks of individuality" (1992, 13). As a student of English at Warsaw University, I decided that the capital city could be my only home in Poland. On a paradoxical, personal level, it was the Palace that symbolized for me some bizarre materiality of freedom that I felt, having moved to Warsaw from my "original" home in the much smaller city of Kielce. The Palace was too big to be true, but it was real; it housed the Party congresses, but also the first Rolling Stones concert; it had a good bookstore and hosted an international book fair every May, which brought some forbidden titles to that temple of socialist public culture. The structure's architectural weirdness, decorative lavishness, and scale made it impossible to see it as a whole with the naked eye. Only fragments, fractured splinters of facade, crenellation, and colonnade could be caught from the human level. When one stood at its base, one could not look at the Palace, but only see the "empty space of the other three parts of the world" (Zielińska 1995, 11).

Fig. 5. A. Kossobudzki-Orłowski, *The Palace and the City*

That was very exciting to me, for the empty spaces could be filled and explored, just as the splintered fragments could be put together into constructions of my own making. It is true that such home-and-identity making arose from a partial blocking (Soviet bloc-ing) of my vision by what the Palace represented, but it also opened up and made even more attractive the unobstructed vistas of the imagination and the world "out there." Kaja Silverman stresses that the "human eye cannot simply be taken at face value. In addition to being the locus of visual perception, it is the faculty through which the image is appropriated in the guise of 'self'" (1996, 163). "My" Palace remained burned into my retina; I saw Warsaw and my homeland through it when I was leaving them in 1987 for the United States and the halls of American academe. It was the last building I could see from the plane circling over Warsaw nearly fifteen years ago. Now, I sometimes see myself as perpetually circling it whenever I try to answer how much of who I am today has been made by what now is taught in Polish schools as the "communist period" in Polish history and culture.

(Lest this be read as an instance of narcissistic authorial exorcism of the past, I want to recall autobiography-affirming work by Susan Rubin Suleiman and Stuart Hall. The latter claims that in order to absolve ourselves from the "burdens of representation" as ethnic critics, we often need to resort to speaking autobiographically: "Autobiography is usually thought of as seizing the authority of authenticity. But in order not to be authoritative, I've got to speak autobiographically" [Hall 1992, 277].)

Around 1988, I was invited to talk about the situation of women in Poland to a seminar of students and realized that some of them may have seen me through Stalin's Palace too, as it were. Telling them that I could only speak for myself, I was face to face with that "burden of representation" as a live specimen from the Other Europe. As such, I realized that, to some in my audience, my body was also supposed to have been marked by my home, that is, according to how Eastern European women's bodies were stereotypically represented in American media or such venues as the *National Geographic*. When, after a pleasant discussion, one of the clearly surprised students told me that I seemed "so young and well groomed," I felt as if I had somehow failed her in upholding the representations of ethnic Polish womanhood that she took for granted. Suleiman's claim that as a critic one always faces "risking who one is" drove home this experience in self-(re)presentation and intercultural dialogue. Because I was born under communism, I am often seen here as having come from a "red" country, and will be seen as such for at least as long as the stereotypical Cold War representations of gender will circulate in the minds of those who look at me. The problem is that I cannot simply go back to Poland and disappear into my "original" home there, either. I don't fit in any more. My mother often tells me that I have become too Americanized, even though I never got rid of my accent.

From the other side of the Atlantic, where I am now trying to feel more rooted after years of nomadic living, David Kranes defines home as a space that combines the illusion of escape with that of power: "Home is what, at heart, we always hope to get-away to. We are all seeking to inhabit that space which most empowers us, which feels most rewarding, most secure, most natural, most intimate" (1995, 93). His idea seems to presume a strict separation between the private and the public aspects of dwelling. Home is the intimate realm, whereas everything else that surrounds it is the alien world out there, over which we have no control, and which is somewhat "unnatural." Home, Kranes emphasizes, "feels centered—as though there were a strong and clear vertical axis going up its core and around which all 'home life' revolves" (94). We rush through alienating public spaces to get home and feel the safe enclosure of what Christopher Lasch (1995) calls "haven in a heartless world," to revolve around that safe core that provides us with a sense of belonging and thus our identity.[27]

Kranes's notion does not include the impact of gender,[28] race, ethnicity, or national identity on one's perception of home and one's perception of the public and private spaces in this country of many homeless people, urban sprawl, gentrified communities, and desperate, impoverished inner cities. How can we be ready to coexist happily in the multicultural or polycultural world, when we cannot do so at home?[29] In posttotalitarian Warsaw, a similar situation begins to develop, as the new and old rich flee into gated communities and everybody is afraid to walk the streets alone after dark. In another seemingly parallel cultural process, Polish right-wing spokespeople often blame the "new woman"—the antidomestic feminist—for this disappearance of safety and stability once provided by the traditional, mythical home. Reactionary nostalgia for what has never been seems to travel freely between the East and West.

Fig. 6. Beata Wehr, *My Home = My Homes,* book no. 16, 1997 (mixed media, 14 × 9 cm)

Taking Sites, or the (New) Woman's P(a)lace

According to bell hooks, "Representation is a crucial location of struggle for any exploited and oppressed people asserting subjectivity and decolonization of the mind" (1995, 3). Western feminist theory has yet to discover the Other Europe and include it as an exciting Second World location and partner in dialogue, although critics like Susan Stanford Friedman and Rosi Braidotti have theorized various international "mappings," "nomadic" subjectivities, and "[trans]cultural encounters."[30] Few scholars of Europe take into consideration too that its real geographic center is in Belarus, and even fewer ponder what such a dislocation of European identity into the realm of its Other might bring about into the discussions on the issues of race, gender, ethnicity, and nationality.

Irit Rogoff claims that the "processes of unsettling geographic, spatial, and spectatorial cultural identity are always, though with varying degrees of consciousness, gender coded and differentiated." She proposes that we "replace a discussion of geography or place with the notion of 'site,' which is fluid and contingent and in which discourses of place, space, positionality, and vision are mutually informing and constitutive. . . . This 'site' is not only the one in which one is located and viewed in relation to the world but also the one from which one looks out at the world as bearer of a located gaze" (1996, 193–94). Being thus "doubly conscious" in our vision—to reiterate and recontextualize W. E. B. DuBois's notion of African American double self-vision in the post-totalitarian context—means to be able to look both outside of one and inward, to see oneself through the eyes of others. It also implies and compels being able to transform one's invisibility into creative expression—what has been the lot of marginalized cultures, women, and ethnic minorities for centuries. In my "chronotope of the local," Polish women artists feature as powerful makers of profound, gendered home sites. I would like to end this inquiry with a brief look at the lives and work of two different women who have creatively transformed the narrative and visual representations of the Palace in Warsaw.

Zofia Kulik's Power of Looking

The first bearer of the "located gaze" is an internationally recognized artist, Zofia Kulik, whose photographic collages, installations, and happenings have

Fig. 7. Zofia Kulik, *Self-Portrait with the Palace*, 1990 (60 × 50 cm), private collection

been among the most provocative art spanning the Cold War era and the present. Kulik's work focuses on fragmented and splintered bodies and sexual, communist, and religious symbols that play on the borders, or in Homi Bhabha's "in-between space[s]" of multivalent cultural discourse. The clashing narratives of (en)gendered Polishness that emerge from various types of her prolific production invite readings located in the overlapping terrains, where woman is interrogated by feminist theory, postcolonial and posttotalitarian studies, as well as cultural studies, architecture, and literary theory. In Kulik's art, these readings are generated and reinvented, they meet, collide, shift, and intersect with one another in the spaces that seem to subvert conventional habitation, spectatorship, and performativity.

Kulik's *Self-Portrait with the Palace*[31] has been described as a powerful site of "memory [which] may take the form of a cultural montage shaped by the scissors of personal experience" (Lajer-Burchardth 1996, 120). It features a nude female body framed with an oval, labialike, "full-body" halo like those surrounding images of the Virgin Mary. The woman stands erect in the center and in both hands, which cover her abdomen, holds a spearlike flag finial. A large red star rests on the tip of the spear and spreads across her chest. A twelve-point white star shines from between her knees. Above her head, turned upside-down as if to imitate the familiar images of the Holy Spirit as a white dove, the Palace hangs, its spire pointed at her head. Against the black background float four male bodies draped in white sheets. The upper two reach toward the Palace, as if trying to support it; the lower two, kneeling, seem to be falling away from the woman's halo or trying to hold onto it.

The image is a seductive, carefully staged, rigidly ordered collage of seemingly incompatible and chaotically coexisting symbols, concepts, and images of Polishness. Like the Palace, it is a hybrid of past and present; like architecture, it stages and presents the (dis)orders of multiple national histories and identities. Kulik's woman-site multiplies and domesticates impossible dichotomies—female sexuality *and* virgin motherhood, the phallic masculine heroism of Cold War monuments *and* the vulnerable bodies of the male figures (which evoke Jesus resurrected,), rituals of the Catholic Church *and* those of communism, Stalin's Palace *and/as* the Holy Ghost. By doing so, she offers an excess of symbols and narratives that lurk beyond the superficial order of the composition. The artist herself refuses to comment much on her work: "I . . . say . . . little and not very well, especially in public —[I am] nearly a mute. I am profoundly concentrated on looking."[32] Kulik's muted images speak volumes on the politics of state-controlled desire. One is drawn into them and has to look at them intensely and closely, while interrogating one's own assumptions about gender and power. And no matter what one takes to be the "masculine" or "feminine" in Kulik's art, the State looms over every viewer's interpretation like the Palace in *Self-Portrait.* Lajer-Burchardth emphasizes Kulik's innovative ways of presenting "a certain masquerade of gender secured by a specific logic of desire at the core of the Communist subjective ideal . . . [her] metaphoric relation between the Communist subject and the State which she thereby reveals to be essentially masochistic" (1996, 126).

Like *Self-Portrait with the Palace,* Kulik's other works featuring this form—*The Guardians of the Spire* and *May Day Mass,* for example—provocatively juxtapose and reinterpret the interpenetration of gendered narratives, political symbols, religious histories, and representations implicit in socialist-realist architecture. At the same time they make palpable the realities of the spaces and bodies once framed by this architecture. Their loaded narrative content invites close reading as careful looking, while their self-referential technique—layering, multiple exposures, images within images—invites the viewer to see them as both windows into the past and mirrors for their present identities.

Kulik's series *Idioms of the Soc-Ages,* features a performance exhibit in which the artist herself is imprisoned between the images of the Palace of Culture while a housewife burdened with heavy shopping bags looks on (Kulik n.d., 15). At the end the artist can be freed from the contraption, but only after her hair has been partially cut off, a part of her body having been incorporated into the structure. Kulik explains that she uses the constricting "soc-form" to practice artistic freedom and confront her fear of subordination (a statement with which bell hooks would undoubtedly agree). Her work reveals and deconstructs some of the ways in which visual culture impacts the stories women tell about themselves as prisoners of, as well as dwellers in, and beholders and transformers of gendered spaces under socialism and beyond (some of her most powerful work deconstructing socialist-realism dates after 1989). In Kulik's works, female bodies, often phallic, sometimes powerfully built and "masculine," sometimes androgynous, are usually juxtaposed with more vulnerable, and "splintered," male ones that often come repeated, refracted, and reflected in intricate patterns like those of prayer rugs.

The women, many of whom are the self-portraits of the artist, seem to play with those cookie-cutter images—a bit butch, sexy, muscular, and androgynous—of females from socialist-realist posters or those sculptures

Fig. 8. Zofia Kulik, *The Guardians of the Spire*, 1990 (240 × 150 cm, 12 panels), private collection

adorning the external niches of the Palace in Warsaw.[33] Even today, they have an empowering, feminist appeal, no matter how much the ideology that constructed their representations subordinated and victimized many living women. Homi Bhabha's notion of writing the nation resonates interestingly with Kulik's gendered and embodied illustrations:

> The current metaphor of landscape as the inscape of national identity emphasizes the quality of light, the question of social visibility, the power of the eye to naturalize the rhetoric of national affiliation and its forms of collective expression. There is, however, always the distracting presence of another temporality that disturbs the contemporaneity of the national present . . . a narrative struggle. . . . National time becomes concrete and visible in the chronotope of the local, particular, graphic, from beginning to end. (1990, 295)[34]

Textually and visually, Kulik's works, much like Kuncewicz's writings, break down the old concepts of Polish female identity and engender new ones. In Kulik's art in particular, this identity seems to have been tinted, or "colored" in a way that paradoxically echoes the inevitably racialized representations and perceptions of Third World female identities described in the epigraph that begins this chapter. In both Kulik and Kuncewicz, the red hue of the so-called system or regime impacts individual self-perception and self-representation, as well as compelling external readings of the Eastern European woman as Other. Being from or living in a socialist or communist country becomes thus a gendered identity aspect that challenges the notions of universal European whiteness, as it links the construction of Eastern European ethnicities to the consequences of the geopolitical divisions of power in the region.

Kuncewicz's and Kulik's autobiographical art in transit demonstrates how autobiographical representations of female identity are contingent on the metaphorics of space, location, and movement in the complex, alternative home spaces of Polishness. While pointing out links between the visual and the literary, their works enable creative readings of liminal narrative spaces—what Susan Stanford Friedman (1998, 3) terms "the interstitial site of interaction, interconnection, and exchange"—where Polish women's posttotalitarian, postsocialist identity is contested, recreated, invented, and performed. Kuncewicz's and Kulik's Poland emerges as a complex homeland,

Fig. 9. The palace, external detail; a sculpture of a woman (photo by author)

an in-between interpretive space that challenges the dichotomies of home and exile, East and West, self and other, public and private, and even male and female. While impacted by the fact of their existence and power to shape human destinies, these artists' powerful visions transcend national and cultural boundaries.

Chronicling the Nation

The second bearer of the located gaze, with whose story I would like to close this meditation on home in Polish visual culture, literature, and autobiography in motion, is Hanna Szczubełek, who for over thirty years has been the chronicler of the Palace of Culture and Science in Warsaw. I interviewed her in her small office on the fifteenth floor of that gigantic building, where she presides over a magnificent panorama of the city. While smoking ferociously and pulling out of a black wardrobe gypsum statues of Soviet architects, indecent cartoons of the building, and leather-bound, original chronicles of the Palace, she told me a story that seems like a good conclusion to mine.

When, early in her career, she was interviewed about her occupation, which placed her in the belly of the beast, so to speak, she trusted a journalist with an unofficial joke about the building that had been circulating around Warsaw in the early sixties: Where is the best view of Warsaw? From the top of the Palace of Culture, because you can't see the damn Palace from there! The journalist, betraying Szczubełek's trust, published the joke, which nearly caused the young chronicler to lose her job.

No matter how trivial it may seem now, this incident illustrates yet another important instance of gendered signification. The transgression of the joke was not so much its explicit critique of the aesthetic value of the Palace as an architectural form, but its implicit desire to rid the city of the atrocious phallic building that symbolized the Soviet domination over Poland. Having come from a woman whose chronicler's role was to guard and reproduce, if not "mother," as it were, the narratives about it, the joke also betrayed the idea of the Palace as a symbol of the socialist home. Not to mention that Szczubełek failed as an ideological guardian of the "House of Culture," rather than supporting it proudly like that famous nameless female in the sculpture by Mukhina, which represents a female worker from a collective farm who is raising an arm interlocked with that of a male industrial worker.

Between her private and public chronicles, Hanna Szczubełek spun anecdotes and fairy tales about the Palace. She pointed out that the unexpectedly luxurious design and execution of the "proletarian" spaces inside it allowed for paradoxical dreams and fantasies about "orientalized" opulence and sensuality for the Soviet architects and other "lovers" of the Palace. (A single woman with, one might say, an alternative personality, Szczubełek herself has been described as having been married to the building, which emphasizes her domesticated role as the keeper of its stories.) She was not ashamed of her liking for the structure and she revealed the interesting ways in which the folklore that had grown up around it had made it into a romanticized national fetish. The Palace could also be seen as a sort of ambivalently eroticized space. Rather tragically, it has been the site of several suicides, and, on a lighter note, its rest rooms, the most luxurious in the country, provided a refuge for homeless lovers of all sexual orientations.

Between Szczubełek's serious stories, lewd cartoons, and hilarious anecdotes, the building began to take on a life of its own, to sport an oral patina independent of the ideological scenarios prescribed for it. But it remained ordinary; "It's just a place to work, you know," Szczubełek shrugged at some point. I thought she might have been understating her loyalty, as did other people on the building's staff—those who tend to it see the Palace as ordinary and yet feel quietly proud of their long service and familial ties to each other. Like Szczubełek, many staff members have been faithfully taking care of the colossus for over twenty years.

At the end of our meeting, Szczubełek gave me a metal pin made in 1955 for the builders of the Palace. In gold letters running around a bright rendering of the Palace against a powder blue sky, it said, "Erector of the Palace of Culture and Science of Joseph Stalin."[35] An Erector? Me? Well, why not? Marked or endowed with it, I felt included in a serious effort of cultural and architectural reappropriation.

As I was leaving, I thought again about that joke that nearly cost Szczubełek her job over thirty years ago. Seen or not, the Palace is always there. Like the dream of home, it is both a poignant absence and an overwhelming presence, a sign of desire for self-signification that we pursue but can never catch up with. Its implicit invitation is to be a process, to embrace identity as change and keep climbing, *not* to the top of the world, but into ourselves and toward others, beyond borders and cultural divides. For that reason, I feel it is good to be in transit, to be at home in the world.

Notes

All translations are mine, unless noted otherwise. All images reproduced in this chapter are used by permission of the authors and copyright holders.

1. I am aware that this can be said of almost any kind of creative expression, but genre exploration is not the aim of this chapter.

2. Beata Wehr, *In Transit,* mixed-media book no. 23 (21 × 21 × 4 cm.), Tucson, March 1998. Wehr's production belongs to the genre of artist's books; its pages are wire and canvas; its spine has a metal wheel attached to it.

3. *Webster's New Universal Unabridged Dictionary* defines *kinesthesis* thus: "[Gr. *kinein,* to move and *aistheēsis,* perception] the sensation of position, movement, tension, etc. of parts of the body, perceived through nerve end organs in muscles, tendons, and joints." In the light of Wehr's art, my own (im)migrant experience, and the larger, post-1989 processes of change in Eastern Europe and the world, this word aims to draw attention to movement and bodily perception in socially constructed space.

4. Doina Petrescu (1999, 2000) has emphasized the need for such readings of Eastern European cultures.

5. See esp. Bachelard's point about "reading" architectural spaces (1994, 14–15), and his claim that "a house constitutes a body of images that give mankind proofs or illusions of stability" in the "veritable psychology of the house" that is based on two principal themes that are especially important for my argument: "1) A house is imagined as a vertical being . . . [and] 2) . . . as a concentrated being [that] appeals to our consciousness of centrality" (17). Jamieson states, "perhaps postmodern architecture is the property of literary critics . . . and textual in more ways than one" (1991, 99). In Caws, see esp. her introduction (1981, xiv–xv).

6. I realize that the theoretical underpinnings of my larger subject are enormous. The limited size and scope of this chapter has prompted me to focus on a wider selection of primary material rather than engage in lengthy theoretical discussions. Such a move is a conscious choice, for it allows me to sketch my argument in broader strokes and introduce less-known examples from Polish culture and my own experience.

7. See Zaborowska 1995.

8. Irit Rogoff argues for linking identity, home, and visual culture: "Geographies have . . . become a great deal more than the scientific location and articulation of the natural world; they are now also a euphemism for concepts of 'home,' 'emplaced

culture,' and 'embodied identity,' which need to be broken down if the complexity of current conditions is to be engaged with and problematized within visual culture" (1996, 193). Rogoff's claim about territorial contingency of the notion of home provides an interesting context for a discussion of its cross-cultural semantics locally and globally. In Poland, it is interesting to observe the ways in which the household-brand advertisements seem to be bringing into people's homes a whiff of multiethnic visual culture that may appeal to local consumers. At the same time, the majority of these advertisements focus on uniform, Western notions of the spatial organization of home and rely on the so-called globalized, commercialized, corporate marketing idiom that in fact erases local differences of site, climate, terrain, and privacy.

9. As in other European countries, women in Poland have been historically relegated to the social and political margin, although they have been mythologized as embodiments of national and spiritual virtue. Always expected to support their men and country, to adorn and nurture their families and temples, they have been objects of ideological contests between church and state, but have rarely been allowed to speak for themselves. This generalization about Polish history and culture does not intend to exclude "nontraditional" Polish women—lesbians, Jews, Roma, Protestants, atheists, and other "others"—but only to signal a few superficial patterns.

For recent explorations of female identity, otherness, and Polish culture see Janion 1996, Walczewska 1999, Borkowska 1996.

10. For my purposes, *house* and *home* will be used interchangeably as spatial concepts, metaphors, and signifiers of location, although I am aware that one could write a separate study concerning semantic and cultural differences between these terms.

11. I am grateful to Jeffrey C. Goldfarb (1989) for coining the term "post-totalitarian mind" long before anybody thought that we could actually live to see the collapse of communism in Europe.

12. Although there has been a wealth of scholarship in English on the sociological, political, and economic aspects of the post-1989 period, few works detailing new developments and East-West exchanges in the arts and humanities have appeared so far. Among them, see Radel 2001, Kennedy 1994, Verdery 1996 and 1999, Verdery and Burawoy 1999, Lajer-Burchardth 1996, Petrescu 1999 and 2000, Zagajewski 1995, and Zaborowska 2001b.

13. Interestingly, even this author does not break down the idea of Europe but refers to it as a universally empowered cultural monolith.

14. The map "functions as a mirror of the world, not because the representation of the earth has the status of a natural sign, but because it aims to invoke a simulacrum of an always inaccessible totality by means of an arrangement of symbols" (Rabasa 1995, 358).

15. In his reading of Mercator's *Atlas,* Rabasa also links Eurocentric notions of humanism to "seeing" history: "The personification of geographic space in terms of

a Eurocentric perspective is inseparable from the . . . definition of history as a visual function: 'the eye of the World'" (1995, 361). See also Radhakrishnan 1996.

16. I am referring to Kundera's argument not so much to endorse his idea of Central Europe, which I find problematic, but to emphasize the political and cultural indifference of Western Europe toward its "other" countries. Nevertheless, Kundera's longing for a united "Europe," where the only recognized marker of difference is nationality, is obviously reductive and essentialist. His desire for a lost paradise of happily cultured Europe that never existed seems especially out of touch with reality at a time when the continent of Goethe and Napoleon is finally having to acknowledge and deal with the challenges of multiculturalism and centuries-long legacies of racism and colonialism. See Kundera 1991, 221, 223. See also Petrescu 2000.

17. See Kennedy 1994, introduction.

18. On Soviet Orientalism, see for example Castillo 1997, 34. Castillo's discussion of Orientalism could be seen in a wider context still, given the *internal*, East-West tensions within the Soviet bloc countries. See also Zaborowska 2001a.

19. See also Hoffman 1990 for an in-depth autobiographical account of the joys and terrors of transcultural and translinguistic domestication.

20. Obviously, Stalin had been dead for two years by 1955, but the cultural and political thaw following his demise didn't come to Poland until 1956. The name of Stalin was removed from the building then and the monumental sculpture of him that was to be placed in front of the building never saw the light of day.

21. Courtesy of Hanna Szczubełek. The original: "Nie nasze były mury / naszej architektury, krwią zlepione pałace, / te ubogiego prace . . . bez serca i urody. . . .

A inaczej ze zwalisk / rośnie, by wróść w socjalism / dla świetlic i bibliotek— / nasz staromiejski gotyk, /nasz renesans i barok, / nasz monument surowy, / nasz fronton koronkowy, / jak spod igły hafciarek, / inaczej nad nim błyska / dachówka sercu bliska."

22. From the ground one cannot actually see the tiles on the Palace's roof, if there are any.

23. It is important to note the literary discourses surrounding the Palace, which should be the subject of a separate study. See Zielińska 1995 and Tomasik 1999, 39, 41–42, 47, 53–56. Tomasik notes that Polish architecture and literature were welded closely together at that time. The task of the former to organize space was seen as instrumental in constructing the "new man" and the "new society," while the latter, as "the leader among the arts," was to express and propagate both products. See also Åman 1992, who claims that no other building in post-war Poland "incurred so much criticism, inspired so much revulsion" (125). For more background on the Palace and its historic, architectural, and cultural contexts see also Dąbrowski 1953, Goldzamt 1956, Kroker and Kroker 1991, Tarkhanov and Kavtaradze 1992, Schmidt 1997, and Tazbir 1996.

The discourses about the Palace as the House of Culture for the masses were meant to obliterate the notion of the bourgeois home and the cult of individuality.

Unlike the nineteenth-century artists, those required to practice socialist realism had to subscribe to the notions of space and home as serving the collective. For a study of homes of Romantic artists, see Mądra-Shallcross 1992.

24. See Zaborowska 1998.

25. In psychosexual terms, the building's phallic presence (see Hayden 1977) embodied Stalin's power as a deliberately planted erection that penetrated, impaled, and subordinated "feminized" Poland, whose position in the Soviet bloc as a body, so to speak, was that of a satellite. Locally, its construction cost lives, uprooted thousands of people, and erased one of the most prominent (largely) Jewish neighborhoods in central Warsaw. In the larger firmament of the Cold War's macho struggle between East and West for hegemony, it symbolized Soviet occupation and Poland's insignificance, for there could be only *two* major adversaries in world politics, countries with acronyms rather than names: USSR and USA. Poland, Hungary, Bulgaria, or Czechoslovakia were spectators, prizes to be awarded one of the big guys after the showdown was over.

26. There are actually efforts to rebuild and return some Jewish spaces to Warsaw. See Zaborowska 2001b.

27. I realize that the issue of gender, or "woman's place," should be addressed at this point, but I am deliberately leaving this discussion for the next section of the paper.

28. On the scarcity of coverage on the gendering of national identity and nationalism, see Sharpe 1996, 97–98.

29. I am not discussing the term *multicultural* here due to lack of space. See Prashad 2000, 110–14 for an illuminating discussion of some of its problems.

30. Perhaps it is instructive to think here about Mary McLeod's statement that the "feminine is different in different places" (1996a, 9) and that the dichotomy between First and Third Worlds does not reflect all, and actually reduces some, important complexities of the polytcultural world. See also McLeod 1996b on the architectural readings of Foucault's theory of otherness.

31. For English-language sources, see Kulik 1997, 1999, and n.d.

32. Letter to the author, 8 November, 1998.

33. In yet another paradoxical accident of cross-cultural translation or symmetry, America's Rosie the Riveter might fit this description too.

34. See also Bhabha: "In the production of the nation as narration there is a split between the continuist, accumulative temporality of the pedagogical, and the repetitious, recursive strategy of the performative. It is through this process of splitting that the conceptual ambivalence of modern society becomes the site of writing the nation" (1990, 297).

35. These pins were never actually given out, as by the time they were ready, the building had shed Stalin's name following the dismantling of the cult of personality.

Works Cited

Alexander, Meena. 1996. *The Shock of Arrival: Reflections on Postcolonial Experience.* Boston: South End Press.

Åman, Anders. 1992. *Architecture and Ideology in Eastern Europe during the Stalin Era: An Aspect of Cold War History.* Trans. R. K. Tanner. Cambridge: MIT Press.

Bachelard, Gaston. 1964. *The Poetics of Space.* Trans. Maria Jolas. Boston: Beacon Press.

Betsky, Aaron. 1997. *Queer Space: Architecture and Same-Sex Desire.* New York: Morrow.

Bhabha, Homi K. 1990. "DissemiNation: Time, Narrative, and the Margins of the Modern Nation." In *Nation and Narration,* ed. Homi K. Bhabha, 291–322. New York: Routledge.

———. 1994. *The Location of Culture.* London: Routledge.

Bloomer, Jennifer. 1993. *Architecture and the Text: The (S)Crypts of Joyce and Piranesi.* New Haven: Yale University Press.

Borkowska, Grażyna. 1996. *Cudzoziemki: Studia o polskiej prozie kobiecej* (Foreigners: Studies in Polish women's prose). Warsaw : IBL PAN.

Braidotti, Rosie. 1994. *Nomadic Subjects: Embodiment and Sexual Difference in Contemporary Feminist Theory.* New York: Columbia University Press.

Castillo, Greg. 1997. "Soviet Orientalism: Socialist Realism and Built Tradition." *Traditional Dwellings and Settlements Review* 8, 2: 33–47.

Caws, Mary Ann. 1981. *A Metapoetics of the Passage: Architextures in Surrealism and After.* Hanover, N.H.: University Press of New England.

Coleman, Debra, Elizabeth Danze, and Carol Henderson, eds. 1996. *Architecture and Feminism.* New York: Princeton Architectural Press.

Colomina, Beatriz, ed. 1992. *Sexuality and Space.* New York: Princeton Architectural Press.

Crossman, Richard, ed. 1965. *The God That Failed.* New York: Bantam Books.

Dąbrowski, Jan. 1953. *Podniebny pomnik przyjaźni.* Warsaw: Wiedza Powszechna.

Derricotte, Toi. 1997. *The Black Notebooks: An Interior Journey.* New York: Norton.

DuBois, W. E. B. 1999. *The Souls of Black Folk.* Ed. Henry Louis Gates Jr. and Terri Hume Oliver. New York: Norton.

Enloe, Cynthia. 1993. *The Morning After: Sexual Politics at the End of the Cold War.* Berkeley: University of California Press.

Friedman, Susan Stanford. 1998. *Mappings: Feminism and the Cultural Geographies of Encounter.* New York: Princeton University Press.

Goldfarb, Jeffrey C. 1989. *Beyond Glasnost: The Post-Totalitarian Mind.* Chicago: University of Chicago Press.

Goldzamt, Edmund. 1956. *Architektura zespołów śródmiejskich i problemy dziedzictwa* (Architecture of inner city complexes and the problems of heritage). Warsaw: Państwowe Wydawnictwo Naukowe.

Greenblatt, Stephen, István Rév, and Randolph Stern, eds. 1995. *Representations.* Special issue of *Identifying Histories: Eastern Europe before and after 1989* 49 (Winter).

Hall Stuart. 1992. "Cultural Studies and Its Theoretical Legacies." In *Cultural Studies,* ed. Lawrence Grossberg, Cary Nelson, and Paula A. Treichler, 277–94. New York: Routledge.

Hayden, Delores. 1977. "Skyscraper Seduction, Skyscraper Rape." *Heresies* 2: 108–15.

Hoffman, Eva. 1990. *Lost in Translation: A Life in a New Language.* New York: Penguin.

hooks, bell. 1995. *Art on My Mind: Visual Politics.* New York: New Press.

Jamieson, Fredric. 1991. *Postmodernism, or the Cultural Logic of Late Capitalism.* Durham: Duke University Press.

Janion, Maria. 1996. *Kobiety i duch inności* (Women and the spirit of otherness). Warsaw: Wydawnictwo Sic'.

Kennedy, Michael D., ed. 1994. *Envisioning Eastern Europe: Postcommunist Cultural Studies.* Ann Arbor: University of Michigan Press.

Kranes, David. 1995. "Play Grounds." *Journal of Gambling Studies* 11, 1: 91–102.

Kristeva, Julia. 1986. *The Kristeva Reader.* Ed. Toril Moi. New York: Columbia University Press.

———. 1994. *Strangers to Ourselves.* Trans. Leon S. Roudiez. New York: Columbia University Press.

———. 1995. *New Maladies of the Soul.* Trans. Ross Guberman. New York: Columbia University Press.

Kroker, Arthur, and Marilouise Kroker. 1991. *Ideology and Power in the Age of Lenin in Ruins.* New York: St. Martin's Press.

Kulik, Zofia. 1997. *An Iconographic Guide* to "All the Missiles Are One Missile." Warsaw: Zachęta Gallery of Contemporary Art.

———. 1999. *Od Syberii do cyberii/From Siberia to Cyberia,* ed. Piotr Piotrowski. Poznań: Muzeum Narodowe.

———. n.d. *Idiomy socwiecza* (Idioms of the Soc-Ages). Trans. Małgorzata Sady. Warsaw: Zofia Kulik.

Kuncewicz, Maria. 1985. "Dom: Wizja przyszłego fin de siècle'u" (Home: A vision of a future fin de siècle). In *Nowele i bruliony prozatorskie* (Novellas and prose sketches), ed. Helena Zaworska, 291–305. Warsaw: Czytelnik.

———. 1997. *Dyliżans warszawski* (The Warsaw stagecoach). Warsaw: Instytut Wydawniczy PAX.

Kundera, Milan. 1991. "The Tragedy of Central Europe." In *From Stalinism to Pluralism: A Documentary History of Eastern Europe since 1945,* ed. Gale Stokes, 217–23. New York: Oxford University Press.

Lajer-Burchardth, Ewa. 1996. "Old Histories: Zofia Kulik's Ironic Recollections." In *New Histories,* 120–36. Boston: Institute of Contemporary Art.

Landes, Joan B., ed. 1998. *Feminism, the Public and the Private.* Oxford: Oxford University Press.

Lasch, Christopher. 1995. *Haven in a Heartless World: The Family Besieged.* New York: Norton.

Leach, Neil, ed. 1999. *Architecture and Revolution: Contemporary Perspectives on Central and Eastern Europe.* London: Routledge.

Lefebvre, Henri. 1995. *The Production of Space.* Trans. Donald Nicholson-Smith. Oxford: Basil Blackwell.

Mądra-Shallcross, Bożena. 1992. *Dom romantycznego artysty.* (The home of the Romantic artist). Kraków: Wydawnictwo Literackie.

McLeod, Mary. 1996a. "Everyday and 'Other' Spaces." In *Architecture and Feminism,* ed. Debra L Coleman, Elizabeth Ann Danze, and Carol Jane Henderson, 1–37. New York: Princeton Architectural Press.

———. 1996b. "'Other' Spaces and 'Others.'" In *The Sex of Architecture,* ed. Diana Agrest, Patricia Conway, and Leslie Kanes Weisman, 15–28. New York: Abrams.

Minh-ha, Trinh T. 1994. "Other than Myself/My Other Self." In *Travellers' Tales: Narratives of Home and Displacement,* ed. George Robertson et al., 9–26. London: Routledge.

Ockman, Joan. 1996. "Mirror Images: Technology, Consumption, and the Representation of Gender in American Architecture since World War II." In *The Sex of Architecture,* ed. Diana Agrest, Patricia Conway, and Leslie Kanes Weisman, 191–210. New York: Abrams.

Petrescu, Doina. 1999. "The People's House, or the Voluptuous Violence of an Architectural Paradox." In *Architecture and Revolution: Contemporary Perspectives on Central and Eastern Europe,* ed. Neil Leach, 188–95. London: Routledge.

———. 2000. "The Microdynamics of Transition." Paper delivered at the Temple Hoyne Buell Center for the Study of American Architecture at Columbia University, New York, February 25.

Prashad, Vijay. 2000. "The Karma of Brown Folk: .com or .comrade?" Paper presented at the Program in American Culture, University of Michigan, Ann Arbor, October 12.

Rabasa, José. 1995. "Allegories of Atlas." In *The Postcolonial Studies Reader,* ed. Bill Ashcroft, Greta Griffiths, and Helen Tifin, 358–64. New York: Routledge.

Radel, Nicholas F. 2001. "The Transnational Ga(y)ze: Constructing the East European Object of Desire in Gay Film and Pornography after the Fall of the Wall." *Cinema Journal,* Summer.

Radhakrishnan, R. 1996. *Diasporic Mediations: Between Home and Location.* Minneapolis: University of Minnesota Press.

Rogoff, Irit. 1996. "'Other's Others': Spectatorship and Difference." In *Vision in Context: Historical and Contemporary Perspectives on Sight,* ed. Teresa Brennan and Martin Jay, 187–202. New York: Routledge.

Sarup, Madan. 1994. "Home and Identity." In *Travellers' Tales: Narratives of Home and Displacement,* ed. George Robertson et al., 93–104, New York: Routledge.

Schmidt, Johann N. 1997. "Architecture as a Joyride: Postmodern Skyscrapers." In *Emotion in Postmodernism.* American Studies, vol. 74. Ed. Gerhard Hoffmann. Heidelberg: Universitätsverlag C. Winter.

Sharp, Joanne P. 1996. "Gendering Nationhood: A Feminist Engagement with National Identity." In *Bodyspace: Destabilizing Geographies of Gender and Sexuality.* ed. Nancy Duncan, 97–108. London: Routledge.

Silverman, Kaja. 1996. *The Threshold of the Visible World.* New York: Routledge.

Smith, Sidonie. 1993. *Subjectivity, Identity, and the Body: Women's Autobiographic Practices in the Twentieth Century.* Bloomington: Indiana University Press.

Stern, Randolph. 1995. "After the Deluge." Introduction to *Representations,* ed. Stephen Greenblatt, Istvan Rev, Randolph Stern. Special issue of *Identifying Histories: Eastern Europe before and after 1989* 49: 10–13.

Suleiman, Susan Rubin. 1994. *Risking Who One Is: Encounters with Contemporary Art and Literature.* Cambridge, Mass.: Harvard University Press.

Szczygieł, Mariusz. 1991. "Kamienny kwiat" (A stone flower). *Gazeta Wyborcza* 299 (December 24–26): 14–16.

Tarkhanov, Alexei, and Sergei Kavtaradze. 1992. *Architecture of the Stalin Era.* Designed and compiled by Mikhail Anikst. New York: Rizzoli.

Tazbir, Janusz. 1996. "Wojna na pomniki" (War of Monuments). *Polityka* 29, 2046: 3–8.

Tomasik, Wojciech. 1999. *Inżynieria dusz: Literatura realizmu socjalistycznego w planie propagandy monumentalnej.* (Engineering of the soul: Literature of Socialist Realism in the Plan of Monumental Propaganda). Wrocław: Fundacja na Rzecz Nauki Polskiej.

Verdery, Katherine. 1996. *What Was Socialism and What Comes Next?* New York: Princeton University Press.

———. 1999. *The Political Lives of Dead Bodies.* New York: Columbia University Press.

Verdery, Katherine, and Michael Burawoy, eds. 1999. *Uncertain Transition: Ethnographies of Change in the Postsocialist World.* Lanham, Md.: Rowman and Littlefield.

Walczewska, Sławomira. 1999. *Damy, rycerze i feministki* (Ladies, knights, and feminists). Kraków: eFKa.

Weisman, Leslie Kanes. 1992. *Discrimination by Design: A Feminist Critique of the Man-Made Environment.* Chicago: University of Illinois Press.

Wilson, Elizabeth. 1992. *The Sphinx in the City : Urban Life, the Control of Disorder, and Women.* Berkeley: University of California Press.

Woolf, Virginia. 1966. *Three Guineas.* New York: Harcourt Brace Jovanovich.

Zaborowska, Magdalena J. 1995. *How We Found America: Reading Gender through East European Immigrant Narratives.* Chapel Hill: University of North Carolina Press.

———. 1998. "Lire l'esprit post-totalitaire (Engendrer l'autre de l'Europe de l'ouest)." (Reading the post-totalitarian mind [Engendering Western Europe's other]). Trans. Johanne Villeneuve and Roch Duval. In *Le mémoire des déchet: Essais sur la culture et la valeur du passé* (Memory of waste: Essays on objects and images in the economy of the past), ed. Claude Dionne, Brian Neville, and Johanne Villeneuve, 207–26. Québec: Nota bene.

———. 2001a. "The Height of (Architectural) Seduction: Reading the 'Changes' through Stalin's Palace of Culture in Warsaw, Poland." *Journal of Architectural Education* (Cambridge, Mass.: MIT Press) 54, 4 (May).

———. 2001b. "Three Passages through (In)Visible Warsaw." *Harvard Design Magazine*, 13 (Winter/Spring).

Zagajewski, Adam. 1995. *Two Cities: On Exile, History, and the Imagination.* Trans. Lillian Vallee. New York: Farrar, Straus and Giroux.

Zielińska, Marta. 1995. *Warszawa—dziwne miasto* (Warsaw—A strange city). Warsaw: IBL.

PART IV

The Writer's Abode

11 At Home with Sienkiewicz

Beth Holmgren

> Oblęgorek, a locale much admired by [Henryk] Sienkiewicz and his many guests, is situated eighteen kilometers northwest of Kielce. It occupies the southern slope of Ram's Mountain in the Oblęgorek range, which was once covered with beautiful firs, oaks, and beeches. Sienkiewicz settled in this area upon receipt of a "national gift"—a small seventeenth-century estate presented to him by his jubilee committee in 1900 during the festivities celebrating his twenty-five years as a writer. Along with the site Sienkiewicz received a house specially built for him; its character and style are still widely discussed. It stands now, as before, in an old park amid orchards and forests, the silhouette of its round turret rising up over the countryside.
>
> This national gift—a small palace in Oblęgorek—came to house the Henryk Sienkiewicz Museum on October 26, 1958.
>
> —Lidia Putowska and Ireneusz Rębosz, *Muzeum Henryka Sienkiewicza*

Henryk Sienkiewicz (1846–1916) was arguably the most popular of all Polish writers, best loved at home for his trilogy on seventeenth-century imperial Polish history (*With Fire and Sword, The Deluge, Pan Wołodyjowski*), and best remembered internationally for his novel *Quo Vadis.* Sienkiewicz knew only a Poland politically dismembered by the Russian, Prussian, and Austro-Hungarian empires during the partitions; he debuted professionally in the subdued aftermath of the failed 1863 uprising against the authorities in Russian Poland; he entertained and heartened his readers for decades with tales of his nation's heroic past; and he eventually won Poland's first Nobel Prize in 1905. Although he died in a Swiss hotel in 1916, where he had settled his family during the war, his body was reinterred, with great pomp and circumstance, in Warsaw's St. John's Cathedral in 1924—that is, in a newly independent Poland. A number of grand memorials mark Sienkiewicz's life in his homeland, from the alpha of his reconstructed birthplace in Wola Okrzejska to the omega of the museum at Oblęgorek,[1] his last Polish residence. Thus, his "national gift" of Oblęgorek, institutionalized by the postwar Polish state, keeps on giving in perpetuity, a public private home remade into a public museum of Sienkiewicz's ostensibly private life.

"The Museum-House of Genius"

> One of the most perceptive guides to the very essence of a writer's work is the author's home.
>
> —Irvin Haas, *Historic Homes of American Authors*

How should we read the writer's home? What might a home afford or cost its creative residents? For the painter, the sculptor, the writer—for any artist who need not work in collaboration or on location—home matters because it often doubles as a work site, as a study or studio enabling private, concentrated work with the tools of one's trade. At the same time, the housed artist cannot help but be a public presence: Property is visible, tangible, shareable, transferable. What terms might the writer's home set for his or her public existence in the world? And what might it signify once it has become a house of the dead?

Speculating about "the most beautiful house in the world," the architect Witold Rybczynski (1989, 172–80) espies a happy symbiosis between writer and home—that is, for such commercially successful writers in the capitalist West as Mark Twain, Robert Louis Stevenson, and Sir Walter Scott. These artists had "earned" the wherewithal to be exacting and indulgent in their building, and their striking homes flaunted their parity with the rich and powerful of their worlds. The idiosyncratic opulence of Twain's home, which boasted both billiard room and mock steamboat pilothouse, codified the Gilded Age he identified and inhabited. Stevenson's tropical estate, Vailima, ensconced on a mountaintop, asserted his prominence in Samoan society. Scott's rambling Abbotsford resembled nothing so much as a "laird's" fanciful castle and inspired genuine royalty to emulate it.[2]

Of course, not every writer in the West could afford this sort of investment. Even the popular Twain went bankrupt on account of it. Stevenson could erect his barnlike structure only incrementally, as royalties permitted. Scott shouldered his writing as necessary payment for cherished additions, admitting, in a letter to his wife, that Abbotsford's projected library, drawing-room, and "better bedroom . . . will cost me a little hard work to meet the expense, but I have been a good while idle" (quoted in Oman 1973, 254). Rybczynski's examples of happy homeowning artists also may be anomalous in their seemingly unambivalent embrace of bourgeois comfort, if not outright upper-class luxury. Or might it be that their extravagance is a matter of degree rather than type? Donald Horne, writing on the museum, claims that the artist's home, or, as he dubs it, "the museum-house of genius," offers "one of the most bourgeois of all tourist experiences," for it so openly celebrates the values of family and private property. The museum-house renders the dead artist's word furniture rather than flesh: "There is the emphasis on genius itself, and on its manifestation in material objects—the actual pen the genius used, the actual chair on which the genius sat—but to these are added the solid consolations of bourgeois domestic comfort. Whether in the Goethe House, Frankfurt, or the Ivan Vasov House, Sofia, the true interest is not the genius or the work, but possessions and furnishings" (Horne 1984, 122).

The tourist industry worldwide has certainly quantified the profitability, if not the bourgeois essence, of the artist's home, categorizing it as a "heritage attraction" that appeals on account of its "connections with people and events" (Herbert 1995, 32). The artist's home constitutes a variant on the "site-museum" or "museums of history where it happened." Site museums derive, in their housing of the authentic and the great, from medieval places of pilgrimage: "When the pilgrimage habit became secularized, one eventually had the beginnings of visits to historic houses and sites, and indeed of tourism as it is now understood" (Hudson 1987, 38, 145–46). Sorting the phenomenon of the writer's home into the material categories of "museum-homes, biographical museums, commemorative rooms, and literary sections of museums," Małgorzata Kucza-Kuczyńska asserts the superior appeal of the authentic residence, the genius loci (Kucza-Kuczyńska 1986, 5). A trip to the writer's home may indeed signify secular veneration of the dead, high purpose. But a recent comparative study of visitors to Jane Austen's Chawton House and Marcel Proust's residence at Cabourg suggests that the appeal of the artist's residence can be quite wide-ranging, drawing both the "discerning" visitor "who wished to learn more about a particular writer" and the casual tourist sampling the available sights of an attractive place (Herbert 1995, 43, 46). For profit reasons or otherwise, the artist's home as museum has proliferated globally to the extent that the International Committee on Museums established an International Committee on Literary Museums in 1977 to catalogue sites worldwide.[3]

Horne's somewhat facile juxtaposition of the Goethe House with the Ivan Vasov House, across the divide between Western and Eastern Europe, raises a further question about the relative value of the "museum-house of genius." Does the connection between artist and home always belie a bourgeois orientation? What happens to this connection when society itself valorizes neither domestic household nor private ownership? What are we to make of the artist's longing for home in the "unofficial" fictions of Soviet or sovietized societies, the writings that are cozily housed in the English phrase "for the drawer"? One can argue that the poet-doctor's inviting desk in Pasternak's retrospective novel, *Doctor Zhivago,* or the basement sanctuary of Mikhail Bulgakov's Master in *The Master and Margarita,* both imagined in the Stalinist years, merely express their authors' nostalgia for a middle-class lifestyle officially, if not literally, denied. But one might also argue that such nostalgia functions subversively, reclaiming the personal and the domestic in defiance of Stalinist collectivization and mass production (Holmgren 1993, 9–10, 15–23). The Stalinist government did proffer material comfort to its artist-producers, a benefit ostensibly available to all, although it was generally the politically conforming or comfortably classic author who secured apartments and dachas from the patron, the Union of Soviet Writers. Official fiction and the press, however, camouflaged such compromise, accenting instead the altruistic statements of the revolution's early social architects, with their visions of an ideal "home commune" and their predictions of the end "of man's present enslavement to material possessions" (and, with this, the end of the bourgeois home) (Andrusz 1984, 116–18, 125). Such harsh ideals were softened somewhat by conservative wartime propaganda and questioned in the post-Stalin era, but they were never officially dislodged.

At Home in Partitioned Poland

A similar ambivalence—personal sanctity versus bourgeois indulgence, sanctuary versus sell-out—obtains in the phenomenon of the Polish artist's home, in part because the Poles for decades had to abide by the same Soviet doublespeak, in larger part because the home could signify and substitute for so much in Poland's troubled modern history. Because Poland entered the modern era as a largely agricultural society top-heavy with gentry, the twin processes of industrialization and urbanization easily shook its foundations, in many cases impoverishing and dispossessing its landed elite and shifting the locus of home from manor to tenement, or manor to simple peasant hut. The genteel poor, or the shabbily housed intelligentsia, were a feature of the Polish landscape long before a sovietized Polish government socialized the housing market in the early 1950s.[4]

This haphazard redistribution of wealth also stemmed from the conditions of Poland's partition by Russia, Prussia, and Austro-Hungary in the late eighteenth century. Poland's erasure as a sovereign nation utterly dispersed and fragmented its space as homeland. The Polish nation cohered only symbolically and, strange to say, textually; the real space of the nation was pigeonholed in discrete households and buildings or smuggled out into exile for safekeeping. In times of Polish revolt against foreign occupiers, the home was first treated as refuge, consequently marked as target, and finally yielded as spoils. The failure of the 1830 insurrection in the Kingdom of Poland uprooted a number of the most affluent families. The aristocratic conspirators in the 1863 uprising were punished with dispossession and deportation to Siberia. The decline of the Polish gentry was abetted by dissidence as well as extravagance, their manor homes not always gambled away, but sometimes forfeited in a noble cause.

The czarist government in the wake of the 1863 uprising effectively redefined political value in economic terms designed to destroy aristocratic outposts of national rebellion and to exacerbate extant tensions between upper and lower classes, between those who could and those who increasingly could or would not subsidize a rather old-fashioned nationalism. Yet the Russians' economic repression misfired in an interesting way. The post-1863, supposedly apolitical Positivist movement of economic and educational betterment scored real political successes in material measures. If divestment and impoverishment were levied to prevent Polish patriotism, then rebuilding and enrichment signified patriotic resilience and rejuvenation. Rebuilding did entail a kind of class re-formation with the emergence of new industrialists and entrepreneurs, the professionalization (in the happiest cases) of impoverished aristocrats, and the general growth of industry and the market. Whatever its "class" of ownership, however, the Polish home—and the manor home, especially—retained its power as a remnant national symbol, as privatized homeland.

This value particularly accrued to the artist's home in the last decades of partitioned Poland before 1917, not only because the artist seemingly stood above the materialistic fray of late-nineteenth-century class relations, but also on account of what I call the abiding textuality of Polish activism and nationalism. The legacy of Polish Romanticism, which conflated word with deed and recognized the real-life leadership of the bard, or *wieszcz,* combined with external political censorship to make it so. In any public representation or commemoration, the Polish artist substituted for the political leader and was hallowed as the nation's treasure and spokesperson (Holmgren 1998, 150–77). Adam Mickiewicz, the wieszcz incarnate, was most often invoked as symbolic hero and resident. His "bronzification" in printed tributes and erected monuments had spread throughout partitioned Poland by the turn of the century. His museums in Paris and Istanbul sowed the émigré diaspora with deposits of Polish glory in the form of his manuscripts, documents, paintings, statuary, photographs, tokens of esteem, the desk on which he composed his famous poem *Pan Tadeusz,* and even his last Turkish inkwell.[5] I must mention here that the Istanbul museum, which commemorates the poet's death place, had itself to be reconstructed after its destruction in a fire. Here was a national erasure that at last could be reversed, on foreign ground and with private money.

Thus, while the national entity of Poland was not allowed to be in the world, the person and property of its greatest native son could be made forever public, accessible, and material, given privately funded shelter and display. Mickiewicz enjoyed tremendous fame in life, but he acquired most of his property in death; the Positivists honored him with the coin of their realm.[6] But what of the living artist? The wide-scale professionalization of the Polish gentry after 1863 by-produced a great many writers and journalists, almost all of whom had to struggle hard to subsist. A poor non-nation had succeeded in building museum-houses for its dead genius. And, in a few remarkable cases, it erected special homes for the living.

Such was Oblęgorek, the national gift bestowed on Henryk Sienkiewicz, the author who afforded Polish society the greatest entertainment, comfort, and flattery in its hard times of nonbeing. Sienkiewicz's deft, flashy fictionalization of imperial Poland's former triumphs and dramas won him a popular audience of patriots burned by Romantic messianism and bored by Positivist edification. He created for them an enjoyable, undemanding nationalism; more, he created in that nationalism an astonishingly popular, world-class export. Sienkiewicz's consequent glory at once refracted and redounded to his nation's glory, as his fellow writer Maria Konopnicka remarked in her correspondence: "We've a thousand chances, in speaking about Sienkiewicz, to speak about Poland, her glory, her bravery, her strength. . . . When we mention *The Teutonic Knights, The Deluge, With Fire and Sword,* everyone knows we are praising the fatherland" (quoted in Putowska and Rębosz 1992, 7).

Like Scott, Twain, and Stevenson, Sienkiewicz succeeded in combining fame with prestige in his lifetime, and he seemed to share both Twain's and Scott's considerable appetites for the good life. Given his earning and spending capacities, he might have disgraced himself before his impoverished peers by financing his own fancy house. But Sienkiewicz was also well schooled in the image making of the patriotic Polish writer and behaved and benefited accordingly. When in 1897 his fans prepared special commemorations of his twenty-five years in the profession, Sienkiewicz opposed them with a counterproject to celebrate the centenary of Mickiewicz's birth. As a result, Cyprian Godebski's statue of the wieszcz appeared in Warsaw in 1898 and Sienkiewicz modestly settled for a private jubilee party among friends. His altruism paid off enormous dividends. By 1900 a Sienkiewicz jubilee committee had rallied, collecting the 70,000 rubles with which it purchased land, livestock, and machinery and commissioned the construction of Oblęgorek, the writer's gift home. At an elaborately choreographed ceremony in Warsaw's town hall (*Ratusz*), four little girls in white presented Sienkiewicz with the deed and the signatures of contributors from all three partitions.

What did this home provide? Sienkiewicz was quick to acknowledge the political symbolism of the bequest—the fact that he, so rewarded in other ways, "lacked this one thing, our land, the land on which we all were raised" (in Rębosz 1996, 2). The otherwise dispossessed Poles had managed to secure a bit of homeland for a de facto national leader, investing in the nation's future glory by sheltering and nurturing his creativity. The home would generate the text that would keep Poland in the mind of the civilized world.

The home itself presented a remarkable national text, compiling deliberate quotations of a glorious past. Sienkiewicz proclaimed that "the country is rewarding my work in the finest, noblest manner, in accord with tradition, for it bequeaths land" (Rębosz 1996, 2). His receipt of Oblęgorek, effected with a courtly flourish, recalled royal bequests of land to loyal subjects—a lavish, kingly, and highly cultivated gesture from Poland's golden age during the Renaissance. The first such documented bequest, made by King Zygmunt I in 1546, presented "our village of Temerówka" to the writer Mikołaj Rej. The village was payment rendered for the works Rej had already dedicated to the king and his daughter, and payment in advance to encourage "further service" (*dalszych wobec nas zasług*) (Bruckner 1988, 56, 174). Near the apex of its domestic power and international prestige, the Polish state thus saw fit to honor one of its newly national writers, one who had made the shrewd move from Latin to Polish, from the lingua franca of civilized Europe to the patriotic vernacular.

As foreign subjects and mere consumers, the Poles in the early twentieth century could commandeer no villages for their greats, but, as it turned out, they could underwrite considerable magnificence. Sienkiewicz's collectively financed bequest resulted in a grand home on the order, if not quite the scale, of an affluent nobleman's estate. A later gift home, bestowed on the poet Maria Konopnicka, adhered to modest dimensions, but Sienkiewicz's Oblęgorek was conceived in a manner befitting an affluent old-style squire, or *szlachcic.*[7] Appropriately enough, the debt-laden property that readers purchased for their living wieszcz had long been in and passed through noble hands, remaining, according to old records, several centuries in the Tarłowie family, then bought at the end of the nineteenth century by the notary Mieczysław Halik, who added a hunting lodge named after *his* family (Halikówka) (Putowska and Rębosz 1992, 11–12). Once the gift was bestowed, the best "artisans" in the land proffered the lord their services. The architect Hugon Kuder, responsible for the monumental St. John's Cathedral in Warsaw (Sienkiewicz's future burial site), donated his design for the manor home, and Franciszek Szanior, the famed creator of Warsaw's Botanical and Saxon Gardens, laid out the estate's lovely park (Putowska and Rębosz 1992, 10).

Oblęgorek incorporated the traditional in theory and practice, for, like other Polish manor houses, its building was, to some extent, self-styled and "organic," utilizing the already erected hunting lodge as its private, informal quarters to the rear.[8] The well-situated "little palace" (*pałacyk*) recalled the

Fig. 1. A front view of Sienkiewicz's "little palace." Muzeum Henryka Sienkiewicza w Oblęgorku (1982)

desired noble amalgam of gentleman farmer and knight in its blend of martial and pastoral features.[9] Kuder's addition, replete with pseudo-Gothic turrets and double-doored entrance, quixotically updated traditional displays of ostentation and power (see fig. 1).

The new front rooms of entrance hall, drawing-room, dining room, and, significantly, the writer's study, were laid out and subsequently decorated for show.[10] Although Sienkiewicz's grand martial exploits were always to be strictly verbal, the entrance hall abutted on a striking watchtower, another citation of the old manor home as necessary fortress; not so coincidentally, this tower also afforded the writer a good view of the ruins of a genuine castle in Chęciny (cf. Łoziński 1969, 72–74). The Sienkiewicz family coat of arms, adorning the entrance, established Oblęgorek as an instant ancestral seat. As if by collective enchantment, the writer's official installment in 1902 prompted a reenactment of patriotically motivated subservience, as local villagers,

Fig. 2. Sienkiewicz's finely decorated study. Muzeum Henryka Sienkiewicza w Oblęgorku

farmhands, and the manor's servants, bearing bread and salt and an arch of green wreaths, greeted and escorted the writer into his new home (Putowska and Rębosz 1992, 12).

Inside Oblęgorek, Sienkiewicz himself labored to maintain the impression of a squire's well-appointed manor house. With his jubilee booty, Sienkiewicz represented a bourgeoisified and distinctly polonized descendant of the fabled aristocratic collectors of Western Europe. He reprised in small the age-old aristocratic practice of the "boastful collection" designed to evoke "the impression of wealth . . . in spectators' minds."[11] Sienkiewicz's study was arrayed, not littered, with fine book editions and works of art, and ennobled, in the Polish tradition, with family portraits, weaponry, hunting gear, and trophies (Putowska and Rębosz 1992, 22, 28; also see fig. 2). The family portrait gallery was a staple of the manor home, a tangible, if not always truthful, guarantor of noble pedigree.[12] Sienkiewicz's was the more imposing due to the renown and talent of his portrait painters, including the famous artist Stanisław Witkiewicz. His display of weaponry reiterated, on a more modest scale, the motif flamboyantly struck by the watchtower. If such goods, influenced by Orientalized notions of costume and a warrior aesthetic, already doubled as weapons and sumptuous apparel in Sarmatian times, their value had redoubled as antiques in Sienkiewicz's day, when, to lift an apt quotation from historian Jan Stanisław Bystroń, "the martial served only for decoration" (1960, 394).[13]

As might be expected of a master of historical fiction, Sienkiewicz also indulged in a kind of "nationalistic collection" of objects tangibly manifesting "a legendary past."[14] He was particularly fond of an old Swedish cannonball extracted from the Jasna Góra monastery walls, a tribute sent him by a fan (Putowska and Rębosz 1992, 24). I should remark here that Sienkiewicz's nationalistic collection was truly a collective effort, comprised in the main of the artifacts and memorabilia his readers discovered, personalized, and dedicated to him as tangible souvenirs of his imagined Poland. In this category fell a casket decorated with the Lithuanian coat of arms that opened to a photograph of Żmudź, the locale of its givers; also an alabaster clock inscribed to Sienkiewicz from the inhabitants of Dzikie Pole and featuring a genuine cannonball and a likeness of Polonia atop a miniature silver steppe burial mound (Putowska and Rębosz 1992, 25). Such kitschy combinations conveyed a fascinating symbolism—of Polish history as the sentimentalized, inscribed, and donated property of the writer's fans (see fig. 3).

In grand sum, Oblęgorek provided Sienkiewicz a permanent home for his burgeoning collaborative collections, a comfortable refuge in which to write, lovely grounds in which to muse and to promenade in the act of musing, and a gracious estate in which to host and impress esteemed guests from around the world, although its castlelike heating deficiencies made it uninhabitable during the winter. Yet did this wonderful gift estate, this *un*official *non*institutional bequest, entail any public costs? Did Sienkiewicz's modern-day patrons demand the "further service" once expected of his royally rewarded predecessors?

Ironically, Sienkiewicz wrote relatively little after his grand acquisition; his energies went elsewhere. But the writer did pay a kingly price for his noble digs, for his peculiar form of public housing also presumed his lifelong public presence and public service. During the twelve remaining years

Fig. 3. The mahogany desk arrayed with some of Sienkiewicz's jubilee gifts. Muzeum Henryka Sienkiewicza w Oblęgorku

he summered at Oblęgorek, Sienkiewicz brought home the holy grail of the French Legion of Honor (in 1904) and the Nobel Prize (in 1905), and he served his people with benefits, donations, committee work, and the founding and staffing of a nursery and a school on his estate. Housed as local nobility, he also obligingly played the part of the lord-benefactor, negotiating land leases that were advantageous to the local peasants. After centuries of devastating and often self-inflicted decline, the Polish gentry happened on a conscientious, photogenic redeemer in Sienkiewicz.

It is this collectively imagined role that fundamentally distinguished Oblęgorek from Scott's Abbotsford and Twain's Gilded Age mansion. The latter writers built themselves homes that made plain their social ambitions and concretized some of their fictional visions. The temptation to conflate life and art seduces the writer as well as the reader; why not realize in wood and stone what one imagines in words? Sienkiewicz lacked neither ambition nor vision and was an active partner in the creation of his estate. But that creation was collaborative, and its funding joint. The artistic visions Sienkiewicz hawked had almost instantly been appropriated by his audience as communal property, as a storybook history that they desperately wanted to be true. The home they bought and built for him willed the link between his fiction and their reality, not only through the inclusion of his fictional characters on its roof and walls, but also through its entire lavish patronage, design, placement, and operation.[15] Here readers and writer worked together to animate and perpetuate the conflation of the real and the imagined characteristic of the institutionalized (read: posthumous) "literary place."[16] Sienkiewicz's fans set him up as a faux aristocrat on a faux estate that would playact a restoration of an imagined imperial Poland. In essence, they furnished their leading actor with an ingenious stage to present an impressive Polishness to the world. The artist's home became their national dream home.

The Sienkiewicz Museum at Oblęgorek

It was a pity, therefore, that the Sienkiewicz family had to vacate the place, the more so because they had labored so hard to maintain it privately after the writer's death. Sienkiewicz's son, Henryk Józef, shouldered its caretaking between the world wars, and, during World War II, distributed much of its collection to local peasants for safekeeping in what is surely the most heroic chapter of the writer's relationship with his faithful public. Yet the war also set the stage for Oblęgorek's institutionalization, for Henryk Józef Sienkiewicz's support of the local partisans resulted in his arrest and Oblęgorek's German occupation. After the war, faced with a ruined property too expensive to restore, the Sienkiewicz children had no recourse but to appeal for enormous sums and protective custody from their only sure patron—the new Polish government.

Nonetheless, their 1948 proposal to reconstruct Oblęgorek into a Sienkiewicz museum was undertaken, like the estate's initial construction, as an official and familial affair, as they joined forces with Aleksandra Dobrowolska, curator of the Świętokrzyskie Museum, to agitate successfully for restoration. The family's involvement intimated a peaceful, voluntary transfer of ownership, not a political appropriation of a class enemy's property. Henryk Józef Sienkiewicz, the aged heir, graced the museum's opening in 1958; subsequently his widow, Zuzanna, served as its curator until 1968. Of course, under the conditions of a sovietized Poland, this postwar reconstruction was state financed and bureaucratically managed. The state, rather than Sienkiewicz's reader-donors, funded Oblęgorek's restoration through the specific channels of the People's District Council in Kielce and the Communal Fund for Capital and National Restoration. The esteemed craftsmen Sienkiewicz had once employed were succeeded by entire departments of the state's arts industries, including a special Sienkiewicz committee attached to the Poznań Cepelia, a high-end division of the Polish folk arts industry that especially catered to foreign tourists (Putowska and Rębosz 1992, 5). Whatever their bureaucratic organization or official socialist persuasion, however, these professionals' attitude toward their work at Oblęgorek harked back to the pseudo-feudal models of the turn of the century, for they construed their renovation efforts as their new "gift to the museum" (Putowska and Rębosz 1992, 5).

The postwar Polish government's restoration of Oblęgorek definitively transformed the estate from private residence (however open it might have been to the public gaze) into a state-run educational institution, outfitting the former home expressly for the functions of "exhibition" and "enlightenment." The chronological sequence of restoration proceeded much as the house introduced itself to visitors—from the public front rooms of the writer's study and salon (1958) through the dining and smoking rooms (1971) to the rear areas of kitchen (the former Halikówka) and the writer's bedroom (1974). An additional five-year renovation (1981–86), during which time the museum remained closed, completed a more thorough restoration, including the family and guest bedrooms upstairs. With admirable timing, the curators thus were poised to reopen a fully restored Oblęgorek exactly seventy years after the master's death.[17] The new curators seemed as savvy as their predecessors in their manipulation of public ceremony and symbolic dates and images.

Yet Oblęgorek's restoration also entailed the imposition of academic control—its supervision and self-presentation as a public museum of a national treasure. The ubiquitous narrative filter of biographical explanations and identifying captions perhaps most clearly redefines this writer's home as any writer's museum. Sienkiewicz had ever obliged in the role of living exhibit at Oblęgorek, yet that role included his own interpretative soliloquies and his dashing pose as landowner and collector. Sienkiewicz spoke for himself as well as for his home and his collections, often in sanguine collaboration with visiting journalists and critics. In his showplace/home-made museum his collections remain in place, but their all-important owner-guide is no more, and Sienkiewicz's life and worldly goods have been inventoried, narrated, and inevitably dulled for pedagogical presentation and mass consumption. Where Sienkiewicz once played host there now stand "biographical-literary displays" that dutifully and impersonally inform and educate. In 1958 this display immediately confronted and initiated visitors in the entrance hall; since 1986 an expanded display fills the upstairs bedrooms, displacing old style hospitality with tourist edification.

In a sense, then, the grand national gift of Oblęgorek, repackaged as Sienkiewicz museum, has been disenchanted and banalized, processed into the standard fare of writer's museums all over the world—a detailed biography printed on fancy posterboards, a series of authentically preserved rooms where the author lived and worked, a collection of the author's artifacts, and a display of the author's tributes. But we must bear in mind the original non-narrated home with its at once self-conscious and self-delusional purpose: that for Poles without a sovereign homeland, making and observing one famous Polish artist at home was perhaps the next best thing to restoring the nation. It would have been far more effective to dispense with museum narratives at Oblęgorek and to staff the place with actors forever playing the Sienkiewicz family. Yet we should note, with cynicism or satisfaction, that such an intentional estate as Oblęgorek, a grand manor of playacted life, has now attained the staid glory and patriotic function for which it was hopefully destined—institutionalized and massively attended as a bonafide museum-house of national genius. Henryk Sienkiewicz did not live to see a free Poland, but his national gift has endured to serve as an official site of national heritage.

Notes

I wish to thank the staffs of the Oblęgorek and Żarnowiec museums for graciously sharing materials about their sites, and Bożena Shallcross for her expert advice and commentary. All translations are mine unless otherwise indicated.

1. Małgorzata Kucza-Kuczyńska (1986) lists three Sienkiewicz museums in her catalogue.

2. "What had started as a cottage, and had grown into a country house, was now transformed into a fortresslike manor, with turrets, towers, and castellated gables—the first example of what was to become known as the Scottish Baronial Style, which was later given royal endorsement by Queen Victoria at Balmoral" (Rybczynski 1989, 174.)

3. Kucza-Kuczyńska (1986, 4) reveals this as the agenda for her catalogue.

4. For more on the postwar situation in Polish housing, see Sillince 1990, 62–63.

5. We learn from Kucza-Kuczyńska's catalogue that the Paris museum, organized by his son, "was opened to the public in 1903" (1986, 110) and the Istanbul museum was fully rebuilt in 1880 after its destruction in 1870 (112).

6. For a fascinating study of Mickiewicz's posthumous cult, particularly the cult of his remains, see Rosiek 1997. My thanks to Bożena Shallcross for sharing this book with me.

7. Konopnicka was the only other Polish writer so honored. Her gift home in Żarnowiec, near Jedlicze, funded through the offices of the Lwów Jubilee Committee, has also been transformed into a state museum. For more information about this site, one can write to the Muzeum Marii Konopnickiej w Żarnowcu, 38-460 Jedlicze, Poland. The museum helped to sponsor the elegant publication *Trzy mowy miane w Żarnowcu w 1903* (Three speeches delivered in Żarnowiec in 1903), an edition of three speeches delivered by the poet.

8. On the *szlachta's* (gentry's) desultory style of building, see Łoziński 1969, 81.

9. According to Łoziński, "The pastoral and the chivalric are the main, almost exclusive features of noble life in times past" (1969, 65).

10. Bystroń remarks on this symbolic division of the house: "In any event, we see in general the tendency to divide the house into two sections, one for daily residence and another for formal entertaining" (1960, 2:400).

11. Wittlin (1949, 23–24) dates this practice to Roman times. Hudson notes the especial status symbol of fine art on display: "Art, in other words, represented conspicuous wealth and, in the aristocratic residences of Western Europe and in the town and country houses of the increasingly prosperous middle classes, large art collections were steadily building up during the seventeenth and eighteenth centuries. Quantity was quite as important as quality. The superabundant display scheme prevailed. Superabundance increased the value of the objects" (1987, 40).

12. As Bystroń wryly notes, "The magnates commissioned these [portraits] from foreign masters; the middle gentry hired anyone to do their portraits, just so they had them on hand. Probably quite a few of these portraits strayed far from the truth, for they mainly served to honor the family" (1960, 2:407–8).

13. Łoziński more fully explains the aesthetics and theatricality of weaponry:

"In speaking about old Polish attire, one shouldn't forget weaponry, which constituted the most indispensable and distinguished part of the costume. The sword was the nobleman's inseparable comrade and lover; he bedecked and adorned it as a lover. . . . The nobility loved rich and decorated weaponry to such an extent that these weapons often lost their defensive function and became objects of fantasy and theatrical pageantry. This was a manifestation of the passion for external show innate in Poles of that time, a passion constantly fueled by the influence of the East, that homeland of fabulously rich weaponry" (1969, 149).

14. Wittlin writes: "Both the ancestral and the nationalistic collection can be encountered in almost any society, in and out of Europe. Both represent a physical link between the living and the dead of a group, be it a relationship by blood or soil. Both tend to represent a particular group in a manner suggesting its superiority to others. The nationalistic collection may imply contempt and hatred of other nations, and the ancestors' gallery may insinuate the inferiority of people not related to the family in question" (1949, 40).

15. Illustrations from and paintings inspired by Sienkiewicz's works hung on the interior walls of Oblęgorek. A sculpted composite of his heroes crowned the entire building: "the stone figure of a hussar, with its distinctive wings, was placed on top of the building. It referred to the heroes of Sienkiewicz's most famous novels. The local people, however, confused the hussar with a guardian angel" (Rębosz 1996, 3).

16. Herbert generalizes that "literary places are the fusion of real worlds in which the writers lived with the worlds portrayed in their novels. Any distinction is unlikely to be made in the minds of visitors" (1995, 33).

17. For more information about the museum at Oblęgorek, write to its director, Lidia Putowska, Muzeum Henryka Sienkiewicza w Oblęgorku, 26-067 Strawczyn, Poland.

Works Cited

Andrusz, Gregory D. 1984. *Housing and Urban Development in the USSR.* Albany: SUNY-Albany Press.

Bruckner, Aleksander. 1988. *Mikołaj Rej.* Warsaw: PWN.

Bystroń, Jan Stanisław. 1960. *Dzieje obyczajów w dawnej Polsce, wiek XVI–XVII* (A history of customs in old Poland, sixteenth and seventeenth centuries). 2 vols. Warsaw: PIW.

Herbert, David T. 1995. "Heritage as Literary Place." In *Heritage, Tourism and Society,* ed. David T. Herbert. London: Mansell Publishing.

Holmgren, Beth. 1993. *Women's Works in Stalin's Time: On Lidiia Chukovskaia and Nadezhda Mandelstam.* Bloomington: Indiana University Press.

———. 1998. *Rewriting Capitalism: Literature and the Market in Late Tsarist Russia and the Kingdom of Poland.* Pittsburgh: University of Pittsburgh Press.

Horne, Donald. 1984. *The Great Museum: The Re-Presentation of History.* London: Pluto Press.

Hudson, Kenneth. 1987. *Museums of Influence.* Cambridge: Cambridge University Press.

Konopnicka, Maria. 1996. *Trzy mowy miane w Żarnowcu w 1903* (Three speeches delivered in Żarnowiec in 1903). Introduction by Zdzisław Łopatkiewicz. Krosno: "HEDOM."

Kucza-Kuczyńska, Małgorzata. 1986. *Polskie muzea literackie* (Polish literary museums). Warsaw: "Kraj."

Łoziński, Władysław. 1969. *Życie polskie w dawnych wiekach* (Polish life in ancient times). Kraków: Wydawnictwo Literackie.

Oman, Carola. 1973. *The Wizard of the North: The Life of Sir Walter Scott.* London: Hodder and Stoughton.

Putowska, Lidia, and Ireneusz Rębosz. 1992. *Muzeum Henryka Sienkiewicza w Oblęgorku.* Kielce: Muzeum Narodowe w Kielcach.

Rębosz, Ireneusz. 1996. *Henryk Sienkiewicz i jego Oblęgorek* (Henryk Sienkiewicz and his Oblęgorek). Warsaw: Voyager.

Rosiek, Stanisław. 1997. *Zwłoki Mickiewicza: Próba nekrografii poety* (Mickiewicz's corpse: An attempt at the poet's necrography). Gdańsk: Słowo/Obraz/Terytoria.

Rybczynski, Witold. 1989. *The Most Beautiful House in the World.* New York: Viking Penguin.

Sillince, J. A. A., ed. 1990. *Housing Policies in Eastern Europe and the Soviet Union.* London: Routledge.

Wittlin, Alma S. 1949. *The Museum: Its History and Its Tasks in Education.* London: Routledge and Kegan Paul.

12 ||| Stawisko

The Home of Jarosław Iwaszkiewicz

Anna Nasiłowska

According to Tradition

THE EXCEPTIONAL CHARACTER of Jarosław Iwaszkiewicz's house cannot be described without reaching far back to the traditions that influenced the shape and character of this family estate. The house itself, which its owners named Stawisko, was built between 1927 and 1928 in Podkowa Leśna, near Warsaw, with funds from the writer's father-in-law, Stanisław Lilpop. Lilpop, overseeing the sizable fortune of his family, bought a large tract of forestland on the outskirts of Brwinów with the idea of dividing it up into building sites. His idea was realized, and with the advent of a local train to Warsaw, the rapid development of a town was made possible, composed of homes in the forest. In the 1930s, it became quite fashionable among the Warsaw intelligentsia to live in Podkowa, where Irena Krzywicka and Stefan Napierski made their homes, among others (Iwaszkiewicz 1957).[1] To this day, Podkowa is one of Warsaw's "good addresses," and owning a house there is a sign of great prestige and prosperity.

The Iwaszkiewicz home was one of the first homes in Podkowa. In the beginning, the Iwaszkiewiczes only summered in the old, ruined villa. The initiative to build the family estate here came from Stanisław Lilpop, although early on his daughter had her reservations about the idea, since Iwaszkiewicz traveled extensively in the early thirties. Between 1932 and 1936, he was often abroad, working as a diplomat in Denmark and Belgium. In 1930, Stanisław Lilpop unexpectedly committed suicide, and his daughter, Anna Iwaszkiewicz, inherited the land in Podkowa. By degrees, the family's existence was supported by the sale of lots there during the thirties and throughout World War II.

Stawisko assumed its function as the family estate when Anna Iwaszkiewicz began to suffer from depression. As her mental state worsened in the thirties, she was sometimes kept from taking an active part in running the house and raising two daughters; these duties were taken over by her aunt, Stanisław Lilpop's sister Aniela Pilawitzowa.

The Lilpop family belonged to the wealthy bourgeoisie. The patterns and values of this milieu, nevertheless, determined the style of this estate only to a degree. Polish culture had not sufficiently formed its own strong bourgeoisie patterns—the circle of "business people" consisted most often of Jews and Germans, who, in deciding on assimilation, often accepted the gentry lifestyle as the most powerful and attractive.

Jarosław Iwaszkiewicz most certainly belonged to the circle of nobility. He was born in Kalnik, in Ukraine, where his family was bonded by blood with local Polish landowners, such as the Iwański and Szymanowski families, from whom the composer Karol Szymanowski is descended. The Iwaszkiewicz family, however, did not own its own land, on which it might depend for its existence. In addition, the author's father, like many young people of his time, was thrown out of the university for his part in the January Uprising and deprived of any possibility of finishing his studies in Russia. He took a rather lowly position as a bookkeeper in a sugar refinery. The house in which the future writer was born was not the property of the family.

A picture of that home may be found in the author's reminiscences, most notably in *Książka moich wspomnień* (Book of my memories), written partly during World War II. It has the typical characteristics of a rural childhood idyll. The first sentence of the memoir points the reader's attention to the distant past:

> Because I was the child of old parents, because I had siblings significantly older than myself, it was as if I reached from the beginning of my existence much further in the depths of the nineteenth century than my date of birth shows. And because Ukraine and her out-of-the-way corners in the twentieth century were connected in many ways with earlier times, it sometimes seems to me that the first years of my life fall somewhat during the time of [Henryk Sienkiewicz's] *Trilogy*—in any case, in the last years of the republic. (Iwaszkiewicz 1957, 7)[2]

Iwaszkiewicz was born in 1894 and so his direct memory does not include the nineteenth century, although in many works, especially in his stories, the times of the uprising are treated as a contemporaneous reality.

The author recognizes his link with the past as an important characteristic involving his ancestry. He treats the part of historical experience inherited from his predecessors as equal to his own and regards it as a harmonious extension of what he has seen with his own eyes. Therefore, his novels cannot repeat the clear form that is proposed by the bourgeois *Bildungsroman.* The hero is born neither as a child of nature nor a tabula rasa; his individual experience is dominated by the history of family, clan, or class, with which he identifies. Such a consciousness favors long existence and is open to the experience of continuity and its confirmation. His own biography is received as a part, a stage of his family history. In addition, history is perceived through family stories and even literary works (such as Sienkiewicz's *Trilogy*), or historical reports are interwoven throughout as elements of reference.

Perhaps such a worldview determined Iwaszkiewicz's decision to have a home and family. From early youth he betrayed homosexual leanings, and throughout his life acted on his preferences. Though this left clear signs in his work, it did not take the form of a specific gay culture. The family home is treated there as a place in which one obtains identity in childhood and in adulthood passes it on to one's own children.

The powerful sensation of cultural continuity, the axis of which is family tradition, arises from identification with the pattern of culture and not from concrete experiences of the family. It would be easy to see in Iwaszkiewicz's earlier biography an enormous number of events that could be interpreted as signs of breaking continuity, breaking with one's heritage. The uncertain position of his family as nonlandowners living among the Polish landed gentry; his relocation from house to house; the death of his father in 1902; numerous changes in his place of residence (Warsaw, Kiev, Elizavetgrad); and finally, the war in 1914 and the revolution, which forced landowners to abandon their estates forever; also, the first years in Warsaw, with their financial instability and uncertainty of position—all these experiences did not affect the impact of his first memories at the center of which was the country cottage, surrounded by a spacious garden, with a veranda, salon, and servants, inhabited by a large family and visited by cordially received guests.

The house in Podkowa Leśna does not attempt a forced imitation of the typical Polish manor. No nostalgic recollections, such as white walls or a typical Polish roof (usually gabled), can be found in its architectural shape. The house is spacious, with the classic shape of a villa. Its furnishing, the nature of its human relations, a few elements of its surroundings constitute the signs of a continuation of tradition, though loosely treated and shaped according to the demands of contemporary needs. The Iwaszkiewicz house is surrounded by a garden, which during its heyday, in the thirties, was tended by a gardener. At the axis of the entrance, decorated with the columns characteristic of the manor, an alley of linden trees is situated, and the driveway to the parade entrance is decorated with a huge circular flower bed (thanks to which it was possible to approach comfortably the entrance in a horse-drawn vehicle). The hall and the ground-floor room are adorned with Stanisław Lilpop's impressive hunting trophies, a decidedly noble, even magnate accent. (Iwaszkiewicz himself did not enjoy the hunt, and did not continue in his father-in-law's passion.) Old furniture and tapestries—an Oriental touch of décor—create expressive signs of continuity.

The naming of the house—Stawisko—has a strong cultural connotation. In Polish gentry customs, it was common to name family estates in the borderlands as well as in central Poland. Sometimes the name of the house was the same as the name of its location, sometimes it came from the name of its owners, in which case the manor, when it changed owners, did not change names, holding over in this fashion the remembrance of the past. It was also common to see old names, with uncertain pedigrees, or those indicative of some local feature. Names such as Zarudzie (from a story written in Taormina in 1974) and Wilko (from "Panny z Wilka"—"Maidens from Wilko") appear in Iwaszkiewicz's works.[3] One of the families close to Iwaszkiewicz in Ukraine had an estate named Stawiszcze. The name Stawisko refers to the ponds (*staw*) found in its surroundings, and the very sound of the word (because of a significant transformation and use of the augmentative suffix *-isko*) creates a feeling of old-fashionedness, of rooted existence. It is, however, a neologism—consciously created by the Iwaszkiewiczes, chosen from a number of other options. The use of this name carries along with it the necessity of a special use of prepositions. In Polish, one does not say "I'm going to Stawisko" (*jadę do Stawiska*), for the preposition *do,* which equates to the English *to,* is used for names of localities. Instead, the Polish *na* is used (*jadę na Stawisko*). Still visible in contemporary Polish, this *na* is a clear designation of gentility because in this case it recalls the archaic, even feudal, *pan na* __ (the lord of __).

The employment of large numbers of servants, the multigenerational family composed of both visiting and permanent relatives—these features also emphasize Stawisko's gentility. The name day of the lady of the house (Saint Anna's day, July 26) became the occasion for harvest festivities, although Stawisko was not an estate. The custom of organizing a harvest holiday most likely has its source in pagan traditions; in the nineteenth century, during the time of great conflicts between gentry and peasants, the cultivation of such activities was meant to foster reconciliation. In Poland proper, this was also a manifestation of national community beyond classes, and in the borderlands, these festivities expressed on the part of the Polish gentry a recognition of and positive interest in local traditions. At Stawisko on the eve of Saint Anna's day, servants and others in one way or another involved with the "manor" were invited, and in the garden guests were treated to vodka, and dances were held. The festivities were not, however, relieved of clear paternalistic accents and were intended to express the gentry's good-natured care of the "people."

The possession of a home, a manor, decidedly distinguished Jarosław Iwaszkiewicz from other artists of his generation. Many of them were of Jewish heritage (Antoni Słonimski, Julian Tuwim), and despite respect for and interest in the traditions of the gentry, they could not regard them as their own. The home of a man of letters during the interwar period was above all a typical intelligentsia apartment: changed rather often, although not deprived of accents of nobility in its interior decoration, it was not a permanent aspect creating an individual identity. Of the group, only Ludwik Hieronim Morstin, a country gentleman by birth, owned a real palace. In his residence in Pławowice (Miechowskie region), he organized a number of meetings of poets, which were also attended by the Iwaszkiewiczes. Yet it is hard to regard even Morstin as a true landowner, for his land was leased by a manager.

Despite a very strong recollection of landowning traditions, Stawisko was not a typical country manor during the period between the wars—those traditional characteristics were joined harmoniously with the function of an artist's home. The Iwaszkiewiczes invited poets and musicians for visits of varying durations and surrounded themselves with friends who could create an artistic salon, an institution steeped in the free exchange of ideas and opinion making. Their salon was supragenerational and served to build community among those who thought alike, seeking in art an outlet for anxiety and metaphysical experiences.

This function of the Iwaszkiewicz home took on additional significance during the war. The house itself was threatened; after the German invasion it was taken by the Wehrmacht to be a vacation home. Its location on the sidelines, however, ensured that it was not intensely used. The owners were allowed to use the upper floors, although until 1941, Wehrmacht soldiers were quartered on the ground floor. In 1941, as their units were transferred to the eastern front, the German army abandoned the house: they did not return until 1944, although by then they were far from their former role as conquerors. It was during this time that the Iwaszkiewiczes organized initiatives to help artists. On behalf of the London government, Jarosław transferred material aid, at times using his own money; Anna ran a kind of a summer house for selected individuals. They also took part in sheltering Jews in the area (these experiences may be found in Iwaszkiewicz's story "Stara cegielnia" [The old brickyard]). They took writers in need of help into their home, some living there permanently and some for a brief respite. These housemates included the poet Roman Kołoniecki and the author Stanisław Piętak. Krzysztof Kamil Baczyński, suffering from asthma, spent the spring of 1942 in Stawisko as if it were a sanatorium, writing, eating large meals, and taking the air, which assuaged his attacks. Although they were not friends, the Iwaszkiewiczes welcomed Baczyński under their roof, viewing it as their duty and as a gesture of respect for the artist:

> Krzyś was very enclosed and I cannot even imagine how it was possible to involve him in any kind of opening of the heart or intimate conversation. He was always very serious and even my wife, who had experience with poets who were rather difficult to interact with, like for example Jerzy Liebert, couldn't get close to him. (Iwaszkiewicz 1979, 150)

Wartime may be recognized as the time of Stawisko's greatest splendor—although not with regard to material conditions, of course. Simply put, the Iwaszkiewiczes felt needed; they bore great difficulties of rationing and discomfort, the cost of their hospitality. Anna Iwaszkiewicz, suffering from depression before the war, manifested an unusual (for her) level of activity, and the condition did not return until the end of her life, during the seventies. At Stawisko, the guests could not only count on aid in difficult situations, but above all on understanding. There it was still as if before the war. Everyone was accepted, including Poles of Jewish descent, even though in Poland this was a very real danger. Irena Krzywicka, who before the war was not counted as one of the persons in the Stawisko circle, found at Stawisko one of very few homes where she was welcomed with good will.

The period just after the Warsaw Uprising was a culminating point, when Stawisko became an open home for refugees chased out of Warsaw. There was no electricity in the house, for the power plant in Pruszków had been blown up. Zofia Nałkowska, who made it to Stawisko on October 16, 1944, noted in her journal that, among others, Maria Dąbrowska, Pola Gojawiczyńska, the Adrzejewskis with their small child, and the wife of Tadeusz Breza and widow of Andrzej Strug all spent time at Stawisko (Nałkowska 1970, 384).[4] A few dozen people lived in the house during this time, and because of the shortage of space, guests even slept in the bathroom and in the hallway. Iwaszkiewicz was forced to give up his study, which became the couple's bedroom temporarily. Even this, finally, had to be shared with yet more guests. The Iwaszkiewiczes slept on one of the beds, on the other slept Wilam Horzyca, the theatrical director and critic, and his wife (Iwaszkiewicz 1984, 58–59).

Stawisko after the War

The appearance of the Red Army in January 1945 in Podkowa took place without much disturbance, but before long the house, which immediately betrayed its associations with the gentry, was treated by the authorities as a threat to the new political system. In October, Iwaszkiewicz visited Maria Dąbrowska in Warsaw:

> He told me the sad conditions of his current domestic situation. Part of his house at Stawisko was taken up by the NKVD and by the Polish army. Both of them stole what they could. The intervention of Borejsza at Bierut in the matter of freeing his home from those billeted there didn't come to anything, in fact it made matters worse, it rankled the lower army authorities that he had gone to higher officials. (Dąbrowska 1996 1:1)

The quartering of officials at Stawisko had two goals: it immediately helped the immense housing shortage and it became an element of political struggle.

"Landlords" and other "property owners" were assigned mandatory lodgers, who in practice were impossible to dislodge. It was a method of separating owners from their property, cautioning them in this by the rule that lodgers must represent a "healthy class" element. In reality, to this day, such situations may be found in certain Warsaw tenements, which are formally private property, although irremovable lodgers from this practice of billeting troops live in divided apartments.

At Stawisko, these tenants did not stay long. Most likely, one of Iwaszkiewicz's interventions with the authorities proved effective. In all, this situation had a strong influence on Iwaszkiewicz's bearing toward the authorities after the war. The statement that the defense of the house against various offenses contributed to his obedience is a certain simplification of matters, although this motivation for his actions seems unusually serious. Iwaszkiewicz, while a member of the noble class, did not accept the nationalist uprisings, and he regarded political conspiracies and rebellion as ineffective, if not ruinous. He regarded the imposition of political duties upon the artist as a misunderstanding. For him, the defense of Stawisko was the more important matter. He regarded the existence of his home, from wartime on, as valuable to an entire circle of authors.

In the meantime, after the war Stawisko returned to its former function as a family home. The connection between it and writing, however, did not carry on without collisions. In a letter dated November 28, 1946, Iwaszkiewicz complains to Jerzy Andrzejewski, then living in Kraków, of his state of health and lack of energy:

> I need more and more strength each day, I have to earn enough to live and take care of the house, and you know how much that costs these days. Now I have a little room in a theater-house in Warsaw, and great comfort from it—I've got peace and quiet, and I think that I'll do good work there. At home the children bawl from morning to night during the week, and on Sunday, the Stachs have guests and vodka, slowly we are coming down to a further plan. . . . this is natural, but it fills one both with sadness and with irritation. (Andrzejewski and Iwaszkiewicz 1994, 44)

Andrzejewski, whose second daughter was born during this time, understood these problems well. Even before the war, Iwaszkiewicz had an apartment in Warsaw that he used as a sanctuary for work. Before the war, this was two rooms at 8 Kredytowa Street, bought by the author after the death of his father-in-law (Iwaszkiewicz 1984, 13). Their modern decoration underlined the fact that this was the apartment of an artist. After the war, Iwaszkiewicz always attempted to ensure that he had some sort of pied-à-terre in Warsaw—but this was a privilege dependent on his position as an artist and on the decisions of the authorities. Stawisko remained the incontestable home, but not necessarily his favorite place to work. Before the war Iwaszkewicz traveled often and he always worked very well on the road. After the war he attempted to continue this same way of life, ensuring himself the privilege of frequent trips to Italy and France and at times, in order to finish a story or essay, traveling to Sandomierz.

The continuing tradition of Stawisko as an artist's home, a salon, serving literary discussion, encountered many difficulties, most often involving political divisions in the literary milieu. The first crisis surfaced at the end of 1946, when Iwaszkiewicz was overlooked for the leadership of the writers' union, his nomination simply passed over. He took it painfully: "After that I went to Stawisko, where during the length of November *no one* came to us (emphasis added). Even Sundays went without visits, which is simply unheard of at our home. I thought then that I was entirely going out of circulation" (letter dated November 30, 1946, in Andrzejewski and Iwaszkiewicz 1994, 46;). The contrast to times not at all previous, when Stawisko was full of guests, could be clearly felt. To make matters worse, Iwaszkiewicz's friendship with Jerzy Andrzejewski constituted yet another political misunderstanding. Andrzejewski, during the war Iwaszkiewicz's closest cooperator in providing material aid to artists and before the war a promising Catholic author, shortly after became one of the most ideologically bound converts of social realism, and looked upon Iwaszkiewicz's moderate stance and distance in the face of history as unforgivable weakness, indecision, or even smacking of political duplicity. Later, after October 1956 and especially in the seventies, Iwaszkiewicz still had not changed his position, but Andrzejewski had become a dedicated member of the political opposition, his position earning him exactly the same criticism he formerly aimed at Iwaszkiewicz.

At the end of the seventies, while differing politically, the two took steps toward reconciliation. They tried to find a formula for friendship, despite the differences that divided them. The most important ground of understanding revealed itself to be the remembrance of times past, and nostalgic references to the role of Stawisko as a shelter to artists:

> You always write so beautifully of Stawisko, about us and our home, and I am always grateful for it, even though you are a scorpion. . . . don't you mythologize the Stawisko of old, and doesn't it seem to be so beautiful and decorative, because you were here when you yourself were young and beautiful, and when you experienced your own great love? Maybe those feelings colored that corner of earth differently for you, and perhaps you simply imagine it all: that there was a beautiful house, that there was a beautiful Hania and a noble Jarosław? (letter dated December 20, 1977, in Andrzejewski and Iwaszkiewicz 1994, 143)

The story of Iwaszkiewicz's friendship with Andrzejewski demonstrates his relation with the literary circle in general. Serving for a number of years as president of the writers' union was a strategic plan on Iwaszkiewicz's part. In the new political system, it would ensure him an unquestionable position, safety for his home, and the possibility of continuing his life as it was up to this point, including travel abroad. Iwaszkiewicz regarded his work for artists during hard times as sensibly replacing his supporting political manifestations and open demonstrations of opposition. He chose moderate methods, looked for personal ways to reach the representatives of the highest authorities. Although he often intervened on behalf of particular people in his circle, this way of doing things aroused more and more reservations.

Attempts to organize anew a social life centered at Stawisko continued. In 1947 the Iwaszkiewiczes celebrated their silver anniversary. A number of people from the artistic and intellectual milieu invited for the occasion remained for a longer stay: the Parandowskis, the Andrzejewskis, the Horzycas, and Paweł Hertz. Fine cuisine meant a lot at Stawisko, and during larger gatherings a special cook was even brought to the house.[5] However, a return to the splendid past is only possible in memory. In the 1977 letter to Andrzejewski cited below, Iwaszkiewicz remembers Christmas Eve 1944, recalling it as the most beautiful moment in the history of his home:

> In the middle of that stormy and deeply intense epoch, [my home] could become an ark, circling over the abyss. I think that the most essential characteristic of that house was that it didn't put out anything for show, that it persisted and continued its daily life, as if nothing happened. I remember

> that our rule was always "Everything as usual." I was asked not too long ago what was the most unusual Christmas in my life; without hesitation I answered that it was Christmas Eve 1944, when at the table at Stawisko sat people who had lost everything—fortunes, children, manuscripts, the work of entire lives—and I, by the greatest exertion of will (for my head was spinning indeed after the "fish"!) I had to be the host, not scream, not laugh scornfully, break the wafer and entertain those gathered with conversation . . . so that they didn't reflect on what had happened. I think that that was the most important part of it, to be as if nothing were going on. (Andrzejewski and Iwaszkiewicz 1994, 143)[6]

Iwaszkiewicz's emotional reactions could be hard to fully understand: where does this temptation to laugh scornfully come from? It is possible that it is tied to the fatalistic historicism visible in many of the works of the author, especially those written during the war ("Bitwa na równinie Sedgemoor" [Battle on Sedgemoor] and "Matka Joanna od Aniołów" [Mother Joanna of the angels]).[7] If the verdicts of history seem to be irrevocable, the most intelligent strategy in times of unrest is to acknowledge self-defense and to attempt to save whatever is essential to the individual. The defense of the home as a place with which particular values are associated becomes a task the size of an epoch, an acceptance of the call of history. Iwaszkiewicz's strategy, in opposition to the traditionally male one of taking part in the struggle for national liberation, appears close to the female pattern of survival as encoded in Polish culture.

The motto "Everything as usual" was no longer in use after the war, even if the inhabitants of the house wanted to remain faithful to it. Stawisko was a denial of normalcy. The house started to be used as a calling card for liberal aspects of the new political system, especially during the unofficial programs of hosting various visits of artists and statesmen. The visit in Warsaw of Queen Elizabeth of England, who came in 1955 for the Chopin competition and unexpectedly extended her visit, was a splendid occasion. The Iwaszkiewiczes were without a doubt the best candidates to host her. Maria Dąbrowska, taking part in a party at Stawisko, does not spare any biting details in the impressions recorded in her diary:

> It's very funny that during the socialist era I ate dinner with a queen for the first time in my life. And how much delight in the fact that it wasn't until the socialist era that a marriage to a rich woman and a lordly residence, worthy

> of hosting a queen, became useful to Iwaszkiewicz. Other than Elizabeth and a few people from her closest circle, and both Iwaszkiewiczes, the only people at the dinner were: Parandowski, Professor Michałowski, Eibisch, Mycielski, and Lutosławski. The meal was exquisite. Elizabeth was filled with grace, conversation carried on easily and smoothly, it was perhaps the most pleasurable social circle in which I have taken part in the last ten years—although without any significance, as light as foam. (1996, 3:11)

In light of the impoverishment of the intelligentsia after the war, a well-appointed villa gave one the impression of a delightful "residence." One could risk putting forth the thesis that in the new era, artists had a chance to become aristocrats. The nobility of the Iwaszkiewicz home after surviving a difficult ideological period stopped bothering the representatives of authority: it was at hand, it amounted to a propagandistically used calling card, an object of snobbery. Of course, the harvest festivities were no longer held, Stawisko no longer had its own gardener—but these were only changes in style that did not transform the home in any fundamental way. Iwaszkiewicz used any occasion to organize recitals at his home: a recital, a chamber concert, or a theater performance—Andrzej Wajda brought actors to perform *Nastasia Filipowna.* These private artistic events best suited Iwaszkiewicz's ideal of a home.

Sometimes it is possible to think that Stawisko amounted to an obstacle in Iwaszkiewicz's contact with his social environment. It was too wonderful, it didn't allow anyone to be on "equal footing." Writers met in the "homes of creative work"—for example, the Warsaw circle customarily spent time in Obory, at the former estate of the Potulickis, where to this day a kind of pension is in operation, allowing peaceful work and time with friends. Stays at Obory (near Konstancin and close to Warsaw) were quite highly valued by Antoni Słonimski after his return from exile. Iwaszkiewicz was excluded from this. The difference in living conditions perhaps appeared natural in his contacts with the younger generation, but young postwar writers did not take any inspiration from Iwaszkiewicz's writing and represented a different style: they gladly underlined their plebeian qualities and distance from the life of an artist. Iwaszkiewicz was important to a generation that was entering life in the thirties, to Andrzejewski and Miłosz, but that situation would not return. Maria Dąbrowska, who after the war bought a small house in Komorowo, notes a strange dream in July 1964: Iwaszkiewicz called her with the news that he had renounced Stawisko and bought a home close by, also in Komorowo (Dąbrowska 1996, 4:298). It was a dream of solving mutual reluctance, victory over distance, and reaching a full understanding. Dąbrowska's house was a typical *kostka mazowiecka* (Mazowian block), a concrete box, devoid of any architectural adornment or aspiration to nobility.

Iwaszkiewicz sought accord with those who remember Stawisko as a place of friendship and mutual understanding between artists. To this end, Stawisko appears in postwar correspondence with Mieczysław Grydzewski, the prewar editor of *Literary News,* and after the war, editor of the London *News.* Iwaszkiewicz knows very well how critical the political emigration toward him was, especially the émigré circle in London. In the letters, however, he does not want to expound differences, but seeks connections between the two. Memories of Stawisko—this was the offering of his hand in agreement—return to idyllic memories tempered by a mild admonition: if the house is still there, then perhaps the émigré opinion of Polish reality is too strong? Iwaszkiewicz, knowing that Grydzewski loves dogs, recalls his dogs, and there were always plenty of them. He presents his current life as a continuation of the good old days. His identification with the house as his own place on earth is complete, even as he is submerged in everyday problems: "In Stawisko, everything has begun to age, but I feel good in this old house, as opposed to Hania, who complains about Stawisko and wants to get rid of it. I believe that her desire is senseless. We should stay there until the end" (Grydzewski and Jarosław Iwaszkiewicz 1997, 35).[8]

After the war, Stawisko became year by year a house of old people. First the older generation died: the grandmother—that is, Aniela Pilawitzowa, who raised Anna Iwaszkiewicz—then Anna's mother, always called Mrs. Śliwińska, then Jarosław's sister, Jadwiga, and finally, Anna, on December 23, 1979. The nearby cemetery became a reference point for the home. Jarosław died on March 2, 1980. In his will he asked that funeral arrangements be made in the tiny church in Brwinów and that they be modest. He also wished that after his death Stawisko would serve writers. Probably, he imagined that it would be a kind of Warsaw-area pension for writers and that it would achieve in that way its own character, as a home for artists. That did not happen. Presently, Stawisko operates as a museum, preoccupied with putting in order and preparing an enormous archive for publication.

The Polish Manor and the Artists' Home

The image of the home appears in Iwaszkiewicz's postwar works, in his memoirs, short stories, and in the three-volume novel *Sława i chwała* (Fame and glory), as well as in his poetry. The epic devices of using this motif were worked out before the war, especially in his short stories. However much Iwaszkiewicz described his prewar reality in novels such as *Zmowa mężczyzn* (Conspiracy of men) and *Pasje błędomierskie* (Błędomierz passions), after the war, he avoids this type of confrontation with the surrounding world. The image of the home is above all a picture of the past, not always distant, but marked with the traits of the bygone.

Those of his short stories which take place in nineteenth-century Ukraine evoke an image of the Polish manor. Even then it is a threatened home, represented on the eve of dramatic events that might bring an end to its existence. "Noc czerwcowa" (June night) represents a situation at the manor on the eve of a young woman's expected departure to join her husband, who is sentenced to exile in Siberia for his part in the January Uprising. We learn that the marriage was not a union of love, and that the couple was divided by a great difference in their ages, but the wife is under the pressure of public opinion, which understands faithfulness in terms of a patriotic act. We only learn the situation through the thoughts and voices of a few people living in the manor house and who are directly interested in its further existence: they are prepared to arrange a romantic meeting between the young wife and a handsome lieutenant, a Russian, in order to save their home. After a hot June night, the young woman stays, and so the house survives. The short story does not evoke a direct confrontation between patriotism and egoism. It is more an attempt at complicating the picture, adding new tension. The short story "Zarudzie" has a similar motif: the hero, young Józio, comes of age in a manor house, unaware that the entire countryside is preparing for the uprising and that he himself is going to be involved. Pretending to be a friend, the ubiquitous Filaret, the son of the Orthodox priest, but in truth Józio's stepbrother, trails him. This is again a struggle over the manor.

In the conversation between a French woman, Miss Goffard, and Filaret, the subject of home is directly discussed: "'In spite of everything, I can't imagine Józio without Zarudzie,' says Miss Goffard. He is himself only against the background of this house" (Iwaszkiewicz 1993, 539). Miss

Goffard here shows a basic tenet of Polish gentry culture: it is based on a complete identification with the home. In this instance, the notion comprises not only the home but also the entire farm, its surroundings, upon which the manor imposes authority. The possession of such a home ensures its owner social status, according to the principle of the Polish gentry republic, in which membership in the gentry community gave one the privilege of participating in democracy. In this sense, the consciousness informed by the writer's family circle is still a part of the seventeenth century. For the hero of "Zarudzie," the possession of this home signifies freedom; a far-off relative and plenipotentiary take on household matters, and Józio can be himself: he spends time reading, playing music, and undertaking spiritual searches. Józio, even if he is not creative, is an artist and belongs to a group of sensitive dreamers, seekers of beauty receptive to metaphysical emanations. This combination of the manor tradition and the modernist mythology of the artist is characteristic of Iwaszkiewicz's works. In Polish culture, the motif of the Polish manor appears quite often; it is, however, connected with an emphasis on patriotism and history. The fusion of modernism and the conservative picture of the manor house universalizes this image and institutes a unique and not always well understood feature of this writer.

The postwar three-part novel *Fame and Glory* represents the subject of the Polish home from all sides. It begins in the Ukraine, as we are first brought into the strange world of that borderland. "It's difficult to get used to our Ukrainian gentry. It smells a little of the seventeenth century," says one of the novel's heroes, the distinguished composer Edgar Szyller (Iwaszkiewicz 1964, 1:11). The concurrence of this statement with the above fragment from *Book of My Memories* is a sign of the writer's strategy: it is not an autobiographical novel, but its material consists of the author's remembrances. In the character Edgar Szyller, the Polish reader should recognize Karol Szymanowski. The heroes of *Fame and Glory* lose their fortunes in dramatic circumstances as a result of the revolution. The revolution means a ruination of homes, manors are burned, the population commits bestial murders, terror reigns. However, the cruelty of the revolution is markedly toned down (see Dunin-Kozicka 1929), and the heroes never forget that the process is irrevocable. They regard the loss of their fortunes with the calm of consummate aesthetes who know that their world was sentenced to disappear in any case.

Between the wars in Poland, the heroes of *Fame and Glory* must organize their lives anew. Edgar and his sister become world-famous artists, whose home is the entire world; Princess Bilińska settles in Warsaw and becomes a grande dame; Count Janusz Myszyński becomes a somewhat bored owner of an estate in the Warsaw suburb of Komorowo; Ola decides on marriage with the good but simple and uncultured pastry baker Gołąbek. Only her aunt, Mrs. Royska, is successful at recreating the old life in the estate at Puste Pola in Podlasie. Her manor is regarded, however, as anachronistic, a relic of the nineteenth century (Iwaszkiewicz 1964, 2:119).

Mrs. Royska rules an entire household, personally and diligently carrying out her farm tasks: "Sitting in black mittens and under a white parasol, on a tiny folding table and reading *The Red and the Black,* she oversees the workers weeding the strawberries. She knows well that no one else can do this" (ibid.). The fact that the household is run by a woman alone is nothing strange in Polish tradition. Women performing "masculine" duties when men are absent always inspire respect. In "Zarudzie," as well, a woman runs the home, guarding young Józio from the responsibilities that would be difficult for this dreamer to assume. Polish culture lacks the usual bourgeois patriarchal forms. This often means that the division of labor should come first and foremost according to individual predisposition.[9] Women's domination over the practical sphere of life in Iwaszkiewicz's works can be contrasted with the position of sensitive youths and contemplatively inclined artists. There are also, however, among his characters women with distinguished careers.

In the summer of 1939, Mrs. Royska is visited at her estate by her grandnephew, Andrzej Gołąbek. Soon, he turns out to be another "sensitive youth." Although his father's position as a pastry baker would place him in the world of bourgeois culture, and his common surname, Gołąbek, leaves no doubt that Andrzej is not a candidate to be a lord, he turns out to be unusually sensitive to the beauty of country life. His artistry and emerging sensitivity open him to this world and ennoble him, for in Iwaszkiewicz's prose the artistic vocation is something higher. In order to be an artist it is not necessary either to create a great work or to gain recognition in the world. Sensitivity and the readiness to feel exceptional moments are primary.

The apology of the manor in Iwaszkiewicz's version has none of the characteristics of the ideology of Blut und Boden (Blood and Earth). It is not birth and inheritance, but internal traits, above all an artistic sensitivity that decides whether or not one belongs to the world of the manor. The legitimate heir of Pusta Łąka estate, Mrs. Royska's son, turns out to be unworthy of his inheritance because he is a fascist ruled by hatred. Even his mother leans emotionally toward Andrzej Gołąbek.

Andrzej, after graduating from high school, prepares to pass the entrance examinations for architecture school. The exam is something to be feared, for his drawings—too artistically inclined and aesthetically subjective—lack the necessary technical discipline. Music, as well, plays an enormous role in his life. He recognizes his stay at Pusta Łąka as his destiny, turning down a trip to the sea with his mother or to the mountains with his father. He comes to the Podlasie region and at once senses that he is in the right place. The aura of the home, the nearness to nature, the night, intensify his existential anxiety; they all favor natural maturation:

> And in the dark night, he felt his body, supple and light, was filled with the current of shadow and wind, with everything that surrounded him. As if he became unified with the momentary rustle, and with that immense silence that stretched far, far over forests and fields, and high above him, where the jumbled clouds brushed against each other. He felt one with the silence, the warmth and scent.
>
> At the same time, he felt that his body required some kind of completion, like those 'Faustian' questions demanding answers. As he sat so peacefully on the porch steps ("on the front step of night," he thought) and petted the head of the old, silent dog, he cast an insistent and huge question into the darkness of the park. He called for something, something that night and wind, and the park, and the scent did not answer. (3:42)

The nights just after his arrival at Pusta Łąka are a time of poetically intense experiences. Andrzej is asking questions of God and Nature, but in truth he does not demand answers. He knows that they are written in his surroundings, in the miraculous space of the park. He is encompassed by peace, he feels prepared to take up the challenge of adulthood. His stay in Pusta Łąka brings him a double initiation: a sexual initiation with Kasia, who works at the manor, and an initiation into the mystery of death. His grandmother stays at the estate and is deathly ill. Andrzej observes close-up the successive phases of disease and at last is witness to her final agony. It is the end of an individual life, but not the end of the mystery of death. With the power of centuries-old rituals, the body of his grandmother, who during her life was not overly respected, takes on dignity and is transformed into a cult object. This death is not a drama but a statement of the higher rights of existence, and only its physiological aspects spur Andrzej's revolt.

Mrs. Royska's home is a place where life reveals its real dimensions, a place of the truth. Iwaszkiewicz always forcefully universalizes the experience of his heroes, removing class or national dimensions. This is the result of a point of contact between the mythology of the manor and the mythology of the artist, both of which in Iwaszkiewicz's works were created before the war. After the war, this means of universalization was often taken as a dodge or proof of obedience to the recommendations of official propaganda.

In *Fame and Glory* there is a scene in which Janusz Myszyński arrives at Odessa in 1936 and finds the Szyllers' villa. At first, he doesn't recognize it:

> The fence was either broken to pieces or stolen. There was no garden, the overgrown acacias, in which Józio hid, and Ola and Spychała talked . . . were no longer there, and the path from the villa to its private beach was overrun as well. The house stood naked and yellow if one stared at it from below, from the beach, and gave the impression of something immeasurably old. It sank into the earth, like a mushroom, from age, and the roof was uneven in places: it surely leaked. (2:317)

Through the windows of the villa, iron beds are visible; a summer camp for children is there. This change from wondrous home to ruin, however, does not evoke an angry reaction. It is the object of peaceful contemplation:

> Never more than when squatting on his heels on the beach . . . and looking at the immeasurably beautiful succession of azure and green strips of sea, on that diminished and abandoned home, like the house of lost childhood, never more than then, Janusz felt his belonging to collective human existence, when his individual traits became incidental. The human collective was like a wave and although he was an ingredient, only a drop in that wave, he tried to apprehend its rising and breaking into foam. (2:318)

Such universalization was received after the war most often as a dodge, another proof of Iwaszkiewicz's conformity, or as an attempt to replace a sharp historical reproach with a "pale" philosophy of expressly modernist character (or, in the Polish sense of the word, with characteristics of Young Poland). Despite its obedience to traditional features of the Polish home,

Iwaszkiewicz's prose is perceived as not "native" enough, filled with some foreign element, too cosmopolitan.

Iwaszkiewicz's memoirs point to a genesis both of a connection between domesticity and the mythology of the artist that is unique in Polish literature, and of a cosmopolitanism. Such a system of values is tied to the Szymanowskis' home in Tymoszówka, in Ukraine. Iwaszkiewicz describes that home a number of times, treating it as the place of his artistic initiation. This idea of "home" points more to family than to a concrete place. The Szymanowskis estate was Tymoszówka, to which they were very strongly tied, treating it as their nest.[10] However, the family often stayed in Elizavetgrad (Kirovograd) or in Odessa. Iwaszkiewicz's *Meetings with Szymanowski* and *Book of My Memories* contain myriad details. As a young man, Iwaszkiewicz's impressions boiled down to the fact that each member in that family was an interesting individual. At home, the newest Polish literature (Wyspiański, Przybyszewski, Kasprowicz) was read, and music always played. Karol Szymanowski's brother, Feliks, and his sisters played music and sang, and Szymanowski's first pieces were performed in the bosom of the family. Sometimes, an orchestra was brought from a neighboring town. Iwaszkiewicz took part in household theatrical presentations as well. In the beginning, as a young and poor distant relative, he was made light of, but his musical education progressed, and with it, his acquaintance with Karol. During World War I, this acquaintance metamorphosed into friendship and bore fruit in a joint work: the opera *King Roger,* with a libretto by Iwaszkiewicz. Conflicts about the writing of the opera renewed a distance between the cousins. *King Roger* contains certain homoerotic accents (as the story of Dionysus' arrival at Sicily, where he must struggle with the strictness of Christian customs).[11]

In the time of the older generation, a strict moral codex was kept and for patriotic reasons no social relations with the Russian neighbors were maintained. After the death of Stanisław Szymanowski, this rule was no longer enforced and Russians began to appear, with whom French was generally spoken. "Incredibly cultured, the Davidov family, long settled in this place, brought into the Szymanowskis' home a special tone of Russian cosmopolitan half-aristocracy, but also a gleaming European polish, contrasting with the provincialism of next-door Polish neighbors" (Iwaszkiewicz 1981, 26). The friendship of Szymanowski and Natalia Davidova (to whom he dedicated his

Second Sonata) turned out to be an understanding beyond national differences, fostered by common spiritual and artistic ground. The villa in Odessa, returning in memories and evoked in *Fame and Glory,* was in actuality the property of the Davidovs. Another recurring guest at Tymoszówka was the pianist Arthur Rubinstein. His presence in the salons ensured that interpretations of classical works for the piano and premieres of Szymanowski's works were perfectly executed. Szymanowski's frequent travels in Europe (Vienna, Paris, London, Switzerland, and Italy) brought him in contact with the newest currents in European music of the beginning of the century (Rubinstein 1973) and ensured that Tymoszówka, situated in far-flung Ukraine, could be recognized as a center of cosmopolitan modernist art.

The Iwaszkiewiczian ideal of home harmoniously connects opposing traits: location at the sidelines is connected with a centrality assured by the rank of the art present there. In Iwaszkiewicz's prose, the interhuman understanding that happens during the playing of music in the salon is based on an extraordinary intuition. In these very moments, the heroes begin to accept their fate not through life events, or as the historic or social effect of their actions and surroundings, but beyond them, as an eternal, universal Destiny. They attain illumination, accept that which is higher, and simultaneously reach a state of agreement with themselves, agreement with transience. It is a musical illumination, filled with sentimentality impossible to render into words, independent and ethereal. Music, by its formal character and its timelessness, is regarded as the essence of art. Poetry, in those moments when it approaches the ideal of pure poetry, contains that same essence.

The Poet's Home

In Iwaszkiewicz's essays and poetry, mythologizations of his own home appear. Stawisko is shown as an exceptional place, an artist's home.

One's own home is a certain place of identification, a permanent point of reference. In the verse written at a congress in Vienna, from the volume *Warkocz jesieni* (Braid of autumn, 1954), beginning with "Autumn Conversations, Hand in Hand," people of different nations can understand each other most fully if each of them calls forth his or her home in thought. The home itself is described in the following manner:

In the center of the world, there is a pine stretching to the sky,
And a home under the pine: Stawisko.
(Iwaszkiewicz 1977, 2:241)[12]

This verse is clearly inspired by socialist realism, as evidenced by its formulaic quality and agreement with the ideology of internationalism. The acceptance of that subject was tied to the author's membership in the Committee of the Defenders of Peace. The use of Stawisko in a socialist-realist argument supporting peace as a universal value seems reckless. However, Iwaszkiewicz entirely overlooks the "aristocratic" character of his home; he attempts neither to dispute the interpretations that might appear nor to attribute some new significance to his home. Instead, he eliminates oppositions and universalizes.

It's important to note that in Polish poetry, especially during World War II, "defense of the home" is a typical metonymical designation for defense of the homeland. We see this topos of patriotic poetry in Władysław Broniewski's poem "Bagnet na broń" (Fix bayonets) from April 1939: "When they come to set fire to the home / in which you live / Poland." The home becomes a synonym for homeland, its most personal form, while exile and wandering are understood to be the state of homelessness (e.g., the classic expression "You who are without a homeland" from Kazimierz Wierzyński). The socialist-realist piece "Autumn Conversation" in *Braid of Autumn* is perhaps the one place in Iwaszkiewicz's works where one can find a similarity to this type of expression, widespread in Polish poetry and calling on the Romantic forms of patriotism.

Iwaszkiewicz's home is always idealized and universally understood. This idealization is not related to the classic topic *locus amoenus,* for the home is above all an inner, mental space. Its exterior or surroundings are no longer important. The home may be designated as a place of happiness as well. In the volume *Jutro żniwa* (Harvest tomorrow, 1963) there is a vision of the small happiness caused by everyday objects: a blue cup, a red toothbrush, toothpaste. Ordinary things create tenderness as they are filled with human presence; they are domestic and friendly, and their presence is a sign of order. This order—visible in one's immediate surroundings—is also a sign of order in the world at large:

It's happiness—that you know how a hedgehog pitters
happiness—that you know how a rabbit patters

happiness—that you know how children pitter-patter
your children

and the children of your children

In school, the teacher said:
brush your teeth
But the teeth decayed and fell out
That is happiness as well

(Iwaszkiewicz 1977, 2:308)[13]

Happiness is not an idyll, but is written in a logic of generation succeeding generation, and so coming to terms with transition. To live to old age is happiness as well. In another poem from the same volume ("Jesienne gwiazdy . . ." [Autumn stars . . .]) a vision of Tymoszówka returns, but the element calling forth memory (a sort of Proustian madeleine) is a sweet plum, most probably from the poet's own garden. The ripe plum, the quintessential fruit of autumn, is a sign of transition as well, but simultaneously an unclear promise of victory over time. Thanks to the cyclical nature of the plum season it is possible to return to the distant past. The plum is tied to an aesthetic ideal as well, as it allows one to follow a reference to the still lifes by Chardin. The great secret of life is contained in that which is close, in domestic life. Iwaszkiewicz returns to this expression repeatedly.

One of the last of Iwaszkiewicz's volumes, *Mapa pogody* (Weather map) ends with a piece that can be called a series of blessings. These are lyric wishes, evoking the order of nature, the forest, storm, water, sky, time, and earth. One blessing that refers to things created by man is the domestic blessing:

May you have good humor in your home
bright room, a full table, white cheese, milk, coffee, cherries, little things, that only we know the origin of photographs, the circumstances of which only we know Irenka, Tadzio, Pani Wodzińska, faces which from the desk go into handbooks once and for all, good humor for houseplants, firs, aloe, good humor for our dogs.
good humor good humor
May good humor on earth be with you . . .[14]

(Iwaszkiewicz 1977, 2:578)

Also in this fragment, the relationship of man to the everyday things that surround him can be expressed as a tenderness, a mutual tenderness. The space of the home is not something that is separated from the space of nature; at home one lives under the protection of water, stars, tender objects, and friendly people.

An element of the mediation between nature and home is the garden, which is treated as an extension of the home. This sense of a garden space is most forcefully expressed in the last part of the essay "Ogrody" (Gardens) published in a collection, *Ogrody* (Gardens), from 1974—a small collection, but one important to Iwaszkiewicz. This slender volume establishes a prosaist pronouncement of the old poet on the subject of transition, an elegiac farewell. Besides this essay, the volume consists of the stories "Sny" (Dreams), a return to Ukrainian youth, and "*Sérenité*" (Serenity), a conception of calming, quieting, or "inner clarity." The garden is the most gloomy of pictures. The author, on a walk at twilight in the company of his dogs and old horse, remembers and sees the present disarray of the garden, overgrown and wild. The garden at twilight is identified with the writer's own age.

In Iwaszkiewicz's later works, an individual symbolism of the home emerges, a kind of private code. The garden is the poet's self, and the dog is a guardian spirit watching the home; at times the dog is perceived as his own soul. A similar significance can be attributed to the dogs from the poem "Stary poeta" (Old poet) and the old bitch in "Muza" (Muse), both in the volume *Śpiewnik włoski* (Italian songbook). These are unclear representations of inner life, shapes that take on the symbolism of the unconscious.

The individual character of this symbolism is outlined even more clearly in the case of the pine. In the poem "Autumn Conversation" from the fifties, Stawisko is referred to as the "home under the pine." The last poem written by Iwaszkiewicz, "Urania" (dated February 2, 1980), during his travels in France, refers to a tree from the park surrounding Stawisko:

> Urania, sister, pine—I call you this way
> For with the finger of your trunk you point to the sky
> The wind, which plucks at your black mane,
> Quiets down below. Sister, I call you.
>
> (Iwaszkiewicz 1980, 3)

The relationship between Urania, the Muse of astronomy, and the pine may at first seem completely arbitrary. The pine is a typical element of the

Mazowian landscape, grows in the sand, and appears in the forests near Warsaw, but the entire fragment rests on a strictly individual symbolism, made clear in *Gardens.* The house at Stawisko is surrounded by pines perhaps two centuries old. At one time there were nine of them, and those close to the writer knew that they were named after the Muses. Later, it became necessary to cut some of the trees, and seven remained. The tree named Urania no longer exists: "Straight as a mast, Urania was opposite the house, in an alley lined by lindens, and she had to be cut" (Iwaszkiewicz 1974, 72). In *Gardens,* this fragment is followed by an angry commentary about the barbarism of cutting trees and the declaration that at times during his walks, the poet caresses the broken bark of the pines. Urania is an inner tree, named in verse as Urania—the protector of the home, "the Muse of the last day," "goddess of the end," "goddess of permanence." There are contradictions in Urania's nature; she is at once allied with death and with constancy, she is the protector and madwoman who brings salvation and perdition. The one solution to the contradictions that tear at the poet is the trust in a protector, at once death and victory over earthly opposition. Instead of a horizontal axis in time she constitutes a vertical one: the dimension of eternity and nothingness at once. The title of Iwaszkiewicz's later lyric "Pan Nicości" (Lord of nothingness) is a designation for God. It has multiple meaning and this potential for various interpretations is consistent with the idea of inner peace: a farewell to contradiction, even to the contradiction between belief and doubt.

The Iwaszkiewicz home is a place in which it is good to live, but something cosmic—the axis of the world—may be found here as well. The representation of the axis as a tree or a column appears in a number of cultures. Trees connect the underworld, the earthly world, and the stars. Stawisko can be understood as a home built under the tree of life. Just as the pine Urania was cut down in the end, however, so the house of life is also a house of nothingness, a house of death.

Translated by Richard Knepper

Notes

1. See also Krzywicka 1992. The critique of the home in Polish culture has been rich, but only occasionally does it discuss the gentry manor as home (see Sawicka 1997).

2. See also Anna and Jarosław Iwaszkiewicz Museum 1994. For the transformations of gentry tradition, see Maciejewski 1999 and the articles by Janursa Maciejewski, Ewa Ihnatowicz, and Ewa Paczoska in that volume.

3. The name Zarudzie appeared as well in Ukraine. See Iwaszkiewicz 1981, 33.

4. See also Gojawiczyńska 1974, 35–39.

5. Much information on this subject is contained in the elder daughter Maria's memoirs on culinary topics: M. Iwaszkiewicz 1980.

6. In the socialist-realist short story "Nim będzie zapomniany" (Before he will be forgotten) by Kazimierz Brandys, one finds the description of the Iwaszkiewiczes' house (slightly changed in form) as the house of Cezary Olborski in Zalesie. The place was represented as the oasis of normalcy and peace amid the war. Brandys's short story is a coded attack against Miłosz after the latter's decision to emigrate.

7. Marian Janion wrote of Iwaszkiewicz's philosophy of history a number of times; see esp. Janion 1984. See also Nasiłowska 2000.

8. For other interesting information about Stawisko, see Mitzner 2000.

9. Very interesting material on Polish gentry customs is displayed in women's novels—for example, in Zofia Kossak-Szczucka, *Dziedzictwo* (Heritage), Hanna Malewska, *Apokryf rodzinny* (Family apocrypha), Zofia Starowieyska-Morstinowa, *Dom* (Home), and Stefania Zahorska, *Korzenie* (Roots).

10. Karol Szymanowski's sister, Zofia, called Zioka, writing about Tymoszówka in her book *Opowieść o naszym domu* (The story of our home), gives a sentimental and idealized description of the manor and forms of family life. The book was not warmly received by Iwaszkiewicz and Szymanowski.

11. A very interesting source for comparing motifs is Szymanowski's novel *Efeb os* (Ephebe of the yellow jackets), which remains in fragments and is known only from Iwaszkiewicz's summary; see Iwaszkiewicz 1981, 58–67. See also Boniecki 1980, 148–52.

12. Pośrodku świata sosna do nieba
I dom pood sosnoą: Stawisko.

13. To szczęście—że wiesz jak jeż tupie
szczęście—że wiesz jak tupie królik
szczęście—że wiesz jak tupią dzieci
twoje dzieci
i dzieci twoich dzieci

14. The Polish word here, *pogoda,* which is difficult to render into English, connotes both good humor and good weather (editor's note).

Works Cited

Andrzejewski, Jerzy, and Jarosław Iwaszkiewicz. 1994. *Listy* (Letters). Ed. Andrzej Fiett. Warsaw: Czytelnik.

Boniecki, Edward. 1980. "W orszaku Dionizosa: Mit dionizyjski Szymanowskiego i Iwaszkiewicza" (In Dionysus' retinue: The Dionysian myth in Szymanowski and Iwaszkiewicz). *Pamiętnik Literacki* 1: 139–59.

Dąbrowska, Maria. 1996. *Dzienniki powojenne* (Postwar journals). Ed. Tadeusz Drewnowski. 4 vols. Warsaw: Czytelnik.

Dunin-Kozicka, Maria. 1929. *Burza od Wschodu: Wspomnienia z Kijowszczyzny* (Storm from the east: Memories from the Kiev region). Warsaw: Dom Książki Polskiej.

Gojawiczyńska, Pola. 1974. *Szybko zapomniane* (Last holidays, quickly forgotten). Warsaw: Czytelnik.

Grydzewski, Mieczysław, and Iwaszkiewicz Jarosław. 1997. *Listy, 1922–1967.* Ed. Bojanowska Małgorzata. Warsaw: Czytelnik.

Ihnatowicz, Ewa. 1999. "Formuła Polaka—posiadacza ziemi. Warianty powieściowe. (Formula of the Pole as a landowner: The novelistic variants). In *Przemiany formuły polskości w drugiej połowie XIX wieku* (Transformations of the formulas of Polishness in the second half of the nineteenth century), ed. Janusz Maciejewski, 97–104. Warsaw: Instytut Badań Literackich.

Iwaszkiewicz, Jarosław. 1957. *Książka moich wspomnień.* Kraków: Wydawnictwo Literackie.

———. 1964. *Sława i chwała.* Warsaw: Czytelnik.

———. 1974. *Ogrody* (Gardens). Warsaw: Czytelnik.

———. 1977. *Wiersze* (Poems). 2 vols. Warsaw: Czytelnik.

———. 1979. "A spieszył się z pisaniem . . ." (And he hurried the writing . . .). In *Żołnierz, poeta, czasu kurz . . . Wspomnienia o K.K. Baczyńskim* (Soldier, poet, the dust of time . . . Memories of K. K. Baczynski), ed. Zenon Wasilewski, 148–52. Kraków: Wydawnictow Literackie.

———. 1980. *Muzyka wieczorem* (Music in the evening). Warsaw: Czytelnik.

———. 1981. *Spotkania z Szymanowskim* (Meetings with Szymanowski). Warsaw: Czytelnik.

———. 1984. *Aleja przyjaciół* (Alley of friends). Warsaw: Czytelnik.

———. 1993. *Najpiękniejsze opowiadania* (The most beautiful stories). Ed. Tomasz Burek. London: Puls.

Iwaszkiewicz, Maria. 1980. *Z moim ojcem o jedzeniu* (About food with my father). Kraków: Wydawnictwo Literackie.

Janion, Maria. 1984. "Iwaszkiewicza mit powstania i ironia czynu dziejowego: Epika życia fantazmatycznego" (Iwaszkiewicz's myth of rebellion and the irony of historical action: The epic of a phantasmagoric life). In *Czas formy otwartej. Romantyczne tematy i media* (The era of the open form. Romantic subjects and media), 363–78. Warsaw: PIW.

Krzywicka, Irena. 1992. *Wyznania gorszycielki* (Confessions of a scandal maker). Ed. and introd. Agata Tuszyńska. Warsaw: Czytelnik.

Maciejewski, Janusz, ed. 1999. *Przemiany formuły polskości w drugiej połowie XIX wieku* (Transformations of the formulas of Polishness in the second half of the nineteenth century). Warsaw: Instytut Badań Literackich.

———. 1999. "Rasa czy principium. O dziejach przemian formuły polskości w XIX i XX wieku" (Race or principium: On the development of the formula of Polishness in the nineteenth and twentieth centuries). In *Przemiany formuły polskości w drugiej połowie XIX wieku,* ed. Janusz Maciejewski, 19–32. Warsaw: Instytut Badań Literackich.

Mitzner, Piotr. 2000. *Hania i Jarosław Iwaszkiewicz: Esej o małżeństwie* (Hania and Jarosław Iwaszkiewicz: An essay on their marriage). Kraków: Wydawnictwo Literackie.

Miejsce Iwaszkiewicza (Iwaszkiewicz's place: On the hundredth anniversary of his birth). 1994. Materials from the conference, February 20–22. Stawisko, Podkowa Leśna: Museum of Anna and Jarosław Iwaszkiewicz.

Nałkowska, Zofia. 1970. *Dzienniki czasu wojny* (Wartime journals). Ed. Hanna Kirchner. Warsaw: Czytelnik.

Nasiłowska, Anna. 2000. "Stary poeta" (The old poet). In *Persona liryczna* (The lyric persona), 173–92. Warsaw: Wydawnictwo IBL.

Paczoska, Ewa. 1999. "Polskość w dobie niewoli—gniazdo czy 'zaścianek'" (Polishness during the era of oppression—a nest or a village). In *Przemiany formuły polskości w drugiej połowie XIX wieku,* ed. Janusz Maciejewski, 105–18. Warsaw: Instytut Badań Literackich.

Rubinstein, Arthur. 1973. *My Young Years.* New York: Knopf.

Sawicka, Grażyna, ed. 1997. *Dom w języku i kulturze: Materialy z konferencji zorganizowanej na Uniwersytecie Szczecińskim przez Zakład Etnolingwistyki* (Home in language and culture: Proceedings of the conference organized at Szczecin University by the ethnolinguistics program). Szczecin: Wydawnictwo Jota.

13 ||| Between Utopia and Parody

The Home for Creative Work

Marek Zaleski

In the vicinity of Warsaw there is a small village named Obory. There we find a charming baroque palace with its meticulously cultivated park and stylish gatehouse. The doorplate informs us that we are in front of the Home for Creative Work for Polish writers. The Potulicki family, a family of landlords, was the last to own the Obory palace and estate, which were confiscated by the Germans during World War II because the younger members of the family were active in the resistance. When the communists came to power after the war, the palace and the estate were nationalized. But it is not the glamour of its past or the charm of the place that impresses visitors. Rather, as one journalist offers, "Five centuries of history look upon you, but the last half of the century is what really counts here, when the writers' paradise was located here" (Żuliński 1995, 6).

The Home for Creative Work at Obory bears a compelling relationship not only to contemporary Polish literature, but to Polish cinema and drama as well, because it was visited by film and theater directors, journalists, artists, and scholars. Numerous poems and novels were written and translated here, not to mention critical essays, screenplays, theatrical pieces, and the like. It is a gold mine for lovers of the anecdotal history of literature.

Obory reveals itself as a very special place to anyone studying the history of the palace. After all, this is the palace with its park where writers were greatly elevated, though that elevation took place in often less than praiseworthy circumstances. One may say then that the Home for Creative Work was an idyllic paradise turned into a velvet prison and a vanity fair. But this history of the extraordinary elevation of writers above their compatriots, who built the happiness of their socialist homeland, makes one think about something quite different, about something quite unexpected: about the strength of modern cultural patterns and those of the distant past, empowered with force enough to moderate an assault on culture. This assault—Promethean and at the same time grotesque—was planned and executed by intellectuals overwhelmed by their passion for constructing social and political reality.

The idea of the Home for Creative Work was born in the Soviet Union in the 1920s. In Mikhail Bulgakov's *The Master and Margarita* we find Griboyedov's House, the mansion that is now the property of the Moscow section of the Union of Soviet Writers. In Bulgakov's devilish vaudeville it was "an old two-storied house, painted cream, that stood on the ring boulevard behind a ragged garden, fenced off from the pavement by wrought-iron railings." We enter through "the paved front courtyard. . . . [I]n summer, shaded by a canvas awning, it became a delightful outdoor extension to the club restaurant" (Bulgakov 1967, 62). The famous Writers' Restaurant there was regarded as the best restaurant in Moscow, where one could eat good food at bargain prices. The menu in the restaurant could make you dizzy, with too many attractions for even the most discriminating gourmand. But let us leave the restaurant because there are several important institutions upstairs. We pass by the office of the Board of Administration, where some folks are badmouthing their colleagues, those lucky enough to get the apartments in the suburban writers' colony. Then we pass sections devoted to sports, travel, fishing; rooms where you can settle up your one-day trip delegation and your paper allocation. There is also a room where the "Housing Problems" are dealt with—the queue here starts on the first floor, near the office of the concierge. And then we are in front of a walnut door with a

> gorgeous poster showing a cliff, along whose summit rode a man on a chestnut horse with a rifle over his shoulder. Below were some palm trees and a balcony. On it sat a shock-haired young man gazing upwards with a bold, urgent look and holding a fountain pen in his hand. The wording read: "All-in Writing Holidays, from two weeks (short story, novella) to one year (novel, trilogy): Yalta, Suuk-Su, Borovoye, Tsikhidziri, Makhindzhauri, Leningrad (Winter Palace)." There was a queue at this door too, but not an excessively long one—only a hundred and fifty people. (63)

Bulgakov's satirical description might also apply to the literary institutions of all the communist countries after 1945, including Poland. By the decision of the Council of State in 1947, the House of Literature was founded in Warsaw; and at the beginning of 1950 the Polish Writers' Union founded its headquarters in two rococo tenement houses, carefully reconstructed in a representative district of the capital. Besides, there were the offices of the union's authorities, the conference room, library and the reading room, and some attic apartments for writers who were located there. The club and coffee house, and the infirmary were located on the first floor, and the restaurant in the basement. The restaurant was not as good as its Moscow counterpart, described by Bulgakov, but the lunches served here were cheaper than in other Warsaw restaurants.

However, the Home for Creative Work in Obory started even earlier, on September 18, 1948. The President of Parliament, the Vice Minister of Culture, some local party activists, the farm council, and representatives of the literary world were present at the opening ceremony. After a year, Obory was fully operational. In keeping with the style of the times, the records in the Memorial Book reveal the writers to be a bit like the "leaders of socialist work": they are politically correct and bursting with enthusiasm. All of them praise the nice atmosphere, excellent working conditions, and the hospitality of the director and the staff. All of them emphasize that they feel almost at home and highly motivated to work.

What was the special attraction of this place besides the amenities? The point was, in this enclave encircled by the palace wall, the dilemmas of the writer's condition were solved. Here, the hiatus between the private and the public (or in Richard Rorty's words, between the need for solidarity with the collective and the need for the narcissistic dream of self-creation and autonomy) was eliminated. For people very much aware of the painful incompatibility between these two dimensions and value orders (as writers are), the Home for Creative Work formed a space where those two antagonistic ideals—*vita activa* and *vita contemplativa*—could find their realization in one harmonious, unified, fulfilled life. It looked like the dream of an "integral man" come true: a writer felt like an artist there, and at the same time like a citizen. Socialist eschatology was a new gospel, bringing hope for the possibility of authentic existence, an existence up until then a victim of its own contradictions. "If authenticity," Charles Taylor says, "is being true to ourselves, is recovering our own 'sentiment de l'existence,' then perhaps we can only achieve it integrally if we recognize that this sentiment connects us to the wider whole" (1991, 9).

According to Taylor, for Romantics, such a wider whole was Nature, and during the Romantic period "self-feeling and a sense of belonging to it were linked" (1991, 9). In the modern world, one inhabited by the people who visited the Home for Creative Work, all forms of order, both natural and spiritual order, were products of modern rationality. They revealed their artificiality and contingency. As Taylor notes, modern instrumental forms of rationality have separated us from Nature, from ourselves, and from our souls, throwing us into a state of alienation.

For those conscious of their uprootedness and alienation, the sense of belonging to a "wider whole" was just a habit of heart and a matter of intellectual and psychic hygiene. But this time, the wider whole was an intellectual fallacy and a trap for people longing for normality and demoralized by the victory over Nazism, the victory of another totalitarianism. This wider whole proved to be a kind of modern captivity and perpetuated an old myth, the myth legitimizing the state, with its administrative and spiritual control. But the consciousness of that fallacy was easily suppressed. Did not the world of the Home for Creative Work seem to be a utopia realized? "In quietness and peace are created the masterpieces that will illuminate the world of your children!" This sentence was written into the Memorial Book at Obory by the president of the municipal council of Obory-Jeziorna on the home's opening day. Even if writers recognized these words to be pathetically pretentious, they accepted them as their proper mission. Writers working on books awaited by the "working masses" felt themselves free of the anxiety of alienation. They also acquired a sense of the importance of their own literary mission as writers ("engineers of human souls," to quote Stalin's famous description). Such a mission was a stigma, making the writer a militant soul from the revolutionary avant-garde.

It looked as if the union of the citizen and the artist could be a historical reality. Not, however, without some conditions. And the main condition was loyalty to the rules: the literary microcosm should mimic the social and political microcosm (that is, the ideological realities of the communist state). Thus, we should not be surprised to see that governmental institutions participated in founding the Home for Creative Work. Writers were evolving into functionaries, and literature into a special emanation of modern rationality, now under the cover of historical and dialectical materialism.

The reasons for writers' and intellectuals' easy appropriation by communism, to say nothing of their vulnerability to leftist rhetoric and their eagerness to identify with the socialist movement, were frequently criticized. Peter Berger (1976), interpreting this enchantment, surveyed several different opinions on this subject. According to Vilfredo Pareto, the loyalty of these groups to communism allowed them to become a social elite. Joseph Schumpeter goes further: the socialist state offered them not only good social position but economic security as well. For Friedrich von Hayek, the economic and social privileges were not the only reasons for this romance, however. As people who blamed themselves for their lack of sense of reality and for their inclination toward abstract thinking, the writers and intellectuals were impressed by the simplicity and rigor of theoretical Marxist constructions.

Undoubtedly, all these arguments are legitimate when one thinks of Polish reality after 1945. Meanwhile, for those who only visited Poland and got very limited insight into that reality, Polish literary life and the economic condition of writers looked like the fulfilled ideals of a sagacious cultural policy:

> One of the most amazing things that ever happened to me was to live at the Home for Writers. I will remember Obory as a place where respect and honor for writers and poets in the People's Democracy made it clear for me how good it is to be here.

This inscription in the Memorial Book was made by an American visitor in 1955.

The eagerness with which men and women from literary circles accepted their isolation can be explained in the same way that Pareto, Hayek, and many others did. But it is worth remembering (as Berger does) the attractive force of the socialist myth. It focused on belief in the progress, the self-improvement, even the self-salvation of man; on the ability of an emancipated mind to destroy prejudice; and on man's ability to create his fate wisely. These assumptions accompanied the Romantic protest against social injustice, combined with the criticism of alienation as the destruction of community, as spiritual homelessness. As Berger says, socialism promises all the benefits of modernity and the elimination of the costs that we should pay for that, including the abolition of alienation. There is nothing strange in this reasoning, given the substitution of socialist myth for religion. If it really is a substitute, one may say that the socialist myth offered by Stalinist ideologists formed the trap described by Theodor Adorno and Max Horkheimer in *The Dialectic of Enlightenment.* It was a trap and an illusion set up by the emancipated mind for his devoted believers, an illusion fabricated when the modern instrumental mind, multiplied in its successive embodiments, became more and more degenerate and adopted the nature of metaphysical beliefs.

In the process, modern *Rationalität* gained its Romantic character, which was syncretic and thus more attractive. The paradoxical affinity between the ideals of avant-garde art or literature and socialist realism illustrates this situation. Boris Groys writes:

> Socialist realism put into effect practically all the fundamental watchwords of the avant-garde: it united the artists and gave them a single purpose, and erased the dividing line between high and utilitarian art. And between political content and purely artistic decisions, socialist realism created a single and easily recognizable style, liberated the artist from the service of the consumer and his individual tastes and from the requirement to be original, became part of the common cause of the people, and set itself not to reflect reality, but to project a new and better reality. (1996, 206)

So as we see, in that model of art, reality was treated as easily manageable material.

However, as I stressed at the outset, the Home for Creative Work, as a part of the larger historical experiment, not only became a sterile laboratory for socialist mandarins or a reservation for the happy few, but, practically from the beginning, happened to be a friendly place and a second home for many of its visitors. Which factors were decisive in the domestication of this place? Czesław Miłosz comments on the attitudes of those who allied themselves with communism: "A big enterprise was at stake. A small, enlightened minority had to transform the ignorant majority of the nation. It was like the Masonic lodge in Mozart's *Magic Flute,* the lodge in conflict with obscurantism—that is, the Queen of the Night" (1998, 237). Those Polish Marxists who were grasping for analogy with the Enlightenment were called mad red Encyclopedists. This invented genealogy and the patterns offered by memory and tradition, ignored the fate of the Soviet avant-garde artists, whose decimation by Stalin soothed revolutionary fervor in Poland. When we take the communist moralistic perspective, there was no room in Poland for this socialist rococo, but it appeared unexpectedly at Obory. Those who spent time at Obory conformed and mimicked (even if not deliberately) the life of those who once walked, chatted, and enjoyed life in the gardens of love and literature, because the world at Obory was a pastoral world. It was a repetition of *locus amoenus,* a representation of an idyllic, friendly, beautiful place, a space of *otium* (leisure), where the writer's labor perhaps could not be identified with leisure but was not far from it.

Obory, as I said, formed a space where the private and the public could meet, an arcadia that, perhaps more than any other place in Poland in those years, was free from the risk and danger (innate in a public space full of the sound and fury of History). It was a place of political truce: differences of literary and ideological beliefs seemed to be losing their poisonous edge, and coexistence was possible. As Aleksander Wat put it in his diary in 1953,

> That summer the weather was perfect: in the Obory park young dervishes and mameluks [young zealots from the Communist Party] spoke in a gentle, discreet, and perhaps tender manner, even to the enemies of the people. . . . Briefly speaking it was a beautiful island of escapism, an island brightened by smiles from the heavens, and full of human goodness, beautiful trees, and sweet breezes. (1986, 11)

One should probably say that conflict between the private and the public was nearly nonexistent, and if it was not, it was certainly losing its edge, losing because the convention was accepted. In other words, as the sophisticated and slightly ironic acceptance of the artificiality of representation was the condition of existence of pastoral literature, the acceptance of theatricality of the model of the world was the condition for which Obory as the oasis of happiness and creativity formed an ideal project.

Theatricality of life at Obory had its antecedents. However, it took on strange new dimensions: idyllic and monumental at the same time. Theatricality, so characteristic of court life at Versailles or at the Petit Trianon at the time of Marie Antoinette, found its successor during Stalinism: "The seventeenth century elaborated the codex of behavior according to which the existence of an individual has an entirely public character. To be oneself meant to represent oneself, and these numerous forms of representation that found their culmination at the time of Louis XIV lasted into the next century" (Siemek 1987, 30–31). Life at Obory was a spectacle, although the games played there were based on different rules than the games played during the *fêtes galantes* of the French court. At Obory, writers represented themselves as eminent literary figures, and even those who were at the beginning of their careers profited from their social status as "laborers of the ideological front." Their eminent position in the strata of society obliged them to obey hierarchies of a different type, those that dominated their inner circle and the etiquette of everyday life. Even if somebody broke official etiquette, it would not have meant that the rules had lost their validity. Obory was a place where one was permitted to abandon one's public role, and one could do that more easily than in any other place: writers felt at home there, but the character of the place and the society gathered there—the "society of the spectacle"—would be revealed anyway. For instance, everybody obeyed a strict sense of hierarchy at the dining room table. Everyone was seated according to his or her importance. In those years, the director of Obory was descended from an old Polish aristocratic family, and she took care of all the domestic ceremonies and rules. That certain positions in such artistic institutions as houses for artists or publishers were held by women (of the gentry or the aristocracy) was significant. Although such people had to respect the hierarchy of guests, their manners and charm helped them soothe the dreadful rigidity of the political reality (see Berberyusz 1997, 9–10). One may add that their presence and their mission evoked and foregrounded the artificiality of the situation and its theatricality. Both the women in charge and the ceremonies they performed were a distant echo of the world of *fêtes galantes,* the world of social rituals and games, of cynical and witty conversations in a milieu of fabricated nature, of luxurious interiors. What happened in Obory was a conjunction of an Arcadian myth and its theatrical parody, the reality and the disguise. Not only was it a place noisy with the clatter of typewriters, it was a modern land of earthly delights, an asylum where, just as in the prewar café, people discussed, chatted, and gossiped. It was also *une maison des rendez-vous.* In many anecdotes, we find this the place stigmatized forever by the ghost of its first landowner, the sister-in-law of a Polish king. The story has it that her temperament and her love affairs embarrassed the king so much that he was glad she was at Obory.

The theatricality of the world there, in its idyllic and monumental dimensions, from the very beginning lent itself to parody. The palace, the annex, and the park were encircled and protected by the wall. Real life spread outside: it was the space of *negotium* (business). There was the farm (now under state administration), the village, where the servants and women who worked in the kitchen lived, and the city of Warsaw, with its rude charm, cynicism, and expectations. The wall and the gate, with a plaque No admittance for unauthorized persons, separated the insiders from the outsiders, as the footlights do in the theater. The dwellers in the Home for Creative Work were aware of their "audience" and of the watchful eyes of the strangers. But living "on the stage," they did not feel alienated because the world outside looked like the pastoral world too. The world with its evil existed, of course. But it was textualized and also unreal. It was the world of "spat-upon dwarves of reaction," the world of embezzlers and kulaks, the world of pathetic reactionaries. And the world divided by frontiers, the imperialistic world ruled by His Satanic Majesty.

From the beginning of the pastoral as a literary genre, duality was its most characteristic representational feature. We deal then with a poetic image of arcadian life, but this image always was opposed to the reality outside the pastoral horizon. The opposition of these two worlds and the resulting confrontation of values always created the very core of pastoral representation (see Ettin 1984, 77, passim). The situation in the poetry of socialist myth was no different. This poetry, as William Empson puts it in his *Some Versions of Pastoral,* was a new, progressive type of pastoral. The inhabitants of the Home for Writers considered themselves the guards and laborers of this new historical reality, the emissaries of revolution. When they sat before the blank sheet of paper, they did not feel alone. "*Saluts fraternels et affectueaux aux poètes et prosateurs polonais, à ceux dont l'oeuvre sera ciment d'un avenir meilleur pour tous les hommes*"[1] reads the inscription by a French poet in April 1954 in Obory's Memorial Book. And we can find earlier inscriptions in Russian, Chinese, German, and English. This community looked like a community with no frontiers, for it was a community where, as I have indicated, the frontier between the private and the public was invisible because it formed a stage for performing mysteries of an idyllic "ideolo" (which Milan Kundera describes in his *Book of Laughter and Forgetting* as a euphoric dance of happy fools). Kundera's metaphor is not casual. *The Master and Margarita* takes place between the House of Writers and a psychiatric hospital, which is significant too. In *The Notebook from Obory,* however, a long poem by Aleksander Wat written in 1953, we find a fragment on the grotesqueness of ideological lunacy.

What I mean to say, using the example of Home for Creative Work at Obory, is that the tradition of socialist myth gained its caricatural embodiment there. The utopia turned into its own parody, an elegant dance of happy men changed into the dance of happy puppets. But one should remember that in postwar Poland, where so many writers returned from deportation camps, from immigration and homeless wandering, and shared the fate of displaced persons, the power of socialist myth was quite distinct.

In modern "city pastoral"—as Renato Poggioli puts it—the pastoral longing for loneliness and independence, for relaxation, for the friendly landscape of a free country, changes into a longing for a lonely place, a cloister's cell, Virginia Woolf's room of one's own, an asylum that is necessary for anybody who wants to work in a creative way (see Poggioli 1957, 149). So maybe there is nothing strange that the House for Writers at Obory changed for many into a Home for Writers. And for many it became a substitute for home, a place where one would want to come back as soon as possible. What is the definition of home? "Home is the only place where you can go out and in. There are places you can go into, and places you can go out of, but the one place, if you do but find it, where you may go out *and* in *both,* is home" (MacDonald 1966, 365; emphasis mine).

Even today, after the change of the political system in Poland, the Home for Creative Work at Obory has, for lack of state subsidies, turned into a house where the writers, mostly retired, who have become addicted to it, spend some time every year. They have to tolerate the presence of casual guests: the palace is let out for wedding parties, family reunions, conferences, and so on. It has to earn its keep. The Memorial Book has changed more and more into a domestic chronicle, where one reads requests and criticism, as well as praise, for the directors. Life, now free from the burdens of the past, from pressing political matters, goes on slowly and in different ways. And in the air the spirit of pastoral elegy now hovers.

Notes

I thank Witold Parczewski, director of the Literary Foundation of Polish Writers in Warsaw, and Artur Czesławski, director of the Home for Creative Work in Obory, for giving me access to the official documents connected with the Home for Creative Work since 1947.

1. "Brotherly and affectionate salutations for the Polish poets and writers whose work will cement a better future for all mankind."

Works Cited

Berberyusz, Ewa. 1997. "Jeńcy Obór." (Slaves of Obory). *Plus-Minus* no. 49, weekly insert to *Rzeczpospolita* 29–30 (November): 9–10.

Berger, Peter L. 1976. "The Socialist Myth." *Public Interest* 44:3–16.

Bulgakov, Mikhail. 1967. *The Master and Margarita.* Trans. Michael Glenny. London: Harvill Press.

Ettin, Andrew V. 1984. *Literature and the Pastoral.* New Haven: Yale University Press.

Groys, Boris. 1996. "The Birth of Socialist Realism from the Spirit of the Russian Avant-Garde." In *Laboratory of Dreams,* ed. John E. Bowlt and Olga Matich. Stanford: Stanford University Press.

MacDonald, George. 1966. A Personal Selection by W. H. Auden and Louis Kronenberger, *The Viking Book of Aphorisms.* New York: Viking.

Miłosz, Czesław. 1998. *Zaraz po wojnie: Korespondencja z pisarzami, 1945–1950* (Just after the war: Correspondence with writers, 1945–1950). Kraków: Znak.

Poggioli, Renato. 1957. "The Oaten Flute." *Harvard Library Bulletin* 11, 2 (Spring): 147–84.

Siemek, Andrzej. 1987. Translator's preface to *Sofa* by Claude-Prosper Jolyot de Crebillon. Warsaw: PIW, 30–31.

Taylor, Charles. 1991. *The Ethics of Authenticity.* Cambridge, Mass.: Harvard University Press.

Wat, Aleksander. 1986. *Dziennik bez samogłosek* (A diary without vowels). London: Polonia Book Fund.

Żuliński, Leszek. 1995. "Dwór w Oborach" (The manor at Obony). *Wiadomości Kulturalne:* 32:6.

PART V

Home Away from Home

14 ||| Home as Desire

The Popular Pleasures of Gender in Polish Émigré Drama

Halina Filipowicz

HOME IS A strategically important object of study, perhaps one of the most important objects of study, for two reasons.[1] First, although homemaking seems to be one of the most universal aspects of human activity, it offers an exemplary case of how the condition called home is in fact a variable function of cultural history. Second, homemaking presents a particularly striking intersection between external forces and internal consciousness, between society and the individual.[2] It follows from this that home is an especially rich site for the multifarious and often contradictory notions of identity to be set in play. A rethinking of the concepts and structures we recognize as home provokes a reassessment of our understanding of belonging. At a moment when we are willing to trouble all sorts of paradigms of identity, we might ask: what can be learned about home/lessness, national identity, and the connection between them?[3]

Now, when such well-worn terms as *homeland, exile*, and *diaspora* have become the focus of lively debate and renegotiation in critical theory, it is possible to preempt the usual circuit of readings and associations and hear not a lament of exile or homelessness, but an active claim for a diasporic vision of home and identity. This claim challenges the opposition between home and exile on which the predominant construction of diaspora (as dehoming or uprootedness) depends, requiring that the notion of diaspora itself be reconceived. Indeed, the potential for this reconceptualization is embedded in the very term *diaspora*, which comes from the Greek *dia*, meaning "apart," and *speirein*, meaning either "to scatter" or "to sow." While in both ancient and modern thought the former meaning has tended to dominate (hence the term *diaspora* has been virtually synonymous with *exile*), the latter meaning, with its promise of rerooting and sprouting new growth, is gaining momentum in critical theory. In this essay, I propose to test this argument in the context of the Polish theater in postwar London.[4]

As Una Chaudhuri has pointed out, "[t]he privileged setting of modern drama is the family home" (1995, 6).[5] A sprawling, now mostly forgotten archive labeled Polish Émigré Drama is no exception.[6] Wiktor Budzyński's *Spotkanie* (The encounter, 1948), Ryszard Kiersnowski's *Dziewczyna z tamtej strony* (A woman from behind the Iron Curtain, 1960), and Stanisław Baliński's *Polka prosto z kraju* (A Polish woman straight from Poland, 1977) are cases in point.[7] Granted, these plays belong to popular culture and hence are a far cry from the touchstone texts of Witold Gombrowicz and Sławomir Mrożek, the canonical figures of Polish émigré drama.[8] One could, of course, remain captive to the dominant narrative of Polish studies, which views popular drama as an unfortunate anachronism on the path to Gombrowicz's *Ślub* (The marriage, 1953) or Mrożek's *Emigranci* (The emigrants, 1974). However, the omission of popular plays from serious scrutiny in Polish studies is short-sighted because, whatever we may think of their art and their politics, they were a significant force in the creation of Polish expatriate culture. It is possible to go much further in marshaling texts to support this claim. I have chosen *The Encounter, A Woman from behind the Iron Curtain,* and *A Polish Woman Straight from Poland* as my primary examples because they bring into focus the twisted skein of diaspora, traveling, and hybridity (or resistance to hybridity). I have selected these particular plays, moreover, because they are separated by roughly fifteen-year intervals and thus offer insights into changing cultural contexts and practices.

First, I will examine the inclusions and exclusions that organize concepts of home/lessness and "Polishness" in *The Encounter, Iron Curtain,* and *Straight from Poland.*[9] Then, to problematize this reading, I will turn to the figure of a Polish woman traveler who, as the titles of the plays suggest, is essential to the plot even though (or precisely because?) border crossings in Poland under communist rule required considerable investments of time, effort, and money.[10] From a dramaturgical perspective, an energetic coming and going of women visitors from Poland is necessary to the intrigue: these women are the object of erotic as well as patriotic desire. Desire for homeland, figured as desire for a woman, is a familiar trope.[11] This, however, is only half the story.

In keeping with the trope of homeland as woman, the women visitors embody the home country. But they also embody the distance from the home country, of which émigrés are always achingly aware. In having the women travel rather than dwell, the plays insist on replacing the cultural figure *native* with the intercultural figure *traveler*. What does it mean, then, that these texts add the trope of intercultural travel to the trope of political exile? I propose that the persistence of the trope of cross-cultural traveling in Polish émigré drama can be enormously productive for questioning Polish culture's long-standing tropes or models of identity formation and for imagining countertropes or figures for alternative modes of being. Thus, the three plays can be seen as figurative markers of characteristic shifts in perspective on the opposition between home and exile. As I will argue, these texts plunge the audience into what I take to be a central concern in identity studies—the difference between a community that defines itself by its national boundaries and one that seeks another, more flexible, less geographically determined frame of knowing.

The Encounter, Iron Curtain, and *Straight from Poland* are tips of now mostly lost icebergs. I approach these plays as both dramatic forms and cultural practices that spoke powerfully to, and about, a particular audience at a particular time and place: the Polish community in postwar Britain, made up predominantly of political refugees. Each play premiered in a Polish-language theater in London. A theater building, of course, is a particular kind of house: a playhouse, a home to plays and actors. Hence it is especially appropriate to speak of drama and theater in the context of houses, homes, and homelessness. It is even more appropriate, I would argue, to speak of émigré drama and theater in that context. The very existence of an émigré playhouse embodies both home (performances are in the language of an émigré community) and homelessness (performances in the language of an émigré community foreground the fact that émigrés do not belong in their host culture). Home, troped as language, has powerful evocative potential for those who seek to represent exile as something other than lack. Since the vicissitudes of history have rendered, for many, the geographic concept of home elusive or fragile, there is always a tendency to claim the vernacular as a kind of homeland. Simply put, language extends the possibility of a home away from home. And what better place to experience this linguistic home-making than an émigré playhouse?

This still leaves (as all performances do) thoroughly and disturbingly open-ended the question of what the relation is between what we as spectators *see* and what we as spectators *want* to see. More specifically, how do the three plays manage to produce so strong a mechanism for recognizing home apart from the fact that, in an émigré playhouse, home is constructed and lived in language? One way, I submit, is by representing home as always already lost. It is not simply that there was once a home there and now it is lost, but that there is from the beginning something profoundly uncanny about "that place." Thus, the issue is not nostalgic regret, but rather the perverse slipperiness of home. Home is familiar precisely to the extent that it is somehow a construction that has never been: a stable, fixed entity, a securely boundaried place that can be grasped in pristine isolation.

Like most Polish plays written and performed outside Poland, *The Encounter, Iron Curtain,* and *Straight from Poland* have attracted almost no scholarly attention. Silently declared to be beneath serious scrutiny, they remain a politely overlooked embarrassment in most studies of Polish expatriate culture. For many reasons, not the least important of which is the need to gain a fuller view of postwar Polish drama, it was these and other plays that came to occupy my attention as I began to rethink the very logic of organizing Polish literature according to the geographic and political boundaries between homeland and outland.[12] The fetishization of those boundaries has produced certain blindnesses that leave Polish studies out of step with advances in theories of identity concurrently developing in many different fields, including anthropology, geography, gender studies, and postcolonial studies. Since the lifting of censorship barriers between Poland and emigration in 1989, there is a growing sense that Polish émigré literature is a more complex, dynamic, and self-contradictory phenomenon than earlier methodological approaches suggested. At the moment, the objects and methods of Polish studies are in an exciting and chaotic state. I will step into this chaos and will try to make at least some sense of it.

Few would deny that the artistic value of *The Encounter, Iron Curtain,* and *Straight from Poland* is open to question. However, the notion of artistic quality does not exhaust the value of cultural objects or the pleasures involved in their consumption: there are many other attributes and effects for which cultural objects may be valued or enjoyed. Though one might dismiss the three plays out of hand as banal and therefore unworthy of analysis, I must admit that their spirited handling of the conventions of popular drama mostly has given me pleasure. Mostly, with one exception. This exception startled me, first by its seeming banality, then by its possible implications. The modest cause of my bewilderment was a throwaway line in *The Encounter,* an incongruous clause of six words rendered in broken English: "*Hwaj dze Poles . . . szut . . . go hom*" (Budzyński n.d., 32) In an act of cultural misprision, the former soldier Ignacy believes that the newspaper headline Why the Poles Should Go Home encourages Polish refugees like himself to feel at home in Britain of 1947. It is obvious that Ignacy has little proficiency in English, but his line of thinking is not without its sterling logic: since Poles fought alongside the British in World War II, they are welcome to stay in Britain. More wrong he could not have been. As this brief scene suggests, the political reality of postwar Britain had a logic of its own. The newspaper headline appears to allude to statements by British officials like Home Secretary Herbert Morrison, who, as Louise London notes, insisted that "at the end of the war the Home Office should require all refugees to depart, not even excepting those who had voluntarily served in the armed forces, and that those refugees who could not emigrate could be repatriated" (2000, 253–54).

It is easy to overlook Ignacy's line and hence to claim that the liberal intent of *The Encounter* is to draw the absolute boundary of difference between a bad, Soviet-controlled Poland, to which the characters are unable or unwilling to return, and a good British society that welcomes them. However, the central fact of *The Encounter* is that the characters are displaced persons in more ways than one. They belong neither there, in Poland under communist rule, nor here, in the place of the play, Britain. This is no longer a simple opposition between East and West, metropole and margins, inside and outside. It was this paradoxical dynamic that caught my attention. That throwaway line, "*Hwaj dze Poles . . . shut . . . go hom,*" suddenly seemed crucial. Poles should go home. But where is home? I wanted to pull out and reweave that loose thread, and many others like it.

To establish a conceptual context for my discussion, it is necessary to look in several directions at once. Taking as her point of departure Benedict Anderson's familiar formulation that "in the modern world everyone can, should, will 'have' a nationality, as he or she 'has' a gender" (1991, 5), Eve Kosofsky Sedgwick argues that "just as every culture has *some* mechanism—different mechanisms—to constitute . . . a 'sex/gender system,' a way of negotiating back and forth between chromosomal sex and social gender, so every *modern* culture and person must be seen as partaking of what we might (albeit clumsily) call a 'habitation/nation system.'" She goes on to describe the habitation/nation system as a "set of discursive and institutional arrangements that mediate between the physical fact that each person inhabits, at a given time, a particular geographical space, and the far more abstract, sometimes even apparently unrelated organization of what has emerged since the late seventeenth century as her/his national identity, as signalized by, for instance, citizenship." As Sedgwick points out, "the existence of habitation/nation systems, and their great variety worldwide, tends to become visible most easily as 'exceptional' stresses on a system (thereby) taken as normal." Among the pressures on a "normal" system, she mentions "personal and political crises concerning exile and expatriation" (1992, 239; emphasis in original).

To modify Sedgwick's formulation somewhat, one could say that among the pressures that expose the arbitrariness of "normal" systems are *gendered* experiences of exile and expatriation. As I will argue, one way to reconceive the opposition between home and exile/expatriation is to run the question of national identity athwart questions of gender and sexuality and to rethink the status of women in home/less discourse. National ideologies often depend on essentializing equivalences between gender/sexuality and nationhood. Women, possibly because of their reproductive ability, have been seen as key symbols of national selfhood, regardless of the actual status of the female population in a given country. They have been construed as biological reproducers of a national collectivity as well as guardians and transmitters of a national culture. Attention to such gender-coded issues necessitates bringing the home, the principal site for performing gender and sexuality, more sharply into view despite the traditional "masculinist uninterest in the home" (Rose 1993, 47).

Before I began this project, I expected *The Encounter, Iron Curtain,* and *Straight from Poland* to reflect the susceptibility of the Polish community in Britain to artistic and political conservatism.[13] Lacking the ironic and self-critical dimensions of high culture, these examples of popular culture would make, I thought, this susceptibility transparent. They would resonate with familiar assumptions about the relationship between national self-identification and national space—assumptions grounded in the conservative discourse of national difference (here, "Polishness"). Tom Nairn notes, "Whenever we talk about nationalism, we normally find ourselves talking before too long about 'feelings,' 'instincts,' supposed desires and hankerings to 'belong,' and so on" (1981, 334). To take his point a step further, one could say that these hankerings to belong need a good home—a national space that at once localizes and stabilizes an individual and collective identity.

First, a brief contextual interjection. It is a truism of identity studies that the spatialization of national identity in conservative discourse is driven by the binary logic of world versus home. It is another truism that the world-home (outside-inside) configuration of social space correlates with the gendered assignment of social roles. The world is the treacherous domain of the pursuit of power and material gain. Typically, it is the domain of the male. The home, presided over by the woman, represents the sanctuary of the "true" self. The presence of the woman, enshrined as mother, a trope of ideal femininity, is crucial. This phantasmic female is the unyielding and faithful guardian of the home and its traditions and hence of national self-identification. Thus both mother and home are implicated in the construction of national difference. In colonial and expatriate contexts, however, home takes on added political urgency and figurative cogency as the most significant bastion against encroachments of foreign difference.

Given the popularity of *The Encounter, Iron Curtain,* and *Straight from Poland* with Polish émigré audiences, I expected these plays to promote a conservative version of Polish nationalism that needs the Polish home to frame transactions of nationalist, us-versus-them axiology in order to fend off foreign difference, both East and West. I assumed that these dramas would be acts of patriotic worship, celebrating the dominant claim in the Polish émigré community—the claim that the Polish nation has escaped social change. These texts would make of female characters a screen on which they project a fantasy (an idealization fueled, perhaps, by the authors' exile) of the Polish nation untroubled by questions of gender inequality. The Polish home would be constructed as a bastion against aberrations of modernity and set up as a fortress of traditional Polish values. Women would tend the flame of domesticity and instill national pride and patriotic morality in the young. The wounded, heavy-breathing, patriotic "we" would spin cobwebs in the Polish home. These were the assumptions I brought to the three plays. Did my reading of the plays bear them out?[14]

| | |

How did Polish émigrés in postwar Britain react to a cultural and political environment that increasingly denied them their Polishness? Weren't they embarrassed by their different manners and customs, by the public exposure of their uncertain or unseemly behavior in an alien land? Faced with such pressures, how could they (re)construct a positive Polish identity? Budzyński's *The Encounter,* Kiersnowski's *A Woman from behind the Iron Curtain,* and Baliński's *A Polish Woman Straight from Poland* know the answer: by having a Polish home. As Ignacy in *The Encounter* says, "Let them say whatever they want, but one feels different in the Polish home" (Budzyński n.d., 22). In other words, the Polish home preserves Polish difference abroad.[15] Here is intimately connected to there. To be sure, the native there has been destroyed, contaminated, rendered illegitimate, or taken over by foreign conquerors. But those forced to remain abroad reconstitute here, in new surroundings, the conditions that existed there before the trauma that necessitated displacement. The issue, however, is more complicated, more paradoxical. Let me begin with a reading of Budzyński's and Kiersnowski's plays. I will come back to Baliński's farce later. The reason for my approach is not difficult to discern: nonnormative practices expose weak links in normative regimes—which is just what I want to do. Normative would not be normative if it were not for the nonnormative.

In Budzyński's *The Encounter,* set in 1947, the Polish home is alive and well—in a boardinghouse in London. The boardinghouse is an ambivalent setting: neither a home nor a hotel. One could argue that the opposition between home and homelessness is recast as the opposition between a lost but stable elsewhere and a contingent, transient here. Unable or unwilling to return to Poland under communist rule, unwelcome in their host country, the characters have no other place to go. The boardinghouse represents their inbetweenness. Without denying this interpretation, I submit that we might expand our understanding of the play by considering the forcefulness with which the action foregrounds Polish sameness versus the alterity of foreigners. How does this sameness come about?

To begin with, the British are invisible in the play. To put this point another way, we do not see the characters engaged in intercultural interaction with what could be called *not-home.*[16] The Polish émigré community closes in on itself and responds with various attitudes of refusal to the host culture. This has a lot to do with the characters' resentment of Western political agendas. They are ruefully aware of the fact that the West has betrayed Poles in the postwar reconfiguration of power in Europe. The betrayal and injustice convince the characters—and, presumably, the audience—that no just recompense could ever heal the suffering that the postwar division of Europe has inflicted on Poles. In the play's reenactment of the spatialized axiology of the home-world and us-them discourse, the Polish home is, predictably, a haven away from the treacherous and corrupt public sphere. Yet I cannot leave this interpretation without asking why Budzyński includes the former war profiteer Jaśkowicz in the Polish home. Nicknamed Rockefeller, Jaśkowicz is a cynical operator, tainted by his collaboration with the Nazis. Why not simply omit him?

In the play's emotionally wounded émigré community, which searches restlessly for clear-cut definitions as a means of clarifying and affirming a moral idea of Polishness, the former war profiteer does not fit. And yet, ultimately, he is forgiven and included, rather than shunned. What are we to make of this? I propose that the figure of Jaśkowicz is crucial. Through him, the play demonstrates the recuperative and amalgamative powers of the Polish home. The play shows that the seductive aura of the Polish home can reform a wayward person like Jaśkowicz and turn a group of strangers into a community by enabling them to recognize the "natural" bond of their Polish origins. Thus, home is rendered nonstatic, not exclusively an aspect of setting, but also an aspect of action. The Polish home in *The Encounter,* then, is a place: a stronghold of Polishness and a frontier outpost that sustains the sense of an enduring moral order despite the moral chaos outside. But the Polish home in the play is also a discursive practice that has agency of its own; it both includes "our kind" and legitimizes the exclusionary, xenophobic attitudes of cultural self-assertion and national survival in an alien culture. In short, this home performs, rather than merely preserves, Polish difference.

According to the familiar cultural myth, however, a home is not a home if there is no woman to preside over the family hearth. Here, the mainstay of the Polish home is Mrs. Zabielska, a maternal woman, nurturing and caring. In her role as hostess and housekeeper, she makes boardinghouse residents feel at home in the Polish home. It is tempting to conclude that she fits the Victorian ideal of the domestic angel. In fact, she fits the Polish ideal of the patriotic mother, who does not shirk her obligation to the cause of Poland's freedom. Accordingly, Mrs. Zabielska volunteered for auxiliary, noncombative service during the war. Still, she feels more comfortable mending men's socks in her living room than participating in public affairs. This is a point to which I will return later.

In the final act, several tenants are about to move out. It is at this point that the characters confront the impending reality of diaspora, understood here as a condition of scatteredness. As one of them says, "We're dispersing all over the world. What will bind us together? What do we all share?" (Budzyński n.d., 62). Jaśkowicz ironizes the force unifying Poles in diaspora is their one-upmanship toward each other and their hostility toward the British. A retired colonel offers a pathos-ridden answer: Poles in diaspora have been united through their participation in the war effort. Mrs. Zabielska, however, has the last word: "It's home, family, comity. That's what gives us strength to survive. And that's what makes our stubborn refusal [to return to Poland under communist rule] meaningful. Ultimately, our home country will understand this refusal" (62). Mrs. Zabielska's pivotal monologue is haunted by a kind of spectral presence, that of an undivided Poland. As she would have it, diaspora is a condition of temporary lack where identity, individual and communal, depends on the idea of a sacred homeland to be recovered in an unspecified future. Yet the defensive tone of the last sentence is puzzling. How are we to understand the anxiety of Poles in emigration vis-à-vis Poles in Poland? Aren't Poles in emigration patriotic heroes who promote the cause of Poland in the international forum and testify with their own displacement to the repressive terms of Poland's Soviet occupation? The conclusion of Mrs. Zabielska's monologue points rather insistently in a different direction. The defensive tone suggests an inequitable power relationship between here and there. Poles in emigration submit to the dominant moral authority of Poles in Poland, who assume the position of silent observer and presiding judge. Thus, the final line adds a subtle yet stunning twist to Mrs. Zabielska's speech: Polish homemaking here is necessary to assure those in the home country that the émigrés are still Poles rather than cosmopolitan, multicultural Others. Identity hardens into essence.

At first glance, then, this is an unbearably pathetic, even saccharine play. Into this world comes Sergeant-Major Anna Maleska. She no more belongs in Mrs. Zabielska's domestic sanctuary than Mrs. Zabielska does in Anna's battalion. Anna was a commanding officer in the underground resistance known as the Home Army. In the Warsaw uprising of 1944, she fought until the last bullet. She enters to the strains of "Warszawianka" (The song of Warsaw, 1831), which originated during the Polish uprising of 1830 against Russia.[17] Thus, she is cast as a spiritual daughter of Emilia Plater, the heroine of the 1830 uprising and the paradigmatic woman warrior of Polish cultural mythology.[18] As soon becomes evident, however, Plater's precedent stigmatizes rather than sanctions Anna's transgression of the traditional norms of gender-appropriate conduct.

Anna arrives to join her husband and son, from whom she was separated during the war. The characters expect to see a woman who has been rendered "unfeminine" by her military service. However, Anna is both feminine and unfeminine, a combination that catches them off guard. She wears an elegant uniform and numerous medals as well as Chanel no. 5. To make matters worse, she is feminine in the wrong way. She has been inducted into the pantheon of patriotic heroes, but her body has not become a marble sculpture. She is a suspect woman with a rapacious appetite for life, rather than a saintly martyr at the altar of homeland. In the Home Army, she was known as "a wild woman of the underground," "a dynamite woman," indeed "a volcano" (30–31). In short, Anna appears to have rejected the ideals of the sacred home, chaste femininity, and social order. How does *The Encounter* handle Anna's transgressive energy and nonnormative behavior? In other words, how does the play protect the Polish community from Anna's multifarious Otherness?

The Encounter does acknowledge Anna's patriotic heroism. When Poland needed her, she chose her country over her family. But the play also makes clear that with women's military service comes their fateful emancipation from inherited gender roles. In wartime Poland, Anna entered the traditionally male realm of military combat; in postwar London, she neglects her family to immerse herself in politics, another "unfeminine" sphere. In a didactic move, the play contrasts Anna with Mrs. Zabielska. Mrs. Zabielska is about to be happily married to the retired colonel, on whom she has had a civilizing effect. She has smoothed out his rough edges, in keeping with women's traditional attributes. Needless to say, Anna faces a failing marriage and her son's delinquency. There is more at issue. Anna's neglect of her family is a harbinger of national doom: gender transgressors like Anna threaten the social stability of the national household. Read thus, the antifamily plot, represented by Anna's emancipation, becomes an alarmist allegory for the national plight.

This instigates the play's anxious search for what lies beneath Anna's Plater-like persona. An operation of stripping away begins. And, inevitably, what lies beneath is what "saves" Anna: her "essential" respectable femininity. Her desire to leave Poland is tied to her role as wife and mother. She has been obsessive about joining her husband and son—she is a good wife and mother, after all. The next step is to clear Anna of the suspicion that she had an affair with the enigmatic Julek, whose name she calls out in her dreams. We find out that Julek is a war orphan whom Anna took under her wing. Thus the play turns a liability into an asset: what seemed to be her infidelity proves to be her displaced maternal feeling. Anna's integrity is vindicated. At this point, it is possible to stage a reconciliation between Anna and her husband, Roman. It goes almost without saying that Jaśkowicz, the former war profiteer, is spared such an elaborate process of exoneration. We simply find out that he used his business deals with the Nazis to aid the anti-Nazi underground resistance. His "essential" masculinity is never questioned.

The Encounter taps into deep fears about women's agency and particularly about women's interventions into male-centered history. Anna becomes suspect because of her "excessive" desire, both patriotic and sexual. However, the gender confusion, which the war provoked, is erased, and Anna's "essential" respectable femininity is restored. With Anna brought back into the domestic fold, social order, which was threatened by female unrule, is reestablished. In more general terms, the play makes the ability of Polish culture to survive dependent on, above all, Polish women's (purported) traditionalism.

My reading has sought to show how *The Encounter* constructs a vernacular home that refuses to admit both foreigners and transgressive Polish women. As this home resists the world outside with its postwar political agendas, social change, and commodifying practices, the home-world divide becomes analogous to the divide between the spiritual and the material. This is an appropriate point at which to take another look at the fact that the Polish home in the play is a boardinghouse. That is to say, this home is not just for home use. Co-owned by Mrs. Zabielska and two veterans, the boardinghouse is both a home and a house for profit, a marketplace commodity. *The Encounter* turns slyly, wryly perverse. The Polish home in the play presumes a distance from the grubby reality of economic hierarchies. This home seems to be the inverse of commodity, indeed a precapitalist Eden, while in fact it challenges the idea that home cannot be commodified for public consumption. Ultimately, then, the play suggests that there is a tangled relation between "Polish" spiritual values, which the residents of the boardinghouse consider immutable, and "Western" marketplace values—a relation sedimented with contradictions at the complex intersection of home/lessness and Polishness in Polish expatriate culture in Britain.

Budzyński's *The Encounter* premiered in the early postwar period, when the essentializing imperatives of Polishness came to preoccupy the Polish public in Britain. The play ostensibly celebrates the traditional, stable, securely boundaried Polish home—if one fails to notice that this home has been recast in market terms. Twelve years later, Kiersnowski's *A Woman from behind the Iron Curtain* seems to resist the polonocentric nativism that plays such as *The Encounter* enacted for an émigré audience. The action takes place during the post-Stalinist thaw of the mid-1950s, when Poland opened up to the West. The setting is an isolated farmstead in Wales where several Polish officers have settled as farmers. The farmhouse meets the essential requirement to qualify as a Polish home: it is presided over by a Polish woman, Helena. However, Helena is involved in a triangular relationship with two of the officers. By the premises of Kiersnowski's play, Helena's illicit sexuality disqualifies her as a Polish homemaker. Not only that. The Polish home in this play harbors a secret: the sudden death of one of Helena's lovers. Was she in any way responsible for his death? Was it the result of despair or an act of protest? And if protest, against what? His daughter, Zosia, arrives from Poland to seek answers to these questions.

By telling the story of a "diseased" home, *Iron Curtain* establishes home as that which is always already its own other. This, of course, is the discovery Freud made when, in his essay on the uncanny, he investigated the German word for "homey." Freud exclaims over the fact the German word for "homey" extends itself to turn into its opposite, that the meaning of *heimlich* moves with a kind of inevitability from cozy, comfortable, and familiar to hidden, secret, and strange, so that one meaning of *heimlich* is identical to its opposite, *unheimlich*. What *Iron Curtain* demonstrates, I think, is that this is exactly what the Polish home is. That is to say, the Polish home in the play is both *heimlich* and *unheimlich*, bespeaking a Polish at-homeness abroad, however fragile or deceptive, *and* serving to duplicate and intensify the ills without.

To destabilize the Polish home even further, *Iron Curtain,* like *The Encounter,* sets it up as a site of travel interaction and cultural translation. With her own modest but modern homemaking back in communist Poland as a yardstick, the woman visitor Zosia finds the Polish home in Wales too awful to contemplate: "I'm glad I don't have to live in Mrs. Dulska's parlor any more. . . . If I were in love with a man and couldn't marry him for some reason, I would live with him even without getting married" (Kiersnowski n.d., 18). She is alluding to Gabriela Zapolska's play *Moralność pani Dulskiej* (The morality of Mrs. Dulska, 1906), a scathing indictment of bourgeois life. Mrs. Dulska's parlor, a figure of conservative, stultifying mentality and repressive morality, has been transplanted into the émigré community. What might seem to be a domestic sanctuary to others is an emblem of airlessness to Zosia. The airlessness of the Polish home in Wales, the notion that the émigrés live cocooned from the larger society, tropes the airlessness of the Polish emigration itself. As in *The Encounter,* the émigré community is insular and self-absorbed, and its members speak only to each other. In *The Encounter,* however, the émigrés had a compelling sense of patriotic mission. In *Iron Curtain,* on the other hand, the larger world has receded, and so did whatever sense of patriotic mission the émigrés had had. Their conversation is increasingly obscurantist, acrimonious, and self-destructive. Their energy seems to be dissipating in squabbles. A response comes from one of the young generation in Poland. Zosia is proof that Polish society back home is neither ailing nor numb, but changed and doing battle. Her dissonance in the Polish home in Wales disrupts the homogeneity of national identity—the amalgamative vision of Poles in Poland and Poles in emigration that defines *The Encounter* and plays like it.

In *The Encounter,* the "deviant" Jaśkowicz is "healed" by the Polish home. In *Iron Curtain,* it is the "diseased" Polish home that needs to be "healed." The émigrés are worn out and embittered, and their home is stuffy. Zosia declares, "This house needs some fresh air, and someone has to shake you up" (39). She is strong, persistent, unsentimental. Confronted with the secret of her father's death, she takes on the role of a detective. The émigrés resent her "unfeminine" conduct, attributing it to the destruction of the traditional social order by the new communist (dis)order in Poland. One of the characters ironizes that Zosia is a product of communist propaganda, which promotes the optimistic image of a strong, happy population. Zosia shrugs off such comments. So what *does* empower her to be so outspoken and assertive? It is her participation in the Warsaw uprising of 1944 and in the anticommunist resistance after the war: "Sometimes we [women] had to be more masculine than men" (46). "While you were making out with your missus, we had to go on fighting for years" (50). "Don't start this [nonsense] with me; I was in the Home Army" (62).

For all her revisionist ways, however, Zosia does not challenge the concept of the Polish home itself. She wants to instill new life into the Polish home while keeping its axiological structure intact. This structure has traditionally been allied with Catholicism. Zosia's unswerving Catholicism comes into focus when she looks for a Catholic church in Wales while planning a memorial service for her late father. Granted, Zosia believes in the primacy of romantic love over the patriarchal institution of marriage, thus rejecting the idea of marriage and family as woman's only route to fulfillment. Still, she insists that she would not be able to fall in love and marry across national lines because she and her non-Polish husband would remain separated by their respective national histories, with all the attendant cultural codes. As she puts it, "All we [Poles] have to say is *Warsaw, uprising,* or *occupation,* and we understand each other perfectly" (36). This might well come from a faith in cultural stability that, by the premise of the play, ensures the sharing of codes. But the logic of the us-them divide, which defines *The Encounter,* is operative here as well. The final scene is paradigmatic for this exclusionist, conservative current. The mutual attraction between Zosia and one of the émigrés leads to a marriage proposal. There may be a whiff of stereotyping here (isn't it the job of women to bring quarreling factions together?), but the anticipated wedding serves as a resolution of conflict—within the émigré community on the one hand and between Poles in Poland and Poles in emigration on the other. *Iron Curtain* has unsentimentally interrogated the seductive pleasures of "feeling at home" in the Polish home only to offer a simple act of renewing it—through reconciliation and marriage.

The characters in Budzyński's *The Encounter* and Kiersnowski's *Iron Curtain* resist the urge to be at home anywhere. In the figure of Ewa Morowiec, Baliński's *Straight from Poland* celebrates the urge to be at home everywhere. Thus his farce clears a conceptual space where one can begin to consider alternative models of identity—a particularly important move in the light of exile's emphasis on loss and dissociation. Let me begin with a cursory reading of the play, to outline the plot and to highlight the intercultural figure *traveler.* The time is the 1970s. Ewa is an attractive, matter-of-factly gritty divorcée who aspires to become a fashion model. She arrives in London to visit her aunt. Yearning for a wider world of freedom, she is scheming to be married so that she can obtain resident status in Britain. She meets a number of interested men, all of them geriatric Polish émigrés who are looking for a clone of the maternal Mrs. Zabielska. The problem is that Ewa is nothing like Mrs. Zabielska. On the subway, while returning home from a performance of Shakespeare in English, Ewa meets Piotr Justyn, a young veterinarian from Poland, who has just completed an internship at Oxford. It is love at first sight. Ewa accepts Piotr's proposal of marriage without realizing that he has a Polish passport. Within hours after their wedding, they leave for Paris, where Piotr has another internship.

Baliński's farce carries an emphatically nonfarcical epigraph, a quotation from Cyprian Kamil Norwid, the most prominent poet of the first post-Romantic generation in Poland: "Poles consider it patriotic to overlook their weaknesses; they haven't developed a language to speak of those weaknesses freely" (Baliński 1986, 44). What are those weaknesses? And, in choosing this epigraph, is Baliński suggesting that his farce is an attempt to develop a language that would address those weaknesses and shock us into a fresh perspective? One way to grapple with these questions is to take the travel metaphor as far as it can go.

Ewa refuses to submit to the palpable constraints (spatial, political, economic, social, cultural) that have defined life in Poland. Tellingly, her last name is Morowiec, which suggests *morowa babka* (Ms. Cool).[19] This Ms. Cool is calmly audacious in making a proposal or demand. She is also assured and unabashed where diffidence might be expected. While the émigrés are patria-centered (even though their patriotism is shown to be shallow), Ewa is shamelessly individualistic. "I don't like family warmth," she declares (47). In Polish culture, this is something little short of heresy. In choosing willed homelessness over family warmth (i.e., at-homeness or a sense of belonging), Ewa demolishes the localizing and stabilizing regimes of the Polish home. In the best (post)modern way, she knows the fundamental fragility of place, and she cultivates a radical skepticism toward the condition called home. She recodes home as a form of travel, as dwelling-in-travel. She grew up in Warsaw, she gets married in London, and she moves on to Paris.

Does Ewa's cosmopolitan mobility mean that she does not have Polish "nationness" as a marker of identity? Or, instead, that her nationness may well have a structure different enough to put into question any single definition of nationness? Ewa's story of dwelling-in-travel is an extreme case, no doubt. But it posits identity as a fluid site rather than a stable and fixed essence. Identity depends on a point of reference; as that point moves nomadically, so do the contours of identity. In the space created by Ewa's story of dwelling-in-travel lies a less amalgamative, more open-ended model of identity and community. To dwell-in-travel, one must necessarily resist seeing the world in terms of the standard, binary paradigm predicated on the distinction between homeland and outland; instead, one must view the world in a decentralized, pluralist way.

Budzyński's *The Encounter* and Kiersnowski's *Iron Curtain* offer the image of a redeemed Polish community in the guise of a utopian Polishness in which the nation is reconstituted as an extended, inclusive family. At the opposite end is Baliński's *Straight from Poland,* which provides a salutary corrective to the amalgamative project of *The Encounter* and *Iron Curtain.* Ewa Morowiec can be seen as a nonessentialist who exposes the complacencies (Norwid's "weaknesses") of Polish culture and subverts the essentialist categories of identity that keep patriotic morality in place. In its modulations between scatteredness (Ewa's dwelling-in-travel) and connection (Ewa's participation in English culture, which leads to her marriage to a Pole), Baliński's farce accepts the necessary brokenness of things and embraces disruption. Reality here is the hard-won, sometimes difficult reality of the reconceived version of diaspora, a version based on passages of wholeness crafted out of a condition of ineradicable scatteredness.

III

A PARTICULAR INSTANCE of intercultural traveling—encounters between Poles in emigration and women visitors from Poland—is one of the major themes in Polish drama written and performed in Britain, represented here by Budzyński's *The Encounter,* Kiersnowski's *A Woman from behind the Iron Curtain,* and Baliński's *A Polish Woman Straight from Poland.* In their own ways, the three plays resonate with a number of recent interrogations of community, including those of Stuart Hall, who views diaspora as the site of an unresolved dialogue between continuity and disruption (see

Hall 1990). *The Encounter* and *Iron Curtain* use a powerful localizing and stabilizing strategy: centering national identity around a particular locus, the Polish home. *Straight from Poland* challenges that strategy. It moves away from privileging relations of dwelling over relations of travel. In doing so, it shifts from promoting a homogenizing vision of Polishness—a vision that links the "essence" of a nation with space, to questioning essentialist formulations, which may lead to nationalist orthodoxies.

Baliński broaches in important and useful ways the possibility of diaspora as a viable model of identity. Writing out of what Rosi Braidotti would call "a nomadic aesthetic," he tropes the nomadic wandering of transnational diaspora. Thus his play sets up a conceptual context for a dynamic account of self and community. By *community* I mean not a securely boundaried, fixed entity, but a diasporic version grounded in the recognition that wholeness and fixity are a transitory proposition—and that any accompanying claim for unity and stability must be tempered by a recognition of the fragility of such a proposal. Therefore I take Baliński's farce as a paradigm of nomadic sensibility. Nomadism, of course, is Braidotti's way of figuring "the subject who has relinquished all idea, desire, or nostalgia for fixity. This figuration expresses the desire for an identity made of transitions, successive shifts, and coordinated changes, without and against an essential unity" (1994, 22). In speaking of nomadism, I am, I realize, introducing yet another trope into an already crowded field. But to represent the nonstatic, varied nature of the concept of home in Baliński's farce, to escape the limiting oppositions (e.g., homeland versus nonhomeland, homeland versus exile, exile versus diaspora, diaspora versus homeland) one must generate a range of terms.

A discussion of Baliński's 1977 farce, which interrupts the normative narrative of the Polish home, might seem to be a foregone conclusion at the turn of the twentieth century. After all, Poles in postcommunist Poland are eager to rejoin the European community. Yet the significance of this play extends beyond Baliński's immediate context and into the early twenty-first century. As I was working on this essay, the online version of the daily *Gazeta Wyborcza* carried an article about the resistance of Rzeszów's municipal authorities to local initiatives to commemorate Rzeszów-born theater director and theorist Jerzy Grotowski (1933–1999). Although he ranks alongside Stanislavski and Brecht in twentieth-century theater, the Rzeszów city council insists that Grotowski does not deserve special recognition. As one member of the city council has put it, "That man was an internationalist. He didn't recognize homelands. First he fled from Rzeszów to Wrocław. Then he fled abroad" (Konieczny 2000). Grotowski's detractors also point out that he ordered his ashes to be scattered over India. In other words, Grotowski is faulted on two counts. First, he refused to center his work around a native locus, the homeland. Second, he refused to return to his native home posthumously. Paradoxically, then, Grotowski's detractors have put their finger on the most important aspect of his life and art: he negotiated a path beyond the identity divide East-West, Polish–non-Polish, native-alien.

The issue that concerns me here is the persistent dichotomy of inside-outside that nationalist discourse deploys with telling effect. As the Rzeszów controversy shows, inside-outside perceptions are still very much alive in Polish culture. What do these perceptions say? The charge that Grotowski failed to "recognize homelands" suggests that, in the name of repressive, essentialist nativism, geography is still seen as the site of Polish identity. Those who assert their independence from the home center and its polonocentric nativism are stigmatized as internationalists, that is, traitors. The opposition between homeland and outland—in its literal and figurative versions—is very hard to get away from. The emphasis on geographically bound notions of self and community, on native belonging, on at-homeness seems to preclude a discourse that would imagine other configurations of identity and community—a discourse that would loosen the hold of national origins on cultural allegiances and practices. We thus return to the pivotal question that resonates in Baliński's seemingly trivial farce: Where and what is homeland?

Notes

This chapter is dedicated to Elwira Grossman and Bożena Shallcross. All translations of source material are mine unless noted otherwise.

1. As will be evident, my use of the term *home* refers not only to a physical structure and to spatial practices such as a style of dwelling, but also to cultural constructions of the idea of home and at-homeness.

2. Thus my perspective differs from approaches that universalize and idealize the comforts of home. See, for example, Gaston Bachelard's classic definition of home as "protected intimacy" (1994, 3). Important to my thinking have been attempts to theorize home as more than a domestic place of one's own, esp. Armstrong

1987, George 1996, Kaplan 1990, Rose 1993, and Vidler 1992. For new insights into the issues of home/lessness, diaspora, and hybridity in the context of performance studies, I am indebted to Loren Kruger (1998). For the most part, I have not attempted to signal specific points of indebtedness, many of which I am doubtless no longer aware of.

3. Theoretically, my argument is framed by the locational discourse of identity. In this context, the term *location* "suggests the variable nature of both 'the home' and 'the self,' for both are negotiated stances whose shapes are entirely ruled by the site from which they are defined" (George 1996, 2). For further discussion of the significance of location and positionality in new ways of configuring identity, see esp. Friedman 1998.

4. For background information, I have relied mainly on Kalemba-Kasprzak and Ratajczakowa 1998, Kiec 1999, Kiec, Ratajczakowa, and Wachowski 1994, Mirecki 1984, and Ostrowski 1964.

5. My thanks to Timothy J. Wiles for this reference.

6. By Jan Ostrowski's estimate (1964, 187), there were over two hundred Polish émigré plays by 1964. Today, the number is roughly four hundred. Most of this writing remains unpublished or buried in rare, inaccessible copies. Dobrochna Ratajczakowa (1992) has made an eloquent case for attending to this archive. For an overview in English of Polish émigré drama, see Ratajczakowa 1995.

7. From this point I will refer to the latter two plays as *Iron Curtain* and *Straight from Poland.* The years given in parentheses refer to the first production. Budzyński (1906–1972) was arguably the most successful dramatist in the Polish theater in Britain. His well-crafted plays were received with equal doses of audience enthusiasm and critical praise. Kiersnowski (1912–1977), a very prolific playwright, was another leading figure. Baliński (1899–1984) is known mainly as a poet; *Straight from Poland* appears to be his only full-length excursion into the dramatic genre.

8. In accord with the conventions of popular drama, *The Encounter, Iron Curtain,* and *Straight from Poland* have a simple, unified plot. The intrigue is triggered by a deviation from the usual order of things: the arrival of an outsider, a woman visitor from Poland. Her arrival is a crucial moment, articulating separate places: the home country and the Polish home in Britain. A series of complications ensue, and the suspense mounts until an unexpected shift (a disclosure of one's "essential" identity, a marriage proposal) intervenes to usher in the dénouement.

9. I use the term *Polishness* (skeptically, as indicated here by quotation marks) as a shorthand for cultural constructions of Polish national difference. For a study of the representation of home in Polish émigré drama as a metaphor of Polish identity and a metonym for Poland, see Ratajczakowa 1998. While the present chapter builds on Ratajczakowa's article, it differs from hers in proposing another conceptual framework (see note 3) and attempting to bring various loose ends into the picture.

10. Typically for Polish émigré drama, the woman traveler arrives from Warsaw. In Budzyński's and Kiersnowski's plays, the importance of Warsaw has to do with its symbolism as the matrix of Polish freedom fighting and, more specifically, the site of the uprising of 1944, in which the women visitors had participated. In Baliński's play, Warsaw seems to be important because it is a metropole.

11. As Laurent Berlant has argued, "a bond between erotic desire and the desire for collective political existence serves the nation, by connecting national identity and more local and personal forms of intimacy" (1991, 7). See also Parker et al. 1992.

12. Reading for geographic or political displacement, though illuminating, is not sufficient. Moreover, reading for "émigréness" foregrounds the autobiographical category of the author, which I find problematic. The rule of full disclosure obliges me to admit that I have argued for a revision of the homeland-outland paradigm in Filipowicz 2001. Now I want to push my argument further.

13. For a critique of the conservative tendencies prevalent in the Polish community in Britain, see Czaykowski and Sulik 1961.

14. For a brief discussion of the gendered division of labor in Polish émigré plays, see Ratajczakowa 1998, 142–43. Ratajczakowa argues that while Polish men in these plays tend to view Polishness as a burden, Polish women cultivate Polishness as a strategy of resisting acculturation in an alien land. While I have no wish to discount Ratajczakowa's valuable work, I want to open up Polish drama to a reading that does not assume gender to be a shared and coherent category of identity either for women or for men. The recent work on gender, exemplified by Friedman's *Mappings* (1998), spins the term outward along dimensions that cannot be subsumed solely under gender and sexuality. As I have argued here, home/lessness—in all its forms, real and figurative—is one of the most important points of departure for examining the ways in which gender and sexuality crisscross with nationality and other identity-constituting, identity-fracturing discourses.

15. Cf. George's point: "Home is a way of establishing difference" (1996, 2).

16. In making this generalization, I am also obliged to point out an exception: Ignacy's two telephone conversations with his English girlfriend, Betty. During the second conversation, Ignacy breaks off their relationship, announcing that he has a girlfriend in Poland and that Betty should date an Englishman. Why doesn't Ignacy stop at the first announcement? Why is he compelled to specify the nationality of the man Betty should date? In effect, Ignacy is policing cultural boundaries and reinforcing the us-them divide.

17. Originally written in French by Casimir Delavigne, with music by Karol Kurpiński, "The Song of Warsaw" urges Poles to rise and break the shackles of foreign oppression in a decisive move that will bring either victory or death.

18. I develop this point in Filipowicz 1996.

19. My thanks to Elwira Grossman for this observation.

Works Cited

Anderson, Benedict. 1991. *Imagined Communities: Reflections on the Origin and Spread of Nationalism.* 2d ed. London: Verso.

Armstrong, Nancy. 1987. *Desire and Domestic Fiction: A Political History of the Novel.* New York: Oxford University Press.

Bachelard, Gaston. 1994. *The Poetics of Space.* Trans. Maria Jolas. Boston: Beacon Press.

Baliński, Stanisław. 1986. *Polka prosto z kraju: Farsa w trzech aktach.* A Polish woman straight from Poland: A farce in three acts). *Dialog* 31, 9: 43–69.

Berlant, Lauren. 1991. *The Anatomy of National Fantasy: Hawthorne, Utopia, and Everyday Life.* Chicago: University of Chicago Press.

Braidotti, Rosi. 1994. *Nomadic Subjects: Embodiment and Sexual Difference in Contemporary Feminist Theory.* New York: Columbia University Press.

Budzyński, Wiktor. N.d. "Spotkanie: Komedia w trzech aktach" (The Encounter: A comedy in three acts). Manuscript in the possession of Dobrochna Ratajczakowa.

Chaudhuri, Una. 1995. *Staging Place: The Geography of Modern Drama.* Ann Arbor: University of Michigan Press.

Czaykowski, Bogdan, and Bolesław Sulik. 1961. *Polacy w W. Brytanii* (Poles in Great Britain). Paris: Instytut Literacki.

Filipowicz, Halina. 1996. "The Daughters of Emilia Plater." In *Engendering Slavic Literatures,* ed. Pamela Chester and Sibelan Forrester, 34–58. Bloomington: Indiana University Press.

———. 2001. "Beginning to Theorize 'Polish Émigré Literature.'" In *Between Lvov, New York, and Ulysses' Ithaca: Józef Wittlin—Poet, Essayist, Novelist,* ed. Anna Frajlich, 225–42. Toruń: Nicholas Copernicus University; New York: Columbia University Press.

Freud, Sigmund. 1953–74. "The 'Uncanny.'" In *The Standard Edition of the Complete Psychological Works,* ed. James Strachey, 17:217–52. Trans. Strachey et al. 24 volumes: London: Hogarth Press.

Friedman, Susan Stanford. 1998. *Mappings: Feminism and the Cultural Geographies of Encounter.* Princeton: Princeton University Press.

George, Rosemary Marangoly. 1996. *The Politics of Home: Postcolonial Relocations and Twentieth-Century Fiction.* Cambridge: Cambridge University Press.

Hall, Stuart. 1990. "Cultural Identity and Diaspora." In *Identity: Community, Culture, Difference,* ed. Jonathan Rutherford, 222–37. London: Lawrence.

Kalemba-Kasprzak, Elżbieta, and Dobrochna Ratajczakowa, eds. 1998. *Dramat i teatr emigracyjny po roku 1939* (Émigré drama and theater after 1939). Wrocław: Wiedza o Kulturze.

Kaplan, Caren. 1990. "Deterritorializations: The Rewriting of Home and Exile in Western Feminist Discourse." In *The Nature and Context of Minority Discourse,* ed. Abdul R. JanMohamed and David Lloyd, 357–68. New York: Oxford University Press.

Kiec, Izolda. 1999. *Teatr służebny polskiej emigracji po 1939 roku* (The utilitarian theater of Polish émigré society after 1939). Poznań: Wydawnictwo Naukowe Uniwersytetu im. Adama Mickiewicza.

Kiec, Izolda, Dobrochna Ratajczakowa, and Jacek Wachowski, eds. 1994. *Teatr i dramat polskiej emigracji, 1939–1989* (The theater and drama of Polish émigré society). Poznań: Acarus.

Kiersnowski, Ryszard. N.d. "Dziewczyna z tamtej strony: Sztuka w trzech aktach" (A woman from behind the Iron Curtain: a play in three acts). Manuscript in the possession of Dobrochna Ratajczakowa.

Konieczny, Grzegorz. 2000. "Grotowski non grata?" *Gazeta Wyborcza,* June 13. <http://www.gazeta.pl/Iso/Plus/Kraj/Ostatnio/890jed. html>.

Kruger, Loren, ed. 1998. *Theatre, Diaspora, and the Politics of Home. Theatre Journal* 50, 1 (spec. issue): 1–150.

London, Louise. 2000. *Whitehall and the Jews, 1933–1948: British Immigration Policy, Jewish Refugees, and the Holocaust.* Cambridge: Cambridge University Press.

Mirecki, Wiesław. 1984. *Wozem Tespisa po obcych drogach* (In Tespis's carriage on foreign roads). Warsaw: Ludowa Spółdzielnia Wydawnicza.

Nairn, Tom. 1981. *The Break-Up of Britain: Crisis and Neo-Nationalism.* 2d ed. London: Verso.

Ostrowski, Jan. 1964. "Dramatopisarstwo" (Drama). In *Literatura polska na obczyźnie, 1940–1960* (Polish literature abroad), ed. Tymon Terlecki, 1:187–208. 2 vols. London: B. Świderski.

Parker, Andrew, Mary Russo, Doris Sommer, and Patricia Yaeger. 1992. Introduction to *Nationalisms & Sexualities,* ed. Andrew Parker et al., 1–18. New York: Routledge.

Ratajczakowa, Dobrochna. 1992. "Nieobecność. Nieznany dramat emigracyjny (1939–1980)" (Absence: Unknown Polish émigré drama). In *Między Polską a światem. Kultura emigracyjna po 1939 roku* (Between Poland and the world: Émigré culture after 1939), ed. Marta Fik, 39–56. Warsaw: Krąg.

———. 1995. "The Light of the Soul and the Lamps of Reason." In *Sacrum in Polish Literature,* ed. Halina Filipowicz. Trans. Joanna Dutkiewicz. *Renascence: Essays on Values in Literature* 47, 3–4 (spec. issue): 167–81.

———. 1998. "DOM emigracyjnego dramatu" (DOM of émigré drama). In *Dramat i teatr emigracyjny po roku 1939* (Émigré drama and theater after 1939), ed. Elżbieta Kalemba-Kasprzak and Dobrochna Ratajczakowa, 123–61. Wrocław: Wiedza o Kulturze.

Rose, Gillian. 1993. *Feminism and Geography: The Limits of Geographical Knowledge.* London: Blackwell.

Sedgwick, Eve Kosofsky. 1992. "Nationalisms and Sexualities in the Age of Wilde." In *Nationalisms and Sexualities,* ed. Andrew Parker et al., 235–45. New York: Routledge.

Vidler, Anthony. 1992. *The Architectural Uncanny: Essays on the Modern Unhomely.* Cambridge, Mass.: MIT Press.

15 ı|ı Gombrowicz's Binoculars

The View from Abroad

David Goldfarb

> . . . *ten tylko się dowie*
> *Kto cię stracił.*
>
> this is known only
> to him who has lost you.
>
> —Adam Mickiewicz, *Pan Tadeusz*

> I draw your attention, dear critics, to all the places in my art where the Inferior, the Younger, creates the superior in its own way, because there you have the most intense poetry I can create.
>
> —Witold Gombrowicz, *Diary*

WITOLD GOMBROWICZ KEPT only the essential items needed for writing at his uncluttered simple wooden desk, writes Rita Gombrowicz in her account of her husband's life in Europe. He used no dictionary or reference books. He kept no notebooks. She recalls that he did his writing "like a schoolboy doing his homework," with only two green Parker ballpoints, an ordinary notepad, his pipe and pipe tools, and a pair of binoculars (Rita Gombrowicz 1984, 318). I asked Mme Gombrowicz in an interview why he needed binoculars for writing and she explained—after the obligatory jest about voyeurism, alluding to Gombrowicz's novel *Pornografia* (Pornography)—that he acquired them in West Berlin during the first year of his return to Europe, to see how people were living on the other side of the Wall.[1] This perspective of the detached observer looking at the world from a distance seems precisely to describe the point of view of Gombrowicz's characteristic narrative persona.

Now that studies of the literature of immigration and migration are developing as a distinct field, we might want to be careful about calling Gombrowicz an exile in Argentina and Western Europe, though that is the term we often apply to Eastern European writers outside their home countries during communist rule. Gombrowicz arrived in Buenos Aires in 1939 as a refugee, the Second World War having broken out during the maiden voyage of the Polish cruise liner *Chrobry.* He might have returned to England, as did most of his fellow passengers, or even to Poland, but he *chose* to seek refuge in Argentina for reasons about which we can only speculate. After the war, Gombrowicz's works were not published in Poland until 1957, during which time we might accurately think of Gombrowicz as a writer in exile. With the publication of the *Diary* and *Trans-Atlantyk,* however, he begins to develop a distinct persona as an outsider—writing in Polish for a Polish and Polish émigré audience, engaging Polish issues, but from the privileged position of a self-consciously adopted critical distance. In his late Argentinian and Western European phase, we might think of Gombrowicz more as an expatriate, standing on the balcony, looking "homeward" through his binoculars, and feeling most at "home" in this posture.[2]

What is Gombrowiczian space? Since the proposed method of this discussion, as I read it at least, is to consider how the idea of home creates and is created by the consciousness of the artist, we might begin by considering the author's own living space as he has constructed it, as it has been represented in images, and as he describes it in his work, most particularly in the *Diary.* Gombrowicz maintained a regularized working environment following his arrival in Buenos Aires, given his previous surprisingly nomadic existence. He preferred for his uncluttered desk to be in a room lit by a large window, almost always with a balcony. Whenever he moved to a new apartment, the window was perhaps the most defining characteristic of the space. When the autobiographical character Witold Gombrowicz in *Trans-Atlantyk* becomes known as an exotic foreign writer in Buenos Aires, he relates:

> Astounded by the abundance of my homages, the proprietress of my Pension would not hear of my staying any longer in that tiny cell of mine and to the best chamber transferred me: so, in these difficult, dangerous times of mine, instead of in a little chamber, in a large Salon with two windows I did find myself. (Gombrowicz 1994, 27)

His final residence in Argentina (fig. 1) is not the one described in the novel, but it provides a sense of his trajectory toward a settled spatial arrangement that felt like "home." When he arrives at his first apartment in Berlin, he describes it in the *Diary* as

> large with an enormous window, stairs from this room to the top, where there is another room, balcony, bed, wardrobe, unpacking, table.
>
> I went out on the balcony: rectangular blocks of fifteen-story buildings in lush greenery, a city garden. I wallowed in these spaces after my Parisian hotel cubicle. (Gombrowicz 1988, 3:107)

Note that the window is the first item observed, and the first destination upon arrival is the balcony.

This room suggests a narrative stance. It gives form to consciousness, and Gombrowicz always describes form as the object of his search: "you look into a crystal ball, into a glass of water, and even out of that comes something out of nothing, a form"—a form that Gombrowicz describes in the immediate context as "architectonic" (). At the same time, however, he reminds the reader that the "subject" of the *Diary* is the self and he resists falling into the trap of travel narration (1:91–92, 3:110). As Gaston Bachelard (1969, 212) observes, as soon as one has a conception of "inside" and "outside" or "this side" and "beyond," even the infinite acquires form. From a balcony, one can address an audience, a vast public perhaps. From the inside, the window is the focal point of the room. From the perspective of the audience, the writer seated at the desk or standing on the balcony is the focal point. This is the private space of an author who writes a personal but public diary that he publishes in the Paris émigré journal *Kultura* over a period of fourteen years. The window provides a vista onto the world and an addressee, but it also gives the imagined public access to this private space.

Here is how Gombrowicz describes the vista from the fifteenth-floor apartment in Berlin where he lived from November 1, 1963 until his departure from the city on May 17, 1964 (figs. 2–4):

> The view from my windows on the fifteenth floor: the white ponds of a broad, slumbering park, about a kilometer beyond it in the Kurfürstendamm, the Zoo, the very center of West Berlin with an American profile, pulsating, winking, blinding, neon lights appear and disappear, hosts of cars speed along the boulevards, an electric streak floods the horizon.

Fig. 1. "Witold Gombrowicz's room at 615, Venezuela St. Drawing, from memory, by Mariano Betelú, Buenos Aires, 28 April 1973" (from R. Gombrowicz 1984). Courtesy of Rita Gombrowicz

Fig. 2. Gombrowicz in his main Berlin apartment (from R. Gombrowicz 1988). Photo: Susanna Fels

From the second large window: gloom and mystery, an enormous silence, beyond the wall spreads East Berlin, with long streets, sad street lamps. Chimneys, towers, blurring in the early dusk of winter, somewhere over there something is shining, I take my binoculars, a multistoried building, maybe on the hillside . . .

This bauble, West Berlin, the last coquetry of luxurious Europe—farther, dead silence as if it were no longer a city but an expanse, gigantic, as far as China. I look with concentration at the mute isolation of winter fields as if I were in the country . . . magic has hidden in this primordial space, of which we know that it is subject to universal and organizing Thought, dominated indivisibly by the Idea.

While West Berlin is a luminous blindness, organizing itself blindly with disorder, on the other side, where there is night, space, earth, winter, darkness, the Idea has settled, dogged, silent. Raw. This annoys. Strange, perhaps painful, that the Spirit is there, not here . . . its closeness fascinates . . . but astounds, depresses, that it is more similar to the rising mists, the

> descending darknesses, the passing clouds, the successive seasons of the year, than to something that would be more human . . .
>
> This primordial quality . . .
>
> "When one looks out a window, it looks gloomy. But, you know, in East Berlin people are much more likable. . . . Friendly, kind . . . Disinterested. Not to be compared with the West Berliner, who is materialistic . . ."
>
> "Aha, you are a proponent of that system?"
>
> "No, on the contrary. The people are better because they live in poverty and are oppressed. . . . It's always like that. The worse the system, the better the person." (Gombrowicz 1988, 3:144–45; ellipses in original; translation adjusted for consistency)

According to Rita Gombrowicz, the binoculars were a gift her husband received in Berlin, but a gift that would become as necessary as the two pens and simple notepad on his desk. When he arrived in Berlin, a scent in the Tiergarten reminded him of his youth in Małoszyce, in Bodzechów (Gombrowicz 1988, 3: 108). The two windows frame separate worlds. Rita Gombrowicz notes that the shade you see over the window on the left in the Berlin apartment was installed at Gombrowicz's request. This is the window providing the view of East Berlin. Gombrowicz's works are being published again in Poland as he writes this and are quite popular, and he could conceivably return, but he never does. He prefers to remain at the binocular distance, in his writer's room, holding an imaginary conversation in his mind, with the readers of *Kultura* listening in, both looking across the Berlin Wall from the fifteenth floor of a building in the West. Elsewhere Gombrowicz observes that places are "more *concrete,* perhaps, at a distance" (Gombrowicz 1988, 3:77; emphasis in Polish version, not in Vallee translation). As the delineation of inside and outside imposes form on the infinite, then, it conversely imposes form on the narrating self—Gombrowicz's object of study. The embattled contradictory "ja" that is Gombrowicz becomes a narrative voice.[3]

"I watch Poland," Gombrowicz writes, "as if through a telescope and can see only the most general outline of their existence, and this invites ruthless disregard" (Gombrowicz 1988, 2:9; translation adjusted for greater precision in this context). The key irony here is in the last word, *bezwzględność*—a "ruthless disregard" for the Other, brought about precisely by the mediation of the viewing instrument. This disregard—a failure of

Fig. 3. Gombrowicz at his desk in Vence (from R. Gombrowicz 1988). Photo: Bohdan Paczowski

vision—is enacted later in a chance encounter across a lecture hall in Berlin after a reading of Gombrowicz's prose (at which Gombrowicz refused to read, because he was given translations of his own works in German, which were incomprehensible to him):

Fig. 4. Gombrowicz on the balcony of his Vence apartment (from R. Gombrowicz 1988). Photo: Bohdan Paczowski

> Then I saw the likable and young Mrs. Kurpiers, but through a telescope in the incomprehensible distance, and she also looked at me through a telescope and cried through the telescope and said, oh please understand our pain and our suffering, we must constantly go on and on and remove ourselves from ourselves and throw ourselves into space, which does not end, which is unearthly, which is beyond. (Gombrowicz 1988, 3:128; translation adjusted for style)

After the encounter Gombrowicz returns to his fifteenth-floor apartment and falls asleep. Who Mrs. Kurpiers is and "beyond" where she throws herself are left ambiguous. The context is a moment of dissociation after a discussion following the reading. Not having understood even his own works in German, he passionately attacks the only other Pole on the panel, Warsaw futurist Henryk Berlewi, and their argument takes on its own absurdist, drunken, self-contained dynamic, like a scene from *Ferdydurke,* because at least they can understand each other. The academics are grinning smugly at their successful presentation of their honored guest as evinced by a lively discussion, largely lost on the audience. Gombrowicz is having a vision of himself floating in space, with the other figures in the lecture hall receding in the distance. Mrs. Kurpiers—perhaps someone in the room like a certain senator or the professor, both mentioned in this vision—becomes one of those figures he imagines as he gazes through his binoculars.

Gombrowicz is clearly working in the same vein as Karol Irzykowski and S. I. Witkiewicz, borrowing key concepts and words from their polemics on form, but Gombrowicz shifts the metaphysical categories in a way that signals the complete shift to come in the work of Bruno Schulz. Rather than valorizing a particular kind of form as pure, in the way that Witkacy would, Gombrowicz maintains a sharper distinction between form and matter. Matter for Gombrowicz is amorphous and "immature," before the imposition of "form," and is identifiable by our tendency to suppress its appearance. Matter in the Gombrowiczian context is, therefore, another vision of the precivilized, a state of nature.

Gombrowicz also claimed Dostoevsky as an important influence, and it would seem that this influence operates precisely in the realm of form and in the form of the psychological duel, which is fundamental to the narrative structure of the works of both authors. Shortly before making his public confession in *Crime and Punishment,* Raskolnikov has an epiphany:

> Ah, it's the form that's wrong, the form is not aesthetically satisfactory! Well, I definitely don't understand why smashing people with bombs in a regular siege is formally more respectable! Regard for aesthetic considerations is the first sign of inability to act! . . . Never, never have I recognized this more clearly than now. (Dostoevsky 1989, 439)[4]

The difference between Raskolnikov and Gombrowicz's characters, however, is that in Gombrowicz no characters ever experience this recognition, which would allow them to break out of the "form" that traps them in incessant cycles of internal and external conflict.

Gombrowicz's foundational novel *Ferdydurke* establishes the formal problematic for all his future works. It might be described as a kind of anti-Bildungsroman, which shows how a well-formed adult could regress into childhood. Józef, the main character and narrator of *Ferdydurke,* returns to his school to visit his old teacher Mr. Pimko. Once he is enclosed in the walls of the institution, the fact that he is a mature adult becomes irrelevant. The place itself seems to force him into the position of the child, because little Józef will always be the student in relation to the teacher, Pimko. What follows is a sequence of tales in which adult characters are "overcome with childishness," collapsing into a narrative morass, or *kupa*—a kind of undifferentiated heap.

The dialectic of matter and form is cast as the struggle between *gęba* and *pupa.* A gęba is an ugly distortion of the face, a mug we might don to conceal our true nature. *Pupa* is a childish word for the buttocks, like *tushie,* that an adult might be embarrassed to use with other adults, but that in Gombrowicz stands as an icon for immaturity. The word itself contains this embarrassment, as an obvious diminutive of the more vulgar *dupa.* An adolescent boy might say *dupa* as a way of adopting the gęba of adulthood. An adult in a position of authority might say *pupa* to an adolescent boy as a way of asserting the boy's inferiority.

While Gombrowicz's works might yield psychological insights, they do so indirectly, as studies of form and logic in language and gesture. At one point in the drama *Ivona, Princess of Burgundia,* Ivona's suitor, Innocent, raises his finger to Philip, shouting, "I protest!" to which Philip responds with a raised index finger. The motif of the raised index finger recurs throughout the play, and in a sense, it does not matter why the finger is raised at any given moment. The play is not really about the feelings of the characters that might cause them to instigate the challenge of a raised finger, but about the congealed forms of language and social life that dictate that a raised finger—or the proposal of marriage, or serving carp rather than pike—is an appropriate and necessary gesture at certain moments. The people do not make the gesture, but the appropriateness of the gesture determines their actions and feelings.

Why does Gombrowicz never return to Poland? To begin to understand this, one must be aware that he must always establish a definitive relationship to places. Should he love Paris or hate it? He decides to hate it, for all the "clothing" and "overcoats" that cover up its "nakedness"—a notion that has its roots in Karol Irzykowski's *płaszczyk* and Stanisław Przybyszewski's *naga dusza*—the idea that rigidified forms of social life conceal our true identities. Aboard a ship to Europe, he wants desperately "to love Argentina," but decides ultimately that he cannot, though he repeatedly thinks of himself as a South American as much as a Pole, having spent twenty-four years there (Gombrowicz 1988, 3:93).

And Poland? "Should I go to Poland?" Gombrowicz asks during his stay in Berlin:

> This question began to plague me on the ship. In Paris they tried to talk me into it: go ahead, what'll it hurt you will see how many friends you have. . . . And it was enough to get close to the window for the northern sky, dark and boiling with clouds, to bear down, confound it, for my prehistory to bear down on me from all sides, from colors, ways of walking, boarding the bus, the caps, the German smile that was right next door to a Polish smile. Go? Don't go? I would not be journeying to Poland but to myself as I was . . . and this I feared a bit. It meant nothing that everything there had been turned inside out and was unrecognizable—I would have found myself. . . . A great opportunity, oh, pencil pushers, to shout in chorus:—Such is the fate of an emigrant and egoist! Nonsense. The fate of any person, at a certain age, whose life has split into two parts. (1988, 3:111; translation adjusted for precision)

The window is as close as he wants to get. The window of the Berlin apartment provides access to Poland at a safe binocular distance, but also maintains a separation from its reality. The window becomes the frame of Gombrowicz's imagined Poland, his object of love and of criticism, often harsh in the *Diary*, and at this point an encounter with the Real might damage the elaborate imaginative construct that he has spent twenty-four years creating. He fears he might be drawn into his former habits, his former consciousness, and thereby lose his privileged outsider's perspective. The Real is thus *less concrete* from the perspective of the author than the imaginary, less immediate, less controllable.[5]

One notable exception in this writing environment was the space in which Gombrowicz wrote his most challenging and adventurous work,

Trans-Atlantyk, which he wrote, at least partially, during his employment at the Banco Polacco when his supervisor was out of the room. Mme. Gombrowicz informed me that in her research for *Gombrowicz en Argentine* she did manage to find one of Gombrowicz's coworkers from the bank, an elderly woman who only recalled him as an odious character who never did any work and smoked constantly at his desk with no respect for anyone else. *Trans-Atlantyk* is also the work that breaks most with the voice cultivated in his other novels and in the *Diary,* stylized in the Sarmatian prose style of the *gawęda,* the most famous example of which is the Baroque memoir of Jan Chrysostom Pasek, whom Gombrowicz lists with Mickiewicz as one of the two Polish writers who most influenced him ("Ostatni wywiad," in Gombrowicz 1986–95, 10:178). In it, he imagines himself a seventeenth-century traveler in the Buenos Aires he found upon first arriving. *Trans-Atlantyk* is to travel narrative, however, what *Don Quixote* is to medieval romance, raised to a higher order of absurdity by virtue of the distance between the writer's parody and its literary object. Of course, there is a much less distant sociocultural object of that parody—the Polish quasi-Romantic nationalism of then contemporary Poland and its émigré community. It is difficult to lay out here all the details, but we might suggest that lacking a real room with a view, the stylization of Baroque memoir becomes a room, a distant point, that brings the characteristic estrangement of the Gombrowiczian narrator and Gombrowicz's own individual persona into relief. The seventeenth-century memoirist is nothing if not an observer, reporting the remarkable and strange findings encountered in his adventures away from home and his brushes with power.

Looking for form and looking for the self, Gombrowicz positions himself inside a space, pushes the interactions in that space to absurdity by means of an arbitrary confrontation, and spirals inward to unmask the self. Bachelard (1969, 214) describes the relation of inside and outside as dialectic, but in Gombrowicz, we might take it as dialogic. In the description of his fifteenth-story room (above), Gombrowicz in fact moves from a first-person objective description to a dialogue between two internal voices. Meanwhile he is writing this dialogue for imagined observers with binoculars of their own, who will attack him for his views. He is anticipating the kupa that the arbitrary conflict between writer and reader will precipitate, as all such conflicts end in the Ferdydurkean world of Gombrowicz's imagination.

Poland, we could argue, remained Gombrowicz's home during his time in Argentina, Berlin, Paris, and finally Vence, as he continued to write in Polish, about Polish characters and the complexities of Polish identity to which they are subject. The home that that identity depends on, however, might be described as pornographic: composed entirely of memory and the fantasies inspired by a detached representation that can only be imagined but never touched.

We can see this in the opening lines of the novel *Pornography,* set in 1943 Warsaw—a Poland that Gombrowicz never knew:

> I shall tell you another of my adventures, one, perhaps, of the most fatal.
> At that time—this had been in 1943—I had been staying in what had been Poland and in what had been Warsaw, at the very bottom of an accomplished fact. (Gombrowicz 1986–95, 4:6)[6]

The opening line frames the *récit* in the manner of the provincial novel, perhaps with a nod toward Irzykowski's avant-garde novel *Pałuba,* which also begins in this manner. While the "I" here is a character named Witold Gombrowicz, in an ironic way, the assertion might be said to have been true of Witold Gombrowicz the author as well, who did choose to "stay" in Poland as it "had been" and not to visit it as it had become.[7] Indeed, a "return" to Poland would have meant leaving the Poland of memory forever.

In *Pornography* the object of desire is provisional, framed by parentheses, kept at a distance, a blank slate for projection. The story recounts Witold's visit to the estate of a certain Hippolit S., where he and a gentleman of similar age, Fryderyk, observe and revel in the flirtations of the young Karol and Henia. Following the conventional plotline of the provincial novel, Henia is expected to marry Wacław, but her true affections are thought to be for Karol.[8] The conventional plotline, however, is merely a formal necessity, an occasion for the author's investigation of Witold's voyeurism. The whole novel is about Witold viewing from a distance, speculating on what the children are thinking, and about his grand fantasies that they are acting for his benefit, when they are really acting for his accomplice, Fryderyk. They never do things for each other, exactly, at least not in the first instance.

The opening chapter ends with Witold falling asleep, then waking in what should be by now a familiar setting: "The next morning a triangle of sun on the wall. A voice from beyond the window. I got up from the bed and opened the shutters. Morning" (Gombrowicz 1986–95, 4:12). Again, he stands at the window, watching the world in its frame. The house where they are staying will provide many such opportunities, "the house with its windows, two rows of windows, downstairs, upstairs, and with its porch" (4:34). This porch will also serve as a frame, like the balcony, from which to observe and project.

Witold's voyeurism begins in earnest in church when, he recounts that "at a certain moment my gaze . . . my eyes . . . eyes in a panic and heavy. Yes, something was pulling them . . . eyes . . . and eyes" (4:18; ellipses in original). All is an exchange of gazes, or at least an imagined exchange. It may be that the eyes that attract his eyes are not themselves attracted. What does he see?

> (a boy)
> (a boy) (4:19)

and throughout the ensuing description he refers to this "(boy)," Karol, and eventually the "(girl)," Henia, parenthetically. Even the narrator, Witold, acknowledges the oddity of this gesture, in yet another parenthetical statement, "(and so sometime I will have to explain why I put the words (boy) and (girl) in parentheses, yes, that too remains to be clarified)" (4:20). I propose that these parentheses do in language what the window and the balcony do in the field of vision. In so doing, they attempt to recreate for the reader the state of consciousness induced by the window and the balcony. Witold's bracketed separation from the (boy) is Gombrowicz's spatial and temporal separation from "what had been Warsaw" and "what had been Poland."

Above all, the form of Gombrowicz's imaginary Poland is what persists in Gombrowicz's prose: an enclosed room with a large window and an ornate balcony from which to observe the wide world of Western Europe. Ultimately, one might even see Gombrowicz's Argentina as such a room. For a refugee turned exile then expatriate like Gombrowicz, that image was comprised not only of his own memory, but by the web of representations in the minds of the émigré community, in their newspapers, journals, cultural events, institutions, and in his quarrels and interactions with them. As such, Witold Gombrowicz could only know Poland as home, as Mickiewicz wrote to his Lithuanian homeland, in the first epigraph at the beginning of the chapter, by having lost it.

"I was a structuralist before anyone else," Gombrowicz claims in his

"Auto-Interview" written in Vence during the 1960s (1995, 9). To take at face value Gombrowicz's statements addressed to "the critics," such as the second epigraph above, would be madness. His work is scattered with numerous such allegedly metafictional land mines that are intentionally contradictory. All Gombrowicz's prose is written in the first person, and in his written and live performances he was always trying on and exchanging masks. The novels that follow *Ferdydurke* might be taken as gestures toward pastiche, where the author adopts certain formal conventions—gothic, the provincial novel, Sarmatian travel narrative, diary—as grounds for the exploration of one or another Ferdydurkean world. While the antistructuralist barb may have been a critical pose aimed from the Gombrowiczian balcony at Barthes and his circle at their height, there is a grain of truth in it. Gombrowicz's earliest stories and his foundational novel *Ferdydurke* tried to demonstrate that in any social setting, if one individual raises a finger, another individual must of necessity raise the binary opposite finger, resulting in a kupa, or heap, of writhing bodies at the end of the scene in spite of any individual intentions, motivations, will, or good breeding on the part of those involved. Meaning, the structuralists would argue, occurs only by virtue of such binary oppositions, but Gombrowicz reveals the binary opposition as a prison, and demonstrates that the artist must strive for the chaos of the kupa to break out of structuralism's logical confinement and create new meaning. In this light, we can read Gombrowicz's notion of immaturity as the *preformal* or the prestructural: primitive matter before the imposition of form.

Notes

1. Interview by the author, New York, March 1996.

2. I have developed the categories of displacement from home here from discussion generated by Bharati Mukherjee, "An Indian Writer's Cosmopolitan Worlds," paper presented at the conference Cosmopolitan Geographies: New Work on the Literatures and Cultures of Cosmopolitanism, Harvard University, 1998. During the entire conference, one of the few sporadic attempts at considering Eastern Europe in the context of issues of cosmopolitanism was a reference by Mukherjee to Gombrowicz as a kindred spirit of sorts, at home everywhere and nowhere.

3. On this subject see Bakhtin 1990, 92–99.

4. Ellipsis in original. In the Russian edition, this quote reads: "A! ne ta forma, ne tak esteticheski khoroshaia forma! Nu ia preshitel'no ne ponimaiu: pochemu lu-

pit' v liudei bombami, prabil'noiu osadoi, bolee pochtennaia forma? Boiazn' èstetiki est' pervyi priznak bessiliia! . . . Nikogda, nikogda iasnee ne soznaval ia etogo, kak teper'" (Dostoevsky 1973, 400).

5. Cf. the first chapter of Delany 1988, where the author introduces his own memoir with a discussion of the problem of the Reality of the imaginary for the autobiographer, often in spite of the reality of what is historically observable.

6. Translations from *Pornografia* are my own.

7. To avoid, or perhaps to exacerbate, the confusion that Gombrowicz intends, I will call the character Witold and the author Gombrowicz.

8. In the Hamilton translation, Wacław's name is changed inexplicably to Albert.

Works Cited

Bachelard, Gaston. 1969. *The Poetics of Space.* Trans. Maria Jolas. Foreword by Etienne Gilson. Boston: Beacon.

Bakhtin, Mikhail M. 1990. *Art and Answerability: Early Philosophical Essays.* Ed. Michael Holquist and Vadim Liapunov. Trans. Vadim Liapunov. University of Texas Press Slavic Series. Austin: University of Texas Press.

Delany, Samuel R. 1988. *The Motion of Light in Water: Sex and Science Fiction Writing in the East Village, 1957–1965.* New York: Plume.

Dostoevsky, Fyodor. 1973. *Prestuplenie i nakazanie.* Ed. V. V. Vinogradov. Vol. 6 of *Polnoe sobranie sochinenii v tridtsati tomakh.* Leningrad: Nauka.

———. 1989. *Crime and Punishment.* Trans. Jessie Coulson. Ed. George Gibian. Norton Critical Edition. New York: Norton.

Głaz, Kazimierz. 1989. *Gombrowicz w Vence.* Kraków: Wydawnictwo Literackie.

Gombrowicz, Rita. 1984. *Gombrowicz en Argentine: Témoignages et documents, 1939–1963.* Preface by Constantin Jelenski. Paris: Denoël.

———. 1988. *Gombrowicz en Europe: Témoignages et documents, 1963–1969.* Paris: Denoël.

Gombrowicz, Witold. 1978. *Ferdydurke, Pornografia, Cosmos.* Trans. Eric Mosbacher, Alastair Hamilton, and Eric Mosbacher, respectively. New York: Grove.

———. 1986–95. *Dzieła.* 12 vols. Ed. Jan Błoński and Jerzy Jurzębski. Kraków: Wydawnictwo Literackie.

———. 1988. *Diary.* Ed. Jan Kott. Trans. Lillian Vallee. 3 vols. Evanston, Ill.: Northwestern University Press.

———. 1994. *Trans-Atlantyk.* Trans. Carolyn French and Nina Karsov. Introd. Stanisław Barańczak. New Haven: Yale University Press.

———. 1995. *Structuralisme, jeunesse, Dante.* Paris: L'Herne.

Mickiewicz, Adam. 1988. *Pan Tadeusz.* Ed. Konrad Górski. Warsaw: Czytelnik.

16 ||| Returns to the Impossible

The Search for Home in the Prose of Gustaw Herling

Włodzimierz Bolecki

IN THE DUTCH town of Delft there stands today, relatively unscathed by the ravages of time, a cluster of houses that were immortalized in a seventeenth-century painting by Jan Vermeer. Though this in itself is ample reason to keep the now famous town in pristine condition (indeed, a matter of life imitating art), it is hardly remarkable, for there are many older abodes in almost every city and town in Western Europe. Such is not always the case as one travels further east. In Poland, for instance, as elsewhere in Eastern Europe, not only houses, but also entire cities, along with all traces of their culture, were wiped off the map—the result of three centuries of war and plunder, beginning with the invasion of Poland by Sweden in the seventeenth century.

Furthermore, in Western Europe the development of civilization had a prevalently urban character, particularly since the advent of the Industrial Revolution. By contrast, Poland had always been primarily an agricultural country. In Western Europe the basis for social growth was the bourgeoisie; in Poland it was the gentry and landowners. Also, in Western Europe literature and art were products of the bourgeoisie, while in Poland literature and national consciousness were formulated in the gentry's manors. This held true up to the start of the Second World War. Many outstanding Polish writers—Witold Gombrowicz, Czesław Miłosz, and Jarosław Iwaszkiewicz—grew up in these manors. Thus the structure of Polish society defined its culture and literature. In contrast too to the bourgeois literary tradition of Western Europe, the Polish home meant not simply a concrete building, or a house providing shelter, but an entire estate consisting of the manor, the barn, servants' quarters, a repair shed, stables, as well as the vast tracts of land on which these domiciles were built. In the Polish language one word defines this conglomeration: *domostwo.* At the same time, *domostwo* has even a broader implication: *dom ojców* (home of forefathers), or more precisely *ojcowizna* (forefathers' estate). *Ojcowizna,* in turn, stands for *ojczyzna* (fatherland), the place of one's birth. (In English the fusion of the words for *dom* and *ojczyzna* form *homeland.*)

During the latter half of the eighteenth century, when Western Europe began the process of modernization, both in society and industry, Poland as a state ceased to exist. This was due to the occupation of Poland by three neighboring countries: Prussia, Austria, and Russia. Thus, while Western Europe moved forward in its grand experiment, the Poles cultivated their memory of the past and of the lost fatherland both as a collective whole represented by the state, and individually, in the confiscation of private property.

In the Polish literary tradition of the eighteenth century (the first partition of Poland took place in 1772), the word *dom* functioned simultaneously as a catchall to describe a dwelling, the surrounding environment, the geographical region, and the state or country; hence the meanings of the private and political, of the individual and social, of time and space were conjoined. Therefore, in Polish literature, home—in the sense of the homeland—includes contemporariness and the past, people and landscapes, language and customs, and so on. Religion, which proved a bastion for Poles after the loss of the state, exercised an enormous influence on this broader understanding of *dom.* In the religious context, what is of particular importance was the biblical understanding of the home as both a spiritual entity and a community (of values).

A few selections from Polish literature would serve well in introducing the question of metaphorical meanings in the notion of the home as expressed in the writings of Gustaw Herling-Grudziński. The poet Franciszek Karpiński (1741–1825), in one of the most popular Polish Christmas carols, in one breath listed as synonyms the words *ojczyzna* (fatherland), *dom nasz* (our home), *majętność cała* (the whole estate), and *wioski z miastami* (villages and towns). Kazimierz Brodziński (1791–1835), in his poem "Do starych" (To the old ones), wrote, "Świat był domem—dziś dom światem" (The world was home—now home is the world). In the nineteenth century, the poetry of Adam Mickiewicz (1798–1855) played a particularly important role in establishing the metaphorical meaning of the home ("dom") both in the sense of *kraj* (country) and *pejzaż* (landscape). In the Polish national epic, *Pan Tadeusz,* one of its characters, Jacek Soplica, in order to persuade Poles to launch an insurrection against Russia, says that one must "oczyścić dom" (clean house). In the poem "Do Niemna" (To the River Neman), Mickiewicz uses the phrase "Niemnie, domowa rzeko moja!" (Neman, you river of my home!). Another acclaimed Romantic poet, Juliusz Słowacki (1809–1849), in his poem *Beniowski,* employed the phrase "Polish homes" to connote Poland in its entirety, while in his famous "Hymn do Boga o zachodzie słońca" (A hymn to God at sunset) he refers to himself as a pilgrim who does not know "rodzinny dom" (the family home) (Słowacki, incidentally, was born after the last partition of Poland). Another important Romantic poet, Cyprian Kamil Norwid (1821–1883), described Poland in *Quidam* as "wielki dom" (a great home).

During the years when Poland was stripped of its identity, appearing nameless on the map, "dom" was also represented by the Polish language. Artur Oppman (1867–1931) wrote in one of his lyrics, "Mowo polska! Ojczyzno i domie!" (Polish language! Fatherland and home!). This meaning of home, memorialized in Mickiewicz's *Pan Tadeusz,* was still quite popular in the twentieth century, in particular, in the émigré literature. The best known usage of this meaning can be found in one of Julian Tuwim's (1894–1953) poems, in which he equated two notions: "ojczyzna-polszczyna" (fatherland–Polish language).

The biblical expression "z domu niewoli" (from the home of enslavement) was given new coinage when Józef Korzeniowski (1820–1869; Joseph Conrad's father) applied it to his exile to Siberia, where he was deported by the Russian authorities for his participation in the preparation for the 1863 uprising against imperial Russia. Later, the phrase, used as a citation, appeared in Juliusz Żuławski's work, as well as the title of Beata Obertyńska's famous memoir about Polish prisoners in the Soviet Union during World War II.

Maria Konopnicka (1842–1910), a Polish woman poet from the Positivist period, defined Warsaw in her poem "W Warszawie" (In Warsaw) as "dom ducha" (the spiritual home), while in another poem she wrote, "budujemy ojczyźnie dom wolności i siły" (we are building for our fatherland a home of freedom and strength). In *Wyzwolenie* (Liberation) by Stanisław Wyspiański (1869–1907), the main protagonist in his Shakespearean monologue confesses that "dziś jest we własnym domu" (today I am in my own home). The moralistic meaning of the home was employed by Gabriela Zapolska in her play entitled *Moralność pani Dulskiej* (Mrs. Dulska's morality) in the expression "brudy swoje prać w domu" (to wash one's dirty laundry in one's own home). Most recently, the critic Jacek Trznadel alluded to this meaning of the home in the title of his book *Hańba domowa* (Domestic disgrace), which he dedicated to the participation of Polish writers in the sovietization of Polish literature.

There are hundreds of such examples in Polish literature. They belong to those aspects of Polish literature that, perceived from the outside and ahistorically, are unintelligible. In this context, Herling-Grudziński's writings give special problems to his critics, especially when they confront his *Dziennik pisany nocą* (Journal written at night). Seemingly, it is a text devoid of literary elements. However, like Gombrowicz's *Diary,* to which Herling's work has been frequently compared, its literariness is deeply hidden and—as in many Polish modernist works—subordinated to the narrator's very personal point of view. In the following chapter, I intend to explore both the symbolic meaning inscribed in the seemingly neutral descriptions and reminiscences, and the unity of landscapes and the mythology of the family home (in the sense of homeland).

Old Stories and Descriptions

In his commentaries on his own works, Herling often uses the type of chronicle narration, which includes a translucent and concise style, stories drawn from real rather than invented events, histories deciphered from ancient scribbles or legends, and, occasionally, somebody else's literary or nonliterary works. In other words, Herling recalls the traditional art of storytelling in which the preciseness of a word, the distinctiveness of the storyteller's role, the sharpness of events and personalities, and above all, the clarity emerging from the story, all turn out to be not only the basis of the narrative art but the writer's artistic and philosophical axiology. *Inny świat* (A world apart), *Dziennik pisany nocą* (Journal written at night), and all his short stories—from "Skrzydła ołtarza" (The wings of the altar) to "Zima w zaświatach" (Winter in the world of the dead) and "Schronisko lunatyczne" (Hostel of lunatics)—exemplify many of Herling's commentaries to his own works as well as his remarks on the contemporary art of storytelling.

Herling, the chronicler, the commentator, the diarist—author of precise, intellectual discourses—overshadows a quite different writer: Herling the storyteller, hidden in shadow, a writer fascinated with ancient history and stories about the secrets of human destiny. This Herling is overshadowed because the stories are not the only stable element of his prose. It is composed of descriptions, especially those of landscapes, which seem to be at first merely narrative pauses in the text: gasps for air between episodes of a story, or, as in *Journal Written at Night* (*JWN*), between commentaries on his readings and political issues or reports of conversations.

It seems obvious that the conventions of a traditional story, to which Herling refers with pleasure, have after all a reserved right to characterize the background for the action, the landscape, the time of day or season. Hence Herling the chronicler or Herling the traveler does seemingly nothing else but fulfill this "narrative duty." He does that with a pious devotion to detail and a sensual feeling for the most delicate changes of smells, colors, and sounds. His descriptions, often metaphorical, seem sometimes to be fragments of the clearest literature, poetic "ornaments of beauty." Comparisons are Herling's favorite stylistic device, bringing additional meaning to his descriptions. They are potential interpretations, comments, and discourses that in a metaphorical shortcut add meaning to the world we look at.[1]

The descriptions of cities and towns, valleys and hills, the landscapes of Umbria, Tuscany, Rome, and Naples, walks in Abruzzo, descriptions of the Bay of Naples, and above all the landscape of Dragonea serve as narrative pauses in Herling's stratified and multilevel discourse.

Landscapes

If we read all of Herling's works, including the *Journal,* as a many-layered literary piece, then these seemingly random and disinterested descriptions of walks or landscapes reveal themselves to be not only a stable poetic motif of his prose but also one of the keys to its hidden meanings and secrets. This is the subject of my research, and I will quote extensively from his writings to illustrate this facet of his work.

> Orvieto, Todi, Assisi, Gubbio, Perugia.
>
> There is a place on the route to Todi where one can pull over and bid farewell to Orvieto from afar. On the other side of the valley, on a hill, the

> morning fog outlines the city's contours. Rose air currents sharpen the lines, and, in turn, feather them into the sky. A herd of sheep with jingling bells moves across the valley, and horses feed on a green meadow beside the path. A row of trees marks the stream's course. Above the scattered houses, columns of smoke spin and wobble. There is something unreal, dreamy, slow, and that is how I will remember the whole of Umbria, a bordered region where time lingers, stops, and then moves on again with laziness. Except for Perugia and Assisi, where tourists and pilgrims congregate, other cities are asleep.
>
> I own a few novelties and additions to this small trip to Umbria besides the confirmed impressions or those refreshed in another piece. It happens that the most important is the process of viewing or, even more, its beginning. (*JWN,* April 20–25, 1975, 105).

With characteristic precision, Herling constructs separate descriptions. The observer's position is very clear and allows him to specify almost perfectly his positioning in the landscape; there are the foreground and the background; one can see even the distances between separate objects observed by Herling. One can see the conscious perceptual activities of the observer, who does not subordinate his sensual fascination with the object even while he expresses his admiration. But the sensuality of Herling's descriptions are more intellectual than expressionistic. Hence they engage nature actively; they are not receptive or passive. The landscape as described by Herling never dominates the observer, nor becomes autonomous: descriptions of landscape in Herling's writings constitute a rare example of keenness for the subject in Polish literature.

Landscape in Herling's prose is not, then, an object that captivates the observer, but rather a kind of perceptual, intellectual, or continual "reading" task. This landscape has something in which the observer notices a barely perceptible characteristic or value, or even a meaning that requires interpretation. In this passage, Herling's landscape is like a great book, language, or text, all common motifs in literature for centuries.

> We entered silence whose deadness constituted a form of stillness of time. Landscapes not only have their own language but also their own cadence, as in a piece of good prose based on an individual and unique enunciation of words. Here, as we were approaching Subiaco, the landscape's cadence was like the pulse of bated breath. (*JWN,* January 8, 1983, 234–35)

Landscape in Herling's prose "exists and enchants," but most of all, it has meaning and symbolism. Let us take as an example the description of "a morning walk with four stops from Dragonea to Cava dei Tirreni," which Herling ends with a characteristic point:

> Tino di Camaino, a famous Sienese painter of the eleventh century, would have called the four stops on the four-kilometer walk from Dragonea Day and Night. Following the style of the illuminated manuscripts of the abbey [where di Camaino is buried] a wise miniature painter could have enclosed in four small pictures the Figure of the World so helplessly and confusedly spoken about in the philosophy books. (*JWN*, July 17, 1984, 56)

Hence, according to Herling, in four stops during an ordinary tourist walk someone could notice "four pictures of the Figure of the World," which is a subject for metaphysical, ontological, and even theological reflections. Therefore the description of a landscape has something that is absent from the landscape itself and that belongs solely to the sight of the viewer. We are a step away from a biblical differentiation between those who look but do not see and those who see even though they are not looking. But in Herling's prose there is a third variant of this motif: to look in order to see more than the eyes take in. To view, in Herling's prose, means to paint as well.

In Herling's narration, descriptions of landscape are accompanied by descriptions of landscapes from paintings by Turner, Corot, Piranesi, de La Tour, and other masters of landscape painting. Herling values in their works what he writes down himself in the reports from his tourist walks, namely the intellectual or sensual margin over the observed object or the whole landscape, what in nonhuman nature is a mystery, a psychological and spiritual value, or an "unspoken speech."

"Landscape painters (no pejorative connotation) calm the storms in people's hearts by contemplation of a landscape. Turner"—Herling calls him earlier "the great drama writer of the landscape"— "reminds a person of his insignificance and fragility in the face of nature" (*JWN*, January 5–10, 1984, 19).

> Baudelaire made it clear in his sketch on Corot's painting: "If one can put together the composition of a landscape with the structure of a man. . . ." One can, although not as Baudelaire, who was fascinated by the "anatomical harmony" of Corot's landscapes. I saw Corot's exhibit in the Orangerie twice in June, and each time I had the same impression: that he painted landscapes like a portrait painter who is in love with his live sitters and possessed by a fever to enter their "souls." (*JWN*, July 20, 1975, 116–17)

> Someone said about [Vermeer's] *The View of Delft* that it is "a still life of a city." He probably meant the hollowing out of a still object in search of its soul. Or the joining of calligraphic precision with the abstraction of an ideal image. To capture and keep forever this one and only brief moment that allows us to see the awakening of life in inanimate matter. . . . Vermeer had distilled from lusterless commonness the clear essence of eternity. (*JWN*, June 19, 1986, 199)

For Herling to describe a landscape is to construct meanings, while to see is to give sight a meaning, to search the depths for the hidden, unseen limits of reality. The description of landscape in Herling's writings is not only a constructive element of his prose but also a constructed element. It is a narrative figure that arranges the meanings (sometimes hidden) of the writer's story. Commentaries on the phenomena of observation, viewing, and contemplation in his narration frequently give cause for reflection. In his narrative writings the sensual powers of viewing and the intellectual powers of reckoning are the two sides of the same page of the mind.

In his comments to Alberto Moravia's novel *The Voyeur*, Herling writes ironically:

> To live with eyesight but without thinking . . . Such a principle leads indeed to the metamorphosis of the art of storytelling into the boring obstinacy of storytelling at all costs, even when one has nothing to tell except for a detailed and circumstantial recording of viewed reality.
>
> I cannot imagine good prose—novel or short story—without a certain, major or minor, sensation of mystery and ambiguity of existence, or without the gift of seeing being unequal to the ability of looking. The danger lies in a rough-hewn explicitness and the fear of the unknown and seemingly inscrutable. The man who looks thoughtlessly, whose "sight school" replaces imagination and intuition, takes from the art of narration its deepest reason for being. (*JWN*, May 20, 1985, 128)

Next, we find in a microstory on the "eighty-year-old antiquarian and erudite V." a commentary quoting both the antiquarian's words and the writer's own point:

> Having taken my hand in his, with calm vision [he] clings to the view that spreads from here . . . To contemplate is to feel with one's rigid, cold fingers the same long-inflicted wounds. When we die, we thank God at least for

> having created us mortal. And we look and look, not knowing where this terrible pain still is coming from. Probably only the pain is clear and real in old age, like the pain of old eyes, washed with tears that cannot be stopped, staring at the remnants of a vanishing world. (*JWN*, November 15, 1976, 185)

Landscape and Memory

What, in descriptions of Herling's landscapes, constitutes the beginning of new meanings?

> A few years earlier during a stay in Munich, in a period of alcoholic escapades from one pub to another, I found myself one April evening in the courtyard of a large old apartment house, a mammoth—such courtyards surely do not exist anymore—filled with the acrid smells of soups, fresh-baked bread, beer and cheap vodka, the yelling and swearing of the janitor, the squabbling of tenants, children's shouts, the familiar uproar of Warsaw's prewar Pańska or Żelazna Streets. (*JWN*, January 5–10, 1984, 16–17)

First is a story of walks in Munich, then a description of an apartment house, of smells and sounds coming from the courtyard, and in the end an unexpected point that establishes a bridge between this picture and the coloring of Warsaw streets as remembered by Herling in his youth.

Herling's description of the viewed landscape becomes a modifier of memories. Looking ahead becomes going inside oneself; a trip in space becomes a journey in time: the observer's eyes, looking at the outside world, are replaced by an inner sight or, as it used to be called, the eyes of the soul. But I am getting ahead of the next analysis—this inner sight completely directs the given functions of most of Herling's descriptions.

> For someone who was raised amid ponds and rivers and has been living at the seashore for thirty years, looking at a countryside river before sunset is as if one's inner sight has been reversed. Old pictures, shaking off a long trance or lethargy, emerge slowly. There are a few horizons, shaded by sand dunes and clumps of osiers, white-rose smoke orchids stuck in the most distant one. Then the pallid rose color gets denser and enters into a thick red; silence also thickens and one can only hear some distant, dull, echoless calling. (*JWN*, June 16, 1984, 50)

In this fragment of *Journal Written at Night,* the pictures of memory are immersed in a long lethargy and rest there asleep, absent, and still; only the landscape, gazed upon by an observer, gives them an impulse to exist. The continuity of the real pictures and those of memory seems to be felt physically. The former are the reverses of the latter, penetrating one another according to the mechanism of a literary or film metamorphosis. It does not suffice to say that the real landscape calls them to life because in their existence there is another secret power of excessive existence, which is their own powerful energy, a power that vehemently seizes the speaker's consciousness. The stylistic animation of these pictures, which suddenly "crawl out" of memory's "lethargy," is particularly suggestive in Herling's description and creates, it seems to me, a characteristic counterpoint to his description of Italian landscapes. Herling the traveler and observer reigns over the viewed landscape with his "outside eye," whereas Herling the writer, preserving the memories aroused by the landscape, seems to totally obey the overwhelming power of pictures that "crawl out" of memory. If in Herling's prose the observer and the traveler decipher the hidden meanings of the real landscape, and even impose them on the landscape, then memory imposes on and dictates to the speaker its own pictures. The creator of the real landscape's meanings is, at the same time, surprised by the power of his own memory's pictures.

Besides the mechanism of metamorphosis, which allows a smooth passage from forms just seen to shapes already entered into memory, landscapes or objects viewed by Herling also liberate a mechanism of sudden evocation. In prose this is, of course, a Proustian motif. It is no longer about a landscape but about a certain object, situation, smell, or color that evokes, almost magically, memory's pictures from the most profound depths:

> How does the power of Proust's madeleine work? Our memory stores still pictures that resemble faded photographs. The madeleine makes them alive at once, as a stone thrown into the still water or the film effect when an interrupted scene is continued. Standing on a bridge, leaning over the balustrade, I closed my eyes, my heart was beating. Landing-stages on the Tiber in postwar Rome, music coming from the old gramophones, dances on shipboard, jumping into the water on hot days, cheap and acidic barrel wine, warming up, happiness. Yes, happiness. We already knew we would not return, that it was the beginning of emigration and exile, but it was an authentic happiness after years spent on prison board beds and in military

> tents. At dusk we would go to *villino* in the Prati district, K. would do the shopping on the way, sometimes we would sit in the tavern Gallo d'Oro. (*JWN*, May 13, 1984, 39)

And here there are two other stories recalled according to the laws of Proust's madeleine. In the following passage, Herling creates a literary myth that shifts the meanings of the world observed with an "outside eye" to the sphere of symbolic meanings, to the mythical area of memory and private cosmology:

> The Eolian Islands off the shores of Sicily. . . .
>
> The first Pearl drawn out of the darkness is Stromboli . . . The second is Panarea, the journey's aim . . . There is no electricity on the island and in the evening they put an oil lamp on the table. What are the oil lamp stories about? Mine are about the moment between childhood and early youth. The things we see, uncover, feel "at the threshhold" belong to our most secret mythology. Poetry consists perhaps in our trying as adults to give back to things and feelings the uniqueness they possess only at first touch. What we call evocation, retreating in time, is an attempt to see the world anew and again, for the second time, in its predesigned form. So in the little house on the pond there was no electricity and in the evening the World of First Elements would be created. A word meant more than a sign. Pond, Meadow, Forest, Windmill, Love, Hate, Fear—almost all clear categories, "in themselves," as gates to regions where the human foot has never stepped. It is later that "reality" opens and pushes clairvoyances, naive symbols, magical spells somewhere down deep. And the whole adult, mature life misses this singleness, uniqueness, clarity, mystery of sight that happens without words until its irrevocable disappearance. Irrevocable? Returns sometimes happen to great writers, the creators of myths. (*JWN Panarea,* June 24–July 2, 1977, 209–11)
>
> But every one of us, deep in the bottom of his memory, stores his own small history, the more vivid, the deeper one goes into childhood. On the way back, we stopped at the sources of the River Sele. Green water with mud, thatch, shrubs on the bank. For the full picture a boy with a fishing rod is missing; a boy sitting in the bushes with his fishing rod, staring for hours at a still float, excited at the sight of young pike jumping out of the water from time to time or of a school of bass that makes a wave swell. Dry and edgy clod in the larynx. (*JWN*, July 7, 1976, 178–79)

These are two of Herling's most self-revealing commentaries in which he uncovers the sphere of the writer's mythology. The literary heritage of these passages is rich, as Herling recalls Leśmian and Schulz, and elsewhere, Czesław Miłosz.

Memory and Dreaming

Dreaming—or the ambiguity of sensations in a state of limbo between consciousness and dreaming—constitutes an intermediary sphere between reality and memory in Herling's writings. This sphere is filled with the vagueness of reality's contours, with an obsession with returns to some of its elements, with the uncertainty of memory's origins, and most of all with the sensed effacement of the border between what is really seen and what is only remembered, recalled from memory but apparently relived with consciousness.

On May 26, 1978, Herling asks himself, "Am I preserving, after many years, Capodimorte's painting or just a dream about it?" (*JWN*, 255). Three years earlier he had written:

> A linguistic dream, I cannot name it in other words. This sudden entering (more precisely: running) into the landscape of childhood and youth is a frequent motif in dreams, although in the case of emigrants it has a special aftertaste. The novelty was that I entered my dream not alone but in the company of my foreign friends and all of a sudden, by a dike in S., all of them began talking to me in Polish. (*JWN*, March 4, 1975, 99)

The sensation of unreality of what is real and of the impossibility of shifting into the past, together with the overwhelming power of pictures that "crawl out" from a lethargy of memory, changes in Herling's writings at times into a state of almost "controlled dreaming." That way, what used to be specific in the past changes its status. While a fact from memory has caused "a clod in the larynx" and a faster heartbeat, a fact from the frontier between dreaming and consciousness becomes a nostalgic feeling of unreality, a mental escape from the world that hurts more as it's emptied of what constitutes the living memory of the observer.

> Wandering around Rome, shortly before midnight, I arrived in the Prati district. Soon after the war we moved into a *villino* owned by a retired conservatory professor. We could use the room we rented and a little glass

> tower on the roof where K. used to paint. In the evenings we would often stop by for a glass of wine at the Gallo d'Oro, located on a neighboring square near the Tiber. The villino with the glass tower is still there, although the professor's nameplate no longer hangs on the gate. Nobody on the square remembers the wine tavern "Under the Golden Cock." Had it been here? No, it had never been here. Maybe in your dreams, Sir. *So lo ha sognato, caro signore.* (*JWN Rome,* July 26, 1971, 65)

The mystery here is clarified by Herling's note, made a month later.

> Before we left for Naples, I would draw my sister out to talk about our home neighborhood. I circled around the Dark Pond, and closing my eyes I would see with an absolute clarity the alder dike, tufts of water lilies, rushes near the meadow, floodgates and a sluice, the shallow brook circling our house, and huge larches standing near it. Does it matter that most of this picture has disappeared, that the pond has been drained and harrowed, and had I troubled a young man about the dark waters of my childhood, he would have muttered in reply, shaking his arms, "Maybe in your dreams, Sir." The reality of childhood is not as fragile and loose as the reality of adulthood. Lucky is he who can preserve it forever in a description. I envy Miłosz his *Issa Valley.* (*JWN Shafuza,* August 21, 1971, 70)

The Mythology of the Home

Herling's descriptions of Italian landscapes are saturated with details of nature and architecture, they vibrate with various colors, puzzle with their great number of emotional shades and meanings given by Herling the observer. Meanwhile, the writer's mythological land, emotionally much more compelling than the Italian landscape, is composed of clusters of memory's pictures. On the one side, Herling evokes the dazzling variety of Italian nature and culture, while on the other side there exists an ascetic world reduced to the magic names from his homeland: Alder Dike, Dark Pond, Water Lilies, Shallow Brook, Little Orchard. What did the objects preserved in them really look like? What happened in these images from the past? What is their "fatal power" about? The answers to these and other questions should be drawn from various of Herling's prose works, separated by anywhere from ten to twenty years. Questions are most frequently broken off, hung, paused—as if they were finishing with words an earlier thought but never said aloud. In any case, this effort would be undertaken in vain, for there is no answer to these questions in Herling's prose. There is none because the landscapes of childhood cannot be resurrected.

> I could quote Proust's chapter on the madeleine, especially the comparable sentence on "drops that bear the heavy construction of memories," but in my case it is not about a comparison. Yesterday, imprisoned by a thunderstorm in a cottage owned by a peasant I am acquainted with, I relived in the raindrops' music on the tiles the birth of evocation. But the passing time gradually destroys the "construction of memories": it used to be a composition of pictures and scenes in motion, of sharp facial features, voices removed, yet alive; now it seems to be a cluster of dead, still photographs, matte, mute, and stained all over. Whose face is this? Whose arms are these and what is this person saying? Where does this path lead? Why is the river silent and disappears in the darkness? Where do shrubs grow? Who is in the group of people on the dike? Was the forest of the first love behind this cloud of smoke?
>
> With my eyes closed I did not feel the fire parching from the hearth but a piercing pain. (*JWN*, November 23, 1976, 186–87)

Even though the motif of Proust's madeleine from *À la recherche du temps perdu* is recalled, different rules govern the evocations of memories in Herling's prose. In Proust there is no piercing pain with one's eyes closed or dry, edgy clod in the larynx. That's why Herling indulges in a subtle struggle with Proust in all the memoirlike fragments of his prose. According to Herling, there is no general memory, or memory in general, identical to everything experienced. Its contents—emotional contents, for example—differ for each person since memory touches, for each, a reality of a different shape. In Herling's prose, pictures that recall Italian landscapes from memory's lethargy toward life belong to the memory of an immigrant, an exiled man, a wanderer, a pilgrim.

And it is not simply memory of the inevitable passage of time in any place but rather memory of the catastrophe of history. It is no longer about contemplating the past or evoking the paradise of childhood but about the secret meaning of individual existence, the roots of one's own destiny and how to determine one's identity. The passing of time is distancing in space as well. Hence memory in Herling's prose is not a contemplation of the past or of lost time but a kind of fever, whereas the journey into the depths of one's personal past is a kind of emotional illness. "Proust contemplates past time and never the passage," notes Herling and adds polemically, "No, not passed time! Time resembling a temperature graph hung by the bed of a hospital patient" (*JWN*, February 7, 1978, 240–41).

> I wondered last year what moved me the most in Dragonea, what (I would have said) allowed me the day after the arrival to "give peace to my nerves." There are two things: one is when just after midnight Casa Rossa is immersed in darkness and the drawbridges linking it with the world seem risen in the skies and dogs bark persistently on the other side of the canyon; the other is the dawn behind the Mountain of the Cross—drowsy yet triumphant. Now I know why. After my mother's death, for a few years, this was how my days would begin and end in S. I commuted on a train to school in K.; in springtime I would leave the house at dawn, it would set in during my forest walk and explode with brightness upon my reaching the railway station, after having seen the train's smoke behind the hill in R.. At dusk I would return to S. and collapse in sleep. I would wake up after midnight to do my homework. Our house was immersed in darkness, cut off from the world, and dogs' barking came from the other side of the pond and the river. Is it then this way that in Dragonea I catch a still-existing piece of my shadow in the past? So do these matte remnants move me and allow me to take a deeper breath? (*JWN*, July 23, 1974, 72)

This is the source of the intensity of emotional experiences and descriptions by Herling the landscape artist. In Italian landscapes the writer notices with his "inner eye" the land of his childhood. He knows that no efforts of his memory will give him back the past. However, the effort of the "outside eyes" so openly focused on the Dragonea's landscape or the waters of the Bay of Naples seems to overcome the shapes of reality. The more precise their description, the more intensive the experience of their colors, smells, game of lights and shadows, the more clearly delineated from their sharp picture the presource of all emotional experiences described by Herling: the Alder Dike and the Dark Pond near the house in S.

> I crawled out of the house in the evening and rolled down the steep lane to the sea. Even the benches usually occupied by prostitutes waiting for clients were empty. Lights on Posillipo and upper Naples turned on like a spider's net. A few sailboats pinned like children's toys to the bay's flat surface.

> Twenty-two years in this city neither beautiful nor ugly, which I have never liked or hated, but felt indifferent. Thirty-eight years ago, I lay on the grass in what used to be our orchard and listened to the murmur of the brook flowing from the dike. Two weeks later, a distant explosion of a bomb came from Skarzysko and reached me in the same place. This much has been left and must be carried further on: "the dark love of the unhappiest of lands." (*JWN*, August 15, 1977, 216)

Four years earlier, Herling had explained why only "this much"—"only" or "so much"—"must be carried further on": "One dies or at least disappears without love for places marked by a supposedly narrow horizon" (*JWN*, May 14, 1973, 216). This "narrow horizon" in Herling's memories constitutes the "orchard" and the "murmur of the brook flowing from the dike," "the alder dike," "shrubs by the pond's shores," "forest." Nothing more.

Polish literature is full of mythical lands of childhood. For at least two hundred years Lithuania has been made to come alive by Mickiewicz; Ukraine by Słowacki, Stempowski, Haupt, Vincenz, Iwaszkiewicz, Odojewski; Wilno by Miłosz and Konwicki; the Great Lithuanian Principality by Józef Mackiewicz—I could name many more such private motherlands, and the list of the writers who described them would be infinite. Herling's prose—in the measure I have reconstructed it here—belongs indisputably to this literary tradition.

However, the mythology of the land of childhood as created by Herling has a place of its own in this tradition. Maybe Miron Białoszewski's room with his wardrobe, table, and the "Mount Carmel" of a pillow create an analogy to universal measures of the "narrow horizon" of Herling's mythological land of his childhood.

The motif of the "land of childhood years" that I have recalled here, which may seem incomparably big when contrasted with the narrow horizon of Herling's memories, is entirely immersed in Mickiewicz's formula: "I see and describe since I am longing after you." All writers—pilgrims, exiles, immigrants—have repeated this formula. Seemingly, Herling does nothing else. However, out of the three dimensions of Mickiewicz's formula, Herling keeps only two: "I see" (that is, "I recall") and "I am longing after you." The third, "I describe," is missing from Herling's narrative prose on the land of childhood. Its absence marks the distinct character of Herling's writings.

Traditionally, this motif sets up the epic character of the memories of the land of childhood, due to the broadened role of description. I probably do not need to restate here what the epic character of this motif is in the works of Mickiewicz, Miłosz, Mackiewicz, Vincenz, Odojewski, or Haupt. It is enough to say that it is composed of the most minute detail of nature and objects, descriptions of traditions or social phenomena, as well as of the whole story of remembered events. We will not find anything from this documentary epic passion in Herling's works. There are no visual details of the homeland or details of short stories. Yet to accuse Herling of not knowing how to write an epic description of a landscape or tell a story from the past is unthinkable.

However, instead of a description of the land of childhood, we have only an evocation of still objects; instead of sensuality of detail, only signs of the author's being moved. Only one explanation comes to mind: in lieu of the detailed descriptions of the land of childhood, as would be required by Mickiewicz's mode, Herling describes the landscapes of contemporary Italy with extraordinary precision.

Now it is fitting to return to Herling's confession that I quoted earlier in the text: "I envy Miłosz his *Issa Valley.*" Herling does not envy Miłosz the Nieważa Valley (the real name of Issa) for his remembrance of his own Dark Pond, but rather for his ability to preserve the memories from childhood in an epic way. It is not solely about the memories, but about the narrative way in which they are presented. I am recalling here the most important, it seems to me, theme in all of Herling's work: the theme of silence and indescribability, the theme of the sphere that is beyond the rule of words.[2]

Reality

Let us leave the myths preserved or created by the author's memory. Herling saw his family's home and the Kielce region for the last time in October 1939. What does this minute land really look like—this "local motherland," this *Heimat* the writer has been looking for so intensively for nearly fifty years in the pictures evoked during his Italian wanderings?

> The pond there does not exist anymore, drained and harrowed after the last war, during which the Germans had ordered to cut down the Alder Dike

> but these are not the only reasons that the old photograph, very "poetic" according to the conventions of the epoch, has a mythological touch (or aftertaste). During my childhood and early youth the Dark Pond was a kind of "infatuation," "amazement" typical for that age. Frankly, it had remained until recently as the only clearly visible point in the gradually misty nostalgia. One misses the source of the first commotion, revelation, and initiation, the scene of the first love encounter, even though one knows well that both the source and the scene have been buried and swamped. After some time, nostalgia becomes one of many habits one can no longer verify. That is, it becomes ordinary, fades, and whitens from loss of blood and takes on the characteristics of a plant in an herbarium or of a butterfly pinned on velvet in a glass case. It exists and becomes tender, time uses it up and at the same time preserves it in some strange way. The inner voice whispers, "You have something of your own, the remains of the roots." Until the moment when a confrontation draws near. Like this photograph, picturing not a still-living past but an irreversibly dead and remote past. Frankly, I have just buried the Dark Pond thanks to this photograph sent to me by K. K. (*JWN*, April 23, 1990; in Herling-Grudziński 1990a)

Nostalgia for the "private motherland" resembles a butterfly "pinned on velvet." This picture has already appeared in Herling's writing: he saw the sailboats in the Bay of Naples pinned on the surface of water. Pinned, therefore momentarily immobilized—momentarily because only the pictures of the land of childhood had been imprinted permanently on the memory. Now even the nostalgia for them is only a dried exhibit of memory.

Is that really the way it is? Only the writer can resolve it in the subsequent narrative parts of *Journal Written at Night,* while a commentator on Herling's prose can only note that this unwritten story about the Dark Pond, Herling's Issa Valley, has been developing in the writer's memory for several decades. It pulsates and waves with the high and low tides of memory and emotion. It may seem a paradox that only memory and not reality acts as the life-giving impulse of his prose. And it is memory, as we well remember, that rules completely over reality. So even though the sight of the Dark Pond photographs forced the writer to "bury" the pictures of "the remote past," the landscapes of Dragonea, Tuscany, and the Bay of Naples can pull them out one day from memory's "lethargy." They "crawl out" without being asked because they are imprinted forever in memory like traces of insects in stone.

Eighteen years earlier Herling wrote:

> I believe in the existence of myth-producing landscapes. After all these years I still can deceive myself, deceived by the memories of childhood, but I would swear that the Świętokrzyskie Mountains are such a fertile region in Poland. Isn't it there where the Stone Pilgrim moves on his knees in a field by the road from Nowa Słupia? A melancholic reflection: I will remember him longer than the landscape he has grown into. (*JWN*, November 3, 1972, 169)

Herling has created out of the memory of the Dark Pond and the Alder Dike in Suchedniów a microcosm of private mythology. Out of the Stone Pilgrim he has created a macrocosm of human history, a symbolic summary of human destiny. He has found in both a formula for his own writing, the meaning and goals of literature. "Stories of initiation"—writes Herling in the margin of *The Death of Ivan Illich* by Tolstoy—"are composed and conducted from beginning to end in such a way that the reader could feel a ritual of initiation into a mystery. . . . Their form is a clear inquiry. And while writing my stories I have always missed this special form, almost humble in its narration" (*JWN*, August 11, 1985, 141). "While writing stories"—but also describing Italian landscapes and evoking the pictures of the Dark Pond and Alder Dike in Suchedniów—Herling was guided by this "dark love of the unhappiest land" "and this is the arrow the bow of exile lets out first."

The narrative returns to the land of childhood in Herling's works are like a palimpsest—one must extract them from underneath several layers of the writer's postwar immigrant life. These returns to the impossible, as I call them, create Herling's private mythology and utopia of youth. However, the stories published in recent years uncover yet another dimension of Herling's memory of his childhood home: the vehement conflict with his father, the longing for his dead mother, and the drastic character of his initiation into the adult world all show a drama of young emotions, still unexpressed by the writer in his works.[3] This autobiographical character of all Herling's stories, at times deeply hidden, allows us to see in them also (or most of all) the continuous search for the truth about oneself.

Notes

1. This function of Herling's descriptions was noticed years ago by Barbara Skarga in her commentary on *A World Apart:* "By composing the facts and contrasting them

with others, by rendering experiences and atmospheres with shades of words, and even by a certain deformation of events, the artist extracts from them a deeper and by far more important meaning. . . . Herling writes: 'One could have been sure that the prisoner when drowning hadn't made a single move, quite the opposite, overtaken by the madness of starvation, he had poured into himself the useless ballast of boiling water and one night would have drowned to the bottom like a stone, and the day after the dawn would have thrown on the shallow waters of his board-bed his monstrously swollen corpse.' How rich this sentence is in information and how greatly put together. . . . One could lecture about it or write a dissertation. They both would be shocking due to the subject. And what kind of menace is brought by this succinct sentence" (1984, 176).

There are many more examples of comparisons that in Herling's prose become interpretative points of descriptions (or stories sometimes) and one can find them in *A World Apart* and other works. In this chapter I am interested solely in *Journal Written at Night* and not in the poetics of descriptions, but in the interpretation of one of their hidden meanings.

2. I discuss this motif in Bolecki 1997b.

3. See Herling-Grudziński 1998. I discuss the previous short stories by Herling in Herling-Grudziński and Bolecki 1997 and 2000.

Works Cited

Bolecki, Włodzimierz. 1997a. *"Inny świat" Herlinga-Grudzińskiego.* Warsaw: Wydanictwa Szkolne i Pedagogiczne.

———. 1997b. "Maisons-Laffitte, 13 December." In *Herling i krytycy: Antologia tekstów* (Herling and the critics: An anthology of texts). Selected and ed. Zdzisław Kudelski. Lublin: "Press Publica" i Wydawnictwo UMCS.

Herling-Grudziński, Gustaw. 1984. *Dziennik pisany nocą, 1980–1983* (Journal written at night). Paris: Instytut Literacki.

———. 1989. *Dziennik pisany nocą, 1984–1988.* Paris: Instytut Literacki.

———. 1990a. *Dziennik pisany nocą . . . Kultura* 7–8: 4.

———. 1990b. *Dziennik pisany nocą, 1971–1972.* Warsaw: Wydawnictwo Res Publica.

———. 1990c. *Dziennik pisany nocą, 1973–1979.* Warsaw: Wydawnictwo Res Publica.

———. 1999. "Sny w pięknym Morodi" (Dreams in beautiful Morodi). In *Opowiadania zebrane* (Collected short stories), ed. Zdzisław Kudelski, 2:295–312. Warsaw: Czytelnik.

Herling-Grudziński, Gustaw, and Włodzimierz Bolecki. 1997. *Rozmowy w Dragonei* (Conversations in Dragonea). Ed. Włodzimierz Bolecki. Warsaw: Szpak.

———. 2000. *Rozmowy w Neapolu* (Conversations in Naples). Ed. Włodzimierz Bolecki. Warsaw: Szpak.

Skarga, Barbara. 1984. "Świadectwo *Innego świata*" (A Witness of *A World Apart*). In "*Inny świat*" *Gustawa Herlinga-Grudzińskiego,* by Włodzimierz Bolecki, 174–85. Warsaw: Wydawnictwo Szkolne i Pedagogiczne.

Notes on Authors

JAROSŁAW IWASZKIEWICZ (1894–1980) was an acclaimed poet, writer, playwright, translator, and critic. As a poet he could be defined as the least typical member of the neotraditional Skamander group because of his cultural background (he came from the Polish gentry settled in Ukraine) and the numerous dualisms that filled his poetry, such as passion for life versus fascination with death, or privacy versus a citizen's involvement. From his debut volume, *Oktostychy* (1919), to his posthumous volume *Evening Music* (1980), his poetry glorified the sensuous qualities of the world and life. Iwaszkiewicz's artistic activity spans several decades, during which he evolved—as a poet—from a youthful enthusiast of life to a man contemplating death; from a master of ornate aesthetic lyrics to a creator of simple, nearly minimalist poems, always rich in cultural associations, in particular, allusions borrowed from Western visual tradition.

His prewar short stories, such as "Maiden of Wilko" and "Birch Wood," remain his most original achievement in the realm of prose fiction (although he also wrote several novels, including *Fame and Glory*), whose tragic vision of life deepened after World War II, as best illustrated in his "The Old Brick Yard" or "The Lovers from Marona." Quite versatile as a critic, Iwaszkiewicz wrote mainly about music, theater, and literature, although his travel sketches and memoirs were equally successful.

CZESŁAW MIŁOSZ (1911–), the most acclaimed Polish poet, received the Nobel Prize in 1980.

Born in Lithuania, educated in Wilno, he moved in 1937 to Warsaw, where he was active in underground cultural activities during the Nazi occupation. At the end of 1945 he entered foreign service and worked as a cultural attaché in New York, Washington, D.C., and Paris. In 1951, disillusioned with the political reality of communism, he broke with the Polish authorities and chose exile. After 1960 he lectured as professor of Polish literature at the Department of Slavic Languages and Literatures at the University of California, Berkeley.

For his poetry, he received numerous awards, among them the Guggenheim Fellowship, the Neustadt International Prize for Literature, and the Nobel Prize.

In his early lyrics, Miłosz was prone to a catastrophic vision; his postwar volume *Rescue,* while retaining the awareness of the crisis of moral and cultural values, discusses the role of a poet during the Holocaust. His inventive approach to poetic genres and styles is fused with irony and objectivity and at the same time retextualizes the tradition of Polish and Western literature. During his American period, enriched by religious meditation, Miłosz focused on such questions as history and mortality, poetic limitations in describing the world, and the role of the poet and poetic language in exile.

While writing poetry solely in Polish, he published numerous volumes of essays in both English and Polish, including *The Native Realm, Visions from San Francisco Bay, The Land of Ulro, Emperor of the Earth: Modes of Eccentric Vision,* and *The Captive Mind,* of which the latter is probably most influential because of the universal aspects of Polish intellectuals' adherence to Communist ideology. Among Miłosz's translations are the writings of Simone Weil and other philosophers, postwar Polish poetry (including translations of his own work), and excerpts from the Bible.

Like Wisława Szymborska and Zbigniew Herbert, TADEUSZ RÓŻEWICZ (1921–) belongs to the generation of Polish poets who were born in the 1920s; he made his debut after World War II. During the Nazi occupation of Poland, Różewicz fought in guerrilla units and cooperated with the underground press. The poet's war experience, his inability to forget about the carnage, and guilt as a survivor were voiced in his first volume, *Niepokój* (Anxiety). His distinctive poetic idiom, which influenced generations of Polish poets, is marked by an economy of artistic means, devoid of rhetorical figures and written in free verse. The lyric persona created by Różewicz, characterized by alienation and confused by the consumer culture, allows the poet to offer his moral criticism regarding the dissolution of cultural and ethical systems of contemporary man, and is particularly pronounced in his poems *Et in Arcadia Ego, Spadanie* (Falling), and *Nonstop Show.*

Różewicz's oeuvre as a playwright is informed by experimentation with an open form; his plays usually are composed of anonymous characters and serve their author to evoke a society in crisis, threatened either by some form of destruction or by a mass-consumption culture.

Although GUSTAW HERLING-GRUDZIŃSKI (1919–2000) had written literary and other essays before publishing *Inny świat* (A world apart; English edition, with Bertrand Russell's introduction, 1951), his worldwide recognition began with the appearance of this work. This nonfiction prose documents the writer's own experience in Soviet labor camps in Siberia; the eyewitness narrative reveals the degradation of any meaningful human interrelationship caused by the social, psychological, and legal mechanisms of the camps. Herling-Grudziński also authored *Dziennik pisany nocą* (Journal written at night), his regular contribution to the émigré monthly *Kultura.* His *Journal* is a mélange of reflections on the exile and an émigré writer's mission, distanced observations of events in Poland, political and literary polemics, and commentaries on the visual arts. Besides his nonfiction prose, Herling-Grudziński also published a few collections of short stories, including *Skrzydła ołtarza* (The wings of the altar) and

Drugie przyjście (The second coming); distinctively different from exilic meditations, these short stories evoke the dark aura of the ultimate mystery of death and solitude, frequently interwoven with his analysis of the emotional ties between man and woman.

TADEUSZ KONWICKI (1926–) made his career as both a writer and a film director. The last two years of World War II he spent in the guerrilla unit of the Home Army in the Wilno district, his native province. After the war, he went to Warsaw, where he worked as a journalist; in the 1950s he adopted the poetics of socialist realism. After this period, he began to write novels in which the past is starkly contrasted to present-day life; this juxtaposition demonstrates the tragic heroism of the past and the grotesque meaninglessness and passivity of contemporary Poles (see, for example, *Kompleks polski* [The Polish complex] and *Mała apokalipsa* [Minor apocalypse]). A different, idyllic mode was employed by Konwicki in his representation of the landscape of his childhood in several novels such as *Zwierzoczłowiekoupiór* (The Anthropos-Specter-Beast) and *Dziura w niebie* (The hole in the sky).

WITOLD GOMBROWICZ (1904–1969) began his literary career by publishing short stories that describe unusual psychological cases (*Pamiętnik z okresu dojrzewania* [Memoir of puberty]). He formulated his main artistic tenets in the prewar novel *Ferdydurke,* in which he critically examines both the Polish cultural tradition and the nature of human relationships. At the outset of World War II, Gombrowicz was visiting Buenos Aires, where he stayed for the next twenty-four years, returning eventually to Europe but never to Poland. During his émigré life he published the novel *Trans-Atlantyk,* whose numerous dualities include a demonstration of spiritual enslavement caused by the Polish national mentality and cultural habits combined with a sophisticated textual exploration of Polish seventeenth-century literary tradition. In *Dziennik* (Diary), *Pornografia* (Pornography), *Kosmos* (Cosmos), and *Operetka* (Operetta) the writer further develops and elaborates his ideas on topics such as the notion of the Human Church, the relationship between inferiority and superiority, and the ambivalent approach to form.

JULIAN STRYJKOWSKI was the pseudonym of J. Stark (1905–1996), a Polish writer of Jewish origin. His Jewish background is most vividly represented in the "trilogy" consisting of the novels *Sen Azrila* (Azril's dream), *Głosy w ciemności* (Voices in the darkness), and *Austeria;* he concluded his exploration of his Jewish themes with the historical novel invoking the Spanish Inquisition entitled *Przybysz z Narbony* (Visitor from Narbona). In his contemporary novels, Stryjkowski examines the complications of ideological choices and blind adherence to communism, as well as the political atmosphere that prevailed in the 1930s. Among his other works are short stories, literary essays, and translations.

Notes on the Contributors

WŁODZIMIERZ BOLECKI is professor at the Institute for Literary Research of the Polish Academy of Sciences and Letters, Warsaw. Among his numerous publications are *Historia i biografia* (History and biography, 1978), *Poetycki model prozy w dwudziestoleciu międzywojennym* (The poetic model of prose in the interwar literature, 1982), *Widziałem wolność w Warszawie: Szkice, 1982–1987* (I have seen freedom in Warsaw: Sketches, 1982–1987), *Ciemny Staw: Trzy szkice do portretu Gustawa Herlinga-Grudzińskiego* (Dark pond: Three sketches for a portrait of Gustaw Herling-Grudziński, 1991), *Pre-teksty i teksty: Z zagadnień związków międzytekstowych w literaturze polskiej XX wieku* (Pre-texts and texts: Problems of intertextual relationships in twentieth-century Polish literature, 1991), *Polowanie na postmodernistów i inne szkice* (Hunting postmodernists and other sketches, 1999).

GRAŻYNA BORKOWSKA is a literary critic and scholar as well as the editor in chief of *Pamiętnik Literacki* and associate professor at the Institute for Literary Research of the Polish Academy of Sciences and Letters, Warsaw. Her books include *Dialog powieściowy i jego konteksty* (Dialogue on the novel and its contexts, 1988), *Pozytywiści i inni* (Positivists and others, 1996), *Cudzoziemki* (Foreigners: Studies in Polish women's prose, 1996), *Maria Dąbrowska i Stanisław Stempowski* (1999).

HENRYK DASKO is a Polish literary journalist, translator, and critic. Educated in Poland and Canada and living in Toronto, he has written extensively on realist Polish prose of the postwar period, including Hłasko, Nowakowski, Brycht, Konwicki, and Tyrmand. He has also produced numerous essays on immigrant writers in North America, including Nabokov, Kosiński, and Tyrmand.

HALINA FILIPOWICZ is professor of Slavic literatures at the University of Wisconsin, Madison, concentrating on performance studies with special emphasis on gender and sexuality in Polish theater and drama. Her publications include *A Laboratory of Impure Forms: The Plays of Tadeusz Różewicz* (1991) and the coedited volume *The Great Tradition and Its Legacy: The Evolution of Dramatic and Musical Theatre in Austria and Central Europe* (2002). To catch Filipowicz in the act of not thinking about sex is rare; when it does happen, she is working on a new book, *Figuring Transgression: The Performance of Polish Cultural Mythology, 1820–1989.*

DAVID GOLDFARB teaches Polish, Russian, and comparative literatures in the Slavic department at Barnard College, Columbia University, where he is assistant professor. He has published articles in *East European Politics and Societies, Philosophy and Literature, Slavic and East European Performances, Proof Texts,* and the *Polish Review.*

BETH HOLMGREN is professor of Slavic literatures at the University of North Carolina, Chapel Hill. Her publications include *Women's Works in Stalin's Time: On Lidiia Chukovskaia and Nadezhda Mandelshtam* (1993) and *Rewriting Capitalism: Literature and the Market in Late Tsarist Russia and the Kingdom of Poland* (1998). Her current research focuses on Russian and Polish émigré culture.

JERZY JARZĘBSKI is a literary critic and professor in the Institute of Polish Philology at Jagiellonian University, Kraków. Among his books are *Gry w Gombrowicza* (Playing Gombrowicz, 1982), *Powieść jako autokreacja* (The novel as self-creation, 1984), *W Polsce czyli nigdzie: Szkice o polskiej prozie powojennej* (In Poland or nowhere: Essays on contemporary Polish prose, 1992), *Pożegnanie z emigracją: O powojennej prozie polskiej* (Farewell to emigration: On postwar Polish fiction, 1998), and *Schulz* (1999).

KIM JASTREMSKI completed her Ph.D. in Slavic literature in May 2000 at the University of North Carolina, Chapel Hill. She spent the 1998–99 academic year on a Fulbright grant doing research in Kraków for her dissertation (of which her chapter is a part), "Apokatastasis in the Work of Czesław Miłosz: The Poetic Restoration of Wholeness." She is currently working on a translation of Olga Tokarczuk's novel *House of Day, House of Night,* and has published several translations of Tokarczuk's short stories.

MADELINE G. LEVINE is Kenan Professor of Slavic Literatures at the University of North Carolina, Chapel Hill. A literary translator, she has published English versions of several of the works mentioned in her essay and has focused her research on Polish literary refractions of the Holocaust.

ANNA NASIŁOWSKA is a literary critic and associate professor at the Institute for Literary Research of the Polish Academy of Sciences and Letters, Warsaw. She has published numerous articles and studies on twentieth-century Polish literature. Her books include *Poezja opisowa Stanisława Trembeckiego* (The descriptive poetry of Stanisław Trembecki, 1990), *Trzydziestolecie: 1914–1944* (Three decades: 1914–1944, 1995), *Literatura współczesna po 1939 roku* (Contemporary literature after 1939, 1996), and *Persona liryczna* (Lyrical Persona, 2000).

RYSZARD NYCZ is professor at the Institute of Polish Philology at Jagiellonian University, Kraków, and at the Institute for Literary Research of the Polish Academy of Sciences and Letters, Warsaw; chair of the Center of Literary Anthropology and Cultural Studies; and editor-in-chief of *Teksty Drugie*. His books include *Sylwy współczesne: Problem konstrukcji tekstu* (Contemporary silvae: The question of text construction, 1984), *Tekstowy świat: Poststrukturalizm a wiedza o literaturze* (The textual world: Poststructuralism and literary scholarship, 1993), *Język modernizmu: Prolegomena historycznoliterackie* (The Language of modernism: Prolegomena to a history of literature, 1993). Among his edited books are *Po strukturalizmie* (After structuralism, 1992), *Postmodernizm* (1997), *Odkrywanie modernizmu* (Discovering modernism, 1998), and *Dekonstrukcja w badaniach literackich* (Deconstruction in literary scholarship, 2000).

BOŻENA SHALLCROSS is associate professor in the Department of Slavic Languages and Literatures at the University of Chicago. She has authored, edited, and translated several books in Polish and English. Her most recent book is *Through the Poet's Eye: The Travels of Zagajewski, Herbert, and Brodsky.*

TAMARA TROJANOWSKA is associate professor in the Department of Slavic Languages and Literatures at the University of Toronto. She specializes in Polish postwar literature, theory, and the history of drama and theater. Areas of special interest are modernity and postmodernity; nationalism; and memory, identity, and gender. She has written articles for Polish, American, and Canadian periodicals and collections of essays (on Gombrowicz, Mrożek, Różewicz, Głowacki, Miłosz, Havel, and the Polish theater of the 1990s). She coauthored *W poszukiwaniu nowego teatru* (On the quest for a new theater, 1988), and has recently completed a book entitled *Identity on Trial: Polish Drama after 1956.*

MAGDALENA J. ZABOROWSKA is associate professor both in the Program in American Culture and in the Center for Afroamerican and African Studies at the University of Michigan and has taught and been a visiting scholar at the University of Oregon, Furman University, and Tulane University. She has written *How We Found America: Reading Gender through East European Immigrant Narratives* (1995) and is the editor of *Other Americans, Other Americas: The Politics and Poetics of Multiculturalism* (1998) and coeditor of *The Puritan Origins of American Sex: Religion, Sexuality, and National Identity in American Literature* (2000). She is currently at work on a book that brings together James Baldwin, architecture, gender, and erotics in transcultural narratives, and is coediting an essay collection on post-totalitarian cultural studies.

MAREK ZALESKI is the editor in chief of *Res Publica Nova* and associate professor at the Institute for Literary Research of the Polish Academy of Sciences and Letters, Warsaw. Among his books are *Przygoda Drugiej Awangardy* (The adventures of the Second Avant-Garde, 1984), *Mądremu biada?* (Woe from wit? 1990), and *Formy pamięci: O przedstawianiu przeszłości w polskiej literaturze współczesnej* (Forms of memory: On the representation of the past in contemporary Polish literature, 1996).

KATARZYNA ZECHENTER is assistant professor of Polish literature in the School of Slavonic and East European Studies, University of London. Her publications include articles on Polish literature for *The Encyclopedia of Modern East Europe, 1815–1989: From the Congress of Vienna to the Fall of Communism* (2000), "Russian Immigrants in Chicago and the Chicago Area" in *The Encyclopedia of Chicago History* (2001), articles on Feliks Gawdzicki, Gracjan Piotrowski, and Wincenty Reklewski, as well as an article on Hipacy Pociej and the Brest Union. Her book *Curse or Glory: Polish History and Politics in Tadeusz Konwicki's Fiction* will be published this year in London.

Index

Page numbers in italics indicate illustrations.